Diversity in Gifted Education

Are national and international systems of education *really* inclusive when it comes to the education of gifted and talented children?

As provision for gifted and talented children becomes more effective and better understood, this timely book calls upon experts from around the world to share their expertise and best practice. This unique collection of different cultural approaches to the education of the gifted highlights, for the first time in one publication, the very best ideas gleaned from a variety of approaches.

The eminent contributors tackle generic and critical issues in the field of disadvantage and diversity. The chapters

- Present an overview of international perspectives on the issues of multicultural and gifted education
- Examine the critical issues related to cultural definitions of giftedness in programming for diverse gifted students
- Present regional real-life case studies, in order to inform practitioners' best practice
- Examine issues of access for gifted students, in relation to culture, poverty, race and gender.

In addition, details of websites and associations which offer support and advice in meeting the needs of diverse gifted students are also provided, making *Diversity in Gifted Education* an invaluable resource for academics, researchers, teachers and parents of gifted and talented children.

Belle Wallace is a consultant on the education of gifted and talented pupils. She is currently president of the National Association for Able Children in Education (NACE), UK and is author of sixty books on language, problem-solving and thinking skills.

Gillian Eriksson is a professor at the University of Central Florida, in the Department of Educational Studies, author, editor and delegate to the World Council for Gifted and Talented Children.

Diversity in Gifted Education

International perspectives on global issues

**Edited by Belle Wallace and
Gillian Eriksson**

Routledge
Taylor & Francis Group

LONDON AND NEW YORK

First published 2006 by Routledge
2 Park Square, Milton Park, Abingdon, Oxon OX14 4RN

Simultaneously published in the USA and Canada
by Routledge
270 Madison Ave, New York, NY 10016

Routledge is an imprint of the Taylor and Francis Group

© 2006 selection and editorial matter Belle Wallace and
Gillian Eriksson; individual chapters the contributors

Typeset in 10/12pt Mono Baskerville by Graphicraft Limited, Hong Kong
Printed and bound in Great Britain by MPG Books Ltd, Bodmin

British Library Cataloguing in Publication Data
A catalogue record for this book is available from the British Library

Library of Congress Cataloging in Publication Data
A catalog record for this book has been requested

ISBN10: 0-415-36105-2 Hbk
ISBN13: 9-78-0-415-36105-7

November 30, 2006

To the Spirit of Africa

Africa: a global perspective

Growing up in a slum area in South Wales, I thought I was a hand-me-down disadvantaged child, especially when I won a scholarship to the local grammar school and met the posh daughters of lawyers, doctors and preachers who lived in a different part of the town in big houses where cups had saucers and matching plates, and sandwiches had thin bread! But when I began working in poverty-stricken African ghettos, I experienced 'disadvantage' on a scale I had never imagined. Yet in this abject poverty, with denial of basic human rights, I lived with people who expressed a joyous resilience to hardship, submerging it with laughter, dance and singing that overflowed my Welsh heart. I worked with young students eager and determined to surmount their deprivation and courage-ously reach out for their dreams. So this book is dedicated to all those students and teachers who took me into their homes and into their lives, sharing their putu, bread and beans and their ringing wide-eyed laughter, showing me the real meaning of joy and resilience, embracing me with the spirit of Africa.

Belle Wallace

Africa: a personal perspective

'Do Good Deeds!' was my father's joking greeting as I left for yet another transatlantic voyage. My father was the epitome of a diverse gifted individual: the third son of Swedish immigrants to Durban, South Africa, whose father died when he was 2, his mother penniless and homeless, he was raised in a children's home, worked as a delivery boy at 11, won a scholarship to Durban High School at 13, matriculated and enlisted, fought for the Allies at El Alamein in World War II, put himself through university, taught at Natal Business School, became a chartered accountant and retired several times. He devoured literature, loved to question and debate, thrilled many with music and song, and had a repertoire of jokes and quotes. An inveterate entertainer and eternal optimist, he was an inspiration to his family: my caring sweet mother, my wonderful talented son, my enduring husband, my three brothers, my sisters-in-law, and my nieces and nephews, all proudly professional and now living on four continents. This 'good deed' is dedicated to that young gifted boy who had the vision and spirit to grasp every opportunity and create a dynamic legacy in South Africa, now reaching around the world.

Gillian Eriksson

Contents

Notes on contributors

Belle Wallace is currently president of the UK's National Association for Able Children in Education (NACE), editor of *Gifted Education International* (AB Academic Publishers) and a well-known national and international consultant for the development of problem-solving curricula. She was formerly co-director of the Curriculum Development Unit (University of Natal, South Africa) and a member of the executive committee for the World Council for Gifted and Talented Children (WCGTC). She has published extensively in the field, specializing in language and cognition, and most recently co-authored with June Maker, *Thinking Skills and Problem-Solving: An Inclusive Approach.* Her particular interest lies in the development of problem-solving curricula across the full range of human abilities. She has recently been elected a Fellow of the Royal Society of Arts (FRSA) for her services to education.

Gillian Eriksson is the coordinator of the graduate program in gifted education and the coordinator of the Office of International, Global and Multicultural Education (IMAGE) at the University of Central Florida, Orlando. She has developed the online Certification in Gifted Education using distributed learning, and teaches both graduate and undergraduate students in multicultural education. As a Fulbright scholar, she completed a PhD at the University of Connecticut in educational psychology, specializing in gifted education. For a decade, she was the director of the Schmerenbeck Educational Center for Gifted Children and lecturer in education at the University of the Witwatersrand in Johannesburg, South Africa. She is the associate editor of *Gifted Education International* and editor of *Discovering Diversity.* She is the current US delegate to the World Council for Gifted and Talented Children and president of Computer Pals Around the World (CPAW), a global education network.

Eunice M. L. Soriano de Alencar, PhD, is Professor of Psychology and Education at the Catholic University of Brasilia. She is the author of numerous articles and books on creativity and giftedness. She serves on the editorial board of many Brazilian and international journals. Her research interests focus on creativity, teacher training and instrument development.

Aisha Arshad spent her early years in Pakistan. She was educated in Saudi Arabia, initially at an orthodox Muslim school and then at an American

International School. She immigrated to the USA with her family and completed High School in Orlando. She graduated in elementary education, and pursued a master's degree in curriculum and instruction at the University of Central Florida. She is currently an elementary school teacher in Orlando.

Stan B. Bailey is a hononary fellow at the University of New England, Armidale, Australia. He is currently a private consultant and has been a member of the coordinating committee of four major government-funded projects on talent development in rural Australia and has served on the executive of the Australian Association for the Education of the Gifted and Talented (AAEGT). He is co-editor of the journal, *TalentEd*, and contributes to its associated website.

Alexinia Baldwin is Emerita Professor at the University of Connecticut, Storrs, CT, Department of Curriculum and Instruction. She has served as the president of The Association for Gifted (TAG), board member of the National Association for Gifted Children (NAGC) and US delegate for the World Council for Gifted and Talented Children. Her publications have focused on gifted underserved students; their identification and curriculum needs, and the masks that hide their recognition. The Baldwin Identification Matrix is widely used. Most recently, she received the 2004 Distinguished Scholar award from NAGC.

Montserrat Casado-Kehoe is a professor in the Department of Child, Family and Community Sciences at the University of Central Florida. She is a member of the Office of International, Multicultural and Global Education, a licensed marriage and family therapist, and a play therapist. Originally from Barcelona, Spain, she presented at the World Conference for Gifted and Talented Children in Barcelona on diverse gifted students. Her research interests include multicultural counselling, marriage and family counselling, supervision and play therapy.

Jaime A. Castellano is a gifted education program administrator for Palm Beach School District, Florida, and he is currently president of Florida Association for Supervision and Curriculum Development. He has served in positions with regard to special populations (NAGC), and the National Association for Bilingual Education, publishing widely in both fields. In Illinois and Florida he has been a special education and bilingual teacher, principal, director of gifted programs, Title VII director, and administrative assistant to the superintendent.

Gil Caudill was formerly an educator and school psychologist. He specialized in gifted, talented and creative children, and children with learning difficulties. He has initiated gifted programs in Oklahoma, Kansas, Indiana, and Florida, USA. He retains his Florida certification in learning disabilities, school psychology and gifted education and his national certification as a clinical hypnotherapist. He is listed in the 2005 edition of *Who's Who Among America's Teachers*.

Graham W. Chaffey is a hononary fellow at the University of New England, Armidale, Australia. He is currently a private consultant involved in collaborative research projects in Australia and Canada using his dynamic testing method

(Coolabah Dynamic Assessment), in field application, to identify high academic potential in indigenous children and mainstream 'invisible' underachievers.

Barbara Clark is Professor Emerita in the Charter College of Education at California State University, Los Angeles. She is the author of the widely used texts *Growing Up Gifted* and *Optimizing Learning* and is the immediate past president of the World Council for Gifted and Talented Children, a past president of the National Association for Gifted Children, and is on the board of directors and a past president of the California Association for the Gifted. She was named California State University, Los Angeles Outstanding Professor of 1978–1979 and nominated for California State Universities and Colleges Trustees Award for Outstanding Professor in 1980–1981 and 1984–1985. She received the World Council International Distinguished Service Award in 2003.

Christina Cupertino is a psychologist, obtaining her PhD degree in creativity at Pontifícia Universidade Católica – SP; she is general coordinator of Objetivo Project for Fostering Talent (POIT) and psycholgy teacher in Paulista University – UNIP, in São Paulo, Brasil. She is also a researcher in gifted education and creativity, and a member of the Brazilian Council for the Gifted – ConBraSD.

Cristina Delou is a psychologist with a PhD in education. She is assistant professor to the Education School/UFF, and responsible for Projeto de Atendimento a Alunos com Altas Habilidades/Superdotação.

Denise de Souza Fleith is a psychologist and an associate professor at the University of Brasilia in Brazil. She is the author of books and articles on creativity and giftedness, a delegate to the World Council for Gifted and Talented Children, and the tutor of the Special Training Program for Psychology at the University of Brasilia.

Vanja Grbic graduated Suma Cum Laude from the University of Central Florida (UCF) majoring in social science and psychology. Vanja received the most prestigious award offered to UCF students 'Order of Pegasus'. Currently, Vanja is completing her Master of Business Administration degree and she is actively participating in the starting of a new technology-based company for the university.

Zenita Guenther is an educational psychologist, with a career in humanistic psychology and gifted education. Since early retirement from the University of Minas Gerais (1993), she started a Community Center for Gifted Children in Brazil, publishing extensively in Brazil and Portugal, where she also gives courses and seminars for teachers and parents. She is an honorary member of the Brazilian Council for the Gifted (ConBraSD).

Carole Ruth Harris is director of GATES Research and Evaluation, Winchester, Massachusetts. She holds a doctorate in education of the gifted from Columbia University where she studied with A. Harry Passow. She lived and worked in Micronesia for several years. Formerly associate in education at Harvard

University, she has also taught education of the gifted, creativity and qualitative research methods at University of Hawaii and University of Massachusetts and is adjunct professor of education at Northeastern University, Boston, MA.

Mary Anne Heng is head of the Early Childhood and Special Needs Education Academic Group at the Nanyang Technological University, Singapore. Her research interests include identifying and providing for the learning needs of precocious children and clinical interviewing as a means of understanding children's thinking.

Maria Herskovits is an educational psychologist and the founder and present leader of the Centre for the Gifted at the Budapest Institute for Educational Services. Previously she worked as a researcher at the Institute for Psychology at the Hungarian Academy of Sciences. She has served as a board member of the European Council for High Ability (ECHA), and is one of the founder members of the Hungarian Academy for the Gifted. Her main interests revolve around the personality, motivation and counselling of gifted children.

Shlomo Kaniel is a professor in the School of Education at Bar-Ilan University. He has been engaged in teaching a wide range of courses and seminars to students in the areas of research, developmental psychology, cognition, decision-making, dynamic assessment, adolescence, interpersonal communication and literacy. He was deputy to Professor Feuerstein at the Hadassah-WIZO-Canada Institute, has been a visiting professor at several universities in the USA and South Africa and vice-president of the International Association for Cognitive Education. He is on the editorial board of two academic journals.

Coury M. Knowles is a specially designed physical education teacher, and is assistant varsity baseball coach at Lake Brantley High School, USA. He is mentor to students with various disabilities, such as the physically impaired (PI), the trainable mentally disabled (TMD), profoundly mentally disabled (PMD), and autistic.

Shirley J. Kokot is a professor in the Faculty of Education, University of South Africa, a practising psychologist and the founding director of a school for gifted children in Johannesburg. She works with both gifted children and those with neurodevelopmental problems causing barriers to learning. She is president of the National Association for Gifted and Talented Children in South Africa, treasurer of the Executive Committee of the World Council for Gifted and Talented Children and an affiliate of the HANDLE Institute in the USA.

Ching-Chih Kuo is currently a professor at the Department of Special Education, and director of Special Education Center of National Taiwan Normal University. She edits *Gifted Education Quarterly* and *Special Education Quarterly* and has published articles on cultural diversities, gifted identification and assessments.

Hikairo Angus Macfarlane is of the Te Arawa tribe of the central North Island of New Zealand. He has worked extensively in Maori contexts where the emphases of his research activities have been in examining successful pedagogies in diverse classrooms. He is a senior lecturer at the University of Waikato.

Krishna Maitra, PhD, is a teacher-educator and actively involved in teaching and research in the area of gifted education. She is a member of the World Council for Gifted and Talented Children (WCGTC), the Council for Exceptional Children, and the Asia-Pacific Federation of the WCGTC. She has written extensively, contributing articles to journals and publishing six books on gifted education.

C. June Maker is Professor of Special Education at the University of Arizona where she coordinates graduate degrees at specialist and doctoral levels. She is principal investigator of the DISCOVER projects, and her current research centres on finding and developing the talents of underserved groups such as Native American, Hispanic American, African American and Asian American students. She is well known internationally as a consultant and has also specialized in topics such as gifted handicapped, gifted minority students, creativity, problem-solving and assessment.

Jacobus G. Maree is Professor of Educational Psychology and Research Methodology at the University of Pretoria, South Africa. His areas of interest include educational psychology, mathematics education and research methodology. He is editor of the journal *Perspectives in Education* and a respected authority in education, receiving the South African Medal for the Promotion of Excellence in Education in 2002 and the medal for Exceptional Research in Education in 2006. Two of his publications include the psychological test *Study Orientation in Mathematics* (SOM) and the textbook *Lifeskills and Career Counselling* (co-edited by Dr L. Ebersöhn).

Ximena E. Mejia was born in Quito, Ecuador, and moved to the USA to complete undergraduate studies in psychology and women and gender studies, and a master's degree in mental health counselling at Stetson University. She graduated with a PhD in counsellor education from the University of Central Florida with a focus on research in counselling Latino population.

Ahmed Hassan Hemdan Mohamed is currently a PhD student at the Special Education Department, College of Education, University of Arizona, Tucson. His interests include the short-term memory of mentally challenged students, creativity across cultures, gifted education, special needs, and educational leadership.

Roger Moltzen is chair of the Department of Human Development and Couselling at the University of Waikato. His teaching and research interests are in gifted and inclusive education. His current research focuses on talent development across the life-span.

Diane Montgomery, PhD, is a qualified teacher, chartered psychologist and Emerita Professor of Education at Middlesex University, London, where she was

Dean of Faculty and Head of the School of Teacher Education. Currently she is director of the Learning Difficulties Research Project in Maldon, UK and programme leader and author of distance learning programmes for Middlesex. Her books include *Gifted and Talented Children with SEN, Improving Teaching through Classroom Observation, Able Underachievers, Reversing Lower Attainment, Spelling and Dyslexia* and *Managing Behaviour Problems*. She is editor of the NACE journal *Educating Able Children*.

Omar M. Muammur is former Assistant Manager for Scientific Affairs at King Abdullaziz and his Companions Foundation for the Gifted (KACFG) In Saudi Arabia. He planned, supervised and evaluated the gifted program that was sponsored by KACFG in 2000–2001. He was a Fulbright scholar at Indiana Academy for Science, Math and Humanities, Ball State University, 2001–2002. He is currently a doctoral student in the Department of Special Education, Rehabilitation and School Psychology, University of Arizona, Tucson.

Prudence Kabirithu Mutuma lived in rural Kenya throughout her childhood, where just going to school was a luxury. She was educated at the Catholic University of Eastern Africa and the University of Central Florida. Currently, she is a language arts teacher at Corner Lake Middle School in Central Florida, USA.

Michele Paule is a senior lecturer working within the fields of able pupils and communication, media and culture at the Westminster Institute of Education, Oxford Brookes University, UK. She leads national training for the Excellence in Cities programme for Gifted and Talented Co-ordinators (Secondary) and the MA in the education of able and gifted pupils. Her research and publications interests focus on able students' identities in and with the media, and on teachers' practice with able pupils.

Susana Pérez specializes in the education of pupils with high abilities graduating from Pontificia Universidade Católica do Rio Grande do Sul state (PUCRS). She is a founder member of the Board and Technical Committee of the Brazilian Council for the Gifted (ConBraSD) and a member of the board and technical committee of AGAAHSD.

Suzanne Rawlins taught middle school gifted students for nine years, then took a one-year sabbatical to work for Harcourt Brace Jovanovich as an associate editor for an elementary science series. Her master's work was completed at Nova Southeastern University in educational leadership. After being an assistant principal at two large middle schools for Volusia County, Florida, she is now the Gifted Program Administrator for that county. Currently, she serves as president elect of Florida Association for the Gifted (FLAG).

Neil A. Reid was formerly chief research officer at the New Zealand Council for Educational Research where he specialized in test development and educational assessment. He also acted as consultant in test development to several government agencies and independent organizations. He has been the New

Zealand delegate to the World Council for Gifted and Talented Children, and a national delegate to the Asia-Pacific Federation of the WCGTC. He has also been a member of the editorial boards for the journals *Gifted Education International* and *Apex: The New Zealand Journal of Gifted Education*.

Sally M. Reis is a professor and department head of the Educational Psychology Department at the University of Connecticut where she also serves as principal investigator of the National Research Center on the Gifted and Talented. Her research interests are related to special populations of gifted and talented students, including students with learning disabilities, gifted females and diverse groups of talented students. She is co-author of *The Schoolwide Enrichment Model, The Secondary Triad Model, Dilemmas in Talent Development in the Middle Years*, and a book about women's talent development, *Work Left Undone: Choices and Compromises of Talented Females*.

Joseph S. Renzulli is a professor of educational psychology at the University of Connecticut, and director of the National Research Center on the Gifted and Talented. He is a fellow in the American Psychological Association and has been designated a Board of Trustees Distinguished Professor at the University of Connecticut; in 2003 he was awarded an Honorary Doctor of Laws Degree from McGill University in Montreal, Canada. Although he has obtained over 20 million dollars in research grants, he lists his proudest professional accomplishment as founder of the summer Confratute program at UConn, which since 1978 has served thousands of teachers and administrators from around the world.

Sylvia Rimm is a child psychologist who directs the Family Achievement Clinic in Cleveland, Ohio, and is clinical professor at Case School of Medicine. She has authored many books including *Rescuing the Emotional Lives of Overweight Children, How to Parent so Children will Learn* and *The 'Jane' Series*. Her book *See Jane Win* was a *New York Times* bestseller. Her parenting column is syndicated nationally through Creators Syndicate; she is also a well-known radio and television presenter.

Achim Runnebaum moved from Germany to the USA when he was about 13 years old. He graduated from the University of Central Florida in psychology, then continued in multicultural studies. Eventually he moved to Japan to teach English. He currently works part time for Berlitz, a world-renowned language company, and also as a private language instructor.

Ugur Sak works as assistant professor in the Department of Special Education, University of Anadolu, Turkey. He achieved his MA in the education of the gifted students at Arizona State University. His main research interest includes assessment of mathematical ability, lives of geniuses, and development of curriculum, assessment and teaching models for gifted students.

Jasmina Šefer is currently an associate professor at the Institute for Educational Research, Serbia University of Belgrade, Department of Psychology. She is author of *Socialisation in the Classroom* and *Creative Child*, and a participant and editor of *Teacher in Practice* and *Recognition of Diversity and Education*. She has written a series of articles in English and Serbian language. Her work has also included research with June Maker, counselling and psychological research at primary and secondary levels, and research for the Ministry of Education.

Jiannong Shi is a past president of Asia-Pacific Federation of World Council for Gifted and Talented Children and focuses his research in the field of giftedness and creativity theoretically and practically. He has authored (or co-authored) more than ten books, as well as more than seventy journal articles, book chapters and conference presentations since 1990. He serves as a director of the Center for Supernormal Children at the Institute of Psychology, Chinese Academy of Sciences.

Susan Sikes, MA, is trained in mental health counselling and play therapy and specializes in working with the gifted, talented, and creative population at all age levels. She is a speaker, writer and consultant to alternative educational groups. She also works through her private practice with the Center for Counseling and Consulting in Casselberry, Florida.

Dorothy Sisk holds the Conn Chair for Gifted Education at Lamar University, Texas. She is the director of numerous associations including, most recently, Even Start, Scientists in Schools and New Steps in Science. Her recent consultations have been for creativity, innovation and leadership, and citizen ambassador programs. She is also an international consultant, holds the Distinguished Service Award for the World Council for Gifted and Talented Children, the American Creativity Award and the E. Paul Torrance Distinguished Scholar Award. Her latest publication (with Paul Torrance) is *Spiritual Intelligence: Developing Higher Consciousness*.

Robert J. Sternberg is the Dean of the School of Arts and Sciences at Tufts University and director of the Center for the Psychology of Abilities, Competencies, and Expertise at Yale. He is a fellow of the American Academy of Arts and Sciences, the American Association for the Advancement of Science, the American Psychological Association (APA), the American Psychological Society (APS), the Connecticut Psychological Association, and the Society of Experimental Psychologists. He has won many awards from APA, APS and other organizations. He is best known for his theory of successful intelligence, investment theory of creativity (developed with Todd Lubart), theory of thinking styles as mental self-government, and balance theory of wisdom.

Trae Stewart is an assistant professor in educational studies at the University of Central Florida where he teaches foundations of education courses, multicultural and international education. He studied French at Université de Bourgogne, France. He has also worked at the Center for Talented Youth and Civic Education Project, Johns Hopkins University and Northwestern University. His research interests and expertise include service-learning, gender and sexuality, qualitative methodology, critical theory and adolescence and identity.

Kai Yung Brian Tam is an associate professor of education in the Early Childhood and Special Needs Education Academic Group at the Nanyang Technological University, Singapore. His areas of research include education of new immigrant students, students at risk and incarcerated youth, empirically based instructional strategies and curricular materials for teaching students with diverse abilities, inclusive education and teacher education.

John West-Burnham is a professor and, until recently, was director of research and development at the Leadership Centre, University of London. He has worked in the Open University, and also at Leicester, Lincolnshire and Humberside universities, UK. He is author of *Managing Quality in Schools*, co-author of *Effective Learning in Schools, Leadership and Professional Development in Schools* and co-editor of *Performance Management in Schools*. He works internationally, and his current research centres on transformational leadership.

Qiong Zhang is a PhD candidate at the Center for Supernormal Children at the Institute of Psychology, Chinese Academy of Sciences. She obtained her bachelor degree of medicine in Hunan Medical University, China, then turned her interest to psychology and obtained her master's degree in the Mental Health Center at XiangYa Medical School, Central South University. She focuses her research interest in the field of intelligence and creativity.

Albert Ziegler, PhD, is Professor of Psychology and a director in the Centre of Educational Sciences at the University of Ulm, Germany. He has published extensively in the field of educational psychology and cognitive psychology. He is director of the state-wide Counseling and Research Center for the Gifted. His main interests in the field of gifted education are the development of exceptional performances, motivational training programs and knowledge acquisition.

Preface

The need for this text developed primarily from the field, from interacting with brilliant children who, despite harsh situations of poverty or special challenges, were optimistic and motivated to seize opportunities and soar. Additional motivation came from panel discussions, conversations and international presentations that stemmed from an ethical concern that many deserving gifted students were not receiving an appropriate curriculum. Children who have been raised in disadvantaged or marginalized communities, however gifted from within their own cultural or microcultural perspectives, face unfair comparisons, standards, prejudices and pressures to relinquish their proud heritage and identity. At the heart of our motivation to create this book was a drive to throw light on these inequities and illuminate the diverse ways in which gifted students show their brilliance, irrespective of culture, language, gender, race, age, religion or exceptionality.

As authors we have traveled to many schools, rural villages and urban cities around the world: a world that is changing and on the move. We needed a book that would reflect world views on diverse critical issues, that examined global perspectives and described international provisions in gifted education. Whilst this text is particularly suitable for certification courses in gifted education that focus on diverse populations, it also examines critical issues as presented from eminent scholars around the world. The principles in the text combine gifted, multicultural, global and international education.

This text has been organized around multicultural issues, including intellectual, socio-cultural, socio-economic, physical, socio-emotional and administrative concerns. The first chapter addresses fundamental aspects of cognition and diverse approaches to intelligence that incorporate cultural perspectives. Following are chapters that address and clarify inhibitors to the development of diverse gifted students, including linguistic dominance, cultural prejudice, classism, racism, religious intolerance, sexism, ableism, ageism and nativism. The mission of global education in the development of world citizens for both gifted students and teachers of the gifted is then identified. Each chapter includes a discussion of the issue with contributions from world educators, and then uses a culturally relative personal perspective or case study, wherein gifted individuals describe their own experiences. Each chapter concludes with key questions and the posing of situations or critical incidents for discussion and conflict resolution. The final chapter on international provisions examines gifted education policies and practices in a selection of countries around the world. The conceptual map will allow teachers to examine these areas of focus and plan a course of study.

Acknowledgments

Contributions to a volume of this scale and complexity require educators who are willing to donate their time, energy and expertise, because they believe in the essential aims of the text. We wanted to portray a truly global perspective, and to involve as many contributors from around the world as was possible. Each contributor brings a depth and breadth of knowledge that is the result of countless contacts with children, parents and teachers across the world. But as well as their expertise, we hope we have encapsulated their humanity and their hope for our global world. It has been a long journey since we were trying to capture ever widening ripples of development and understanding.

Our sincere thanks to all the contributors.

We would also like to give our sincere thanks to Harvey B. Adams, who spent many hours patiently checking the entire text.

Belle and Gillian

1 Cognition and underachievement
Motivation and self-esteem
Self-regulation
Self-monitoring
Language and emotion
Multiple abilities
Metacognition
Successful intelligence

2 Bilingually enriched
Respect and self-esteem
Bilingual strengths
Acceptance of difference
Transcending culture
Multiple criteria identification
Diversity of curriculum
Transition and continuity

3 Culturally diverse
Cultural strengths
Differentiated curriculum
Content and process
Personalized learning
Collaborative working
Flexible organization
Long-term support

4 Socio-economic
Resilence and transcendence
Cognitive modifiability
Metacognition
Self-regulation
Opportunity and support
Developing intelligence
Real-life problem-solving

5 Ethnic promise/prejudice
Language and emotion
Self-esteem
Opportunity and support
Acceptance of difference
Non-school achievement
Teacher training
Whole school ethos

Diversity in Gifted Education
International perspectives on global issues
Belle Wallace and Gillian Eriksson

6 Ethical perspectives
Universality of meaning
Self-actualization
Language and emotion
Connected learning
Peak experiences
Life values and purposes
Philosophical issues

7 Gender issues
Self-esteem and self-concept
Inner locus of control
Life role models
Mentoring and support
Acceptance of difference
Equal opportunities
Appropriate teacher training

8 Exceptionality issues
Underachievement
Inclusive education
Cognitive curriculum
Learning difficulties
Internal and external barriers
Informed diagnostic support
Appropriate teacher training

9 Developmental and age issues
Changing family structures
Generational conflict
Role conflict
Self-esteem
Cultural adjustment
Opportunity to achieve
Assessment and counselling

10 Global education
Intercultural competencies
World citizenship
Equality of opportunity
Acceptance of cultures
Communication
Problem-solving/decision-making
Interdependence

11 International profiles
Legislation and practice
Multiplicity of approaches
Definition and assessment
Teacher training
National curriculum
Acceptance of cultures
Gender issues

Concept map

Introduction

Applying multicultural and global education principles to the education of diverse gifted and talented children

Gillian Eriksson

Objectives

In this book we address diversity issues in gifted students who are marginalized: the central objective is to overcome the stereotyping, prejudice and discrimination that many gifted students face around the world. We aim to provide guidelines for developing culturally responsive and appropriately differentiated curricula. These students are often an afterthought, considered 'second best', as we modify our identification systems or 'water down' gifted programs. We need to infuse planning and transform programming with multicultural perspectives for all gifted students, and focus on the wonderful intercultural competence and diverse brilliance that these children display.

Key areas of focus

Who are these diverse gifted students who have not had a fair chance to succeed?

Culture

Are diverse cultural skills irrelevant to a dominant culture classroom? Children who have been enculturated into indigenous cultures often perceive the world from perspectives different from the dominant macro-cultures, and learn skills that are adapted to their own context, environment and motivations. Their stories, artwork, songs, dances, beliefs, dietary preferences and customs are often not reflected nor appreciated in the curriculum. Certain behaviors, such as not looking at the teacher, are culturally relevant but interpreted negatively by dominant culture teachers as insolence or inattentiveness.

Ethnicity and race

What minorities still suffer oppression that denies their social, political and educational rights? The Harvard Civil Rights Project (Orfield and Chungmei 2005) and the Southern Poverty Law Center (2005) have shown that minorities are present in disproportionate numbers in special education and underrepresented in gifted education. In American gifted programs, African-American, Hispanic, Alaskan and Native American students are underrepresented (Ford 1994; Grantham 2004; Callahan and McIntire 1994).

Socio-economic class

Does gifted education replicate segregation? Dr Gary Orfield (Orfield and Chungmei 2005) conducted research on desegregation in US schools and found that 50 years after the landmark Brown vs. Board of Education Act that disbanded segregation, it is pervasive in the United States nowadays. In low-income schools there is greater diversity and concentrated minorities, particularly Hispanic and African-American children. In most states, there are far fewer students in gifted programs at low-income schools, favoring high-income students (Davidson et al. 2004). The US Jacob K. Javits Act 1989, aimed at gifted underserved populations, has shown the dramatic results of intervention with low-income gifted children, largely minorities in 125 projects (US Department of Education 2005).

Language

Why identify by a deficiency in a dominant language? The domination of English as a major world language has marginalized gifted students whose linguistic heritage is denied while their English deficiency is stressed, i.e. 'Limited English Proficient' (LEP). In a monolinguistic US school system, these children are now labeled 'English Language Learners' (ELL), masking their gifted abilities. Approaches to bilingual education vary according to the degree of incorporation of multicultural perspectives. The trend toward English immersion, demonstrates the pressure to conform to the English macro-culture. This assimilation of minority languages into the dominant culture language throughout the world not only creates inequitable classrooms, but also denies the ethnic identity of diverse gifted students.

Gender

Is gender equity merely a question of access? Even though there are increasing numbers of girls taking math and science, the reality is that gifted girls tend to drop out of gifted programs in high school, and still choose occupations that have lower status and lower pay. In higher education, teaching is dominated by females, and other professions such as engineering, medicine and economics are dominated by males (Cushner et al. 2003). In many cultures, despite the high abilities of girls, they are expected to remain subservient and focus on domestic duties. Globally, the incidence of harassment, violence and abuse against women continues, escalating into rape and 'honor crimes'. Of increasing concern are the dropout rates, violent behavior and suicide rates among gifted boys. The concept of 'family' and 'marriage' is being redefined to include single parents, blended, extended, multiracial, immigrant families, foster and adopted parents. Victimization can also extend to the homosexual and lesbian community, leading gifted lesbian, gay, bisexual and transgender (LGBT) students to be marginalized.

Religion and ethics

What inhibitions, prejudices and discriminatory practices do gifted students from diverse religions face? Religious fundamentalism inhibits creative and critical thinking, and the conservative trend limits the right to choose for these gifted students. Alternatively, there are also new age religions that incorporate universal truths and question the reality of academic achievement as an end in itself. With global tragedies such as the World Trade Center and Asian Tsunami, there is an increasing need to define meaning and wisdom, to focus on spirituality. The need to validate diverse personal ethics while maintaining an objective and comparative approach to religion in schools, remains a challenge for teachers of diverse gifted students.

Age

'Ready' for what? The myth of the average classroom assumes that children of a certain age have common academic and socio-emotional needs. Precocious children display gifted abilities very early. Children who suffer from chronic illness need special modifications. Children who are underachieving may mask a learning disability. Tragically, so many children are subject to child labor and physical and sexual abuse. The highly gifted suffer from the notion that they are socio-emotionally immature, despite long-term studies that demonstrate positive adjustment (Hollingworth 1927; Gross 2004). The considerable skills of the highly gifted make them model world citizens who demonstrate their knowledge and impact on world issues.

Exceptionality

What are the real limits to intellectual ability? The move towards inclusion of exceptional students has led not only to an acceptance and normalizing of disability and appropriate modifications, but also to a social revolution in defining what is 'average' and 'gifted' academically. However, many disabled individuals still suffer prejudice and have to endure the assumption that physical disability implies intellectual inferiority. Role models for diverse disabled should include the achievements of gifted blind, gifted deaf, gifted physically disabled, gifted learning disabled and the global reality of chronically ill gifted (HIV-positive).

Key issues

Marginalized 'second-best' gifted

The evolution of the field of gifted education has been largely created by theorists in developed countries from a macro-cultural perspective to identify high ability students whose needs can be appropriately met in school systems that have the resources, funding, facilities and teachers to do so. Even though definitions of giftedness have tried to incorporate the wider context of intelligence, and personal characteristics such as creativity and motivation, they have not adequately addressed the micro-cultural inhibitors that prevent the development or expression of gifted abilities clarified above. We are still at the stage where gifted programming is predominantly for the affluent and powerful (Davidson et al. 2004).

Culturally diverse concepts of giftedness

In Native American cultures, where value is placed on community over individual, giftedness is seen as social wisdom in harmony with natural and spiritual powers equated with altruism, rather than competitiveness and personal achievement. In African cultures, Afrocentrism embodies the principle of *uBuntu*, where community, nature and universality are valued. In developing nations today, gifted students embody both principles of individual ambition with community integrity, the vision of a citizen who reaches both worlds (western and traditional) and has intercultural competence.

Dominant culture conformity

In the past, children who did not 'fit' the dominant or macro-cultural perspective were deemed 'culturally deficient' and trained to assimilate into the middle-class classroom within a specific language and religion seen as superior and desirable. Throughout the world, children who were enculturated into minority or indigenous cultures had to conform to colonized systems of education. This is still the reality for immigrant children; the loss of their personal and cultural identity can lead them through stages of shock, denial, grief and acceptance (Cushner et al. 2003).

Equity and excellence

This focus on inadequacy led to use of the term 'culturally different'. The term 'disadvantaged' describes those who have been economically impoverished through lack of resources, access, and skills. The brilliance of children within their own cultural context, their unique skills, high abilities and talents, must be valued. The concept of excellence has to be defined culturally, to reflect the values and norms of the gifted students' heritage, and internationally, as it relates to differential standards of achievement and national educational objectives. The world is evolving beyond cultural pluralism, where each unique culture is validated and celebrated, to an egalitarian society, where the diverse gifts and talents of our students are actualized in addressing world problems. As educators of the world's most brilliant children, we have a responsibility to preserve and celebrate the abilities of these endangered cultures. Not only is the loss of this potential one that is individual to these gifted children, but also a loss for the world at large.

The constructivist perspective and cultural relativism

It is with this perspective that the focus has become one of celebrating 'diversity', an impartial inclusive term. We need to incorporate principles of constructivism, an understanding of how a student constructs knowledge from a socio-cultural perspective (Oakes and Lipton 1999). Cultural relativism is clarified as viewing the world relatively and empathetically through the eyes of the student's own experiences (Cushner et al. 2003). Each marginalized gifted student has a personal and unique story to be validated and demands an appropriately differentiated curriculum. The profile of the student's cultural competencies needs to be defined in identification. Teachers need to develop their own intercultural competencies to meet the needs of these diverse gifted students.

Prejudice and discrimination

Eriksson Sluti (2001) defined the term 'giftism' as

> a system-wide justification of unequal treatment of those who do not meet the school criteria for admission into the program, as well as the belief in the inherent superiority of the gifted student. This view leads to segregated social and educational programs, propagates arrogance and fosters prejudicial attitudes.
>
> (Eriksson Sluti 2001: 11)

To reduce prejudice, we need to respect and celebrate cultural and ethnic heritage, broaden cultural experiences, challenge cultural stereotypes and incorporate cultural positives into curriculum. Teachers need knowledge and contact with diverse communities as they transform the curriculum to reflect multiple perspectives, learning styles and ethnic preferences (see Table I.1).

Global perspectives

In the examination of gifted education policies and practices around the world, the stresses of assimilating for marginalized gifted students need to be addressed. Comparative education, defined by Kubow and Fossum (2003), examines the role that education plays in national and individual advancement of developed and developing countries across multiple disciplines. Global education, defined by Swiniarski and Breitborde (2003), includes basic education, lifelong learning, cooperative learning, social action, economic education, technology, creative

Table I.1 Developing a multicultural perspective for gifted students

Objectives of multicultural education	Corresponding skills	Appropriate strategies/ multicultural activities
Examination of issues of social justice and equity	Critical thinking about social and cultural injustices	Independent research on key issues and concerns
Developing intercultural understanding	Developing a culturally relative view of others' experiences and intercultural competence	Mentorships and internships in challenging diverse settings
Self-awareness of ethnic perspectives and lifestyle assumptions	Analysis of own heritage and prejudices	Enrichment activities beyond own cultural perspective: talks, trips, service-learning
Examination of how knowledge is constructed from cultural perspectives	Developing a constructivist perspective on knowledge	Accelerative study in social and behavioral sciences; and multiple disciplines to expand knowledge perspectives
Problem-solving and conflict resolution	Creative productivity that is ethnorelative	Developing real solutions to diversity problems

Source: Adapted from Banks and McGee Banks 2001; Cushner et al. 2003; Ford and Harris 1999.

and critical thinking, moral and multicultural education, supports a sustainable environment and enhances the spirit of teaching and learning. Each nation encompasses a range of cultural, linguistic and ethnic perspectives. This text differentiates international provisions from the mission of global education, which is one that transcends political and social policies of nation states to examine the impact of education of gifted students on the future of the planet (see Table I.2).

Culturally responsive curriculum

Gay (2000) clarified 'culturally responsive pedagogy' as having the following characteristics: validating, comprehensive, multidimensional, empowering, transformative and emancipatory. Many theorists in gifted education have tried to identify content and multiple disciplines so that curriculum is meaningful and developmental. In addition, the report *A Nation Deceived* has shown the positive impact and importance of accelerating gifted students (Colangelo et al. 2004). An appropriate curriculum for diverse gifted students must be relevant to their cultural positives (Torrance 1977).

Accountability

What assumptions underlie identification? We assume that most children have had equal opportunity to learn and equal access to resources as well as sufficient

Table I.2 Global education principles applied to gifted education

Global Education	Gifted Education
Rights of child	Right to appropriately differentiated curriculum
State of the planet	In-depth first-hand research to critical issues in sciences that is action oriented
Futures perspective	Developing future problem-solving strategies and speculation about alternative futures
Virtual learning	Transforming learning environment through multiple media, developing literacy skills
First-hand experiences	Use of mentors, internships and service learning as sources of information and higher-level investigation
Global village	Interdependence and interdisciplinary approach to addressing key issues of equity and excellence in cultures, languages
World citizens	Creative productivity that has world impact while challenging abilities

Source: Adapted from Swiniarski and Breitborde 2003.

motivation to actualize their abilities. In most countries, teachers come from the dominant culture and may not understand the skills and abilities of multilingual or multicultural children. Research has shown that teachers need careful training in identifying gifted students, even more so when these students are diverse (Smutny 2003). It is clear that to include multiple perspectives, approaches to research should incorporate ethnographic studies within the context of the culture.

Key trends

These issues are timely as we face environmental and natural threats and social and political terrors around the world. The dangers of not identifying diverse gifted students are underachievement, depression and alienation, brilliant but destructive students, global ignorance, destruction of indigenous culture, and world domination of popular culture. Saddest of all, we are losing our future innovators, inventors, problem-solvers and peacekeepers. We need to transform the 'second best' gifted students into culturally excellent achievers. This is not merely an educational need, it is a global mission.

References

Banks, J. A. and McGee Banks, C. A. (eds) (2001) *Multicultural Education*, 4th edn. New York: John Wiley and Sons.

Callahan, C. M. and McIntire, J. A. (1994) *Identifying Outstanding Talent in American Indian and Alaskan Native Students*. Washington, DC: US Department of Education, Office of Educational Research and Improvement.

Colangelo, N., Assouline, S. G. and Gross, M. U. M. (2004) *A Nation Deceived: How Schools Hold Back America's Brightest Students*. The Templeton National Report on Acceleration. Iowa City, IA: University of Iowa Press.

Cushner, K., McClelland, A. and Safford, P. (2003) *Human Diversity in Education: An Integrative Approach*, 4th edn. New York: McGraw-Hill.

Davidson, J., Davidson, B. and Vanderkam, L. (2004) *Genius Denied: How to Stop Wasting our Brightest Young Minds*. New York: Simon and Schuster.

Eriksson Sluti, G. (2001) The gifted game: overcoming stereotyping in gifted education. *Gifted Education International*, 15(2): 178–187.

Ford, D. Y. (1994) *The Recruitment and Retention of African-American Students in Gifted Education Programs: Implications and Recommendations*. Storrs, CT: National Research Center on the Gifted and Talented.

Ford, D. Y. and Harris, J. J., III (1999) *Multicultural Gifted Education*. New York: Teachers College Press.

Gay, G. (2000) *Culturally Responsive Teaching: Theory, Research, and Practice*. New York: Teachers College Press.

Grantham, G. (2004) Multicultural mentoring to increase black male representation in gifted programs. *Gifted Child Quarterly*, 48: 232–245.

Gross, M. U. M. (2004) *Exceptionally Gifted Children*. London: Routledge Falmer.

Hollingworth, L. (1927) *Gifted Children: Their Nature and Nurture*. New York: Macmillan.

Kubow, P. K. and Fossum, P. R. (2003) *Comparative Education: Exploring Issues in International Context*. Upper Saddle River, NJ: Pearson Education.

Oakes, J. and Lipton, M. (1999) *Teaching to Change the World*. Boston, MA: McGraw-Hill.

Orfield, G. and Chungmei, L. (2005) *Why Segregation Matters: Poverty and Educational Inequality*. Office of Civil Rights. Cambridge, MA: Harvard University. Retrieved 15 March 2005 at: http://www.civilrightsproject.harvard.edu/

Smutny, J. F. (2003) *Underserved Gifted Populations: Responding to their Needs and Abilities*. Cresskill, NJ: Hampton Press.

Southern Poverty Law Center (2005) *Teaching Tolerance*. Retrieved 21 March 2005 at: http://www.splcenter.org/index.jsp and http://www.teachingtolerance.org

Swiniarski, L. B. and Breitborde, L. B. (2003) *Educating the Global Village*. Upper Saddle River, NJ: Pearson Education.

Torrance, E. P. (1977) *Discovery and Nurturance of Giftedness in Culturally Different*. Reston, VA: The Council for Exceptional Children.

US Department of Education (2005) *Jacob K. Javits Gifted and Talented Students Education*. Retrieved 25 April 2005 at: http://www.ed.gov/programs/javits/index.html

1 Cognition and underachievement

1.1 The triaxial bond of emotion, language and cognition: TASC – Thinking Actively in a Social Context

Belle Wallace

We are sentient, dynamic beings capable of change: but we can be trapped not only in the learned sense of what we are not, but also in a powerful negative mirror image of ourselves that we perceive emanating from others. Yet, we can be released through enabling interactions with those special mentors who offer constant and strong scaffolding that we are, indeed, of great worth and significance as individuals with potential.

Personal empowerment through self-esteem fuelled by praise

The greatest challenge that teachers can face is maintaining learners' motivation to *want to learn*, particularly when learners' life experiences are different from the mainstream school culture and customs. It is important then, that teachers understand the internal processes that underpin motivation. Maslow's (1968) discussion of universal needs is still essentially relevant today: the individual needs to belong to a group, needs to feel self-esteem and self-worth, needs to experience fulfilment of personal potential through self-expression, ownership of learning and creative endeavour. Lack of motivation arises when learners feel insignificant and undervalued, and experience frequent failure. Usually learners attribute this to internal factors, such as their lack of ability over which they have no control. Children who are in a minority culture often perceive school knowledge, defined by the dominant culture, as a series of topics quite unrelated to their fragile world concept. Many feel it is useless to apply effort when faced with a difficult task, and sink into chronic underachievement and low self-esteem: they succumb to the syndrome of *learned helplessness* (Weiner

1985). However, when the school fully accepts learners' cultures, not only celebrating but also integrating the cultures into the whole curriculum, pupils develop self-esteem, have a sense of belonging and experience a sense of personal significance.

As well as having a deep sense of personal significance, self-regulation and a sense of self-efficacy form the essential scaffolding for the development of high self-esteem, leading in turn to motivated learners with the belief that they are capable of learning. Central to the discussion of attribution theory, the empowerment of learners derives from learning to control their own learning: leading to the development of independent, autonomous learners (Pintrich and Schunk 1996; Weinstein and Van Mater Stone 1994). Self-regulation is the ability of learners to evaluate their own learning: to reflect on what and how they are learning, to monitor the processes of learning and to identify when there is a breakdown of understanding. Learners can then modify their approach to tasks to ensure effective learning; and this leads to the belief in self-efficacy, self-empowerment and the feeling of ownership of the learning process. Consequently, key elements that influence the development of self-efficacy lie within the processes teachers use to conduct lessons: the processes ranging along a continuum from enabling, interactive, inclusive, discursive processes to disabling, didactic, fixed content delivery. (The enabling processes are discussed more fully below.) Moreover, the feedback given by the teacher to each individual learner needs to convey a belief in the ability of the learner to succeed – positive *feed-forward* for success. Through verbal and non-verbal behaviours, teachers very powerfully convey their attitudes towards and expectations of the learners in the classroom: gradually the learners move closer to the teachers' expectations – the self-fulfilling prophecy deriving from learners' internalized reflections of themselves mirrored by people in 'authority' over them (Ames 1992; Dweck and Legett 1988).

Personal empowerment through communication fuelled by language

However, important though positive self-concept is for learner motivation and empowerment, the processes of learning interactions depend on how learners receive, understand and communicate through language – both verbal and non-verbal. Although there is growing acceptance of pupils' differentiated personal profiles of strengths across the full range of human abilities (Wallace et al. 2004), essentially language is the dominant mode of communication between people. Not only is language central to informal and formal learning, but also it is essential to the processes of thinking. We rationalize and make sense of the world through language which establishes our cognitive map of processes and meanings. But our language and cognitive development are inextricably bound up with our emotional development: the earliest exchanges of language reinforce our sense of self, our feelings of worth, our emerging identities. It is to be hoped that our first experiences of the world are of loving, reinforcing, secure exchanges of soothing reassuring words, sounds and expressed feelings.

Our 'first' language is non-verbal and we never lose the intuitive awareness of understanding expressions and body language – that sense of feeling in communication with others. But we need verbal language to give symbolic structure to thought, and it is in developing appropriate structures and expressions, that we become truly human (Schlesinger 1993). Although debate continues as to whether thought precedes language or language precedes thought, it is obvious that the two processes are closely intertwined. Lev Vygotsky (1978) argues that the quality and quantity of children's language development depends heavily on interaction with adults and more capable peers. When language is developed through interactive dialogue in the active process of problem-solving, then the more capable learner leads the less capable learner through the stages of the uncertainty of not knowing and not understanding, to the full realization of knowing and crystallization of meaning and understanding. The adult learner reaches out to identify the level of understanding of the child, and constructs and builds understanding within the child's 'zone of proximal development'. We can see immediately what this means for the teaching–learning interaction: through active problem-solving, mediated by appropriate language, the child understands and gains mastery and is ready for further learning.

There are many children who enter school with underdeveloped *home* language (L1), even from homes in the so-called developed world, where parents are so busy earning a living in order to survive, or are working long hours to buy material luxuries: these children have had insufficient time with their parents for quality, mediated interaction, and negotiation of language and understanding through problem-solving play activities (Wallace, in progress). Such children enter school lacking the extensive building blocks of language that they need to begin more formal learning, and teachers in nurseries and playgroups are finding that they need to develop the essential language for early school learning through verbally interactive and experiential play. In many so-called developing world communities, parents necessarily work away from home finding jobs in the cities, and children are often left to fend for themselves, consumed by the need to emotionally and physically survive, and often with the additional domestic chores of carrying water and cooking over a wood fire (Wallace and Adams 1993a). In both the developed and developing world contexts the learners are *under*developed with regard to having the verbal tools in L1 to express their thinking and feeling, especially in the context of school.

When the school language for learning (L2) is different from the home language (L1), children are faced with the huge challenge of negotiating meaning and understanding. However, learners with well-developed home language, with appropriate mediation, can more easily build bridges and *acquire* the school language of learning because they have a rich internalized language structure, and can draw parallels and make the cognitive links between the two languages. Even so, the children's home language needs to be accepted and celebrated since it is closely linked with their emotional development, sense of personal identity and sense of self-efficacy. The acceptance and practice of *additive bilingual* language acquisition as the means of learning and making meaning, celebrates both home and school language. Learners can switch between the second language (L2) used in school and their home language (L1), negotiating the meaning from one to the other (Wallace et al. 1996 ongoing). Additive bilingual learning, however, is still dependent on the learning being related to the social context of the learners: their culture, home background, sense of values, etc. The heavy cognitive load of negotiating meaning by straddling two languages is lessened when learners can identify with the content and find relevance within their own lives (Wallace et al. 1997, 1998, 1999). Moreover, the processes of teaching and learning using an additive bilingual approach are necessarily inter-active with learners having the time and opportunity to think, negotiate meaning and communicate. In addition, the rules and grammatical structures are initially of secondary importance to the understanding of meaning: when the teacher makes the input comprehensible, the rules of the second language (L2) become internalized naturally by the learner and are used automatically (Omaggio 1986). We can find a parallel to this process when we analyse how children acquire first language expressions, structures and syntax in a richly verbal home that accepts, celebrates and mediates the child's tentative language efforts, while supporting and extending the base of the child's own emerging language.

However, with children who have underdeveloped home language (L1), the problems of acquiring the school language of learning are exacerbated. The school language can be a second language in two senses: different, more formal modes of the same language (extended L1) or a different language (L2). In both cases, children have not learned a rich range of expressions and structures within their home language (L1), and when faced with learning in the *extended* L1 of school language, or the L2 of school language, they do not have the parallel or compensatory structures to build bridges linking home language and school language. The same principles of mediation and extension of language through negotiation of meaning, apply to the development of both extended L1 language and L2 language. Teachers need to begin language mediation from the base of the learners' own language: the language of the street, the peer group, and the home language, extending this to incorporate 'new' language for more formal learning. The teacher input *has to be comprehensible* to learners: Dromi (1993) and Krashen (1981) identify three variables which relate to learners' being able to access the meaning of teacher–pupil exchange:

- When learners' motivation is high, they can take risks with expressing ideas, however tentative that expression may be.
- When learners have high self-confidence and good self-image, they tend to be more open to accepting adaptations to their everyday home language (L1) and to accepting a new language (L2).
- Low levels of personal and classroom anxieties are indispensable for the acquisition of both extended L1 and L2 language.

Personal empowerment through language and thinking fuelled by active engagement in problem-solving

Wallace and Adams (1993b) maintain that successful teaching and acquisition of language, and the teaching of problem-solving and thinking skills, are inseparably fused together and, consequently, share the same common aims and purposes:

- Both should seek to develop language and cognitive skills through purposeful real-life situations that provide learners with authentic and meaningful contexts for learning.
- Both should view the acquisition of language and learning to think effectively as active processes. It is not sufficient for learners to learn *about* them; they need to *do* something constructive with the acquired skills.
- Both should see language and thinking skills as vehicles for self-expression, personalisation and ownership of the learning processes.
- Both should see the development of language and thinking as skills to be used and transferred across the curriculum.
- Both should develop a curriculum and teaching/learning processes that develop learners' positive self-image, internal locus of control, and the belief in lifelong learning.

The development of the TASC Project: Thinking Actively in a Social Context

Background

In 1984, Belle Wallace and Harvey Adams established the Curriculum Development Unit attached to the Faculty of Education, University of Natal, South Africa. They began a project which lasted for fifteen years, the overall aims of which were to research the needs of the disadvantaged Zulu population in the then apartheid Homeland of KwaZulu, to develop teachers' and learners' L1 and L2 language skills, to develop a range of appropriate thinking skills to promote self-esteem, independence and empowerment, and to design curricula which were relevant to and contextualized in Zulu culture. They worked within a spiral framework of action research, using a constructivist approach involving pupils, teachers, educational psychologists and parents or carers whenever possible. Importantly, Wallace and Adams did not work from a deficit framework of the skills the learners lacked, but from a framework of skills the learners already had: namely strong powers of memory due to their oral culture; well-developed group listening and leadership skills; democratic ways of working through discussion and sharing of ideas; ease of, and enjoyment in, cooperative learning; a tremendous motivation to learn as a means of self-development; and a deep and incisive awareness of the political, economic, social and emotional dimensions within a country wracked by division and inequality.

The existing situation in KwaZulu was one of mainly rural subsistence farming; high dropout rates from school due to lack of money for school fees, or long walking distances to the nearest school; high levels of failure in the regular 'control tests' and perceived self-inadequacy as learners; classes had over seventy pupils crowded into small, dark classrooms resulting in lectures for rote learning of facts; all lessons were conducted in the learners' L2 language. (Wallace and Adams 1993a). The project began with a group of twenty-eight mid-secondary school students identified by their teachers as the 'most able': this assessment was based on the fact that these students were achieving relative success in the school. The project was gradually extended to involve mixed-ability, class, year-groups, and both primary and secondary schools. It came to be known as 'TASC: Thinking Actively in a Social Context', its name evolving from a series of workshops where the students and their teachers identified the needs and problems they faced in both home and school. It is important to stress at this point that the learners perceptively expressed their need to work in ways already discussed in this chapter: they cemented through their personal experience and insight the application of the theories of learning and teaching outlined above. They also identified the overall need to be able to think in ways that made the western curriculum manageable, but could not yet identify these particular skills. Generalizing from these discussions and clarified by the current theory and research, the following tenets of TASC emerged:

- *Thinking*: although all learners can and do think, there is a vast range of 'formal' thinking tools and strategies that learners need to develop, so that the capacity of every learner increases. All learners can cope with complexity if they understand the task and can communicate effectively. The power and confidence to engage in effective thinking stems from the individual's belief in self-efficacy and self-regulation. Although language is a major tool for thinking, people can think using the full range of human abilities, for example, through dance, art, music, architecture, etc.
- *Actively*: learners need ownership of their learning; they need to play active roles in decision-making about how and what they learn, and they need to be involved in discussion of both immediate and long-term goals.
- *Social*: cooperative learning is powerful in its mediatory function; learners need to learn with and from each other. But there is also a need for learners to know how to work independently; and additionally, there is a need for learners to realize that they are globally responsible and enviro-dependent.
- *Context*: learners need to start learning in a context that is practical, real-life and concrete. The context needs to be relevant and meaningful so that they can relate to it and bring their own knowledge into the learning situation. As they develop mastery, they move into deeper, more abstract contexts, but these contexts are still related to their own world and level of understanding. (Since the early development of the TASC Project, the 'western' curriculum has been revised to produce a curriculum more relevant to learners in a multiracial, multicultural context.)

Theoretical underpinning of TASC

The theoretical underpinning of TASC evolved from the work of the theorists briefly outlined earlier in this chapter. The work of Vygotsky is central: the importance of social and cultural transmission and construction of knowledge as the fundamental vehicle of education, runs parallel with the vital role of mediation for understanding and mastery. Through cooperative, interactive learning, pupils negotiate language and meaning, internalizing concepts and gaining conscious control over their thoughts and actions. As they develop these understandings, they form language and thinking tools for further learning: the role of the teacher is to scaffold the task until learners become independent. Modelling thinking behaviour and thinking language is another key strand in TASC: the senior learner demonstrates, verbalizes and facilitates the active learning situation. A further element underpinning TASC is the essential requirement to develop self-esteem, self-efficacy and self-regulated learners through relevant context, constant success even in small stages, and positive assessment that feeds forward to further learning (Eggen and Kauchak 1997; McCown et al. 1996; Bandura 1982).

When we consider the range of thinking skills and strategies encompassed within TASC, then the work of Robert Sternberg (1985, 1997; Sternberg et al. 2001) has had a dominant influence. Sternberg proposes that 'intelligence' consists of three interrelated aspects:

- The contextual sub-theory in which intelligence is viewed as mental activity directed towards the purposeful adaptation to, selection of, and shaping of real world environments relevant to life. There are clear indications in this for the recognition of cross-cultural differences in cognition.
- The experiential sub-theory which proposes that intelligent performance on any task requires: the ability to deal with novel tasks; and the ability to automatize the processing of information.
- The componential sub-theory that specifies the strategy for information processing, i.e.

  - the executive (meta) processes that are used to plan, monitor and evaluate strategies used in problem-solving
  - the performance components used to carry out the task
  - the knowledge acquisition components that are used to learn how to solve problems in the first place.

All three components outlined above are interactive and need to be trained in parallel.

Many theorists stress the importance of metacognition, but the particular influence of the seminal work of Campione et al. (1984), Borkowski (1985) and Sternberg (1985) is particularly evident in the development of the TASC Framework. Metacognition is viewed as a component of intelligent behaviour used throughout life, as a process of generalizing effective thinking strategies and

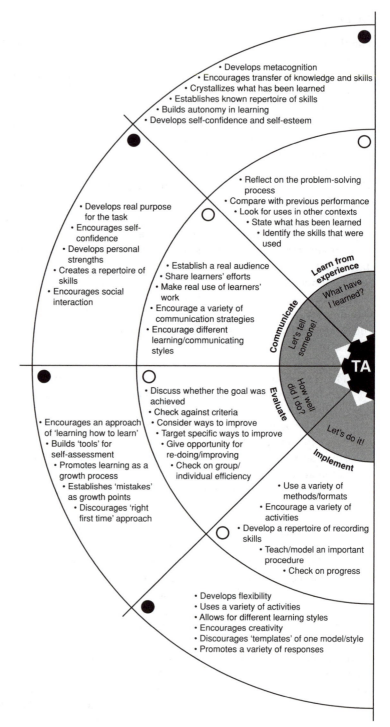

Figure 1.1.1 TASC Problem-solving Framework.

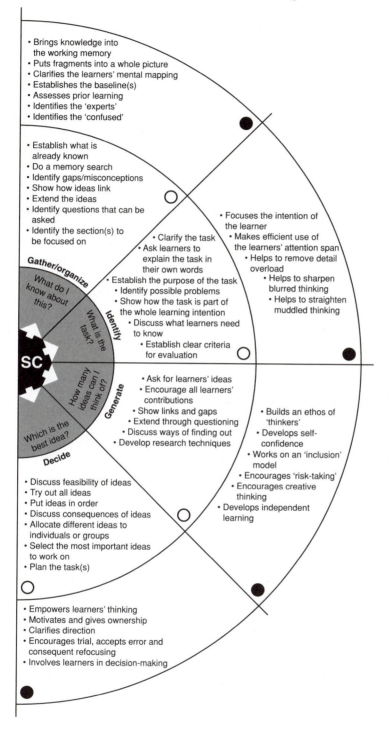

- Brings knowledge into the working memory
- Puts fragments into a whole picture
- Clarifies the learners' mental mapping
- Establishes the baseline(s)
- Assesses prior learning
- Identifies the 'experts'
- Identifies the 'confused'

- Establish what is already known
- Do a memory search
- Identify gaps/misconceptions
- Show how ideas link
- Extend the ideas
- Identify questions that can be asked
- Identify the section(s) to be focused on

Gather/organize
What do I know about this?

What is the task?

Identify

SC

How many ideas can I think of?

Which is the best idea?

Decide

Generate

- Clarify the task
- Ask learners to explain the task in their own words
- Establish the purpose of the task
- Identify possible problems
- Show how the task is part of the whole learning intention
- Discuss what learners need to know
- Establish clear criteria for evaluation

- Focuses the intention of the learner
- Makes efficient use of the learners' attention span
- Helps to remove detail overload
- Helps to sharpen blurred thinking
- Helps to straighten muddled thinking

- Ask for learners' ideas
- Encourage all learners' contributions
- Show links and gaps
- Extend through questioning
- Discuss ways of finding out
- Develop research techniques

- Builds an ethos of 'thinkers'
- Develops self-confidence
- Works on an 'inclusion' model
- Encourages 'risk-taking'
- Encourages creative thinking
- Develops independent learning

- Discuss feasibility of ideas
- Try out all ideas
- Put ideas in order
- Discuss consequences of ideas
- Allocate different ideas to individuals or groups
- Select the most important ideas to work on
- Plan the task(s)

- Empowers learners' thinking
- Motivates and gives ownership
- Clarifies direction
- Encourages trial, accepts error and consequent refocusing
- Involves learners in decision-making

as a key link between intelligence, self-knowledge and self-regulation. Through the process of metacognition, learners reflect upon their learning, crystallizing and automatizing thinking skills and processes.

Teaching principles of TASC

- Adopt a framework of the problem-solving process, and share and evaluate this with learners and teachers through the active solving of problems relevant to learners.
- Negotiate and use relevant language for thinking: naming strategies and skills appropriately to enable reference to and recall of these strategies in further problem-solving.
- Give attention to motivational aspects through praise and positive reinforcement of thinking behaviour.
- Model relevant thinking strategies then provide experiences for learners so that they use the strategies and perceive themselves as successful problem-solvers.
- Use cooperative, interactive teaching and learning methods with pupils working in small groups.
- Encourage self- and group-monitoring, evaluation and reflection on success, ways of improving and opportunities for transferring skills and strategies to other contexts.

Outline of the TASC problem-solving processes of teaching and learning

Figure 1.1.1 outlines the basic parameters of the TASC Framework, together with a selected range of key teaching and learning thinking skills and strategies.

Conclusion

There is not the space here to discuss the full extension and application of the TASC Framework and its applications to teaching and learning: however, readers are referred to the development and practical implementation of TASC in the following publications.

TASC applied in the context of the developing world

Wallace, B., Pandaram, S., Modiroa, T., Thomson, C., Mattson, E., Maltby, F. and Mungoshi, D. (Series authors) (1996 ongoing) *Language in my World: Grades 1 to 12*. Cape Town, South Africa: Juta Educational.
Wallace, B. and Baker, P. (Series authors) (1997, 1998, 1999) *Reading in my World: Grades 1 to 3*. Cape Town, South Africa: Juta Educational.

TASC applied in the context of the UK

Wallace, B. (2002a) *Teaching Thinking Skills across the Early Years: A Practical Approach for Children Aged 4–7.* London: David Fulton.

Wallace, B. (2002b) *Teaching Thinking Skills across the Primary Years: A Practical Approach for All Abilities.* London: David Fulton.

Wallace, B. (ed.) (2002c) *Using History to Develop Thinking Skills at Key Stage 2.* London: David Fulton.

Wallace, B. and Bentley, R. (2002) *Teaching Thinking Skills across the Middle Years: A Practical Approach for Children aged 9–14.* London: David Fulton.

Wallace, B., Maker, C. J., Cave, D. and Chandler, S. (2004) *Thinking Skills and Problem-Solving: An Inclusive Approach.* London: David Fulton.

Key questions

1 Discuss the issues which need to be addressed in developing multilingual classrooms. How would you begin to address these issues?
2 What are the issues that give precedence to a content-based curriculum rather than a process-based curriculum? What strategies need to be in place to transform the teaching-learning interaction?
3 Design a series of lessons around a global issue that emphasize problem-solving strategies and thinking skills.

References

Ames, C. (1992) Classrooms: goals, structures and motivation. *Journal of Educational Psychology*, 84: 261–271.

Bandura, A. (1982) Self-efficacy mechanism in human agency. *American Psychologist*, 37: 122–147.

Borkowski, J. E. (1985) Signs of intelligence: strategy generalisation and metacognition, in R. S. Yussen (ed.) *The Growth of Reflective Thought in Children.* New York: Academic.

Campione, J. C., Brown, A. L., Ferrara, R. A. and Bryant, N. R. (1984) The zone of proximal development: implications for individual differences and learning, in B. Rogoff and J. Wertsch (eds) *Children's Learning in the 'Zone of Proximal Development'. New Directions for Child Development* no. 23. San Francisco, CA: Jossey-Bass.

Dromi, E. (1993) Language and cognition: a developmental perspective, in E. Dromi (ed.) *Language and Cognition: A Developmental Perspective, Volume 5.* Norwood, NJ: Ablex.

Dweck, C. S. and Legett, E. L. (1988) A social-cognitive approach to motivation and personality. *Psychological Review*, 95: 256–273.

Eggen, P. and Kauchak, D. (1997) *Educational Psychology: Windows on Classrooms*, 2nd edn. Upper Saddle River, NJ: Merrill.

Krashen, S. D. (1981) *Second Language Acquisition and Second Language Learning.* New York: Pergamon.

McCown, R., Driscoll, M. and Roop, P. G. (1996) *Educational Psychology: A Learning-centered Approach to Classroom Practice*, 2nd edn. Boston, MA: Allyn and Bacon.

Maslow, A. H. (1968) *Toward a Psychology of Being*, 2nd edn. Princeton, NJ: Van Nostrand.

Omaggio, A. C. (1986) *Teaching Language in Context: Proficiency Oriented Instruction.* Boston, MA: Heinle and Heinle.

Pintrich, P. R. and Schunk, D. H. (1996) *Motivation in Education: Theory, Research and Applications*. Englewood Cliffs, NJ: Prentice Hall.

Schlesinger, I. M. (1993) If de Saussure was right, could Whorf have been wrong?, in E. Dromi (ed.) *Language and Cognition: A Developmental Perspective, Volume 5*. Norwood, NJ: Ablex.

Sternberg, R. J. (1985) *Beyond IQ: A Triarchic Theory of Human Intelligence*. New York: Cambridge University Press.

Sternberg, R. J. (1997) *Successful Intelligence*. New York: Plume.

Sternberg, R. J., Nokes, K., Geissler, P. W., Prince, R., Okatcha, F., Bundy, D. A. and Grigorenko, E. L. (2001) The relationship between academic and practical intelligence: a case study in Kenya. *Intelligence*, 29: 401–418.

Vygotsky, L. (1978) *Mind in Society*. Translated and edited by M. Cole, V. John-Steiner, S. Scribner and E. Souberman. Cambridge, MA: Harvard University Press.

Wallace, B. (in progress) *Lifting the Lid off Underachievement* (working title).

Wallace, B. and Adams, H. B. (eds) (1993a) *Worldwide Perspectives on Gifted Disadvantaged*. Oxford: AB Academic.

Wallace, B. and Adams, H. B. with F. B. Maltby and J. Mathfield (1993b) *TASC: Thinking Actively in a Social Context:* Oxford: AB Academic.

Wallace, B., Maker, C. J., Cave, D. and Chandler, S. (2004) *Thinking Skills and Problem-Solving: An Inclusive Approach*. London: David Fulton.

Wallace, B., Pandaram, S., Modiroa, T., Thomson, C., Mattson, E., Maltby, F. and Mungoshi, D. (Series authors) (1996 onwards) *Language in my World*. Cape Town, South Africa: Juta Educational.

Weiner, B. (1985) An attributional theory of motivation and emotion. *Psychological Review*, 92: 548–573.

Weinstein, C. E. and Van Mater Stone, G. (1994) Learning strategies and learning to learn, in T. Husen and T. N. Postlethwaite (eds) *International Encyclopedia of Education*, 2nd edn. New York: Pergamon.

1.2 Developing teachers' and learners' autonomy through reflection and meta-consciousness

Shlomo Kaniel

This chapter argues for the development of reflection and meta-consciousness (RMC) as a powerful process for developing teachers' and learners' awareness of their inner processes, so that they are able to manage and justify their thinking and actions. It is suggested that when RMC is the goal of the curriculum, teachers and learners enhance their thinking and increase motivation, as well as developing both intrapersonal and interpersonal awareness. RMC can also be an effective vehicle for differentiation across cultures, abilities and individual rates of progress.

The concept 'reflection' (Schön 1987) has its roots in education, whereas the term 'metacognition' (Sternberg 1999) stems from cognitive psychology. This chapter will redefine the core of both concepts within a framework of information-processing, and will seek to integrate both concepts (Anderson 1993; Estes 1999; Sternberg 1999).

Underlying concepts necessary to understanding reflection and metacognition

Cognition and consciousness

Originally, 'cognition' referred to processes, such as perception, memory, thinking, intelligence and imagery, and excluded emotions such as motivation and psycho-physical areas such as sensitivity thresholds. Recent research, however, has shown that components of emotions, cognition, motivation and behavior are intermixed. As a result, the concept 'cognition' has expanded and now encompasses most areas of psychology, from thinking, attention, memory, feelings and motivation to complex processes of intergroup, inter-organizational and interpersonal relations.

Working memory and stream of consciousness

'Working memory' refers to that part of consciousness which holds and processes relevant data such as contents, cognition, emotions and motivations (Baddely and Logie 1999). Working memory generates a stream of consciousness which continues throughout waking and dreaming hours. For processing to occur, sensory messages must encounter stimuli coming from memory storage such as languages using words, pictures and graphics; movement (dance, body language, non-verbal communication); numbers; sounds and musical tones. Somewhat like a river in changing states of flow, the contents of consciousness flow throughout one's life: although the contents themselves vary, the stream remains constant.

Reflection

The core of the concept 'reflection' refers to focused scrutiny of *something*, in order to examine it thoroughly. For the present purposes, that 'something' is oneself: one is reflected as if by a mirror. Self-observation allows people to gather data about their thoughts, feelings, physical appearance: this reflection underpins both interpersonal and intrapersonal communication. Reflection is also expressed when people fill out self-report questionnaires for surveys about attitudes, self-image, locus of control, and degrees of motivation or satisfaction.

Metacognition

Metacognition (Flavell 1979) is often defined as 'thinking about thinking', introspection or insight (Sternberg 1988; Bartsch and Wellman 1995). Accordingly, metacognition can be defined as 'a person's awareness of the workings of her or his own mind'.

'Meta-consciousness' rather than metacognition

We will use the concept meta-consciousness rather than metacognition to refer to the inner eye scanning everything flowing within the stream of consciousness. Then reflection becomes reflection about the body, about apparel, speech etc. and combines with meta-consciousness (RMC) which refers to the inner eye scanning stream of consciousness – emotions, motivation, cognition etc.

The components of RMC (Reflection and Meta-consciousness)

RMC can be organized around three major tiered components: the inner eye; knowledge about oneself, including knowledge about consciousness; management of the self, including management of consciousness. These three elements are accompanied by justification within the processes and contexts where they occur (Brown 1987; Flavell 1985; Nelson 1999).

The inner eye

In analysing RMC, the concept 'inner eye' becomes the first stage of the RMC processes: an inward gaze upon the self (reflection) or on the stream of consciousness (meta-consciousness). The spotlight is directed towards the observer and the eye scrutinizes one's own actions. For example, after a lesson, a teacher might say to herself: 'I get a headache every time I teach about the causes of World War II (reflection about her pain). Perhaps it's because my mastery of this material is inadequate (meta-consciousness).'

Following practice lessons, a teacher-trainer might ask trainees to look back at 'yourself-in-the-act-of-teaching'. In this situation, reflection will be expressed as reporting actions, and metacognition as recounting the stream of consciousness that passed through one's mind. The second possibility is that people themselves, on their own initiative, will look inward. The need to do this can arise from problems: after a class attains low grades, a teacher might examine her teaching; or if he has lost the desire to teach, he might investigate his feelings. Of course, it is best if the need for RMC is felt not only when one must cope with difficulties but also as a comprehensive and complex attitude combining cognition, emotions and behavior. This approach also includes the idea that people are responsible for themselves (internal locus of control) and achieve full functioning when they control and guide their mental processing.

Knowledge about the self, including knowledge about consciousness

After the inward gaze, one must analyse the content of the observation and judge whether the observation is correct and precise. This analysis of knowledge about the self (reflection) and about consciousness (meta-consciousness) can be organized within two possible categories.

The first possibility is that knowledge can be classified as declarative, procedural and conditional (Anderson 1990). *Factual or declarative knowledge* answers the question: 'What do I know about myself, about the task, and about the various strategies I can use in this task?' The term 'declarative' was chosen because the knowledge exists within consciousness and learners can report about it whenever necessary. *Procedural knowledge* answers the question 'How should I do this?' It involves a system of specific rules and principles for problem-solving within a knowledge domain. These inform the learner how to combine task components in ways that facilitate an optimal solution to the problem at hand. *Conditional knowledge* tells us when and why specific strategies should be used for each task. The three types of knowledge form a structure with progressive tiers.

A second possibility is to assign knowledge to three categories: knowledge about the *self*, about *tasks* and about *strategies* (Flavell et al. 1993). *Knowledge about the self* refers to areas such as knowledge about one's body, which includes elements such as body-image and proprioception; knowledge about various attention, memory and inference processes; knowledge about characteristics of the self (personality), which includes concepts like self-image, locus of control, sense of efficacy; teachers' knowledge about their instructional methods and learners' knowledge about their typical ways of learning; knowledge about one's strengths and weaknesses, personal attributes that influence task implementation (anxieties, self-image, locus of control); levels of expectation and ambition; emotional problems.

Knowledge about a task refers to the degree of task familiarity, how the task is structured, how much time is required, inherent risks and possibilities, past experience with tasks of this sort and, estimation of the task's difficulty. For instance, teachers planning an instructional unit (e.g., causes of World War II) must base their work on knowledge of historical facts, content structure, how much time pupils will need to achieve the lesson's goals, and conclusions drawn from previous teaching.

Knowledge about strategies concerns knowledge about appropriate strategies for performing a task and regulating processes of consciousness. The strategies should be effective in a wide range of situations and for a long period of time. There should also be reasons that justify the strategy's use (Kaniel 2001).

The two categorization possibilities presented above are examples of the importance of organizing knowledge. Organizing systems can be varied and represented graphically (picture, table, flow-chart). Importantly, since organization operations depend on people and not on the objects being sorted, one can predict that there will be significant difference within and among people and cultures.

Management of the self, including management of consciousness: goals, planned monitoring, control and feedback

Management of the self involves planning, performance and feedback so that all the components of learning work as a whole.

A number of constituents of management of the self can be outlined:

- *Goals:* goals are formulated, justified and defined, in terms of products.
- *Planning:* people select and sort elements of knowledge about themselves, the task, required time and strategies, and combine them in a manner which makes it possible to plan the problem's solution.
- *Monitoring and control:* monitoring refers to observation of the process and control refers to using the observations as the basis for action. This serves as feedback to the monitoring system, and the cycle continues. Combining monitoring and control within metacognition manifests as an internal dialogue between 'I as monitor/observer' and 'I as decider/executor/controller' (Nelson 1994). Continually keeping an eye on performance can be expressed as questions: 'Am I implementing this strategy correctly?' 'Am I working at the right pace?' 'Do I understand what I am doing?' For example, a teacher might estimate that, in order to prepare a lesson plan, she must perform a number of operations (gathering data, defining goals). Through monitoring, she may discover that she is already familiar with some of the material and can dispense with some of the work. Accordingly, she reduces the number of planned operations (control) or the time invested in learning.
- *Feedback and conclusions:* effective feedback must answer three major questions: 'Which of the things I did was effective and correct?' 'Which things were done badly, and therefore should be discontinued or changed?' 'What should be done next time?' In teaching, these questions should be answered at the end of every lesson, throughout the school year. In practice, there should be formative and summative evaluations to transform teachers into independent learners who develop and change throughout their careers. The whole RMC process should be constantly analysed and justified so that increasing self-knowledge transforms the apprentice learner into an expert learner.

Development of RMC components

RMC systems and mediation to the self (self-management) form a continuous multidimensional process and are an integral part of all aspects of consciousness, such as feelings, locus of control, sense of efficacy, motivation. However, there are considerations to be taken into account when developing RMC:

- *Cognitive overload:* too much immersion in RMC can be paralysing, overloading consciousness and working memory (Paris and Winograd 1990; Sweller 1994).
- *Poor interpretation:* RMC and self-talk can contain biased inferences, erroneous conclusions of causality (Hewstone 1989).
- *Mind (cognitive) closedness:* RMC and mediation to the self can be biased or overconfident, maintaining existing beliefs (Kruglanski and Webster 1996).

- *Overgeneralization:* many theorists contend that the components of RMC and self-talk are domain specific and carry the risk of overgeneralization (Gruber et al. 1999; Hirschfeld and Gelman 1994; Kelemen 2000; Kaniel 2001; Sternberg and Wagner 1994; Salomon 1993).

Application of RMC to education and teaching

Although perceptions of education differ, all provide a central place for RMC: the inner eye observing teaching knowledge, and management of instruction and learning. Four components must be explored: curricula, learning communities in challenging environments, use of advanced technologies and training teachers as RMC expects.

Curricula

A curriculum for developing RMC must have the following characteristics:

- The centrality of RMC as the curriculum's goal should be evident (Kaniel 1995).
- Concerning contents, the emphasis should be on the acquisition of knowledge about the functioning of consciousness and the central cognitive processes (attention, memory, working memory, mental images, reflection, metacognition, etc.). The curriculum should focus on decision-making, problem-solving and transfer of strategies, combining cognition, feelings and motivation.
- Learning tasks should provide many opportunities for success, thus improving pupils' self-image and motivation. Tasks should be set at various levels of difficulty, and classes should be flexible and differentially adaptable to group work, peer teaching, and computers. Thus, both strong and weak pupils can progress at their own rates, with appropriate challenges and successes. More able pupils will ascend the ladder of success with large steps, and less able pupils with smaller ones.
- In the specific context of RMC, multidisciplinary tasks with many solutions, such as research projects, should be chosen or designed. Through these tasks, learners can understand various processes for problem-solving. Tasks should be relevant, linking the classroom with real life.
- Teachers must model RMC. They must share, explain and consult with their pupils about RMC processes.

Learning communities in challenging environments

RMC is established through processes of acquisition, organization and storage of schemas relevant to different cultures (Lave and Wenger 1991; Van-Oers and Forman 1998). An effective environment and linguistic mediation can 'stretch' RMC towards more distant ranges of development (Vygotsky 1988). A good curriculum for developing RMC is embedded in novel situations (Kaniel and

Feuerstein 1989). A challenging environment must also include multifaceted communities which learn together (Campione et al. 1995), developing a culture of reflection and meta-consciousness expressed as much 'thinking out loud' and 'sharing'.

Use of advanced technologies

It is important to integrate advanced technologies whose central goal is expertise in RMC (Mason 1993; Jonassen et al. 1999). The primary advantage of computers is that they can provide modeling of RMC processes similar to experts (Venezky and Osin 1990). Effective software facilitates manipulations and interactions with various partners, such as teachers, computers, teaching materials and other pupils. Computers can also show pupils that learning takes place inside their heads; they direct it and are responsible for it.

Training teachers as RMC experts

Like teachers of any discipline, RMC teachers must have expertise above that of their pupils. Therefore, all the principles detailed above regarding curricula for pupils must also be part of teacher-training programs.

- Primarily, RMC creates integration among cognitive, personality and motivational factors which influence processes of learning and teaching with regard to different abilities, environments and cultures. A teacher expert in RMC will know what to teach, how to teach, when and why to teach.
- It is important to integrate teacher-training, teaching in schools, and life experiences focusing on problem-solving and decision-making.
- Teachers must be taught to make their own RMC processes transparent to pupils explaining and involving them in the process. Parents also need to be involved so that they can use RMC with their children.

Conclusion

Thus, through thinking about the self (reflection and meta-consciousness), a person will move from understanding the self to understanding the self of another. Such insight facilitates 'marching in another's moccasins' and contributes to greater tolerance and understanding.

Key questions

1   Reflect on your own sense of being in control of your own learning. What teaching and learning experiences enabled you to develop ownership of your learning?
2   Analyse the learning experiences you think trainee teachers need in order to develop their pupils' reflective and metacognitive processes.

3   Design a class topic for an age group of your choice. Indicate the teaching strategies you would use in order to develop the pupils' reflective and metacognitive processes.

References

Anderson, J. R. (1990) *Cognitive Psychology and its Implication*, 3rd edn. New York: Freeman.

Anderson, J. R. (1993) *Rules of the Mind*. Hillsdale, NJ: Erlbaum.

Baddeley, A. D. and Logie, R. H. (1999) Working memory: the Multiple-Component model, in A. Miyake and P. Shah (eds) *Models of Working Memory: Mechanisms of Active Maintenance and Executive Control*. New York: Cambridge University Press.

Bartsch, K. and Wellman, H. M. (1995) *Children Talk about the Mind*. New York: Oxford University Press.

Brown, A. L. (1987) Executive control, self-regulation, and other more mysterious mechanisms, in F. Weinart and R. Kluwe (eds) *Metacognition, Motivation, and Understanding*. Hillsdale, NJ: Erlbaum.

Campione, J. C., Shapiro, A. M. and Brown, A. (1995) Forms of transfer in a community of learners: flexible learning and understanding, in A. McKeough, J. Lupart and A. Marini (eds) *Teaching for Transfer: Fostering Generalization in Learning*. Mahwah, NJ: Erlbaum.

Estes, W. L. (1999) Models of human memory: a 30-year retrospective, in C. Izawa (ed.) *On Human Memory: Evolution, Progress, and Reflections on the 30th Anniversary of the Atkinson-Shiffrin Model*. Mahwah, NJ: Erlbaum.

Flavell, J. H. (1979) Metacognition and cognitive monitoring: a new area of cognitive developmental inquiry. *American Psychologist*, 34: 906–911.

Flavell, J. H. (1985) *Cognitive Development*, 2nd edn. Englewood Cliffs, NJ: Prentice Hall.

Flavell, J. H., Miller, P. H. and Miller, S. A. (1993) *Cognitive Development*, 3rd edn. Englewood Cliffs, NJ: Prentice Hall.

Gruber, H., Law, L., Mandl, H. and Renkl, A. (1999) Situated learning and transfer: implications for teaching, in P. Murphy (ed.) *Learners, Learning and Assessment*. London: Paul Chapman.

Hewstone, M. (1989) *Causal Attribution*. Malden, MA: Blackwell.

Hirschfeld, L. A. and Gelman, S. A. (1994) *Mapping the Mind: Domain Specificity in Cognition and Culture*. Cambridge: Cambridge University Press.

Jonassen, D. H., Peck, K. L. and Wilson, B. G. (1999) *Learning with Technology*, Upper Saddle River, NJ: Merrill/Prentice Hall.

Kaniel, S. (1995) Quality control for curricula. *Curriculum and Teaching*, 10: 3–6.

Kaniel, S. (2001) Transfer from the learner's point of view. *Journal of Cognitive Educational Psychology*, 3: 266–293.

Kaniel, S. and Feuerstein, R. (1989) Special needs of children with learning difficulties. *Oxford Review of Education*, 15: 165–179.

Kelemen, W. L. (2000) Individual differences in metacognition: evidence against a general metacognitive ability. *Memory and Cognition*, 28: 92–114.

Kruglanski, A. W. and Webster, D. M. (1996) Motivated closing of the mind: seizing and freezing. *Psychological Review*, 103: 263–283.

Lave, J. and Wenger, E. (1991) *Situated Learning*. Cambridge: Cambridge University Press.

Mason, R. D. (1993) *Computer Conferencing: The Last Word?* Victoria, BC: Beach Holme.

Nelson, T. (1994) *Metacognition*. London: Allyn and Bacon.

Nelson, T. (1999) Cognition versus metacognition, in R. J. Sternberg (ed.) *The Nature of Cognition*. Cambridge, MA: Bradford, MIT Press.

Paris, S. G. and Winograd, P. (1990) Promoting metacognition and motivation of exceptional children. *Remedial and Special Education*, 11: 7–15.

Salomon, G. (ed.) (1993) *Distributed Cognitions*. New York: Cambridge University Press.

Schön, D. A. (1987) *Educating the Reflective Practitioner*. San Francisco, CA: Jossey-Bass.

Sternberg, R. J. (1988) *The Triarchic Mind: A New Theory of Human Intelligence*. New York: Viking.

Sternberg, R. J. (ed.) (1999) *The Nature of Cognition*. Cambridge, MA: Bradford, MIT Press.

Sternberg, R. J. and Wagner, R. K. (eds) (1994) *Mind in Context: Interactionist Perspectives on Human Intelligence*. Cambridge: Cambridge University Press.

Sweller, J. (1994) Cognitive load theory, learning difficulty and instructional design. *Learning and Instruction*, 4: 252–312.

Van-Oers, B. and Forman, E. (1998) Introduction to the special issue of learning and instruction. *Learning and Instruction*, 8: 469–72.

Venezky, R. and Osin, L. (1990) *The Intelligent Design of Computer Assisted Instruction*. New York: Longman.

Vygotsky, L. S. (1988) *Thought and Language*. Translated, revised and edited by A. Kozulin. Cambridge, MA: MIT Press.

1.3   Creativity, intelligence, problem-solving and diversity[1]

C. June Maker

The world we have created is a product of our thinking; it cannot be changed without changing our thinking.

Albert Einstein

Need for changes in beliefs

Since the early 1900s, educators have limited their beliefs about intelligence and superior abilities to research and theories from psychology, particularly from the research on 'individual differences' even though this research has been conducted mainly on groups, especially those from advantaged and mainstream cultural backgrounds, with generalizations based on averages and 'standard' deviations rather than individual behavior (Ceci 1996; Nielson 1994). Ideas, results of empirical research, and theories from cultural anthropology, sociology, genetics, neuroscience, developmental psychology, education, and the new field of cognitive science must be integrated into our thought systems to form a more complete view of the multifaceted, multidimensional phenomenon we call giftedness. My life work has been to make changes in educators' ways of viewing children that are respectful of their differences and challenges as well as their strengths and capabilities.

A new framework: from theory to practice

The primary goal of my research has been to transfer theory and research into classrooms and communities by designing an assessment and curriculum model integrating the theoretical frameworks proposed by Ceci (1996), Sternberg (1997, 1999), and Gardner (1983, 1995), which are excellent examples of integrated perspectives. According to Ceci, a prerequisite for cognitively complex behavior in a given realm is the possession of a well differentiated yet integrated knowledge base that gets operated on by efficient cognitive processes: 'The knowledge and beliefs we possess in a specific domain . . . provide the raw materials for the operation of various cognitive processes during moments of problem solving' (1996: 22). Gardner (1983: 60–61) defines intelligence as 'a set of skills of problem solving enabling the individual to resolve genuine problems or difficulties that he or she encounters . . . , to create an effective product, and . . . the potential for finding or creating problems – thereby laying the groundwork for the acquisition of new knowledge.' Sternberg's ideas are similar. He emphasizes problem solving as a key element of competence, and, like Ceci, examines success in broader contexts than academic and professional ones with his theory of 'successful intelligence.'

To make Ceci's, Sternberg's, and Gardner's ideas applicable in education and easily understandable to teachers, my work on defining levels of content enabling students to see how facts and experiences are connected to 'big ideas' (Maker 1982; Maker and Nielson 1995) was integrated with the early work of psychologist Mihalyi Csikszentmihalyi (Getzels and Csikszentmihalyi 1967; 1976). Shirley Schiever and I elaborated and extended this work to create a continuum of problem types that could be used to develop assessments and curricula.

The framework of DISCOVER was designed to create a better alignment between the definition of problem solving, its assessment, and its development in an educational context. In Csikszentmihalyi's early research, the ability (and willingness) to structure an open-ended or ill-structured problem, or 'problem-finding' as it was later labeled, was the single trait that most accurately predicted the later creative achievements of artists. This research had a significant effect on the field of education for gifted students, leading to the development of numerous teaching models in which problem-finding was valued over the solving of already-defined problems or problems with known solutions (Gallagher et al. 1992; Maker and Nielson 1995). Using the DISCOVER Model, assessments and curricula include a balance of all types of problems, and incorporate all levels of content – from data to concepts, principles, and theories.

Since the publication of my first books on curriculum design and teaching (Maker 1981, 1982), I advocated the design of learning environments for gifted students that are learner centered, knowledge centered, assessment centered, and community centered (Bransford et al. 2000). Discovering Strengths and Capabilities while Observing Varied Ethnic Responses (DISCOVER) was created to extend these principles and practices into schools with high concentrations of culturally and linguistically diverse, geographically isolated, and low income students – helping administrators, teachers, parents, and communities to adopt a 'strength-based' instead of 'deficit-based' view of students (Maker 1993, 2001; Maker and King 1996; Maker et al. 1994; Maker et al. 1996).

The purpose of this chapter is to present a brief summary of DISCOVER – one model for eliminating barriers and increasing facilitators in identification and the design of curriculum and instruction for students from groups tradition-ally underrepresented in programs for the gifted. The chapter is not intended as a review of several approaches or a comparison of similar and different methods, but rather as an overview of DISCOVER. Information in this chapter is taken from a monograph published by the National Research Center on the Gifted and Talented (Maker 2004).

The definition of giftedness used in the DISCOVER framework is consistent with Stephen Ceci's (1996) Bioecological Theory of Cognitive Complexity and Sternberg's and Gardner's theories of intelligence: 'Giftedness is the ability to solve the most complex problems in the most efficient, effective, or economical ways.' In addition, gifted or highly competent individuals 'are capable of solving simple problems in the most efficient, effective, or economical ways.' (Maker 1993: 70) I believe that observation by competent, open-minded professionals, paraprofessionals, and community members is an important basis for decision-making across assessment and curricular contexts and consistent with these the-ories. The ideas presented in this chapter have evolved over the years, beginning with the study of gifted individuals with disabilities, then designing assessment and curriculum models based on Gardner's Theory of Multiple Intelligences and Sternberg's Triarchic Theory, and finally, rethinking and re-examining these assessment and curriculum models within the context of Ceci's Theory and the results of over sixteen years of research.

Barriers and facilitators: assessment and curriculum

Test makers and publishers continue to insist their instruments have no bias – yet those who score at the highest levels do not include equitable numbers of children from culturally and linguistically diverse groups, and programs for gifted students continue to be dominated by children and youth from mainstream, middle and upper socioeconomic environments and backgrounds (Coleman and Gallagher 1995; Ford and Harmon 2001; Gardner 1995; Maker 1996). A definite problem exists with the use of these instruments and the practices associated with them (Clasen et al. 1994; Cummins 1985, 1991; Ford and Harmon 2001). New instruments and procedures must be created, used, and evaluated.

Since intelligence and giftedness are complex constructs, and our world is in a constant state of change, programs and curricula also must be multi-dimensional and complex. Frameworks for program and curriculum development, as well as the practices that result, must be reframed so they are consistent with new beliefs, recent research, and new identification procedures. If learning is viewed as a transformation of an individual's knowledge and experiences rather than as an accumulation of new knowledge and experience, practices will be consistent with the latest information about how people learn (Bransford et al. 2000), and will be more culturally responsive to the changing faces of the children included in these programs.

The traditional and emerging paradigms (thought systems), that guide practice and research in education of the gifted (Feldman 1993; Treffinger 1991) are quite different, and can be examined both to gain an important perspective on the reasons why certain groups have continued to be underrepresented in special programs and to generate alternatives with the potential to change this national problem. In the traditional paradigm, giftedness is seen as equal to a high IQ, stable and unchangeable, identified based on psychological tests, elitist in orientation, authoritarian or 'top-down', school-oriented, ethnocentric, and expresses itself without special intervention. In the emerging paradigm, giftedness is perceived as having multiple forms, being developmental and process-oriented, based on performance, collaborative at all levels, and field-oriented. Excellence rather than elitism is the focus, diversity is central to its mission, and the context in which giftedness is assessed and developed is crucial to its expression. The traditional paradigm includes many barriers to the identification and provision of appropriate services for children from diverse groups, and examining this perspective carefully can help educators understand why certain groups remain underrepresented in special programs for the gifted. The emerging paradigm includes many facilitators – beliefs and practices that can help in identifying and providing appropriate services for underrepresented groups – so DISCOVER was designed from the viewpoint of the emerging paradigm. The aim of our teams of researchers and practitioners (Maker 1996) was to minimize barriers and increase facilitators both for identification and programming.

The DISCOVER Assessment

A fundamental belief in the equal distribution of abilities across diverse groups led to the creation of the DISCOVER Assessment. I believed that an emphasis on problem solving would be an important way to access the abilities of students from 'at risk' populations. When testing a student's knowledge, often we are assessing exposure, not the ability to learn the information. The ability to learn is the key. Producing sophisticated products also is influenced by exposure to ways of organizing and presenting information. Emphasis on use of effective strategies has the potential to 'level the playing field,' enabling students who solve problems on a daily basis to demonstrate their abilities. 'Little Claudia,' a five-year-old Mexican American girl, who was responsible for dressing her two-year-old brother and making sure he was taken to daycare before she went to kindergarten class, had extensive practice in problem solving. However, she was not exposed to advanced knowledge through visits to museums or a home environment with many sources of information, nor was she given opportunities to produce sophisticated products through special courses, lessons, or other opportunities afforded to children from middle and upper socioeconomic status (SES) families. Many children from diverse economic, geographic, and cultural groups face challenges similar to Little Claudia's. Research on the DISCOVER assessment is showing that, without lowering standards or changing criteria, when DISCOVER is used to identify gifted and talented students, the ethnic, economic, and linguistic balance in the identified groups parallels the balance of these groups in the community (Nielson 1994; Powers 2003).

Repeated assessments, revisions, feedback, and on-going data collection have resulted in a set of activities for each of four grade levels (K-2, 3-5, 6-8, 9-12), standardized procedures and directions, a behavior checklist to provide consistency in evaluations, and a 'debriefing' process for increasing inter-rater reliability. Assessments are conducted in the familiar classroom environment. The students' teacher is the facilitator. The observers who assess children are other general classroom teachers; specialists in education of the gifted, bilingual education or special education; pre-service educators; counselors; community members; administrators; and other experts. Students, in groups of four to five peers, are encouraged to interact and meet the challenges presented. Bilingual observers and teachers present instructions and interact with children in the dominant language(s) of the students.

Current and future efforts

During the past 16 years, colleagues, graduate students, and I have conducted studies of various aspects of the DISCOVER Assessment: consistency and reliability; inclusion of students from diverse linguistic, cultural, and economic backgrounds; theoretical or construct validity; concurrent validity; and predictive validity. Some studies have been published, some are master's theses or doctoral dissertations, and a few are internal reports designed to help us refine the assessment or detect problems we need to resolve.

Results from research on the DISCOVER Assessment provide support for its use to identify students from culturally, linguistically, and economically diverse groups. More studies have been done with this 'alternative' assessment than with most other such instruments in use in our schools. Clearly, however, more research is needed, especially predictive validity studies with different populations.

The DISCOVER assessment, however, cannot be separated from curriculum and teaching strategies, especially when they are designed to be interdependent. After a DISCOVER assessment is completed, administrators, teachers, parents (and the students themselves, especially at the high school level) receive information about the students' strengths (inter-individual and intra-individual) across the domains assessed, as well as very detailed reports of the problem solving behaviors observed during each activity. Problem solving behaviors are reported for each domain, core competencies within each domain, and for creativity and task commitment clusters. Teachers, parents, and students are assisted in the process of planning ways to build on student strengths as well as to compensate for weaknesses.

The DISCOVER Curriculum Model

In the DISCOVER Curriculum Model 'at-risk' students are viewed as being 'at-promise' for success due to their problem solving strengths in diverse cognitive domains. When students' strengths are identified and teaching approaches developed so that strengths are used as vehicles for developing academic and real-life skills, students from all groups, including those considered to be 'at-risk' experience greater success in school (Maker 1992; Maker et al. 1996). Children and their teachers and caregivers develop more positive and realistic beliefs about children's potential to succeed. When academic skills are taught within the context of real-world problem-solving, these academic skills take on new meaning, and students perceive them as relevant.

A consistent message of school reform efforts is that students in America's schools must learn to think and solve problems rather than memorize facts and mindlessly apply algorithms (National Council of Teachers of Mathematics (NCTM) 2000; President's Committee of Advisors on Science and Technology Panel on Educational Technology (PCAST-PET) 1997). A second consistent message is that a 'constructivist' (rather than a 'reductionist') approach is the most effective way to achieve the new national standards, and that certain key elements characterize this approach:

- active building of new knowledge from experience and prior knowledge
- acquisition of higher-order thinking and problem-solving skills
- basic skills learned while undertaking higher-level, 'real-world' tasks whose execution requires the integration of a number of skills
- information resources available to be accessed by the student at that point in time when they actually become useful in executing the task at hand
- fewer topics covered and explored in greater depth
- students as active 'architects' rather than passive recipients of knowledge (PCAST-PET 1997; NCTM 2000).

The DISCOVER curriculum is based on a constructivist philosophy, and involves using the principles of a good program for gifted students to enhance the learning and raise the standards for all students. Curricula and teaching strategies for gifted students are characterized by

- integrated, interdisciplinary content
- higher-order thinking, appropriate pacing, self-directed learning, and complex problem solving processes
- development of unique products for real audiences
- student interaction, interaction with experts, and learning environments with physical and psychological flexibility, openness, and safety.

The environment is rich in resources, and the teacher usually acts as a guide rather than a dispenser of knowledge as the students make choices based on interest and ability (Maker 1981, 1982; Maker and King 1996; Maker and Nielson 1995, 1996). These principles advocated for programs for gifted students characterize successful bilingual education programs (Cummins 1994; Nieto 1996; Ramirez 1991; Tharpe 1989), effective schools (Weissbourd 1996), and early childhood programs incorporating developmentally appropriate practices (Bredekamp and Rosegrant 1995; Maker and King 1996). In addition to these principles, the DISCOVER Curriculum Model includes two other elements to broaden its applicability to students with diverse backgrounds and personal traits, including types of abilities. These two important elements are arts integration, especially visual arts, music, creative dance/movement, and theater arts, and development of a wide range of problem-solving abilities.

Research on the DISCOVER Curriculum Model has shown that when teachers use this exciting approach consistently, their students learn more information, develop higher skill levels, improve their problem solving skills, and become more creative. In addition, when a high percentage of teachers in a school use the model consistently, the performance of all students at the school can increase steadily, and sometimes dramatically. Clearly, however, more research is needed, and this work is continuing. The most significant study currently in progress is an analysis of changes in student creativity, math performance, and written linguistic proficiency in classrooms of high, medium, and low implementers of the DISCOVER Curriculum model from the most recent project. We are developing and testing a new method for scoring the creativity test administered so that an acceptable level of inter-scorer reliability can be reached. Once this new system is in place, data have been collected about its effectiveness, and all tests have been re-scored, the analysis can be completed.

DISCOVER around the world

The framework and ideas forming the basis for DISCOVER are not only appropriate for honoring diversity in gifted children and youth in the United States, but also are important ways to meet the needs of diverse gifted learners in an international context. My work with educators in other countries has been rewarding, and has enabled me to develop a richer, deeper understanding of diversity.

China

DISCOVER now has partners in all three parts of China. After several colleagues and I took American students to Beijing for a Creative Problem Solving program, many discussions with educators from the Beijing Institute of Education resulted in my sponsorship of a Chinese scholar and several presentations to various groups interested in DISCOVER. In the summer of 2000, the DISCOVER in China project was born. A group of researchers interested in educational reform and Multiple Intelligences theory started a cooperative project that has grown and blossomed. Over 700 schools have been involved in various aspects of the project, and government officials are very supportive of our efforts because the goal of the project is development of students' abilities, creativity, and personality – the goal of new curricula in China. The project shows how this new goal can be integrated with the goal of mastering basic knowledge – the goal of traditional curricula in China. Educators involved in the project have combined 'the best of both worlds' by integrating the strengths of Western Education with the strengths of traditional education in China and other countries in the East.

In 2002, in addition to visiting interesting programs, I heard many teachers and other educators tell about the problem solving activities and experiences they have designed. Here is one excellent example from a science teacher of young children in Beijing:

- *Type I problem solving experience:* students made careful observations of different animals, looking at the relationship between the position of the animals' eyes and their eating habits.
- *Type II problem solving experience:* students looked at the eyes of different animals. They categorized the animals, and found that those with eyes in front ate meat and those with eyes on the sides of their heads ate grass and plants.
- *Type III:* students were asked to think about why the animals' eyes are in different positions.
- *Type IV:* students were asked to think about the principle and to form a hypothesis about the relationships between plant and animal structures and functions.
- *Type V:* students conducted their own investigations about structure and function in nature and outside of nature.

In one province, the DISCOVER Problem Continuum is being used to construct questions on college entrance examinations.

In 2003, Aibi Chen, the first Chinese scholar to study DISCOVER, completed an innovative book (Chen 2003). In it, she constructed an instruction through problem solving model with Chinese characteristics based on the continuum of problems used in the DISCOVER Projects. In this book, she offered both practical and theoretical discussions of ways to localize and adjust the problem-solving continuum so that Chinese teachers could see how to meet the goals of the new curricula in China. She included an excellent discussion of the stages of development of instruction through problem solving in China. The first stage is 'exploring' in which the teachers are led to change their way of teaching from a 'transferring-accepting' model to problem-based teaching, in which they change 'content' or result to 'problem'; change 'well-structured' problems to 'ill-structured' problems, and 'closed' problems to 'open-ended' problems. The second stage is the 'standard stage' in which the teachers are led to apply the problem continuum, to form a norm of teaching through a problem solving model in which the value of each type of problem is explained, and the principle of designing each type of problem is provided. The third stage is the 'reframing stage.' After internalizing the problem continuum, teachers are encouraged to implement it in a more flexible and creative way and with personal style, so that instruction through problem solving is shown as a perfect integration of 'science and art' in teaching. The principle of designing instruction using the problem continuum is also provided in this stage.

In Hong Kong, the DISCOVER Assessment has been used in an international center for the gifted since 1998. Students' creativity and problem solving are assessed as a part of a comprehensive measure of the abilities of gifted students and students with learning difficulties. Dr Hing Fung Tsui, from the Hong Kong Institute of Education, and I are working to design research and create various cooperative projects between the University of Arizona and the Hong Kong Institute of Education. This year, an exciting new book entitled *Creativity: When East Meets West* was published by World Scientific Publishing Company, Ltd, containing a chapter on DISCOVER. The book contains many excellent chapters resulting from a conference on creativity sponsored by Hong Kong Baptist University's Child Development Center, another DISCOVER partner.

Taiwan

In Taiwan, the University of Arizona has a cooperative mentoring and research program with Kang Ning College. This includes exchanges of scholars and presentation of curriculum design workshops. In 2003, under the direction of Dr Ching-Chih Kuo, I also became involved in a cooperative research project at National Taiwan Normal University (NTNU). The purpose of this project is to identify and nurture multiple intelligences and problem solving abilities in gifted/talented handicapped and non-handicapped preschool children. NTNU has received funding from the National Science Council to support this work.

Korea

Science and math teachers participate in an action-packed workshop on the University of Arizona campus in which they solve science and math problems using a combined model we are recommending for science and math. The curriculum framework is the DISCOVER Curriculum Model (with the Human Abilities from the Prism Model I will describe later), Thinking Actively in a Social Context (TASC) is the process for solving problems, and Problem Based Learning (PBL) is the model for designing complex Type IV problems that lead to students' identification of their own Type V Problems. The Hilda Taba Teaching Strategies (HTTS) are used to structure teacher discussions about student research, and the Schoolwide Enrichment Model (SEM) serves as an administrative framework. During a follow-up visit to the teachers, I established cooperative research agreements with Busan National University of Education and the National Center for the Gifted directed by Dr Seokhee Cho.

Mexico

In Mexico, a physician interested in early development started a school based on the DISCOVER Curriculum model and began adaptation of the DISCOVER Assessment for Mexican children. He also started an exciting community program for children and parents called a children's museum. In this biannual event, children and their parents come to the University of Juarez on the weekend. They participate in problem-solving activities in all of the multiple intelligences. Children have fun while parents learn more about their children and about the theory of multiple intelligences. Children can choose from a variety of activities, and can stay as long as they choose in any of the areas. At the children's museum in 2002, for example, several activities captured the children's attention; the most interesting one was making rockets from recycled plastic bottles and then launching them!

United Kingdom, United States, and Thailand

In three countries, an exciting cooperative action research project is underway. Together with educators from two very different countries, one in Europe and one in Asia, I have developed a theoretical framework and practical applications in which our research and development experiences are integrated. One book has been published and one is in progress as well as several action research projects in which we are designing, implementing, evaluating, and revising our model and applications. Similar action research projects in the United States will be initiated, and new ones are welcomed.

The new framework represents an integration of DISCOVER with the Thinking Actively in a Social Context (TASC) model originally developed in response to concerns about underachievement, dropout rates, and the standard instructional practice of rote memorization in KwaZulu/Natal schools in South Africa (Adams and Wallace 1991; Wallace and Adams 1993), and subsequently applied with aboriginal children in Australia and with children in England; and the Exploring Centers model developed originally for use in a private school in Thailand, and subsequently adopted by public and private schools all over Thailand, including alternative schools and programs operated by the Thai Red Cross (Anuruthwong 2002). The Exploring Center's use has spread to other Asian countries as well. The description is updated and excerpted from other publications: Maker and Anuruthwong (2003) and Wallace et al. (2004).

The prism of learning model

> Prism (priz'em) n. a crystalline solid with at least three similar faces paralleling a single axis, for producing or analysing a continuous spectrum.

A prism is the metaphor we use for this new learning model. The mind of a child is like the beautiful light coming out of a prism – an iridescent rainbow with a spectrum of colors. Each mind is unique, with its own combination of colors, shades, and shapes.

The prism of learning has three sides. On one side is the environment, another the competencies or outcomes we expect from learners, and on the third side are the learning processes. In the middle, or the axis, are human abilities. Often, the three dimensions are not in harmony, and seldom do we synchronize these dimensions with the inner, natural abilities of children. Our responsibility as guides in the learning process is to create more harmony in all dimensions so that the full spectrum of abilities can be integrated and separated in the same way that a prism refracts the light. We must provide the kind of environment that will enable each child to be illuminated from within. Educators can be the most important 'illuminators,' especially for children without advantages in their home environments.

Problem solving: the key construct in intelligence and creativity

At the heart of all theories of intelligence and creativity is the concept of problem solving. Various theories exist to explain the abilities needed to resolve everyday problems as well as to create new knowledge. We use a simple definition: a problem is 'a question or situation that presents doubt, perplexity, or difficulty; a question offered for consideration, discussion, or solution' (Webster's II: *New Riverside University Dictionary*, p. 937). A problem is not necessarily bad. It is a challenge: something we want to resolve, change, or create. Problem solving, then, is the process of answering questions, resolving difficulties, creating solutions, and investigating perplexing situations.

To solve problems, people must use six general capacities – memory, creativity, reasoning or logic, metacognition, intuition, and sensitivity, and metacognition – and ten types of human abilities: social, emotional, somatic, visual/spatial, auditory, mathematical/symbolic, linguistic, mechanical/technical, scientific, and spiritual. A short definition of these capacities and abilities is provided in the following sections. To solve problems, people also must use certain learning processes and acquire certain competencies. Integration of general capacities, human abilities, learning processes, and competencies in an exciting learning environment is the essence of the prism model.

General capacities

- *Memory:* remembering information and experiences.
- *Creativity:* the ability to think of, develop, or implement unique and appropriate ideas or solutions.
- *Reasoning or logic:* the general capacity to think in systematic ways.
- *Metacognition:* self-awareness and the ability to monitor one's own thinking.
- *Intuition:* the ability to know something immediately – without going through steps or sequences of thought. Intuition is the language of understanding,

and can be considered our real first language while the words, symbols, and sounds an individual learns are part of their *second* language.

- *Sensitivity:* emotional and sensory openness to experiences; the capacity to respond to experiences and feelings, and to respond with emotional awareness and intensity.

Human abilities

At the most specific level, humans have ten different types of abilities: social, emotional, somatic (touch, movement, taste), visual/spatial, auditory, mathematical/symbolic, linguistic, mechanical/technical, scientific, and spiritual. People have a spectrum of abilities – a broad range of related qualities that are combined in many different ways to solve problems, meet challenges, and create new products. In all activities and careers several of these basic abilities are needed. However, most activities and careers have two or three that are dominant, and therefore essential to success.

- Social abilities are skills we need to get along with other people.
- Emotional abilities are the skills we need to manage our emotions.
- Mathematical/symbolic abilities consist of the use of abstract models, numbers, mathematical figures and objects that symbolize abstract ideas.
- Somatic abilities include large muscle movements as well as small muscle movements, and also include touch, taste, and smell.
- Visual/spatial abilities include seeing things accurately and clearly through one's physical eyes as well as seeing images clearly in one's mind.
- Auditory abilities are skills in hearing, producing, and manipulating sounds.
- Linguistic abilities are skills in using words.
- Mechanical/technical abilities are the skills needed to understand, create, and repair machines or other devices that perform or help perform human tasks.
- Scientific abilities include observing, identifying, describing, classifying, studying, and explaining natural phenomena.
- Spiritual abilities include knowledge, ability, and willingness to see beyond bodies and objects to develop awareness and understanding of phenomena related to the human soul or spirit.

Learning processes

Learning processes can be explained by using the metaphor of a tree. Some learning processes include observing, feeling, connecting, decoding, remembering, imagining, composing, duplicating, symbolizing, translating, developing, crystallizing, transforming, playing, listening, searching, reflecting, sensing, enjoying, producing, exploring, engaging, and inventing. Some learning processes are conscious and some are subconscious, corresponding to the roots (subconscious) and branches (conscious) of the tree. Some processes are above the surface while others are below the surface, and all are essential to the growth and development of the tree.

Learning processes also include the problem-solving processes used to meet the challenges of life! As people meet important challenges, they go through a series of steps – either consciously or unconsciously – that result in selecting or implementing a particular solution. Many develop effective methods, while others struggle, use trial and error ineffectively, or select the first idea that comes to mind rather than considering the consequences of several solutions. We believe that both children and adults can benefit from learning a flexible problem-solving process they can apply in many and varied situations. Thinking Actively in a Social Context (TASC), the process we advocate, is a 'wheel' with eight spokes: gather/organize, identify, generate, decide, implement, evaluate, communicate, and learn from experience. Usually, the process begins with gathering and organizing, and proceeds around the wheel. However, generating ideas may sometimes be the first step, and one may need to revisit certain steps in a spiral fashion. TASC includes all the learning processes and helps both teachers and children structure their problem solving experiences, becoming more effective problem solvers.

Competencies

Competencies are the things we want children to learn as a result of school or life experiences. Often, educators attempt to categorize or compartmentalize competencies, separating academic subjects in artificial ways. Knowledge is connected and interdependent just as our bodies and all natural systems are connected and interdependent.

We define key ideas for each age and grade level and recommend ways to integrate important information and competencies from the traditional academic disciplines into each of these themes. For example, individuality, change, patterns, relationships, cycles, and environment are key ideas for young children in preschool and early grades (Grades K to 2), while conflict, communication, cooperation, interaction, and structures are important ideas to internalize during the middle elementary years (Grades 3 to 5). Middle school students (Grades 6 to 8) need to understand concepts such as culture, extinction, exploration, diversity, and systems. Secondary students (Grades 9 to 12) need to struggle with ethics, beauty, harmony, invention, and interdependence. Secondary school students also must revisit all the other themes with an emphasis on development of competencies needed for life success.

Learning environment

The learning environment has two major components: physical and dynamic. The physical environment includes color, shape, temperature, light, sound, textures, and materials. The physical environment includes buildings, playgrounds, trees and other natural things as well as the way the teacher sets up the classroom, organizes the chairs, puts posters on the walls, and organizes input or stimuli. The dynamic environment includes the teaching methods and processes as well as the ways teachers interact with children. The activities the teacher organizes, the questions she asks, the reinforcement or punishment methods, and the classroom management techniques are part of the dynamic environment.

How to make effective, joyous learning happen

We believe that the best way to make effective, joyous learning happen is to set up a learning center (as big a room as possible) with a 'corner' or special place for each of the human abilities except social and spiritual. Put in a creative, empathic, knowledgeable teacher/guide, include both individual and group activities that are challenging and engaging; bring in the children, and let them explore and discover! The teacher designs a learning environment to facilitate learning, maintains this environment, and develops ways to motivate and challenge students while allowing sufficient time for exploration and discovery. In this environment, learning is fun for both the teacher and the children!

A center can be in an individual teacher's classroom, or can be a large room in a school, serving all children in the school. We can identify advantages and disadvantages to both these models, so educators can choose the model that works best within their budgets or school space limitations. Belle, June, and Usanee are working on manuals and examples to provide guidance to everyone who wants to make learning effective and joyous by using the prism of learning model.

Conclusion

Across these diverse settings, and resulting from the research presented in the boxes, general principles and recommendations emerge that can provide a useful guide to educators (policy-makers, principals, coordinators of special education and programs for gifted students, and teachers) wishing to increase the participation of and improve services to students from underrepresented groups in programs for the gifted. Only if educators are committed to the goal can they accomplish it, and the goal will be accomplished more quickly if we work at all levels, both simultaneously and cooperatively.

Policy-makers are urged to implement pilot programs in which the progress (success in the program or in regular classrooms) of students identified by various instruments is monitored, analyse these data, and report the results to others using or considering certain instruments; and to create policies requiring that all students be served in ways consistent with their strengths and challenges. Program coordinators are asked to include many types of screening and referral procedures (such as performance-based measures like DISCOVER), to supplement teacher referral as a first step in deciding which children to test or examine further, and to develop services for gifted students instead of 'a program.' Principals are urged to interview or find other ways to elicit teacher statements or information to identify the beliefs of teachers, determine whether teachers' views are consistent with the traditional or emerging paradigm, and initiate discussions and study groups to examine consistencies or discrepancies between beliefs and practices, and devise ways to resolve discrepancies. Teachers are urged to examine their own beliefs about giftedness and think about how they evolved, expand options provided for all students, and to try the DISCOVER curriculum approach if it fits within their belief systems. Detailed recommendations are presented in the monograph from which this material was excerpted (Maker 2004).

Many resources are available for those wishing to implement the DISCOVER Assessment and Curriculum Models. Readers are invited to visit the website at www.discover.arizona.edu and to contact the DISCOVER team of professionals to gather more information or request other resources listed on the web site.

Key questions

1   Discuss the concept of 'intelligence' proposed in this chapter. Analyse the characteristics of your own 'intelligent' behavior which correspond with the concept proposed in this chapter.
2   Discuss the characteristics of 'intelligence' that you would try to develop in the pupils in your classes. How would you do this?
3   Design a series of lessons around a global theme that would allow pupils to engage in open-ended problem-solving.

Note

1   This chapter is extracted from C. June Maker (2005) *The DISCOVER Project: Improving Assessment and Curriculum for Diverse Gifted Learners.* Storrs, CT: National Research Centre on the Gifted and Talented.

References

Adams, H. B. and Wallace, B. (1991) A model for curriculum development. *Gifted Education International*, 7(3): 105–113.

Anuruthwong, U. (2002) Exploring center: ignition key to children's potential and thinking, in U. Anuruthwong, S. Hiranburana and C. Piboonchoil, *Igniting Children's Potentials and Creativity: Proceedings of the 7th Asia-Pacific Conference on Giftedness* (pp. 92–93). Bangkok: Center for the Gifted and Talented, Srinakharinwirot University.

Bransford, J. D., Brown, A. L. and Cocking, R. R. (2000) *How People Learn: Brain, Mind, Experience, and School.* Washington, DC: National Research Council.

Bredekamp, S. and Rosegrant, T. (1995) *Reaching Potentials: Appropriate Curriculum and Assessment for Young Children*, Volume 1. Washington, DC: National Association for the Education for Young Children.

Ceci, S. J. (1996) *On Intelligence: A Bioecological Treatise on Intellectual Development*, 2nd edn. Cambridge, MA: Harvard University Press.

Chen, A. (2003) *DISCOVER in China: Curriculum Reform and Instruction Through Problem Solving.* Beijing: Beijing University Press.

Clasen, D. R., Middleton, J. A. and Connell, T. J. (1994) Assessing artistic and problem-solving performance in minority and non-minority students using a nontraditional multidimensional approach. *Gifted Child Quarterly.* 38: 27–37.

Coleman, M. R. and Gallagher, J. J. (1995) State identification policies: gifted students from special population. *Roeper Review*, 17: 268–275.

Cummins, J. (1985) *Bilingualism and Special Education: Issues in Assessment and Pedagogy.* San Diego, CA: College Hill.

Cummins, J. (1991) Institutionalized racism and the assessment of minority children: a comparison of policies and programs in the United States and Canada, in T. J. Samuda, S. L. Kong, J. Cummins, J. Pascual-Leone and J. Lewis (eds) *Assessment and Placement of Minority Students* (pp. 97–107). Kingston/Toronto: Intercultural Social Sciences Publications.

Cummins, J. (1994) Primary language instruction and the education of language minority students. In California State Department of Education (ed.) *Schooling and Language Minority Students: A Theoretical Framework*, 2nd edn. Los Angeles, CA: Evaluation, Dissemination and Assessment Center.

Feldman, D. H. (1993) Has there been a paradigm shift in gifted education?, in N. Colangelo, S. G. Assouline and D. L. Ambroson (eds) *Talent Development: Proceedings from the 1991 Henry B. and Jocelyn Wallace National Research Symposium on Talent Development* (pp. 89–94). Boston, MA: Trillium Press.

Ford, D. Y. and Harmon, D. A. (2001) Equity and excellence: providing access to gifted education for culturally diverse students. *Journal of Secondary Gifted Education*, 12: 141–148.

Gallagher, S. A., Stepien, W. J. and Rosenthal, H. (1992) The effects of problem-based learning on problem-solving. *Gifted Child Quarterly*, 36(4): 195–200.

Gardner, H. (1983) *Frames of Mind: The Theory of Multiple Intelligences.* New York: Basic Books.

Gardner, H. (1995) Reflection on multiple intelligences: myths and messages. *Phi Delta Kappan.* 77: 200–209.

Getzels, J. and Csikszentmihalyi, M. (1967) Scientific creativity. *Science Journal*, 3(9): 80–84.

Getzels, J. and Csikszentmihalyi, M. (1976) *The Creative Vision: A Longitudinal Study of Problem Finding in Art.* New York: John Wiley and Sons.

Heckman, P. E. (1996) *The Courage to Change: Stories from Successful School Reform.* Thousand Oaks, CA: Corwin.

Maker, C. J. (1981) The gifted hearing-impaired student. *American Annals of the Deaf*, 126: 631–645.

Maker, C. J. (1982) *Curriculum Development for the Gifted.* Austin, TX: Pro-Ed.

Maker, C. J. (1992) Intelligence and creativity in multiple intelligences: Identification and development. *Educating Able Learners: Discovering and Nurturing Talent*, 27: 12–19.

Maker, C. J. (1993) Creativity, intelligence, and problem-solving: a definition and design for cross-cultural research and measurement related to giftedness. *Gifted Education International*, 9: 68–77.

Maker, C. J. (1996) Identification of gifted minority students: a national problem, needed changes and a promising solution. *Gifted Child Quarterly*, 40(1): 41–50.

Maker, C. J. (2001) DISCOVER: Assessing and developing problem solving. *Gifted Education International*, 15(3): 232–251.

Maker, C. J. (2004) Creativity and multiple intelligences: the DISCOVER project and research, in S. Lau, N. N. Hui and Y. C. Ng (eds) *Creativity: When East Meets West.* Singapore: World Scientific.

Maker, C. J. (2005) *The DISCOVER Project: Improving Assessment and Curriculum for Diverse Gifted Learners.* Storrs, CT: National Research Centre on the Gifted and Talented.

Maker, C. J. and Anuruthwong, U. (2003) The miracle of learning: the prism model. *Proceedings of the 15th Biennial World Conference of the World Council for Gifted and Talented Students.* Adelaide, Australia: World Council for Gifted and Talented Students.

Maker, C. J. and King, M. A. (1996) *Nurturing Giftedness in Young Children.* Reston, VA: Council for Exceptional Children.

Maker, C. J. and Nielson, A. B. (1995) *Teaching/Learning Models in Education of the Gifted,* 2nd edn. Austin, TX: Pro-Ed.

Maker, C. J. and Nielson, A. B. (1996) *Curriculum Development and Teaching Strategies for Gifted Learners,* 2nd edn. Austin, TX: Pro-Ed.

Maker, C. J., Nielson, A. B. and Rogers, J. A. (1994) Giftedness, diversity, and problem-solving: multiple intelligences and diversity in educational settings. *Teaching Exceptional Children,* 27(1): 4–19.

Maker, C. J., Rogers, J. A., Nielson, A. B. and Bauerle, P. (1996) Multiple intelligences, problem solving, and diversity in the general classroom. *Journal for the Education of the Gifted,* 19(4): 437–460.

National Council of Teachers of Mathematics (NCTM) (2000) *Principles and Standards for School Mathematics: An Overview.* Reston, VA: NCTM.

Nielson, A. B. (1994) Traditional identification: elitist, racist, sexist? New evidence. *CAG Communicator: The Journal of the California Association for the Gifted,* 3: 18–19, 26–31.

Nieto, S. J. (1996) Affirming Diversity: *The Sociopolitical Context of Multicultural Education,* 2nd edn. New York: Longman.

Powers, S. (2003) Evaluation report for Project LISTO: Paradise Valley Unified School District, Arizona. Creative Research Associates, Inc., 2030 E. Broadway, Suite 221, Tucson, AZ, 85719.

President's Committee of Advisors on Science and Technology Panel on Educational Technology (PCAST-PET) (1997) Report to the President of the use of technology to strengthen K-12 education in the United States.

Ramirez, J. D. (1991) *Longitudinal Study of Structured English Immersion Strategy, Early-exit Transitional Bilingual Education Programs for Language-minority Children.* Final report to the US Department of Education, executive summary. San Mateo, CA: Aguirre International.

Sternberg, R. J. (1997) *Successful Intelligence.* New York, NY: Plume.

Sternberg, R. J. (1999) Intelligence as developing expertise. *Contemporary Educational Psychology,* 24: 259–375.

Tharpe, R. G. (1989) Psychocultural variables and constants: effects on teaching and learning in schools. *American Psychologist,* 44: 349–359.

Treffinger, D. J. (1991) Future goals and directions, in N. Colangelo and G. Davis (eds) *Handbook of Gifted Education.* Boston, MA: Allyn and Bacon.

Wallace, B. and Adams, H. B. with F. B. Maltby and J. Mathfield (1993) *TASC: Thinking Actively in a Social Context.* Oxford: AB Academic.

Wallace, B., Maker, C. J., Cave, D. and Chandler, S. (2004) *Thinking Skills and Problem-solving: An Inclusive Approach.* Oxford: AB Academic.

Weissbourd, R. (1996) *The Vulnerable Child.* Reading, MA: Addison-Wesley.

Table 1.3.1 Beliefs about giftedness

Traditional paradigm	Emerging paradigm
Gifted = High IQ	Multiple Forms
Trait Theory: Stable, Unchangeable	Developmental, Process-oriented
Identification Based on Tests	Based on Performance
Elitist in Orientation	Excellence a Focus
Authoritarian, Top Down	Collaborative at All Levels
School-oriented	Field-oriented
Ethnocentric	Diversity Central to Mission
Giftedness Expresses Itself Without Special Intervention	Context Is Crucial

Sources: Feldman 1992; Treffinger 1991.

1.4   Understanding learning: creating a shared vocabulary

John West-Burnham

Any discussion about the nature of learning in the future risks indulging in a false optimism – seeking to describe Shangri-la. This is not the purpose of this discussion; rather it is to try to identify current knowledge and trends and extrapolate from them what our emerging understanding of education might lead to. We create the future, the decisions that we take now will determine the nature of schooling, educating and learning in the future.

Understanding the learning process

The historically dominant paradigm of learning as the product of teaching is being replaced by a recognition that teaching is a necessary, but not sufficient, condition for learning. We will focus on three areas where our understanding of the learning process is developing rapidly:

- the science of learning
- learning as a social relationship
- intelligence and learning.

For many educators, the concept of learning is implicit and assumed. In some usages it implies what the learner does in response to teaching, 'If you don't pay attention to me you won't learn this'. A common usage equates learning with memorization, 'I want you to learn this for a test tomorrow'. Although the situation is now changing, many schools do not have a shared vocabulary as to

Table 1.4.1 Modes of learning

	Shallow	*Deep*	*Profound*
Means	Memorization	Reflection	Intuition
Outcomes	Information	Knowledge	Wisdom
Evidence	Replication	Understanding	Meaning
Motivation	Extrinsic	Intrinsic	Authentic
Attitudes	Compliance	Interpretation	Creativity
Relationships	Dependence	Interdependence	Autonomy

what constitutes learning – it is usually judged as a product rather than a process – 'I have learned this'. What 'learning this' actually involves is elusive and not codified. There is little doubt that this is, to a significant extent, the result of a curriculum that is focused on information transfer and means of assessment that value the 'correct' answer. Most national schooling systems focus on this narrow, instrumental and reductionist view of learning and this is reinforced by prevailing models of accountability, which value outcomes that allow for generic comparability rather than individual capability.

What follows is an attempt to develop a model of learning which provides the basis for meaningful dialogue about the learning process and its related outcomes (see Table 1.4.1).

This model is not intended to be hierarchical; it is rather descriptive of the characteristics of different modes of learning. In some contexts, shallow learning is entirely appropriate – my knowledge of how my car's engine works is shallow, but I hope that the mechanic's is deep if not profound. Equally, it is important not to impose academic values on this model; profound learning is not only about the more arcane branches of philosophy, but also about the qualities of a counsellor, the skills of a joiner, and the moral insights of a child.

In many important respects, shallow learning is synonymous with the prevailing patterns of schooling – it is based on the memorization and replication of information. While it does not preclude deep and profound learning, schooling does limit and inhibit the potential to move beyond the shallow. Shallow learning has been adequate for a world, which operated on high levels of compliance and dependence in the work place and society. Shallow learning may have been an acceptable foundation for life in a relatively simple world with fewer choices and greater hegemony, but it is clearly inadequate in a world of complex choices and limited consensus. A simple illustration of this is the present place of sex education in the curriculum. It is taught as a subject but it does not really seem to impact on behaviour – Britain, for example, has the highest level of teenage pregnancy, abortion and sexually transmitted diseases in western Europe. Surely, the basis for sex education has to be the creation of understanding and the confidence that comes with personal wisdom. Perhaps the most negative aspect of shallow learning is the emphasis that it places on extrinsic motivation, compliance and dependence.

Deep and profound learning occur in every classroom and school every day, but often this is in spite of the prevailing curriculum, patterns of assessment and modes of teaching. The major issue now facing us is how to optimize the likelihood of deep and profound learning being available to all as an entitlement, and as the core purpose of the school. Deep learning occurs when understanding is achieved, and this is fundamental to any aspect of life, driving a car, medical research, writing poetry, preparing a meal, becoming a moral person. A focus on deep and profound learning would produce the following definition of the learner in the future:

> The Autonomous Learner knows how to learn and has a disposition to do so. They can identify, on their own, and/or with others, a problem, analyse its components and then marshal the resources, human and non-human, to solve it. They continuously question themselves and others as to whether they are employing the best methods. They can explain the processes of their learning and its outcomes to their peers and others, when such a demonstration is required. They are able to organize information and, through understanding, convert it into knowledge. They are sensitive to their personal portfolio of intelligences. They know when it is best to work alone, and when in a team, and know how to contribute to and gain from teamwork. They sustain a sharp curiosity and take infinite pains in all they do. Above all, they have that security in self, built through a wide and deep set of relationships and through their own feelings of worth fostered in part by others, to be at ease with doubt, and to welcome questioning and probing of all aspects of their knowledge.
>
> (This model was developed by Christopher Bowring-Carr)

The boundaries between deep and profound learning are infinitely permeable, and it would be inappropriate to try to define a specific instance where deep becomes profound. The transition from knowledge to wisdom is subject to multiple permutations and does not apply equally to all domains of human activity and experience. Thus the wisdom of the child prodigy musician or mathematician will probably not be reflected in comparable wisdom in human relationships. Moral and spiritual understanding and wisdom may not be paralleled by kinaesthetic or mathematical ability.

The specific components of deep and profound learning might be itemized as:

- the ability to demonstrate understanding
- being able to engage with the understanding of others
- relating new knowledge to prior knowledge and project its future implications
- the ability to demonstrate a synthesis and develop holistic models
- being able to demonstrate the causality in an argument
- demonstrating awareness of different types of knowledge
- being as aware of the learning process as of the outcome.

Engagement in deep and profound learning has much in common with what Maslow (1968) describes as self-actualization:

> on-going actualisation of potentials, capacities and talents, as fulfilment of a mission (or call, fate, destiny or vocation), as a fuller knowledge of, and acceptance of, the person's own intrinsic nature, as an increasing trend towards unity, integration or synergy within the person.
>
> (Maslow 1968: 25)

For Maslow, this type of learning is unselfconscious immersion in the learning process. This has powerful echoes in the work of Csikszentmihalyi (1997) and his definition of 'flow':

> These exceptional moments are what I have called 'flow' experiences. The metaphor of flow is one that many people have used to describe the sense of effortless action they feel in moments that stand out as the best in their lives. Athletes refer to it as 'being in the zone', religious mystics as being in 'ecstasy', artists and musicians as aesthetic rapture. . . .
>
> Thus the flow experience acts as a magnet for learning – that is, for developing new levels of challenge and skills.
>
> (Csikszentmihalyi 1997: 29, 33)

Deep and profound learning are the means by which the artist, the mystic, the athlete, the mathematician, the surgeon, the chef and the engineer achieve their full personal potential, creative knowledge and enhance the lives of others.

The science of learning

There is no synthesis available of the wide range of scientific research that may impinge on our understanding of the learning process. However, research into genetics, neurological functioning and cognitive psychology do seem to point to the possibility of increased empirical knowledge about how we learn.

Hard scientific data about learning is very elusive, but there are significant developments which may lead to profound changes in the conceptual framework that informs our thinking about the nature of learning. The completion of the Human Genome Project has led to equal outbursts of optimism and pessimism about the future of the human race. For some there is hope that genetic engineering will remove most of the ills that assail humanity and the positive attributes will be enhanced and extended. This prospect has led others to reinforce the centrality of human experience as the key determinant of our lives i.e. we come into the world as blank slates. Educational theory and practice has been very largely dominated by a view of the world that, according to Pinker (2002), divides matter from mind, the material from the spiritual, the physical from the mental, biology from culture, nature from society, and science from the social sciences.

(Pinker 2002: 31)

Not surprisingly, educationists have believed that the schooling process is the means by which the tabula rasa or blank state is filled. As Pinker (2002: 22) caricatures it, 'children come to school empty and have knowledge deposited in them'. For Pinker:

> Education is neither writing on a blank slate nor allowing the child's nobility to come into flower. Rather education is a technology that tries to make up for what the human mind is innately bad at.
>
> (Pinker 2002: 22)

Our genetic and evolutionary inheritance means that we have a predisposition to speak; we do not have such a predisposition to write. Education is a process of compensating for gaps in our biological inheritance and adapting natural predispositions 'to master problems for which they were not designed' (Pinker 2002: 223).

> And this offers priorities for educational policy: to provide students with the cognitive tools that are most important for grasping the modern world and that are most unlike the cognitive tools they are born with.
>
> (Pinker 2002: 235)

This is an argument for both a better understanding of the impact of our genetic inheritance, and recognition that the blank slate and genetic determinism arguments are both wrong. As Ridley (2003: 280) argues:

> Nature versus nurture is dead. Long live nature via nurture.

Our capacity to learn is the result of complex interactions at the most fundamental level of what makes us human. The most powerful expression of this interaction is our neurological functioning. The brain is the most powerful example of the interaction between our genetic make-up and the environment in which we live. The starting point for this discussion has to be a very simple but highly contentious proposition – learning is a physical process. There is no 'ghost in the machine'.

> So everything we think and feel can ultimately be boiled down to this alternating sequence of electrical and chemical events. The electrical signal arriving along the axon is converted into a chemical signal that carries it across the physical barrier, the synapse, between the neurons.
>
> (Greenfield 2000: 39)

Our capacity to learn is the result of an incredibly complex equation of which neural processing is only a part. However, as our knowledge of neurological functioning improves it might be increasingly possible to help individuals understand the optimal circumstances that inform their potential to learn. Any summary of these issues is bound to be a parody but it is possible to identify a range of implications for educators about research into the brain:

- There is a need for a much greater understanding of the development of the brain, and learning potential, in the early years.
- Effective learning is an individual phenomenon – every brain is unique – and there needs to be much more explicit recognition of individual dispositions to learn.
- Teaching needs to pay more attention to the variables influencing engagement with learning, e.g. choice of learning activities, time-on-task, appropriate levels of challenge, development of cognitive skills and strategies, especially memory.
- The psychological aspects of learning need greater recognition – even though the effects may be long term. Health is a vital component of effective brain functioning.
- Human relationships, especially in the family, have a profound impact on learning capacity. Effective neurological functioning is significantly determined by the emotional state of the learner.

Learning as a social relationship

The increasing recognition of the importance of emotional intelligence in all aspects of human collaboration is firmly rooted in neurological science. The core proposition is very simple – our emotional responses to the world are so powerful that they can overwhelm most cognitive processes. For Greenfield (2000):

> The question of emotions is one of the most important that a brain scientist, or indeed anyone, can explore. We are guided and controlled by our emotions. They shape our lives as we attempt to maximise some, such as happiness, and obliterate others such as fear.
>
> (Greenfield 2000: 107)

Inevitably, the picture is much more complicated than EQ versus IQ, in that our behaviour, and therefore our capacity to learn, is the result of a complex series of interactions in the brain, which are in turn the result of our learnt experiences.

> This tight orchestration of thought and feeling is made possible by what amounts to a superhighway in the brain, a bundle of neurons connecting the prefrontal lobes, behind the forehead – the brain's executive decision-making center – with an area deep in the brain that harbors our emotions.
>
> (Goleman 1998: 24)

As our understanding of this relationship grows so do the implications for the management of the learning process, and Pinker (2002: 40) argues that it is possible to identify three interacting components of the brain:

- It has distinct interaction processing systems for 'learning skills, controlling the body, remembering facts, holding information temporarily, and storing and executing rules.'
- Second, there are mental faculties 'dedicated to different kinds of content, such as language, number, space, tools and living things.'
- Third, there are the systems for motivation and emotion, the 'affect programs.'

Pinker concludes:

> Behaviour is not just elicited or emitted, nor does it come directly out of culture or society. It comes from an internal struggle among mental modules with differing agendas and goals.
>
> (Pinker 2002: 40)

From this perspective brain functioning, and therefore learning, can be seen as a complex interplay between information processing, mental faculties and the affect programs. These factors, what Pinker calls 'combinatorial software', are the essence of our capacity to learn and to use that learning. Our knowledge of these three elements is limited; even more uncertain is how the multiple permutations they offer might be better understood and managed. What is clear is the potential to develop and enhance each of these elements and so enrich their 'combinatorial' capacity.

This may be the very heart of learning *in* the future and learning *for* the future – developing strategies to enhance the potential and capacity of every person: replacing knowing *what* to knowing *how*. The work of Gardner (1999) and others on multiple intelligences and Goleman (1998) and others on emotional intelligence demonstrate the potential for building the capacity to learn on the basis of focused interventions.

Gardner (1999: 81) identifies seven implications for educators growing out of brain and mind research:

1   The tremendous importance of early experience.
2   The imperative 'use it or lose it'.
3   The flexibility of the early nervous system.
4   The importance of action and activity.
5   The specificity of human abilities and talents.
6   The possible organizing role played in early childhood by music.
7   The crucial role played by emotional coding.

Each of these is an intervention – the result of learning and teaching strategies, which have the potential to develop (nature via nurture!) all aspects of human potential. The development of appropriate learning strategies will create richer, stronger and more resilient networks of neurons, which, with repetition, will become the brain's default option – our automatic and spontaneous response. Our emotions inform our learning at the neural, personal and interpersonal levels. Developing our interpersonal relationships and our capacity to understand our emotional selves has a direct impact on our neural functioning. The health of the neural network is a product of the health of the social network and vice versa.

One way of understanding the social implications of deep and profound learning is to reflect on the quality and potential significance of the various social relationships that are constructed. Much of the debate around effective teaching and learning in schools has centred on class size. Anything below 30 is perceived as progress and yet this approach is posited on teaching rather than learning. The following list summarizes the outcomes of various group interactions.

1   *Autonomous learning:* fully conversant with self-as-learner, metacognition and self-motivation.
2   *Coaching and mentoring:* perhaps the most powerful developmental relationship to support the move from shallow to deep and profound.
3   *Small group learning:* high social and cognitive interdependence.
4   *Team-based learning:* the optimum balance between effective social relationships and the breadth and depth of skills and knowledge.

Any group larger than seven will inevitable tend towards a focus on the teacher and so dependence resulting in shallow learning. This can be highly effective and appropriate but will always be constrained in its potential to optimize deep and profound learning.

Intelligence and learning

The debate around the nature of intelligence is central to any view of learning in the future. Most education systems are still dominated by four fundamental assumptions about intelligence:

- intelligence is expressed through logical and reasoning abilities
- those abilities can be measured quantitatively
- such measures are predictive
- intelligence is fixed for life.

These assumptions have led to patterns of schooling, assessment, the nature of the curriculum, models of accountability and dominant modes of teaching. A key influence in Britain was Cyril Burt who argued that intelligence was 80 percent genetic in origin – which might explain the confidence in predestination implicit to many education systems. However, according to Ridley (2003) reviewing studies of twins:

IQ is approximately 50 percent 'additively genetic', 25 percent influenced by the shared environment and 25 percent influenced by factors unique to the individual.

(Ridley 2003: 90)

Ridley points to two other crucial findings: first, living in poverty has a profound impact on IQ – environment outweighs genetics. Second, ageing reduces the effect of family environment on IQ and genetic factors become more significant. If these points are accepted, then many of the fundamental assumptions under-pinning schooling are called into question. Schooling fails to come to terms with environmental issues and what we are learning about the influence of genetics. To build an educational system around IQ, which is so culturally and chrono-logically specific, is to deny the full human potential of an individual.

I view giftedness as being of multiple kinds, as would be retardation. Componential, experiential and contextual strengths and weaknesses can all lead to different patterns of giftedness or retardation, and hence, for me, giftedness and retardation are in no way unitary phenomena.

(Sternberg 1990: 299)

Sternberg's view has, of course, much in common with Gardner's (1999) view of multiple intelligences: both offer a response to the potentially inhibiting model based around IQ. If our understanding of intelligence moves from a unitary to a federal model then a range of assumptions about the nature of the curriculum, the role of the teacher, the patterns of assessment and accreditation are all called into question. Gardner shows just how fundamental the challenge is:

For those who believe that human beings have a desire to explore and to understand the most fundamental questions of existence, and that curricula ought to be organized around the teaching of these epistemological concerns – familiarity, the true, the beautiful and the good.

(Gardner 1999: 226)

The response to this challenge lies in what Gardner (1999: 226) characterizes as 'literacy skills, disciplinary skills and the possibility of multidisciplinary or inter-disciplinary approaches'. A further challenge to the historical model of intelligence is the recognition that intelligence is, partly, a social construct based on interactions.

I want to capture the important fact that intelligence, which comes to life during human activities, may be crafted. There are both social and material dimensions of this distribution.

(Pea 1997: 50)

Intelligence is constructed socially through relationships and interactions; the material dimension is in response to the environment and artefacts. Intelligence can thus be said to be constructed, in fact, intelligence can be learned and can be taught, if we change the definition of intelligence. We have changed our definitions of democracy, family and culture; so it may now be time to develop a new understanding and shared usage around the concept of intelligence.

Conclusion: learning for the future

Based on what has been discussed above, it is possible to draw some tentative conclusions about what actions might be taken now in order to create a model of learning *in* the future and learning *for* the future. The fundamental issue is to create an effective dialogue between professional educators and those carrying out research into all branches of neuroscience and cognitive development. At present educationists are working by inference and innuendo, feeding off the crumbs when they need to be sitting at the table as equal participants. There is an obvious need for a radical change in the perception as to what constitutes professional knowledge and the creation of new communities of practice centred on the application of scientific research to professional practice in schools.

The implications of such a partnership might include:

- A focus on the need to design learning programmes around the individual as a unique learner rather than as a member of a class. This implies much more than the diagnosis of learning styles, rather a detailed profile of all the variables that are likely to have an impact on the individual's ability to learn. In medical terms this is like moving from an X-ray to a full body scan.
- A recognition of the impact of the social environment as a crucial determinant of educational success. The significant improvements in public health in the nineteenth century were partly the result of improvements in medical practice, but were substantially the result of improvements in the basic infrastructure, i.e. clean water and sewers. Real improvement in the learning of all will come only when the issues of social equity are addressed.
- The introduction of programmes to enhance cognitive ability; what might be called the 'cognitive curriculum' that might take the form of a range of interventions to enhance the skills that Gardner (1999) outlines above. The content-based curriculum would become the vehicle for the cognitive curriculum rather than, as at present, an end in itself.
- As part of the cognitive curriculum, far greater emphasis needs to be placed on the cultivation of personal and social skills, the concept of emotional intelligence. This has implications for effective learning, the development of social skills, employability and, crucially, the social expression of moral principles.
- A review of our understanding of assessment, both what is assessed and how it is assessed, in essence moving from summative to formative, from assessment of learning to assessment for learning.

- A radical rethinking of the role of the teacher, moving from the manager of information to the facilitator of the learning of the individual. Central to this change is the development of the role of the educator as coach, as the pivotal relationship in the facilitation of learning.
- A focus on the development of ICT to support the learning process, especially the development of cognitive skills such as memorization, problem-solving, analysis and information management.

Fundamental to all of these points is an emphasis on the early years of learning; neurologically, socially and morally, investment in the early years seems to be the one thing that is most likely to create a learning society. It would be wrong to underestimate the barriers to the changes outlined in this discussion: the more profound the changes, the more fundamental is the need for leadership that is focused on transformation.

Key questions

1   What changes would you like to see in education that would accommodate the principles outlined in this chapter?
2   Research the latest findings in the field of neuro-science discovery of how the brain works. How can this new field guide change in educational practice?
3   Discuss the view of an autonomous learner presented in this chapter.

References

Csikszentmihalyi, M. (1997) *Finding Flow*. New York: Basic Books.
Gardner, H. (1999) *The Disciplined Mind*. New York: Simon and Schuster.
Goleman, D. (1998) *Working with Emotional Intelligence*. London: Bloomsbury.
Greenfield, S. (2000) *Brain Story*. London: BBC Worldwide.
Maslow, A. (1968) *Towards a Psychology of Being*. New York: Van Nostrand.
Pea, R. D. (1997) Practices of distributed intelligence and designs for education, in G. Salomon (ed.) *Distributed Cognitions*. Cambridge: Cambridge University Press.
Pinker, S. (2002) *The Blank Slate*. London: Penguin.
Ridley, M. (2003) *Nature via Nurture*. London: HarperCollins.
Sternberg, R. J. (1990) *Metaphors of Mind*. Cambridge: Cambridge University Press.

2   Bilingually enriched students

2.1   Bilingual education issues: Haitian and Haitian-American students in gifted education

Jaime A. Castellano

Historically, students of Haitian descent have been excluded from gifted education programs in the schools and districts they attend. However, current paradigms in gifted education call for a more inclusionary process for identifying and serving our academically best and brightest students. When the identification net is cast far and wide the hope is that we capture more students who are poor, culturally and linguistically diverse, and others who have been underrepresented in programs for gifted students. Students of Haitian descent fall under this category.

In many cities across the United States, the community Diaspora is woven with the rich culture, language and heritage of those citizens of Haitian descent. They contribute to their community fabric economically, politically, socially, culturally and educationally. Many speak multiple languages, including Creole, French, Spanish and English. Parents believe in the value of education and encourage their children to do their best. Within this group of school-aged children are those that exhibit a remarkable aptitude and propensity for learning and who exhibit characteristics of gifted behavior.

According to Diaz (2002), a sizeable body of literature exists regarding identification and programming issues for gifted and talented students who are from different cultural backgrounds. Nonetheless, most of the literature neglects the linguistic component, thus leaving only a few significant yet scattered pieces of literature available and the research specifically on Haitian descent students who speak Creole in gifted education, is scarce.

Castellano (2003) maintains that gifted and talented students transcend cultural, ethnic and linguistic ties, conditions that are disabling, sexual orientation, poverty and geography. In every possible subgroup of students there are those who deserve, by right, not privilege, the benefits of gifted education programming.

Bernal (2002) adds that as the demographics of our society have been changing inexorably toward greater proportions of minority students in our schools, minority gifted youth will have to be found and educated.

Factors that confound the identification of Haitian descent students for gifted education include a language (Creole) whose history as a formal written language is in its infancy. Poverty is another socioeconomic reality that must be considered. In Florida, the vast majority of Haitian descent students enrolled in schools in Palm Beach, Broward and Miami-Dade Counties are eligible for free or reduced lunch (Title I Program). Differences in learning styles also contribute to their under-representation. What is being advocated here is an inclusionary rationale that believes in revealing the success of students in the classroom through traditional and non-traditional approaches while honoring and respecting who they are, what they know, and what they can contribute.

Haitian descent students attending public schools are a heterogeneous group. Much like the work from Kitano and Espinosa (1995), this diversity suggests a need for a broad range of programs that provides options, different subject matter interests and talent areas. Collaboration and commitment between the schools, community, parents and stakeholders must occur in order to establish a process that is fair, meaningful and meets expectations. Students of Haitian descent, and their advocates, must also be part of the process to ensure that students' unique needs are being considered and met within the context of program development.

The culture of Haitian descent students

About 95 percent of Haitians are of African descent, the rest mixed Caucasian–African ancestry. French is one of two official languages spoken by only about 10 percent of the people. All Haitians speak Creole, their other official language. English is increasingly spoken among the young and in the business sector. About one of every six Haitians lives abroad, with large-scale emigration to the United States, Canada, the Dominican Republic and the Bahamas. In recent years, there have been efforts to reform Haiti's educational system to make education more accessible and relevant to the poor. In 1978, primary schools were restructured by the National Department of Education (DEN) into ten years of basic education and three years of secondary education. Curriculum and materials were also changed using Haitian Creole as the language of instruction in the first four grades. Other instructional innovations were grouping by ability and the emphasis on discovery learning rather than memorization.

Despite the reforms, the majority of Haitians do not have access to it. As of 1982, more than 65 percent of the population over the age of 10 had received no formal education at all, and only 8 percent of the population had received more than a primary education. Even though education is technically free in Haiti, it remains beyond the means of most Haitians, who cannot afford the supplemental fees, school supplies and uniforms required. Thus, education remains a privilege of upper and middle classes, with fluency in French a marker for success. Although plans for further implementation of reforms have not been abandoned, the current economic and political crisis in Haiti has overshadowed educational concerns.

The education of Haitian descent students

Students who have participated in the Haitian educational system will exhibit different behaviors and certainly have values and expectations different from their American counterparts. A major difference between the two educational systems is in styles of teaching and learning. The Haitian curriculum requires learning many subjects in detail. Rote learning and memorization are the norm. Haitian students will not be used to the analysis and synthesis that US teachers expect of their students. The number of right answers that are sometimes possible when solving problems will also puzzle them. Haitian students must be overtly taught that thinking for oneself is highly valued in American schools. In Haiti most schools are coeducational; desks are joined together; textbooks and visual aids are scarce; special education is not provided; and parent groups do not exist.

Haitian students may also be disturbed by the informal teacher–student relationship in the United States, perceived as a lack of respect. In Haiti, the teacher addresses all students by their last names and has total authority over the class. A student speaks only when asked a question. As a sign of respect, Haitian students do not look their teachers in the eye, but keep their heads down in deference. American teachers should not be misled by this body language; Haitian students need to be taught that Americans value eye contact.

In one of its English to Speakers of Other Languages (ESOL) instructional courses, the Department of Multicultural Education of the School District of Palm Beach County, Florida has developed a participant booklet which details the cultural characteristics of Haitian students. Many of these students deliberately try to isolate themselves from the negative stigma of being a Haitian refugee or 'boat people', as they try to assimilate. They may show isolation from others; fear of rejection; fear of being known as one of the 'refugee' boat people; low self-esteem; school adjustment problems due to academic frustrations; hostile if rejected or ridiculed; may be very docile if educated in Haiti; have few role models in the schools; be impoverished and not able to participate in extra-curricular activities; be secretive about family due to immigration fears; exhibit different customs and habits; have frequent absenteeism due to family responsibilities (translating, babysitting, etc); can mimic African-American peers' behavior to 'fit in'; can resist critical independent thinking.

How the Haitian community perceives giftedness in its own children

According to Castellano (2003) virtually no research exists on issues of giftedness in Haitian descent school-aged children, including how the adult Haitian community perceives giftedness in its own children. As a result, and under this author's direction, a town meeting was held with the Haitian community of Palm Beach County, Florida in 1998. At the meeting participants identified the following primary characteristics of giftedness in their own children:

- ability to problem solve (though may not be able to articulate process in English)
- ability to code-switch (using two languages interchangeably to transmit message)
- ability to translate from one language to another at a high degree of accuracy
- high levels of internal motivation
- easily adapts to new environments
- easily learns new skills, concepts and ideas
- curiosity/inquisitiveness (wants to know)
- creativity (musical or artistic talent, kinesthetic, performance-based)
- strong memorization skills (related to the importance of rote learning in Haiti)
- ability to multi-task
- demonstrates leadership behavior in formal and informal contexts

Additionally, when cultural values and their behavioral differences were matched to what generally are perceived as absolute aspects of giftedness, the Haitian participants generated the information in Table 2.1.1. For those parents who only spoke Creole, translators were provided.

This information documents many of the same types of behavior also found in other under-represented groups of students identified as culturally and linguistically diverse. In attempts to validate the gifted behavioral characteristics generated by the Palm Beach County Haitian community, the research was shared with other Haitian educators from Broward County, Miami-Dade County, New York City, and Boston during a national conference on bilingual/multicultural education. There was a general consensus that the information was on target and did, in fact, reflect behaviors of gifted or potentially gifted Haitian/Haitian-American students.

Characteristics of giftedness and/or potential giftedness in other culturally and linguistically diverse students

Students of Haitian descent who demonstrate gifted potential often exhibit many of the same characteristics of other historically under-represented groups, particularly English language learners. The focus on language skills makes sense, as all individuals learn a new language through the same language acquisition process. Haitian descent students who are bilingual share many characteristics of both groups and are reflected in Table 2.1.2.

Table 2.1.1 Characteristics of giftedness and cultural values of Haitians and the behaviors resulting from their interactive influence

Absolute aspects of giftedness	Connection to Haitian cultural values	Behavioral differences
High level of verbal ability	Haitian Creole spoken at home and church	Strong communication skills, even when limited in the language; English at school, Creole at home
Emotional depth and intensity	Strong physical and spiritual foundation	Takes problems of others personally; touching as a sign of affection
Unusual sensitivity to feelings and expectations of others	Male is the head of the family, but does not dominate the family; strong matriarchal sense; women responsible for discipline	Children may assume adult role with/for parents; high respect for friends, teachers, peers
Conceptualizes solutions to social and environmental problems	Strong nuclear and extended family ties	Often assumes responsibilities for family, younger siblings, and other relatives within the extended family
Unusual retentiveness; high capacity for processing information	Traditional culture; places value for knowing about African ancestors	Successfully adapts to both mainstream and home culture; American during the day, Haitian when at home
Leadership	Sense of being competitive; has capability of being collaborative	Can function equally well individually or in small groups

Aguirre and Hernandez (1999) generated the characteristics as a result of their work with Project GOTCHA (Galaxies of Thinking and Creative Heights of Achievement) in over fifteen states (1987–1996), developed to meet the needs of high-ability learners who were not proficient in English, including students of Haitian descent. Bernal (1974) combines both qualitative and quantitative characteristics in his identification of gifted Hispanic English language learners. His work reveals the importance of going beyond what is commonly held to be true about gifted behaviors and considers the influences of culture and other factors. These characteristics are also consistent with behaviors exhibited by Creole speaking students of Haitian descent. In conducting research on characteristics of other historically under-represented student groups, I concluded that the characteristics generated by the work at Kent State University in 1992 transcend culture, ethnicity and linguistic differences and speak to universal traits. When asked how giftedness is perceived in their own children, Haitian and Haitian-American adults identified many of the same characteristics.

Table 2.1.2 Characteristics of gifted English language learners

Aguirre and Hernandez (1999)	Bernal (1974)	Kent State University (US Department of Education 1992)
Eagerly shares his/her culture	Enjoys intelligent (or effective) risk-taking behavior, often accompanied by a sense of drama	*Exceptional learner* (acquisition and retention of knowledge)
Shows strong desire to teach peers words from his/her native language	Exhibits characteristics, which are defined by the students' native culture as fulfilling the characteristics of gifted children	• exceptional learner • learns quickly and easily • advanced understanding
Has a strong sense of pride in cultural heritage and ethnic background		*Exceptional user* (application and comprehension of knowledge)
Translates for peers and adults at a high degree of accuracy	Has older playmates and can easily engage adults in lively conversation	• exceptional use of knowledge • advanced use of symbols • demands a reason • reasons well
Balances appropriate behaviors expected of the native culture and new culture	Is able to keep busy and entertained, e.g., imaginative games and ingenious application, such as getting the most out of a few simple toys and objects	
Possesses advanced knowledge of idioms and native dialects with ability to translate and explain meanings in English		*Exceptional generator* (creator of knowledge) • highly creative • atypical thinking • keen sense of humor • curious
Understands jokes and puns related to cultural differences	Exhibits leadership behavior and emphasizes interpersonal skills	
Reads in native language two grades or more above grade level	Is 'street-wise' and recognized by others as possessing the ability to 'make it' in the dominate 'White' society	*Exceptional motivator* (pursuer of knowledge) • perfectionism • initiation • reflective • long attention span • leadership • intensity
Functions at language proficiency levels above that of non-gifted peers who are LEP	Rapidly acquires English language skills once exposed to it and given the opportunity to use it expressively	
Able to code-switch	Accepts responsibilities at home normally reserved for older children, e.g., supervision of younger siblings, etc.	
Possesses cross-cultural flexibility		
Has a sense of global community		
Learns a second or third language at an accelerated pace		
Excels in math achievement		

Testing Haitian descent students for gifted education

In an attempt to be proactive and responsive to the needs of Haitian descent students, it is necessary to consider alternative means of identification and assessment that, when coupled with more traditional conventions, serve as a more inclusionary model for admitting these students into programs for the academically talented. The use of multiple criteria refers to the process of obtaining comprehensive information about a student's abilities by gathering and analysing results from such formal and informal procedures as

- standardized measures of aptitude, achievement, and creativity in the child's native or English language
- nominations by teachers, parents, the student themselves, peers, and community or cultural groups with which the student identifies
- ethnographic assessment procedures whereby the student is observed in multiple contexts over time
- evaluations of student products or performances (performance-based or non-verbal), such as portfolios, writing samples, and samples of creativity
- observations using rating scales and behavioral checklists
- past-school performance
- parent interviews.

There is wide agreement that the use of multiple criteria undoubtedly serves to include more culturally and linguistically diverse students in gifted education.

Academic achievement

A student typically demonstrates need for a gifted education program through advanced academic achievement in math and/or reading. At this point a more rigorous curriculum may be required. A look at the student's current report card combined with results from local or state administered assessments can also serve as supporting evidence. Need for a gifted program can also be demonstrated by how a student performs on chapter, unit and/or end of the book type tests, computer-based assessments and any other combination of academically based assessments or evaluations that accurately reflect the student's math and/or reading ability. The results of a norm-referenced standardized test of achievement such as the Woodcock-Johnson or the Kaufman Test of Educational Achievement will also demonstrate need. Achievement criteria for demonstrating the need for a gifted education program vary across school districts.

Legal issues

Legal requirements in the United States, under the No Child Left Behind (NCLB) legislation, mandate testing of Haitian descent students if they are designated limited English proficient (LEP), participate in a Title I program, or with the exception of gifted education, are tested for special education (Pompa 2003). Furthermore, for students with special needs the federally mandated Individual with Disabilities Education Act (IDEA) stipulates appropriate use of tests and assessments. Each public school must ensure that first, tests and other evaluation materials used to assess a child are selected and administered so as not to be discriminatory on a racial or cultural basis, and are provided and administered in the child's native language or other mode of communication, unless it is clearly not feasible to do so; and second, materials and procedures used to assess a child with limited English proficiency are selected and administered to ensure that they measure the extent to which the child needs a special education (ILIAD Project 2002). Although gifted education is not mandated by the IDEA, requirements should be part of a best practices approach to testing culturally and linguistically diverse students for gifted education.

Strategies for recruiting Haitian descent students in gifted education

The strategies or activities that a school district implements in order to recruit and identify under-represented students for their gifted education programs vary from voluntary proactive measures to court ordered mandates. Paying attention to the idiosyncrasies of any particular student group will allow the school district to tailor a process that allows access and opportunity, and should be reflected in the identification process. Castellano (2003) identified strategies to recruit Haitian descent students and other under-represented groups for gifted education. They are:

- gather data from multiple sources rather than a single criterion
- use former students as ambassadors to assist in the recruitment process
- plan and conduct recruitment fairs in the local community, for example, at malls, grocery stores and churches
- use community resources for communication, such as newsletters, websites and other multimedia resources, in the heritage language(s) of the parents and community
- develop programs and activities both in and out of school to help students increase awareness of their own talents
- design and implement student mentorship programs to include shadowing, internships and sponsorships
- increase the diversity of teachers with gifted education endorsements
- increase the selection pool of under-represented students by using non-traditional measures, such as portfolios, performance-based projects and activities, and opportunities to demonstrate the student's unique skills and talents
- develop strategies as part of the school improvement plan designed to target and identify under-represented students as part of the talent pool for gifted education programming

- provide potential candidates with learning strategies to be successful in the transition to a gifted education classroom
- select relevant curriculum and instructional methods that are culturally sensitive and that meet the student's cognitive and academic needs
- develop after-school programming with academic components that support and nurture the achievement of poor and/or minority students.

Strategies for retention

Castellano (2003) writes that once students of Haitian descent are enrolled in gifted education classrooms, it is imperative that program staff and administration implement initiatives in the areas of curriculum and instruction, staff development, counseling, assessment, and parental involvement to keep the students in the program. The gifted program should develop a culturally relevant curriculum that is equitable and addresses the sensitive values, attitudes and heritage of participating students. Instruction should be individualized to the child's learning style and modality, with accommodations provided to meet unique needs. It is also important that teachers consult the research for curriculum adaptations for under-represented students. To showcase the talents of diverse gifted students, program teachers and administrators should consider having them participate in local, state and national competitions. The positive aspects of competition will be a selling point to students and parents. Finally, the use of bibliotherapy to enhance self-concept and to teach inquiry skills through content makes this approach an important part of the learning process.

Retaining diverse gifted learners in appropriate programs necessitates an improvement in the transition from elementary to middle, and middle to high school. Staff development opportunities that bring transition teachers and administrators together ensure a continuous gifted education experience. The counseling of gifted students may include a mentorship program that offers internships and career awareness. Peer counseling in the form of meetings, conferences, tutoring and the like are also viable options. Recruiting parents into a network of volunteers, mentors, experts in residence, and resources adds to the overall gifted education experience. If the parents are non-English or limited English speaking, interpreters or translators need to be present.

Although the majority of Haitian students are poor, they are as capable and as deserving as any other group. Furthermore, because giftedness can be viewed as multidimensional and process oriented, Haitian (Creole) and other culturally and linguistically diverse students stand a better chance of gaining access to nomination and identification processes.

Having their say: what students of Haitian descent say about being gifted

Despite the under-representation of Haitian descent students in gifted education, they can be found. They are bright, intelligent, and academically capable. They compete with white middle-class students, proudly represent their schools and communities, and aspire to be the best. Students of Haitian descent currently enrolled in gifted education programs offer the following thoughts.

> What I like most about being gifted is knowing that I am smart and that I can be selected to attend our nation's top colleges because of what's in my head.
>
> (Seventh grade female)

> If there was one thing I could change about being gifted it would be to change the amount of regular classes that we must attend. I don't like being ignored by the teacher all the time.
>
> (Seventh grade female)

> If there was one thing I could change about being gifted I would want more challenging work.
>
> (Fourth grade male)

> I want my teacher to know the 'real' me. The sensitive me, inside.
>
> (Fourth grade male)

> If there was one thing I could change about being gifted I would ask for more exciting educational experiences.
>
> (Fifth grade male)

> What I like most about being gifted is people knowing that I am smart. It makes me feel different. It also allows me to establish a good state of mind.
>
> (Seventh grade female)

Resources

In a gifted program that represents diversity in terms of intelligence styles, ethnicity and language, curriculum materials must reflect this dynamic mosaic while maintaining a focus on rigorous standards and high expectations. When curriculum materials and resources are aligned with the strengths that gifted students bring to the classroom, the learning is deeper, more complex and challenges the students. For gifted education programs serving students of Haitian descent, Educa Vision Inc. (EVI) is a resource for curriculum materials highlighting their culture and heritage in language arts, science, social studies, and mathematics. The children's literature available through EVI can serve as the foundation for the use of bibliotherapy with Haitian descent students. Castellano (2003) writes that bibliotherapy can take into account the demographic make-up of a classroom, thus offering a multicultural perspective to teaching based on guiding principles that make up a gifted education program committed to equity and excellence. That is, bibliotherapy can target particular problem-solving skills, knowledge, cognitive development, creativity, affective development and 'personal' stories. Books are chosen for a purpose that often leads to self-understanding, growth and acceptance. For students of Haitian descent this is especially important as many must learn to balance the often-competing values of their home, school, community and peer group.

Conclusion

Students of Haitian descent who demonstrate characteristics of gifted behavior are more likely to gain eligibility to gifted education programs when the identification process is inclusionary and multi-criteria based. Programs that promote equity and access typically include wide stakeholder support and an infrastructure with leadership that acknowledges and accepts diversity. Alternative, or different approaches to identify Haitian and other culturally and linguistically diverse students for gifted education are needed. Confounding issues of gifted behavior include language proficiency, culture, and quite often, poverty. Only when school districts acknowledge this will we see gifted education classrooms reflecting the demographics of its school community.

Diaz (2002) writes that the United States is a country in transition because considerable demographic changes are taking place. Its racial, cultural, and linguistic diversity is unparalleled. A better understanding of these students, through an expanded body of knowledge and increased awareness, calls for a type of education that capitalizes on the growing cultural and linguistic diversity in the United States by assisting these students to tap their potential and sources of talent.

Haitian descent students are a heterogeneous group. However, they are united by customs, language, religion, and a value system that reflects the degree of their acculturation. These differences are crucial when considering the identification and development of giftedness among them. According to Castellano (2003) inclusionary methodology dictates that any process implemented to evaluate the academic and cognitive ability of underrepresented students for gifted education must be flexible enough to accommodate their individual needs. In the final analysis, Passow (1991) concludes that if giftedness is to be nurtured, then schools must create a climate for excellence for all, one in which a variety of outstanding talents are understood, valued and rewarded. This is true for students of Haitian descent. This is true for all students.

Key questions

1   Despite a best practices approach to the identification of gifted students from culturally and linguistically diverse backgrounds, why do they continue to be underrepresented in gifted education programs? Suggest possible approaches to solve this.

2   How can we best align the influence of the Haitian culture in an identification process that is meant to identify academically talented students? Suggest alternative approaches.

3   What does placement in a gifted education program do to the social-emotional state of students whose worlds (home, school, community/peer

group) may be in conflict, are merging, or are congruent? As a teacher, how would you deal with this?

References

Aguirre, N. M. and Hernandez, N. E. (1999) *Characteristics of the Culturally and Linguistically Diverse Gifted Child.* Baton Rouge, LA: Project GOTCHA; Title VII; Academic Excellence Program; Modern Language Services.

Bernal, E. M. (1974) Gifted Mexican-American children: an ethnico-scientific perspective. Paper presented at the annual meeting of the American Educational Research Association, Chicago, IL, April.

Bernal, E. M. (2002) Foreword, in J. A. Castellano and E. I. Diaz (eds) *Reaching New Horizons: Gifted and Talented Education for Culturally and Linguistically Diverse Students.* Boston, MA: Allyn and Bacon.

Castellano, J. A. (2003) *Special Populations in Gifted Education: Working with Diverse Gifted Learners.* Boston, MA: Allyn and Bacon.

Diaz, E. I. (2002) Introduction, in J. A. Castellano and E. I. Diaz (eds) *Reaching New Horizons: Gifted and Talented Education for Culturally and Linguistically Diverse Students.* Boston, MA: Allyn and Bacon.

ILIAD Project (2002) *Determining Appropriate Referrals of English Language Learners to Special Education: A Self-assessment Guide for Principals.* Arlington, VA: Council for Exceptional Children.

Kitano, M. K. and Espinosa, R. (1995) Language diversity and giftedness: working with gifted English language learners. *Journal for the Education of the Gifted*, 18(3): 234–254.

Pompa, D. (2003) Accountability: measuring ELL success under the new federal law. *National Association for Bilingual Education News*, 26(3): 16–20.

United States Department of Education (1992) *Early Assessment for Exceptional Potential.* Jacob K. Javits Gifted and Talented Students Education Act. Grant R206A00160 awarded to Kent State University: Washington, DC.

2.2   Case study: insights into bilingual gifted – example of curricular intervention 'Flora' (Excerpt from full case study)

Carole Ruth Harris

Flora was a profoundly gifted bilingual (English and German) girl aged 7. A voracious reader, very strong in verbal and music, Flora read on an adult level and enjoyed both facts and fantasy. She was intense, responsive, cooperative, friendly and affectionate, with strong focus and excellent concentration. Flora had an extraordinary ability to problem-solve and to engage in abstract reasoning. She loved literature and history and had interests in science, math and geography. Flora had unusual tactile ability and could construct highly detailed objects from clay. She was playful, creative, highly competitive and willing to experiment, with a great sense of humor. At the same time she was well-organized, goal-oriented and craved challenge.

Flora was lonely and longed for a companion her own age who was 'also smart'. No school had been able to accommodate her bilingual and academic needs so Flora was home-schooled with her gifted 11-year-old brother. Flora was very interested in women's rights. Acutely aware of color in art and textiles, she expressed an interest in design and historical costumes. To accommodate all of her interests, a curriculum cluster theme was developed, entitled *Queens*. Socialization, humor, advanced reading, problem-solving and creativity were incorporated into the curriculum (see Box 2.2.1).

At the last parental report, Flora was excited about her studies and her final curriculum project, the coronation of Queen Flora, with other children who would also be smart, dress as nobles and ambassadors and royalty and attend the coronation. She is still being home-schooled and participates in university classes but joins classes and enrichment activities and socializes with a variety of other children of different ages.

Box 2.2.1   Curriculum unit on queens for Flora

Activity	Rationale
Read Gatti, A. (1997) *The Magic Flute*. Mozart, W. A. (1756–1791). *Zauberflöte* (with CD). San Francisco, CA: Chronicle Books.	**Introduces** opera. **Utilizes** unit theme with musical connections.
Listen to the CD. Compare and contrast the Queen of the Night with the Snow Queen. How were they similar or different?	**Assists** creativity. **Reinforces** goal-orientation through alternate means of sharing impressions.
Watch the videotape, *The Magic Flute*. Tell how the music and costumes reflect the characters Mozart portrays.	
What happens in the music when the Queen of the Night appears? Do you think she is truly evil? Why?	
This opera has many charming, and some frightening aspects. Tell about these in any way you wish: tape, chart, drawing, essay, or collage with felt.	
Look at the costumes Braun and Schneider. *Zur Geschichte der Kostüme*. Munich/New York. (Republished version).	**Introduces** period dress in alternate version.

Make copies of the dress of the periods of the queens you are studying and place beneath your timeline, color them in.

Initiates comparison. **Reinforces** visualization within timeline concept.

Browse Langley, A. (1999) *Renaissance*. Eyewitness Books. New York: Alfred A. Knopf.

Art related to your studies of queens. Add important facts to your timeline.

Look at pp. 211–307 Wilson, E. (1973) *Erica Wilson's Embroidery Book*. New York: Charles Scribner's Sons. You will see how embroidery for the queens was done.

To try your own *Black Work*, draw a design on white linen with a black felt tip pen. Put the fabric on an embroidery hoop. Follow the directions for making a chain stitch on page 60 of *Erica Wilson's Embroidery Book*. Work a chain stitch over the black lines with thin black crewel wool and a tapestry needle.

Read the stories, 'Selim and the Snake Queen' and 'The Queen's Children', Manning-Sanders, R. (1978) *A Book of Kings and Queens*. New York: E. P. Dutton.

Tell about the special magic of these queens.

Introduces fantasy. **Encourages** lateral thinking. **Initiates** plot analysis.

Read pp. 77–79 in Czarnota, L. M. (2000) *Medieval Tales that Kids can Read and Tell*. Little Rock, AR: August House.

You are Queen Eleanor of Aquitaine and you have just returned to England. Your son, Richard, must become king and you write a letter to the rich nobles in England to raise money for his ransom. In the past, they have regarded you as a schemer and many were glad that Henry II imprisoned you as he did. You invite them to a banquet at the palace; they cannot refuse to come, but how are you going to gain their cooperation? Write a letter to these nobles that indicates you want their support and their friendship. Plan the banquet and give directions to the palace staff about the food and entertainment.

Initiates critical thinking. **Encourages** creative problem-solving. **Provides** vehicle for creative writing.

2.3 Personal perspective: coping with war, a new culture and new language

Vanja Grbic

My language and ethnic background are very diverse; my family members speak Serbo-Croatian, a western group of the South Slavic languages. Our family reunions used to be very interesting: we all speak with different dialects and accents because every city in former Yugoslavia has its own unique expressions.

The war in former Yugoslavia started because of disagreements between three religions – Muslim, Serb and Croatian. Life before the war seemed like an unreachable fairytale after all the horrific events started unveiling around me. Every day was the same; the ground was shaking with each rumble created by enormous explosions of bombs and missiles. I would often watch the night sky that was set on fire by thousands of projectiles flying on their bloodthirsty mission. I knew that every bomb was going to end numerous lives, and I hated them for it.

There was no school at the beginning of the war because everyone hoped that the madness would soon be over. But it continued and we had to move to another city in order for me to attend a school that was pierced by thousands of bullets, grenades and bombs. Our classes had to end early numerous times for safety. One of my teachers was so racist that she wouldn't allow us to read books that were written by authors who belonged to a different religion than hers, she even burned certain books in our library.

My family were fortunate to have grandparents who had a farm, and could produce at least some food for us. Hunger was very typical; people were so desperate for food that they started eating roots. I lost my grandparents during one of the bloodiest battles. We went hungry and homeless. I had nightmares for over three years, flashbacks of situations I was placed in during the war.

We were forced to leave our family, friends and possessions behind and go to a completely different country, the United States. It was an extremely stressful transition for my entire family; my parents weren't sure if they were doing the right thing. If we were to stay in a war-infested country there would be no guarantee that we would all stay alive.

When we first arrived in Florida my family was exposed to an enormous culture shock; a completely different language and people who live by different rules. For the first four months I was afraid to leave our apartment; I looked at pictures from Yugoslavia, read letters from my friends, and listened to music in tears. I became extremely introverted, and I wasn't eager to talk to anyone because I wasn't able to communicate efficiently in English. Since my parents didn't speak English at all, I took care of our household, paid bills and translated whenever necessary. This was extremely hard for me because I only manipulated with enough vocabulary to hold basic conversations. I was forced to grow up overnight.

Going to school was particularly difficult. I was always a high academic achiever and I felt restricted by my inability to communicate with others proficiently. The school system was completely different to former Yugoslavia – I had been taking fourteen subjects, and in Florida as a sophomore in High School, I only had to take six. That amazed me because I wasn't used to such a light load of academic requirements. I was placed in two ESOL classes; the ESOL teacher was an incredible man who cared greatly about my development, unlike other teachers who did not pay much attention to the ESOL students, viewing them as 'little pests' who always require additional explanation. After only one semester, I was placed in an ESOL class for students with higher language proficiency and was able to excel at a greater pace. In junior year, I joined a regular English class and was finally able to blend in with the rest of the students.

My parents were very proud of me. I was able to see great differences in the treatment I received in public places: more respect, patience and enthusiasm. This fact is very disturbing when I think about how many immigrants, like my parents, get poor treatment because they are not able to express themselves fluently. It discourages them from trying to communicate using English. I started a foundation to support immigrant students.

All these experiences inspired me to become a teacher. I have now graduated in the College of Education at the University of Central Florida and I have received numerous awards (President's and Dean's Lists, Alumni Association Distinguished Student for the year of 2004). I was actually able to speak at the opening ceremony for the Academy for Teaching, Learning, and Leadership – an enormous success considering my limited English mastery just a few years ago! I was awarded the highest achievement the university confers, the 'Order of Pegasus'. Our actions are stronger than words, and humankind can survive only if we all demonstrate through our actions that we all speak the language of peace, prosperity, tolerance and love for each other. As a result of my hard work and dedication I have been able to achieve numerous things I never thought would be possible. My life experiences have taught me that nothing can stop persistence and dedication, and I hope that my story will inspire others to follow their dreams and never give up.

2.4   Conflict resolution 1: bilingual

Suzanne Rawlins

A new program for gifted services was being developed in an elementary school in a small, rural community in the United States supported by Hispanic farm workers. Spanish was their primary language. The principal, teachers and program director went to great lengths to assure that all published information was available in both English and Spanish. The night of the Parent Orientation arrived. Parents and students quietly entered the school media center where the program would be explained in both languages. All the school officials were excited to be offering a full-time program in this primarily Hispanic community.

The principal and program director outlined the plans for the parents. Teachers were introduced. Curriculum was shared. As the lengthy translated bilingual presentation drew to an end, the program director eyed a father in the front row of the audience. A single, tiny tear was shed down his cheek. The professionals in the room were confused by his reaction. Rather than draw attention to his surprising emotional display, the program specialist asked if anyone had any questions. The father slowly raised his hand. He said, 'Are you telling me that my child is smart? I thought there was a problem. We only hear from the school if there's a problem. My child is smart?'

Not once in the communication in two languages had it stated that the parents were being summoned to the school because their child was smart.

3 Culturally diverse students

3.1 Curriculum compacting: a research-based differentiation strategy for culturally diverse talented students

Joseph S. Renzulli and Sally M. Reis

Tom Bernard, a fifth grade teacher in an urban school, walked into the teachers' room, sank into the worn sofa in exhaustion and frustration, and started to speak without really caring who was listening: 'I just don't know what to do with Miguel. He's so bright, and he finishes his math before everyone else, but he's started getting restless, and now he doesn't even want to do the assignments at all. He says he already knows this stuff, and it's boring to have to do all the problems. I know how he feels, and I've tried to have him help the other kids, but he's not really interested in doing that. It's the same in reading, but the others need so much help, and the state tests are coming up. I feel guilty because I know I am not challenging Miguel, but I just don't know what to do.'

Ms Castellano, another fifth grade teacher, listened intently: 'I know exactly how you feel. Brandy, in my class, is the same way. She was zipping through her math so quickly that I decided to let her take the next few chapter tests and she sailed through them even though we haven't covered the material yet in class. I've been letting her read while the others have been working on math, and she's picked up a book with excerpts from Shakespearean plays and really has gotten into it. I have an idea. I suggested to Brandy that she should try acting out a scene from one of the plays. She really likes *Taming of the Shrew* and wants to do one of the scenes, but needs a Petruchio. Miguel is very dramatic. Maybe he would like to work with her during the times that the others are working on things that he already knows and they can dramatize the scene.'

These teachers face a common problem, and they need a strategy to differentiate for high achieving and high potential students called curriculum compacting (Renzulli and Smith 1979; Reis et al. 1992). Curriculum compacting can be used in all classrooms to help students who have proven mastery of material that must be covered by other students. 'What do I do now?' is a refrain that causes frustration in many teachers and students, and curriculum compacting has been demonstrated to be a successful intervention to keep high potential students engaged.

In urban areas where many students begin to underachieve due to repetition of content and the attention that must be given to students who are scoring below grade level or are unmotivated, pressure to raise test scores permeates a teacher's day. In some urban schools, the most able academic students are at-risk for becoming underachievers because of the lack of challenge they experience.

Since the mid-1990s, a disproportionately low number of culturally diverse urban students have been identified to participate in these programs, and equity issues are justifiably raised by parents, journalists and the Office of Civil Rights. Some parents of culturally diverse children are frustrated by the traditional identification strategies that often overlook their children, while others fight any attempt to change instruments or procedures, stating firmly that they do not want 'watered down' identification or programming for their children.

Barriers for the participation of talented urban youth in gifted and enrichment programs and the rise of underachievement have been attributed to several factors, such as the use of definitions of giftedness that reflect middle-class majority culture, values and perceptions (Frasier and Passow 1994), standardized tests that do not reflect the exceptional abilities of minority children (Ford 1994; Ford and Harris 1990; Kitano and Kirby 1986) and the effects of low socioeconomic status and/or differences in environmental opportunities that enhance intellectual achievement (Ford 1996; Ford and Harris 1990). Crocker (1987) has also found that social factors have been underestimated and that the effects of discrimination and low socioeconomic status have profound effects on the achievement of urban youths. High ability students may often be affected more severely, as their intellectual strength often goes hand in hand with emotional sensitivity and a sense of social justice (Silverman 1993; Neihart et al. 2001) causing psychological impediments that Ford (1992) believes have a negative impact. Many American born minorities, in contrast to immigrant populations, consider obstacles to their achievement insurmountable, thus the key to change must be within the educational system (Ogbu 1987).

A number of factors have been found that relate to success in talented urban students. These factors are true for all children, but even more imperative for the child who faces the societal obstacles posed by minority and low socioeconomic status. A study of talented students who either achieved or underachieved in an urban high school identified several factors that characterize high levels of achievement and success in school (Reis et al. 1995). Students who achieved:

- developed a belief in self and a vision of a hopeful future
- had relationships with supportive adults (teachers or parents) in their lives

- interacted regularly with high achieving peers
- encountered intellectual challenge in honors or advanced classes
- participated in extracurricular activities and opportunities to develop their talents.

A study of twenty successful programs identified five strategies that can be successfully used with urban students:

- high expectations for students, program and staff
- personalized attention
- innovative structure and organization
- experiential learning opportunities
- long-term support (James et al. 1999; Keith and Cool 1992).

Strategies for curriculum and instructional differentiation

In order to accommodate for the simultaneous inclusion of diverse students and the increasing elimination of gifted programs in economically strapped urban areas, many school districts have adopted a variety of within-classroom strategies collectively referred to as differentiated instruction. Differentiation is an attempt to address the variation of learners in the classroom through multiple approaches that modify instruction and curriculum to match the individual needs of students (Tomlinson 2000). Tomlinson (1995) emphasized that when teachers differentiate curriculum, they stop acting as dispensers of knowledge and instead, serve as organizers of learning opportunities.

Renzulli (1977, 1988; Renzulli and Reis 1997) defined differentiation as encompassing five dimensions: content, process, products, classroom organization and management, and teachers' own commitment to change themselves as learners as well as teachers. The differentiation of *content* involves adding more depth to the curriculum by focusing on structures of knowledge, basic principles, functional concepts and methods of inquiry in particular disciplines. The differentiation of *process* incorporates the use of various instructional strategies and materials to enhance and motivate various students' learning styles. The differentiation of *products* enhances students' communication skills by encouraging them to express themselves in a variety of ways. To differentiate *classroom organization and management*, teachers can change the physical environment and grouping patterns they use in class and vary the allocation of time and resources for both groups and individuals. Classroom differentiation strategies can also be greatly enhanced by using the Internet in a variety of creative ways. Last, teachers can differentiate *themselves* by modeling the roles of athletic or drama coaches, stage or production managers, promotional agents and academic advisors.

Curriculum compacting is a differentiation strategy that incorporates content, process, products, classroom organization and management and teachers' personal commitment to accommodating individual and small group differences.

The scenario at the opening of this chapter describes the need for this strategy, and how two teachers who wanted to improve instruction for talented youth used a similar strategy that emanated from their common experiences. This approach can benefit teachers of all grades in many subject areas, and addresses the demand for more challenging learning experiences designed to help urban youth achieve at high levels and realize their potential.

Curriculum compacting: definitions and steps for implementation

Curriculum compacting streamlines the grade level curriculum for high potential students to enable time for more challenging and interesting work. This differentiation strategy was specifically designed to make appropriate curricular adjustments for students in any curricular area and at any grade level. The procedure involves:

- defining the goals and outcomes of a particular unit or block of instruction
- determining and documenting the students who have already mastered most or all of a specified set of learning outcomes
- providing replacement strategies for material already mastered through the use of instructional options that enable a more challenging, interesting, and productive use of the student's time.

Most teachers indicate that they are committed to meeting students' individual needs. Yet, many teachers do not have background information to put this commitment into practice as related research demonstrates that many talented students receive little differentiation of curriculum and instruction and spend a great deal of time in school doing work that they have already mastered (Archambault et al. 1992; Reis et al. 1993; Westberg et al. 1992). Too often, for example, some of our brightest students spend time relearning material they already know, which can lead to frustration, boredom and, ultimately, underachievement. Curriculum compacting has been effective in addressing underachievement when the compacted regular curriculum is replaced with self-selected work in a high interest area, making schoolwork much more enjoyable (Baum et al. 1995; Reis et al. 1993).

Most teachers who use compacting learn to streamline or 'compact' curriculum through a practical, step-by-step approach to the skills required to modify curriculum, and the techniques for pretesting students and preparing enrichment and/or acceleration options based on individual areas of interest. Practical issues such as record keeping and how to use the compacting form are also necessary to help guide teachers toward implementing this strategy. Once they have tried to compact for students, these guidelines can help to save valuable classroom time for both teachers and students.

Curriculum compacting, as presented in this chapter, has been field tested since 1975. It has been used with individuals and groups of students with above average ability in any academic, artistic or vocational area. Most important, research demonstrates that compacting can dramatically reduce redundancy, and challenge gifted students to new heights of excellence (Reis et al. 1993). It can be particularly meaningful for high ability students who are underachieving as it provides one clear way to eliminate work that may be too easy and replace that work with self-selected opportunities in an area of interest.

An overview of the curriculum compacting process is best provided by the use of the management form 'The Compactor', as presented on page 78, that serves as both an organizational and record-keeping tool. Teachers usually complete one form per student, or one form for a group of students with similar curricular strengths. Completed compactors should be kept in students' academic files, and updated regularly. The form can also be used for small groups of students who are working at approximately the same level (e.g. a reading or math group), and used as a addendum to an Individualized Education Plan (IEP) in states in which services for gifted students fall under special education laws.

The Compactor is divided into three columns:

- The first column includes information on learning objectives and student strengths in those areas. Teachers should list the objectives for a particular unit of study, followed by data on students' proficiency in those objectives, including test scores, behavioral profiles and past academic records.
- In the second column, teachers should list the ways in which they will pre-assess whether students already know the skills that will be taught in class. The pretest or pre-assessment strategies they select, along with results of those assessments, should be listed in this column. The assessment instruments can be formal measures, such as tests, or informal measures, such as performance assessments based on observations of class participation and written assignments. Specificity of knowledge and objectives are important; recording an overall score of 85 percent on ten objectives, for example, sheds little light on what portion of the material can be compacted, since students might show limited mastery of some objectives and high levels of mastery on others.
- The third column is used to record information about acceleration or enrichment options; to determine these options, teachers must consider students' individual interests and learning styles. We should not uniformly replace compacted regular curriculum work with harder, more advanced material that is solely determined by the teacher. Many years of research and field-testing have helped us to learn that when teachers do this, students will learn a major lesson. They learn that if they do their best work, they are rewarded with harder and more work. Instead, we recommend that students' interests should be considered. If for example, a student loves working on science fair projects, time to work on these projects can be used to replace material already mastered in a different content area. Teachers should be careful to help monitor the challenge level of the material being substituted. Too often, talented students do not learn and understand the

INDIVIDUAL EDUCATIONAL PROGRAMMING GUIDE
The Compactor

Prepared by: Joseph S. Renzulli
Linda M. Smith

NAME: _____ AGE: _____ TEACHER(S) _____

SCHOOL: _____ GRADE: _____ PARENT(S) _____

Individual Conference Dates and Persons
Participating in Planning Of IEP
_____

CURRICULUM AREAS TO BE CONSIDERED FOR COMPACTING. Provide a brief description of basic material to be covered during this marking period and the assessment information or evidence that suggests the need for compacting.	PROCEDURES FOR COMPACTING BASIC MATERIAL. Describe activities that will be used to guarantee proficiency in basic curricular areas.	ACCELERATION AND/OR ENRICHMENT ACTIVITIES. Describe activities that will be used to provide advanced level learning experiences in each area of the regular curriculum.

☐ Check here if additional information is recorded on the reverse side.

nature of effort and challenge because everything they encounter in school is too easy for them. Teachers must attempt to replace the compacted material with work that is engaging and challenging.

How to use the compacting process

The first of three phases of the compacting process consists of defining the goals and outcomes of a given unit or segment of instruction. This information is readily available in most subjects because specific goals and outcomes are included in teachers' manuals, curriculum guides, scope-and-sequence charts, and some of the new curricular frameworks that are emerging in connection with outcome based education models. A major goal of this phase of the compacting process is to help teachers make individual programming decisions; a larger professional development goal is to help teachers be better analysts of the material they are teaching, and better consumers of textbooks and prescribed curricular materials.

The second phase of curriculum compacting is to identify students who have already mastered the objectives or outcomes of a unit or segment of instruction that is about to be taught. Many of these students have the potential to master new material at a faster than normal pace, and knowing one's students well, is, of course, the best way to begin the assessment process. Standardized achievement tests can serve as a good general screen for this step because they allow us to list the names of all students who are scoring one or more years above grade level in particular subject areas.

Being a candidate for compacting does not necessarily mean that a student knows all of the material under consideration. Therefore, the second step in identifying candidates involves the use of assessment techniques to evaluate specific learning outcomes. The process is slightly modified for compacting content areas that are not as easily assessed as basic skills, and for students who have not mastered the material, but are judged to be candidates for more rapid coverage. First, students should understand the goals and procedures of compacting, including the nature of the replacement process. Underachieving students often regard compacting as a bargain as they may be able to compact out of a segment of material that they already know (e.g. a unit that includes a series of chapters in a social studies text) and the procedures for verifying mastery at a high level should be specified. These procedures might consist of answering questions based on the chapters, writing an essay, or taking the standard end-of-unit test. The amount of time for completion of the unit should be specified, and procedures such as periodic progress reports or log entries for teacher review should be discussed and selected.

Providing acceleration and enrichment options for talented students

The final phase of the compacting process can be one of the most exciting aspects of teaching because it is based on cooperative decision-making and creativity on the parts of both teachers and students. Time saved through curriculum compacting can be used to provide a variety of enrichment and acceleration opportunities for the student.

Enrichment strategies might include a variety of strategies such as those included in the Enrichment Triad Model (Renzulli 1977) that provide opportunities for exposure to new topics and ideas, methods training and creative and critical thinking activities, and opportunities to pursue advanced independent or small group creative projects. This aspect of the compacting process should also be viewed as a creative opportunity for a teacher to serve as a mentor to one or two students who are not working up to potential. We have also observed another interesting occurrence that has resulted from the availability of curriculum compacting. When some previously bright but underachieving students realized that they could both economize on regularly assigned material and 'earn time' to pursue self-selected interests, their motivation to complete regular assignments increased; as one student put it, 'Everyone understands a good deal!' Several strategies have been suggested for differentiating instruction and curriculum for talented or high potential students, ranging from substitution of regular material with more advanced material to options such as independent program or specific content strategies, such as Great Books or Literature Circles. Many of these strategies can be used in combination with compacting or as replacement ideas after students' curriculum has been compacted, as can acceleration, that enables students to engage in content that is appropriately challenging (Stanley 1989; Southern and Jones 1992) by joining students in a higher grade level class or by doing advanced curriculum materials while in the same class, a form of content acceleration.

Case study of Rosa and the use of compacting in language arts

Rosa is a fifth grader in a self-contained heterogeneous classroom in a lower socio-economic urban school district. While Rosa's reading and language scores range between four or five years above grade level, most of her twenty-nine classmates are reading one to two years below grade level. This presented Rosa's teacher with a common problem: what was the best way to provide differentiated services to Rosa? He agreed to compact her curriculum, and taking the easiest approach possible, he administered all of the appropriate unit tests for the grade level in the Basal Language Arts program. He subsequently excused Rosa from completing the activities and worksheets in the units where she showed proficiency (80 percent and above). When Rosa missed one or two questions, the teacher checked for trends in those items and provided instruction and practice materials to ensure concept mastery.

Rosa usually took part in language arts lessons with the rest of her classmates for one or two days a week; the balance of the time she spent with alternative projects, some of which she selected. This strategy spared Rosa up to six or eight hours a week with language arts skills that were simply beneath her level. She joined the class instruction only when her pre-tests indicated she had not fully acquired the skills or to take part in a discussion that her teacher thought she would enjoy and spent as many as five hours a week in a resource room for high ability students with an enrichment specialist. This time was usually scheduled during her language arts class, benefiting both Rosa and her teacher, since he didn't have to search for all of the enrichment options himself.

Rosa also visited a regional science center with other students who had expressed a high interest and aptitude for science. Science was a second strength area for Rosa, and based on the results of her *Interest-A-Lyzer*, a decision was made for Rosa to proceed with a science fair project on growing plants under various conditions. Rosa's Compactor, which covered an entire semester, was updated in January. Her teacher remarked that compacting her curriculum had actually saved him time – time he would have spent correcting papers needlessly assigned! A copy of her compactor form was also included in her permanent record folder and provided for Rosa's sixth grade teacher, and a conference between the fifth and sixth grade teachers and the resource teacher helped to ensure continuity in dealing with Rosa's advanced curricular needs.

Research on curriculum compacting

A national study completed at the University of Connecticut's National Research Center on the Gifted and Talented (NRC/GT) (Reis et al. 1992) examined the use of curriculum compacting for use with students from a wide diversity of school districts. A sample of 465 second through sixth grade classroom teachers from 27 school districts throughout the country participated in this study. Several urban schools were included in the study, including a magnet school for Hispanic students in California.

Classroom teachers were randomly assigned to participate in either the treatment (implemented compacting) or the control group (continued with normal teaching practices). Treatment and control group teachers were asked to target one or two candidates in their classrooms for Curriculum Compacting, and all participating students in treatment and control groups were tested before and after treatment with out-of-level Iowa Tests of Basic Skills (ITBS). Next-grade-level tests were used to compensate for the 'topping out' effect that is frequently encountered when measuring the achievement of high ability students.

The most important finding from this research might be described as the more-for-less phenomenon. Approximately 40 to 50 percent of traditional classroom material was compacted for targeted students in one or more content areas. When teachers eliminated as much as 50 percent of regular curricular activities and materials for targeted students, no differences were observed in post-test achievement scores between treatment and control groups in math concepts, math computation, social studies, and spelling. In science, the students who had between 40 and 50 percent of their curriculum eliminated actually scored significantly higher on science achievement post-tests than their peers in the control group. And students whose curriculum was specifically compacted in mathematics scored significantly higher than their peers in the control group on the math concepts post-test. These findings point out the benefits of compacting for increases on standard achievement assessments.

In another recent study, teachers were asked to use both curriculum compacting and self-selected Type III enrichment projects (self-selected projects based on students' interests) as a systematic intervention for a diverse group of under-achieving talented students. In this study, underachievement was reversed in the majority of students, and the use of compacting and replacement of high interest projects (Renzulli 1977) specifically targets student strengths and interests to reverse academic underachievement (Baum et al. 1995).

Use of compacting in the future

In research on compacting (Reis et al. 1992), participating teachers were asked whether they would continue to use curriculum compacting in the future, and why they would make this decision. Responses to this question from almost 400 teachers were coded into three categories: positive, negative and uncertain. More than two-thirds of all teachers indicated that they would continue to use curriculum compacting procedure in the future, and most who responded positively explained why, including the following representative comments from urban teachers:

> Yes. I feel that the time talented students are in my classroom is better spent doing more challenging work than it is doing assignments on material they already know. When they share projects and reports with the class, it also enriches their [other students'] learning experiences.

> Yes, I will continue this method of differentiation because it has shown me a very meaningful strategy to use with students who already know grade level material. In turn this enables students to become interested in independent learning they would like to pursue. The capable students are less likely to be turned off by this approach. This was a strategy that kept all students challenged in my class. I will use this next year in Math and hopefully other areas as well.

> Definitely! This is such an exciting way to teach! The students involved in the compacting program had the opportunity to become such active, independent learners. They had a taste of learning through their own actions not just the material spooned out through limited textbooks. It was amazing to watch this learning process in action! Sparks flew in my classroom this year! Now that I'm familiar with compacting, I can't wait for next year to begin!

Teachers who responded that they were uncertain about continuing with compacting discussed their concerns about available planning time, a need to learn more about compacting, and students' lack of independent skills. The reasons cited by the small number of teachers who gave negative responses about the future use of compacting included comments about large class sizes and a preference for their own method of meeting students' needs. While curriculum compacting is a viable process for meeting the needs of high ability students in the regular classroom, it does takes time, effort and planning on the part of classroom teachers. With urban teachers, especially those who work with students placed at risk because of poverty, compacting requires different types of efforts, particularly in finding different materials to substitute in environments that often rely primarily on addressing deficits and remedial instruction.

Many factors contribute to the creation of a supportive school environment for the use of curriculum compacting, such as administrative support, encouragement, availability of materials and resources for substitution of the regular curriculum, the availability of guided practice and coaching, and teachers' increased ease and reflections about how to fit compacting into their professional practices.

Advice from successful teachers who implement compacting

Research (Reis et al. 1993) showed that the most successful teachers to use compacting, many of whom taught in urban areas and/or taught culturally diverse talented students, implemented the following strategies to successfully implement compacting. First, they worked with a colleague or colleagues with whom they shared a common bond. They wanted to improve their teaching practices and were not afraid to ask each other for help or support. Second, they started with a small group of students and not their entire class. The successful teachers understood that this process would take some time and organization and became committed to trying to work with a group who really needed the process first. By not trying this with all students, they reduced the stress and challenges they would have encountered if they tried to do too much in the beginning of the process. Third, they asked for help from their liaisons, the district content consultants and each other. In each successful district, teachers asked each other how they were handling pre-testing and assessment. They shared strategies for management and for replacement, and visited each other's classrooms at their own suggestions or because a liaison suggested it. The modeling and sharing success stories made a difference. Fourth, they also understood that like a novice practicing piano scales, they would continue to improve by trying and reflecting on their work in this area. The teachers who did the best work consistently asked their colleagues and liaisons what had worked best and how current practices could extend and improve this practice. By reflecting on what had worked, they were able to modify and change their own attempts, and consistently improve. In the most successful schools, teachers were provided with time to work with liaisons, small amounts of material funds for curricular replacement costs and substitutes to enable them to visit and observe direct modeling in each other's classrooms.

Conclusion

The many changes that are taking place in schools require all educators to examine a broad range of techniques for providing equitably for *all* students. Curriculum compacting is one such process. It is not tied to a specific content area or grade level, nor is it aligned with a particular approach to school or curricular reform. Rather, the process is adaptable to any school organizational plan or curricular framework, and it is flexible enough to be used within the context of rapidly changing approaches to general education. The research described in this chapter, and the practical experiences gained through several years of field testing and refining the compacting process, particularly in urban areas and in schools that serve culturally diverse students, have demonstrated that many positive benefits can result from this process for both students and teachers, and particularly, talented students who may be placed at risk for underachieving in school.

Like any innovation, curriculum compacting requires time, energy, and acceptance from teachers. Yet, educators we have studied who compact effectively indicate that it takes no longer than normal teaching practices. More importantly, they reported that the benefits to all students certainly make the effort worthwhile. One teacher's comment about the compacting process reflects the attitude of most teachers who have participated in research about compacting:

> As soon as I saw how enthusiastic and receptive my students were about the compacting process, I began to become more committed to implementing this method in all my classes.

Key questions

1   How is the strategy of compacting for diverse gifted students different than that for other gifted students?
2   What collaborative efforts are required to compact successfully?
3   How can compacting be used to include cultural perspectives?

References

Archambault, F. X., Jr., Westberg, K. L., Brown, S., Hallmark, B. W., Emmons, C. and Zhang, W. (1992) *Regular Classroom Practices with Gifted Students: Results of a National Survey of Classroom Teachers.* Storrs, CT: National Research Center on the Gifted and Talented.

Baum, S. M., Renzulli, J. S. and Hébert, T. P. (1995) Reversing underachievement: creative productivity as a systematic intervention. *Gifted Child Quarterly*, 39(4): 224–235.

Crocker, A. C. (1987) Underachieving, gifted working class boys: are they wrongly labeled underachieving? *Educational Studies*, 13(2): 169–178.

Ford, D. Y. (1992) Determinants of underachievement as perceived by gifted, above-average, and average black students. *Roeper Review*, 14: 130–136.

Ford, D. Y. (1994) *The Recruitment and Retention of African American Students in Gifted Education Programs: Implication and Recommendations* (RBDM 9406). Storrs, CT: National Research Center on the Gifted and Talented.

Ford, D. Y. (1996) *Reversing Underachievement among Gifted Black Students: Promising Practices and Programs*. New York: Teachers College Press.

Ford, D. Y. and Harris, J. J. (1990) On discovering the hidden treasures of gifted and talented Black children. *Roeper Review*, 13: 27–32.

Frasier, M. M. and Passow, A. H. (1994) *Towards a New Paradigm for Identifying Talent Potential* (Research Monograph 94412). Storrs, CT: National Research Center on the Gifted and Talented.

James, D. W., Jurich, S. and Estes, S. (1999) *Raising Minority Academic Achievement: A Compendium of Education Programs and Practices*. Washington, DC: American Youth Policy Forum.

Keith, T. Z. and Cool, V. A. (1992) Testing models of school learning: effects of quality of instruction, motivation, academic coursework, and homework, on academic achievement. *School Psychology Quarterly*, 7(3): 207–226.

Kitano, M. and Kirby, D. (1986) *Gifted Education: A Comprehensive View*. Boston, MA: Little, Brown.

Neihart, M., Reis, S. M., Robinson, N. M. and Moon, S. (2001) *The Social and Emotional Development of Gifted Children*. Waco, TX: Prufrock Press.

Ogbu, J. U. (1987) Variability in minority school performance: a problem in search of an explanation. *Anthropology and Education Quarterly*, 18(4): 312–334.

Reis, S. M., Burns, D. E. and Renzulli, J. S. (1992) *Curriculum Compacting: The Complete Guide to Modifying the Regular Curriculum for High Ability Students*. Mansfield Center, CT: Creative Learning Press.

Reis, S. M., Westberg, K. L., Kulikowich, J., Calliard, F., Hébert, T. P., Purcell, J. H., Rogers, J., Smist, J. and Plucker, J. (1993) *An Analysis of the Impact of Curriculum Compacting on Classroom Practices* (Technical Report). Storrs, CT: National Research Center on the Gifted and Talented.

Reis, S. M., Hébert, T. P., Diaz, E. I., Maxfield, L. R. and Ratley, M. E. (1995) *Case Studies of Talented Students Who Achieve and Underachieve in an Urban High School*. (Research Monograph 95120). Storrs, CT: National Research Center on the Gifted and Talented.

Renzulli, J. S. (1977) *The Enrichment Triad Model: A Guide for Developing Defensible Programs for the Gifted and Talented*. Mansfield Center, CT: Creative Learning Press.

Renzulli, J. S. (1988) The multiple menu model for developing differentiated curriculum for the gifted and talented. *Gifted Child Quarterly*, 32: 298–309.

Renzulli, J. S. and Reis, S. M. (1997) *The Schoolwide Enrichment Model: A Comprehensive Plan for Educational Excellence*. Mansfield Center, CT: Creative Learning Press.

Renzulli, J. S. and Smith, L. H. (1979) *A Guidebook for Developing Individualized Educational Programs for Gifted and Talented Students*. Mansfield Center, CT: Creative Learning Press.

Silverman, L. K. (1993) *Counseling the Gifted and Talented*. Denver, CO: Love.

Southern, T. W. and Jones, E. D. (1992) The real problems with academic acceleration. *Gifted Child Today*, 15(2): 34–38.

Stanley, J. C. (1989) A look back at educational non-acceleration: an international tragedy. *Gifted Child Today*, 12(4): 60–61.

Tomlinson, C. A. (1995) *How to Differentiate Instruction in Mixed-ability Classrooms*. Alexandria, VA: Association for Supervision and Curriculum Development.

Tomlinson, C. A. (2000) *Differentiation of Instruction in the Elementary Grades*. (Report ED 443572). Champaign, IL: ERIC Clearinghouse on Elementary and Early Childhood Education.

Westberg, K. L., Archambault, F. X., Dobyns, S. M. and Salvin, T. J. (1992) *An Observational Study of Instructional and Curricular Practices Used with Gifted and Talented Students in Regular Classrooms* (Technical Report). Storrs, CT: National Research Center on the Gifted and Talented.

3.2   The detection and nurture of the culturally different gifted and talented in Aotearoa/ New Zealand

Neil A. Reid

New Zealand is a nation of barely 4 million people largely of British stock (Europeans/Pakeha) with a sizeable minority (21 percent) of Polynesians, plus a burgeoning number of Asian newcomers, currently 7 percent, but projected to reach 15 percent by 2021. Both English and Maori are official languages. While 70 percent of the population is concentrated in a few main urban areas, many people live in coastal sub-cities or rural towns.

Development of concern for the gifted in New Zealand education, 1940–2000

The development of gifted and talented education in New Zealand is largely the outcome of the commitment and effort of dedicated individuals. Concern for the welfare of gifted children has waxed and waned over the years, and in the absence of any Ministry of Education policy on meeting their special needs, provisions for their education have been either non-existent or small-scale and localized. Despite major developments since 1990 requiring all schools to cater for the gifted under the charters by which they must now operate, as Moltzen (1999) observed:

> Our record in this area is hardly an enviable one. There have been a number of occasions this century that seemed to hold great promise for our students, but almost inevitably this promise was not fulfilled, and gains made seemed to disappear almost overnight.
>
> (Moltzen 1999: 66)

Identification strategies

Although several prominent educators have advocated a broad concept in identifying giftedness using multiple criteria and techniques, and a team approach involving teachers, parents, peers and educational specialists, the majority of classroom teachers still tend to consider only academic achievement. While this conservative view is common worldwide, it is worth pondering how long it will take to modify the concept of giftedness as largely intellectual ability, and to include multiple forms of giftedness. In New Zealand, some teachers are making an effort to provide opportunities for all children to develop their potential: nonetheless, many gifted children are finding their school experience boring, and lacking in challenge. New Zealand espouses a distinctive philosophy towards an 'egalitarian' state: regrettably, this frequently means 'the same for all', rather than 'equal as fitting'.

Gifted: definition of the term

In New Zealand, the rise and fall in popularity of particular concepts and definitions has followed the general pattern for most of the western developed countries. Nowadays, we have an array of definitions. Until recently, 'children with special abilities' was the term used by ministry officials and by most teachers, and the definition is sufficiently vague and broad to include most varieties of talent. But with the publication of a handbook for schools *Gifted and Talented Students: Meeting their Needs in New Zealand Schools* (Ministry of Education 2000), 'gifted and talented' has become the preferred term. However, many New Zealand educators still think of 'giftedness' primarily in terms of a very high level of academic achievement, although they would also acknowledge special talent in art, music, drama and sports, with a limited acceptance of 'creativity'. But are those with *differing* ethnic and cultural backgrounds considering exactly the same 'thing' in any discussion about giftedness and talent?

Research and experimentation undertaken from 1980 onwards (Reid 1983, 1985, 1989, 1990, 1991, 1992; Doidge 1990; Doidge and Leilua 1992; Cathcart and Pou 1992; Bevan-Brown 1993, 1996, 2000, 2002) has revealed different conceptions of giftedness, which if unrecognized will disadvantage minority children in New Zealand's multicultural classrooms.

Pakeha/European conceptions

While New Zealand's largely middle-class Pakeha society values intelligence and to a lesser extent creativity, current national and international economic and social developments have led to a focus on very specific gifts or talents which can be utilized for technological progress and economic advancement: computer know-how, export marketing, business wheeling-and-dealing, marine and agricultural sciences, macro-economics, and of course sport, are highly prized by the dominant culture. Meanwhile, the talents of potential poets, writers, social and political leaders, musicians and artists are less valued. This narrow focus is also evident in the schools which promote mathematics, science, computer science and technology as first-order subjects, largely eclipsing the 'softer' options of history, foreign languages, music and art.

Maori conceptions

The evidence from the literature, research and collected opinion suggests that Maori, while not denigrating the intellectual and the academic, place more value on the kind of 'cleverness' epitomized in the speechmaking and oratory on the *marae* (centre of tribal life) and in the lobbying and politicking on tribal councils.

Prized characteristics are more people-oriented: the warmth and support of the family and the community bound by *aroha* (understanding) and shared activities. Getzels and Dillon (1973) drew attention to 'life talents' – talents for 'being something'. This is similar to the Maori concern for being of service to others, for coping with dignity especially in times of crisis such as birth, marriage and death. There is also a spiritual dimension which is largely ignored by Europeans: for example, Maori informants will cite personal 'gifts' such as astral travel, healing through touch, *matakite* (foretelling) and *makutu* (sorcery) – a 'darker' talent. The holistic nature of Maori concepts depicts a rich tapestry of attitudes, values and beliefs, markedly different from the dominant culture (Bevan-Brown 1996).

Pacific Islander conceptions

The Pacific Islanders lie between the two extremes of Pakeha and Maori. Torn between integration, as a means to achieve success in the host society, and a desire to maintain their distinctive cultural identities, their dilemma is disturbing. Generally, these Polynesian immigrants have coped with the problems of culture shock and a new way of life, reflecting the strength of their social institutions. Their adjustment to city life and an industrialized society is amazing, given their small island village and agricultural background.

In contrast to the revival of Maori cultural identity, many of the Pacific Island immigrants are submerging their own rich cultures to assimilate and benefit from the material fruits of the Pakeha culture. Fairbairn-Dunlop and Makisi (2003) summarize the situation thus:

> The Pacific Island community has shown resilience and determination to succeed in the past. However, there is a sense of fragility and some insecurity today. . . . Our Pacific Island leaders must appreciate these changing times and guide us through them, leaving our identities intact, our uniqueness unique, and our spirits alive.
>
> (Fairbairn-Dunlop and Makisi 2003: 41–42)

To balance this conscious cultural integration, some Pacific Island families save money for trips back to their home villages to maintain kinship ties and feelings of belonging. But presently, young Pacific Islanders lack adult role models in New Zealand society, particularly in positions of leadership. Even the church, a meeting place, solace and identity for Pacific Islanders, is less vital for the increasingly disaffected urban youth. Sefulu Ioane, a Samoan, says, 'There are already more than enough young [Islanders] in our streets today whose values are neither Pakeha, nor Polynesian' (Ioane 1982: 16). Melanie Anae (2003) captures the Polynesian youth's predicament in this poem:

I am – a Samoan, but not a Samoan . . .
To my *aiga* [extended family] in Samoa, I am a *Palagi* [European]
I am – a New Zealander but not a New Zealander . . .
To New Zealanders I am a 'bloody coconut' at worst,
A Pacific Islander at best
I am – to my Samoan parents, their child.

(Anae 2003: 89)

Asian conceptions

It is tempting to try to define a homogeneous Asian concept of giftedness, but 'Asians' come from some eighteen different countries from Afghanistan in the west to Korea and Japan in the east. While some, like Japan, are ethnically homogeneous, countries such as Malaysia, Indonesia and the Philippines comprise several distinct ethnic groups. A significant number of Chinese began to arrive during the 1860s Otago goldrush; Indian labourers were recruited in the 1890s to work on farms. Most Asians qualify for immigration through the business/skilled category, those selected being young, well-educated, highly skilled and wealthy. Two-thirds of Asian New Zealanders were born in Asia, and a quarter of them have a bachelor's degree or a higher qualification – double that of the total population.

Spoonley et al. (1996) write of the increased flow from Hong Kong on the return of sovereignty to the Chinese, ethnic Indians fleeing racial discrimination following military coups in Fiji and ethnic Chinese from Malaysia and Indonesia escaping discriminatory practices. The majority desire an improved quality of life, better education for their children, less crowded housing and a cleaner, pollution-free environment. But Asians have not looked to government for their success: despite being 'disadvantaged' especially in terms of language, Asian migrants have adapted readily to the dominant culture; parents 'value education very highly and are prepared to bear enormous sacrifices so that children of the family can receive the best educational opportunities' (Thakur 1995: 275). Further, Asians are making a huge impact in the business sector, the professions, the arts and in certain sports, e.g. table tennis, hockey, martial arts and golf. Asian New Zealanders can be referred to as a 'model minority' (Tsai 1992) and have 'long been known for their gentle care of children, esteem for the elderly and all-round fine citizenship' (Brown 2003: 49).

Clearly, any concept of giftedness for Asians must accommodate all those intellectual traits valued by European New Zealanders. But there are other dimensions evident. The teachings of Asia's great religions are practised and the language and customs of the homeland maintained, certainly by older immigrants. And in this there are close parallels with Pasifika peoples. The notions of sagehood and reverence for ancient philosophies are also apparent (Kuo 1992). Accomplishments in the arts and physical prowess are recognized and respected, together with Polynesian conceptions of giftedness: spirituality, 'wholeness', humility, morality, honour for the family and in the serving of others.

Identification

While it is universally accepted that gifted and talented children may be found in all ethnic groups, unless focused efforts are made to both find and nurture minority group youth, they remain an untapped source of potential intellectual and creative talent. In New Zealand, Polynesian children are under-represented in the ranks of the gifted and talented. The biggest barrier to identification in the school context is the prevailing conception of giftedness, emphasizing those traits valued by the dominant culture of monolingual, mainly middle-class Europeans that rejects or ignores other characteristics valued by minority cultures.

Undeniably, the majority culture does recognize and value certain talents among its Polynesian minorities. The Polynesian's prowess in many athletic activities requiring physical skill, stamina and psychomotor abilities is con-spicuously represented in national and school sports teams. Cultural clubs and multicultural schools are also a feature of communities with large numbers of Polynesian residents. Their members' talents are frequently on display for tourists and visiting dignitaries and the groups proudly perform *haka* (action-songs), *waiata*, *poi* and *siva* dances. Polynesian skills in arts and crafts, wood, stone and bone carving, weaving fine mats, baskets and *tapa* (cloth-making) are admired. In the visual arts, many Maori artists have been involved in a recent renaissance in Maori art, combining traditional and innovative approaches. Belatedly, New Zealanders are recognizing the richness of ancient Maori verse and music, and recent years have witnessed a burgeoning of talent in the field of poetry, play, film and television script, short-story and novel writing by Polynesian authors.

But brown-skinned New Zealanders are usually not considered as potential participants in gifted programmes, whereas Asians and some other ethnic and cultural minority children are 'over-represented'. Maori and Pasifika children are generally not perceived as a talent pool by European teachers: all too often, cultural difference is viewed as cultural disadvantage. Hill maintained as far back as 1977: 'Where a cultural group places a high value on a certain form of art or creativity or human performance, it is likely to produce better performances in that area' (Hill 1977: 9).

Identifying giftedness and talent in New Zealand's ethnic and cultural minorities

Teacher identification

Teacher identification is dependent on the teacher's understanding and ability to interpret student characteristics and behaviours appropriately. In New Zealand, the vast majority of teachers are middle-class, monolingual, monocultural Europeans working in an education system that is predominantly ethnocentric.

Teachers' low expectations of Maori children's capabilities have been noted by Clay (1985), Benton (1986), Jones (1987), Cathcart (1994) and Bevan-Brown (2002). Many teachers still subscribe to the 'deficit' ideology and make statements about Polynesian children such as: 'they . . . tend to answer in monosyllables . . . almost pidgin English . . . they're limited in many ways', and phrases like 'limited language', 'limited experience', 'restricted codes', 'non-standard English', 'lack of preschool experience' are employed frequently alongside more common labels such as 'lazy', 'unmotivated', 'withdrawn', 'short attention span' to 'explain' the underachievement of their students. Clearly there will need to be conscious efforts to suppress culturally determined prejudices and to accommodate different ways of thinking, feeling and doing. If schools are to become multicultural in the fullest sense, teachers will need to consider differences in positive terms, as desirable strengths rather than incompetences.

Already Pakeha New Zealanders have had to accept Maori who have clung tenaciously to their *Maoritanga* (Maori traditions, practices and beliefs). More recently, with the steady inflow of Pacific Island immigrants and the flood of people from Asia, European teachers have been reminded that there are other ways of perceiving and doing things, even in such matters as establishing eye contact, and in social courtesies, like opening the door for females and standing when guests come into a room, using appropriate forms of greeting and address, and in matters such as borrowing money and property belonging to others.

Walford (1979) summarized the position thus:

> Aside from the consideration that all children, whatever their culture, have a right to the full development of their potential, their community needs their talents as future leaders to fill the role of the elder. We, as teachers, have a moral obligation to treat all children as important human beings, with feelings, attitudes, experiences and interests that are worthy of our attention and respect.
>
> (Walford 1979: 3)

Her statement, made in the late 1970s, still rings true today.

Educational and psychological assessment

Internationally, teachers reveal with monotonous regularity that the objective data provided by standardized tests are considered to be highly effective in identifying gifted students for the typical school-based enrichment and acceleration programmes. But Renzulli's (1973) caution warrants consideration:

> In view of the heavy cultural loading of most standardised tests of intelligence and achievement, it is apparent that an identification process that depends mainly on traditional measures of performance will discriminate against youngsters who have not participated fully in the dominant culture.
>
> (Renzulli 1973: 439)

And Sternberg (1984) reminds us that,

> Tests work for some people some of the time, but they do not work for other people much of the time. . . . Applied conservatively and with full respect to all of the available information, tests can be of some use. Misapplied or overused, they are worse than nothing.
>
> (Sternberg 1984: 14)

Tests, including tests of general ability and scholastic achievement that are nationally standardized, do not operate in a cultural or social vacuum. Test constructors ensure that their measures reflect accurately the values of the dominant culture, and thus the formal education system as a facet of that society. Such tests attempt to assess those abilities required to deal effectively with the dominant language, numbers, symbols and abstractions. The tests are then unashamedly culturally loaded if they are to do the job required of them for the majority.

Attempts to circumvent this problem through the development of culture-fair or culture-free tests have been largely unsuccessful. They have failed to yield measures that neutralize the influence of important factors in intellectual growth and most that have been produced are far from free of cultural bias. One such test currently in vogue is Raven's Standard Progressive Matrices (SPM), a non-verbal measure which purports to assess the components of 'g' – the 'general' factor in intellectual ability. The SPM manual (Raven et al. 1991) states,

> If, . . . the 'Progressive Matrices' is used to select students for 'gifted' educa-tional programmes, the chosen students will not necessarily excel if the programmes operate along traditional academic lines. Some form of 'multiple talent' programme will be required to nurture such students' abilities.
>
> (Raven et al. 1991: 7)

Tests are usually used to assess present functioning: what the student knows and can do *now*, and to predict progress in the *immediate future*, the concern is with present performance and potential anticipated on the basis of current accomplishment. As with all sensitive test interpretation, test users must take into account the student's circumstances: in the case of minority group students, their opportunities to learn those behaviours incorporated in the tests, and their motivation to perform to the best of their ability on the tasks presented. This is essentially a judgement about the test's validity – there is no dodging it!

Apart from the more sensitive and searching interpretation of test scores, or possibly the use of separate norms for minority ethnic groups (which is political dynamite), the alternative is to resort to non-test methods, such as checklists, observational schedules, inventories, rating scales and the like. There are disadvantages here, too. Such methods are time consuming and they do not have the same degree of objectivity as psychological and educational tests. Nor do they usually have demonstrated validity and reliability. However, several useful checklists which attempt to take account of minority culture values have been devised since the mid-1980s (Baldwin 1984; Mitchell 1988; McAlpine and Reid 1996).

Parent nomination

Maori and Pacific Island parents, when judged by European, middle-class terms, are frequently considered to adopt less-than-adequate child-rearing practices in matters of health care, attention and supervision. Mention is often made of parental indulgence in babyhood, the rejection and alienation of children as the family grows, and the capricious and often sharp punishment practices employed by Polynesian parents.

It has also been noted that poorly educated, working-class Maori parents are wary of the school and suspicious of teachers. Some have had little secondary schooling themselves and consequently are in no position to guide their children at high school. Many teachers feel that Maori and Pacific Island parents lack involvement in their children's education. They cite non-attendance at school functions, and the lack of minority ethnic groups on Boards of Trustees. However, lack of confidence, a feeling of self-consciousness about their poor English, a belief that their educational duties as parents cease once their children have entered the formal education system, and for purely practical reasons such as both parents needing to work, leaves them little time to help their children or to take on additional responsibilities.

There is generally an absence of academic tradition in most Maori families, although there is an acknowledgment of the necessity for secondary and vocational education. There is also the suggestion that success in the Pakeha system will take their children away, make them consider their origins and parents as 'inferior', and most of all, that they might lose their Maoriness – their *Maoritanga*. Many Maori university and college of education graduates tell of the alienation of their friends and relations on returning to their tribal *marae* (community) after time away in the cities. This attitude lingers nowadays among *kaumatua* (tribal elders) where there is a distrust of 'book learning' and the university educated. The extended family has been dislocated: city houses are too small to accommodate grandparents and relations, although the effort is often made to extend customary hospitality, leading to overcrowding and sub-standard living conditions in what are rapidly becoming depressed inner-city ghettos.

As a consequence of these circumstances, children often lack adult models who would inculcate those behaviours valued by Maori, such as sharing, respect for elders and getting along with people. In the past, grandparents frequently nurtured budding talent: for example, a young Maori woman activist says:

> I was trained as a leader by my grandmother. There's usually one or two in each *whanau* [extended family] that are designated for leadership from birth really . . . I was always very bright and outspoken and . . . I was preened for leadership from birth.

The model of the more tight-knit, middle-class, suburban family is being forced on both Maori and Pacific Islanders by social pressures and economic circumstances: urban living is slowly breaking down the child-rearing patterns typical of the traditional rural communities.

The typical Maori home, again judged by middle-class European standards, lacks a computer, books, pictures, printed resource and reference materials. Hence the environment is evaluated as being unstimulating in terms of those experiences that underlie scholastic achievement, and communication between parents. But what is unrecognized by Europeans is that Maori children are exposed to aural and visual stimulation of kinds not acknowledged by those brought up in a culture that stresses the written word. Sympathetic teachers have demonstrated that Maori children from supposedly deprived backgrounds can, given appropriate stimuli and support, produce superbly accomplished and imaginative work.

Ranginui Walker, a Maori academic, writes:

> According to the 'deficit' theories of Reissman and others, Maori were under-achieving because they were 'culturally deprived'. Because Maori families were impoverished, their houses thought to be less stimulating than those of their Pakeha counterparts . . . children from working-class homes spoke a 'restricted language' code which stopped them from succeeding at school. These 'deficit' theories appeared to validate the conventional wisdom that Maori failure was due to poor English and lack of family support.
>
> (Walker 1990: 98)

Generally, there appears to be conflict between home and school standards, and Maori children often seem to lead two discrete lives. As Witi Ihimaera, one of New Zealand's leading writers, recalls, 'I'd go to school and be in one culture and I'd go home and be in another' (Shepheard 2003: 51). Many Maori children find that what they have already learnt at home and in their community is unaccepted, misinterpreted or unrecognized at school where they are expected to have mastered quite different skills.

However, since the early 1990s there have been significant changes taking place: with the advent of *Kohanga Reo* (Maori language pre-schools) and the Pacific Islands language nests modelled on them, and the establishment of *Kura Kaupapa Maori* (Maori-medium schools), parents have been drawn into the education process to a much greater degree than ever before. Preliminary evaluations of these initiatives (Ministry of Education 2001) indicate that parental interest and involvement is high.

Obviously, this view of Maori parents is over-generalized, but there are some disturbing statistics that have emerged recently. Nearly half of all Maori families may now be sole parent, and more than 75 percent of these parents have no school qualifications; and of greater concern, nearly 60 percent of child neglect cases reported to the authorities each year involve Maori children. Maori sole parents stand out as a large, disadvantaged group within the sole parent population. They are disadvantaged in income, housing, education, occupation and employment, compared with European sole parents.

In sharp contrast to the alleged lack of support given to teachers by Maori parents, Pacific Island parents place high value on a good education for their children. Their enthusiasm is recognized in a report: 'Pacific Island parents have high expectations for their young people, and these community aspirations are a positive resource on which schools can build' (Ministry of Education 2001: 77). However, any scheme for identifying and educating gifted Pasifika students will not succeed unless it accords with the way Polynesian parents consider their children should be treated at school. And the students themselves, through loyalty to the community's adults, will not cooperate with the teachers. 'Giftedness' for Pacific Island parents would have to be compatible with the cultural values of the community. And 'giftedness' as a trait that sets one apart from the community is unlikely to be valued highly.

Peer nomination

Compared with the vast majority of European children, Maori youngsters are strikingly independent at an early age. Since adults rarely interfere in their games, fights and other activities, the behaviour patterns are determined by the children's own standards. However, it has been observed that children who show any special gifts and who attract attention through leadership ability or marked independence are criticized, ridiculed by their peers until they conform. A somewhat similar set of dynamics is to be found in Pacific Island children's group behaviour. Peer group loyalties are strong and there is solid conformity to group standards. Independence is little valued; group cooperation and cohesion are considered vastly more important.

Bound up with Maori group behaviour are two complex concepts embodied in the words *whakaiti* and *whakahihi*. Roughly translated *whakaiti* means being humble, putting yourself down. As Metge (1986: 86) explains, 'From the Pakeha point of view *whakaiti* is disadvantageous when it causes the able to play down their ability. To Maori it is a praiseworthy preference for fellowship over individual eminence'. Maori children will disguise their ability so that they do not rise above their peer group. And *whakaiti* is seen as a desirable quality in great leaders.

The second, *whakahihi*, is the opposite: boasting, making yourself out to be somebody. A Pacific Islands (Samoan) version is *fia poto* (trying to be clever); Tongans have an almost identical term. Again, Metge (1986) informs us that one of the most damning criticisms one Maori can make of another is to accuse him/her of being *whakahihi*. Polynesian parents ensure that their children do not attract the *whakahihi/fia poto* label by squashing any signs of childish pride and withholding praise when outside the family circle. However, this situation is compensated for by *whanau* and/or other members of the *hapu* (subtribe) or *iwi* (tribe) who give encouragement and support (Bevan-Brown 1996: 105).

The *whakaiti–whakahihi* dimension is very strong and has greater significance for Maori. The pressures can be intolerable: some high-achieving Maori students have had to abandon their friends if they wished to succeed academically; others succumb to peer pressure. Some students ask to be taken out of top-stream classes, others deliberately fail tests, and some children beg their teachers to deduct marks from their assignments and tests so that they would not appear to have done so well!

Self-identification

Attention has been recently focused on students identifying themselves for gifted programmes, for example, Renzulli's 'revolving door' strategy. Mitigating against such a self-identification strategy is a complex phenomenon called *whakama* in Maori (shame, alienation). The rough Samoan equivalent is *musu*, and elsewhere in the South Pacific, *ma*. When confronted with unfamiliar situations, or authoritarian figures, Maori children or youth may be emotionally immobilized by *whakama*. The emotion can be so intense that they may have difficulty in expressing what they feel, much less the reasons for it. Some investigators have considered *whakama* a more significant potential difficulty than Pakeha prejudice in providing for Maori fulfilment, and much less easy to eliminate.

Maori research respondents give accounts of being singled out as the only Maori, say, as a member of a sporting team. Through their own skills and abilities they had earned selection, but being 'the only Maori' together with the isolation from ethnic peers resulted in withdrawal. In psychological terms, it could be said they suffered a failure in confidence, suddenly doubting themselves and their capacity to achieve. But, interestingly, although acknowledging *whakama* as a powerful phenomenon, most informants thought it less potent than reported by the research psychologists. Nonetheless, many Maori become *whakama* when they are separated from their peers and placed in a 'special' category be it superior, inferior or just different.

In the school context *whakama* may be triggered by a sense of shame, for example, for not being able to speak Maori well, or by feelings of injustice or guilt. But other examples may involve being called upon to give an impromptu talk or to read orally. While *whakama* causes most Maori to withdraw, some individuals treat it as a challenge and strive to regain *mana* (prestige, status) by achieving well. Metge (1986: 117) believes that the difference between profiting from *whakama* and being disabled by it are probably due to 'security of identity, upbringing and personality'.

Musu is similar to *whakama*. People afflicted by *musu* become withdrawn; they have a 'dead pan' look and restrict answers to monosyllables. *Musu* is common among Samoans, Cook Islanders, Tongans and Niueans. European teachers with little training in handling multicultural classes are baffled by such behaviour, and frequently misinterpret these actions as sulkiness, insolence or rejection of authority.

As a further complication, psychologists report that Maori children have a low self-concept, seeing themselves as inferior in many ways. They know that they belong to a 'brown' minority that is subordinate to the Pakeha majority; that they have been brought up in ways that differ significantly from those of the dominant culture, with obvious differences in material wealth and social position. The subsequent loss of pride, poor self-image and low self-esteem (*whakama*) is probably the greatest disadvantage the Maori child suffers in competition with the Pakeha.

Efforts have been made to boost Maori children's confidence, self-esteem and academic standing by introducing *Taha Maori* (literally 'the Maori side') and *Maoritanga*. However, research undertaken during the 1980s and 1990s indicated that 'teaching' *Maoritanga* in isolation helps self-concept and academic success hardly at all. This is not surprising to those who claim that *Maoritanga* cannot be taught – it is something that is lived.

Criticism has been levelled at both the concept and the development of *Taha Maori* by Maori educators such as Penetito (1984), Walker (1985), Smith (1990) and Smith and Smith (1996). Smith (1990) states uncompromisingly:

> The introduction of *Taha Maori* into schools relates to the interests of the dominant Pakeha population, in particular to the preservation of Pakeha social, cultural, economic and political privilege . . . *Taha Maori* [is] more concerned with educating Pakeha pupils.
>
> (Smith 1990: 188)

We have the familiar scenario of middle-class Pakeha capture of innovation to strengthen the dominant culture in the education system.

Non-Maori commentators have also expressed doubts. Hames (2002) queries whether there really are specific Maori ways of learning that would assist Maori in a predominantly European world and whether the present enthusiasm for bilingual education might not lead to 'further ghettoising Maori and widening any [social and educational] gaps' (Hames 2002: 64). Ramesh Thakur (1995) is also sceptical:

> It is difficult to see how individual Maori or Maoridom collectively will benefit by abandoning the opportunities of the mainstream schools for parallel schools. Unless immersion in Maori language is accompanied by improvements in English, scientific and numeracy skills, separate Maori-medium curricula will become part of the problem [of Maori underachievement] . . . This is not to dispute or reject the benefits of self-esteem conferred on Maori as they learn and preserve their language. But native-language fluency and self-esteem are the beginning, not the end of the process.
>
> (Thakur 1995: 276)

What has been said about *Maoritanga* and *Taha Maori* also applies equally to other attempts to introduce Pacific Island elements into the school's activities. There has been a quiet resentment of all this by Polynesian parents who see clearly through the few items of ethnic entertainment and superficial attempts at multiculturalism. As Ioane (1982: 13) stated, 'the real spirit and practices of the schools are still fashioned on the monocultural beliefs of the past'.

Obviously, in the light of the foregoing discussion, any identification and selection procedures which are going to make children feel 'different' from their peers, will have little appeal for Polynesian students. They are highly unlikely to volunteer for inclusion in such programmes, should they ever consider themselves as suitable candidates.

Responsive environment identification

Such an approach is premised on teachers providing a stimulating and challenging learning environment which fosters student self-identification. Given the background, training and experience of New Zealand teachers, how likely is this approach to prove successful in multicultural classrooms? And given that 90 percent of Maori and Pasifika students attend mainstream schools, how accurate will any identification be when what goes on in the classroom differs dramatically from what is considered traditionally appropriate for these students?

If conceptions of giftedness differ, might it be that aspects of the education system, such as content and learning styles might also be viewed differently by ethnic and/or cultural minorities? There appears to be widespread recognition that New Zealand curricula have been 'based squarely within one cultural tradition, that of the Pakeha, and on theories and practices imported from other western countries . . . its stress is on the objectification of knowledge and individual competitiveness in its pursuit' (Metge 1990: 33). The attempts made during the 1990s to produce national curricula relevant to minority cultures, were cosmetic and almost exclusively for Maori, i.e., bicultural. As a Samoan secondary school teacher enquired, 'how can subjects such as mathematics, physics, chemistry and computer studies be changed to be culturally appropriate?' These subjects are unpopular with Polynesians and viewed as distinctly 'un-Polynesian'. Nonetheless, even with the 'directions' suggested in ministry publications, change in curricula will not happen unless teachers are convinced that change is necessary.

Teachers need to learn that other cultures organize bodies of knowledge differently from Europeans. Instead of compartmentalizing knowledge into subject areas, Maori and other Polynesian cultures, stress the wholeness and interconnectedness of life and knowledge. The fragmentation of the field of knowledge by specialization, modules and timetabling is alien to people of these cultures.

Teachers also need to accept that the knowledge, beliefs, values and insights of other cultures are as valuable as those of the dominant culture. All ethnic groups in New Zealand should, as Metge (1990: 33) states, 'be recognised and valued for their own sake and for their past, present and potential contributions to our national society and culture'.

The new national curriculum is supposedly flexible enough to allow for a maximum of local input and adaptation. It is anticipated that the school system will accept its role in retaining, preserving and fostering Maori language and culture, as well as other minority cultures. Such initiatives should provide gifted minority ethnic/cultural students with opportunities of reaching their potential.

As long ago as the early 1960s, a concerted approach, especially in the Auckland area, led to the recognition that:

- cooperative learning, with group goals are more appropriate for Maori and Pasifika students
- memorizing and rote learning are valued and culturally appropriate methods
- non-standard language codes are not inferior to standard English.

Metge (1990: 62) writes: 'Maori *kaiako* give a central place to fostering of language. [The] emphasis is put on direct communication, especially (but not exclusively) in oral interaction'. Listening as well as speaking skills are encouraged. *Whakarongo* (active listening leading to understanding and response) is one of the first words a child learns in a Maori language environment.

Kaiako also actively promote the association of intellectual activities with things that have a physical dimension. Factual information, stories and values are expressed, not only in speech and writing, but also in song-poems, action-songs, enactments, painting, carving and weaving. Music, dance and the visual arts are moved from the fringe of the curriculum into the core.

Memorization is used as a learning method far more than is found in the typical preschool or junior school, and cooperation and sharing are stressed heavily. Metge (1990) states:

> individuals take turns as leader emerging from and then returning to the group, while the less proficient build up expertise and confidence as group members. Individuals are singled out publicly as little as possible, praise or blame being directed at the group or bestowed privately and often non-verbally. Even when doing their own work, children are encouraged to work together and help each other.
>
> (Metge 1990: 62)

Such teaching programmes in *Kohanga Reo* and *Kura Kaupapa Maori* are thoroughly integrated – they blur the boundaries between curriculum subjects, between inside and outside the classroom, and between school and community. In considering these features alone, there are obvious differences in both teaching and learning approaches between Maori and Pakeha. How, then, is the typical teacher expected to create a fitting classroom environment in which a Polynesian student's special abilities will 'surface', enabling identification?

Educational provisions

Segregation

While there have been examples of special short-term teaching programmes – either during school hours (opportunity clubs) or out of school hours (museum classes, explorers' clubs, music, drama and art classes) – most formal teaching of the gifted and talented takes place in mainstreamed classroom teaching. Provision is essentially in-school and in-class, and 'official' policy endorses integration, rather than segregation. Yet New Zealand schools display a double standard: while decrying the special treatment of intellectually able children, no such barriers operate for the most able athletes, dancers, singers, musicians and actors who are identified, segregated, and given intensive coaching during the school week. Competition is fierce, and selection confers status and special privileges. Yet, the selection of students on the basis of intellectual abilities invariably stimulates antagonism and charges of elitism.

It has not been claimed by New Zealand educators that there must be special classes for the gifted, nor for those who are deaf, mentally and / or physically handicapped or emotionally disturbed, and there are valid arguments for integrating children in the normal classroom. What is being suggested is that the needs of the gifted child be met fundamentally – and not administered in tiny daily doses as an extracurricular activity, or at one-day or weekend classes.

Enrichment and acceleration

Enrichment is the popular catch-phrase for most educational provision for the gifted because it is 'safe' and tolerable because of the favourable spin-off effect for the average child. The basic notion is that enrichment classes provide opportunity to study, in some depth, subjects that are not available within the curricular pattern. Yet, how should the other teaching that the gifted receive during the rest of the time in school be described? Enrichment often becomes 'more of the same', a quantitative increase of work on the usual level through projects of momentary interest with no connection to the curriculum. Nothing precedes these programmes, and nothing logically follows.

Acceleration is equated most often with the idea of skipping year levels (grades). Exaggerated drawbacks of the effects of acceleration abound; many teachers believing that social and emotional maladjustments will result, despite copious research evidence to the contrary. It is commonly thought that while intellectual interests and activities may be shared, the gifted cannot participate as equals in activities of a social or physical nature since some will be emotionally immature. This is a gross overgeneralization, particularly when it is recognized that for many gifted children their intellectual, social, and emotional peers are those who *are* older!

Professor Clem Hill (1977) commented:

Acceleration of a kind must occur in any scheme for it is impossible to range wider and deeper intensively without going on. . . . Let us avoid the tyranny of breadth of learning. The importance of breadth for balance is accepted. Yet this can easily lead to a diminished 'altitude in ability'.

Similarly, in New Zealand the Department of Education (1972) stated, 'Few programmes enrich horizontally without leading vertically into the higher levels'. But, despite official sanction for at least some acceleration (Ministry of Education 2000: 38), it is little utilized in New Zealand schools (Townsend and Patrick 1993; Townsend 1996).

Teachers and teacher training

Since the vast majority of gifted children in New Zealand are taught in the regular classroom, the quality of teaching and teacher training is of critical importance. If the classroom teacher is not predisposed towards identifying gifted children, what chance is there of catering for their special needs?

It is fair to state that the majority of New Zealand's teaching force is unable to cope adequately with the range of abilities found in the heterogeneous, multicultural, mainstreamed classes. They are insufficiently trained to teach children with special needs at the extremes of the ability continuum, nor are they taught to recognize and foster talent among the socially and culturally 'disadvantaged'. Maori and Pacific Island teachers are still under-represented in New Zealand classrooms, despite strenuous efforts to recruit, and there remains a chronic shortage of Polynesian teachers teaching across the curriculum in secondary schools.

Some of New Zealand's teacher training establishments offer courses in teaching students with special areas of exceptionality, including the gifted. However, the majority are optional courses and are limited in scope, and hundreds leave with little notion of how to identify, stimulate and extend gifted children. Almost without exception, the training establishments would all like to do more in this area if specialist staffing were available. Fortunately, there are some in-service training courses but these are irregular: New Zealand's 'record in in-service professional development in this aspect of education is appalling. In this regard the gifted must surely represent the most neglected group in our school system' (Moltzen 1999: 63).

On a more positive note, undergraduate and graduate 'gifted' courses are offered at Massey, Waikato and Flinders (Australia) universities, and have a steadily increasing number of enrolments. A welcome innovation has been the introduction of a course at Massey University, devoted exclusively to the study of educating the gifted and talented in a multicultural context.

Looking to the future

In considering the education of the gifted and talented in New Zealand, the following problems need swift resolution:

- First, New Zealanders must decide whether they value excellence in education. If they do, then they must be willing to support the values with tangible assistance in terms of money and personnel. Second, New Zealanders must examine whether 'equality of educational opportunity' has become distorted so as to promote mediocrity, rather than ensuring the maximum growth of individual abilities.
- The central education authority has promoted biculturalism; the rationale being that the majority culture needed to address the Maori–Pakeha relationship first before a multicultural approach could be developed. The anticipated move to foster multiculturalism in education – to celebrate the diversity of New Zealand's cultural heritage and to overcome educational 'disadvantages' – is long overdue, and is, given the country's rapidly changing ethnic composition, becoming increasingly pressing.
- New Zealand educators' current notions of giftedness must accommodate the entire range and diversity of human talents and break free of the dominance of the IQ metric. Teachers should consider humanistic/ non-academic/creative/multi-talented notions of giftedness as well as the utilitarian/academic/intellectual.
- Identification of giftedness should be preceded by the kind of education which makes its manifestation possible. Identification should involve multiple methods with records accessible to all teachers including those in tertiary level.
- Opportunities to explore ideas and to be creative in a stimulating and supportive school environments must be provided. The curriculum for the gifted child should not be some 'beefed-up' version of the common core, nor doses of 'busy' or project work, euphemistically termed 'enrichment'.
- A policy of integration for all children should be supported by enlightened, well-trained and empathic teachers. Every classroom teacher will be a teacher of at least one gifted child, yet the present pre-service and in-service training are inadequate to equip them to meet the challenge.
- Significant changes are required in both school and classroom administrative practices and organization:
    - There must be more flexibility: children working out of class and out of school where appropriate; more individualized programmes; flexible promotion practices; less rigid timetabling, particularly in the secondary schools; opportunities to attend university classes; mentorships and opportunities to work alongside professionals in the community.
    - More consideration should be given to teams of teachers, supported by paraprofessional and community resource personnel, working cooperatively with groups of gifted children on a regular basis. The concept of the 'one teacher in one classroom for one year' approach must be modified.
    - A far better job must be done of planning, monitoring and evaluating the enrichment programmes that exist. The fact that everybody involved appears to be enjoying the experience will not suffice.

- New Zealand's multicultural setting, and the recognition of different ideas, interests, beliefs, values and abilities of gifted and talented children from minority cultures needs rigorous research to uncover the magnitude of the problem, and also to suggest possible solutions.
- New Zealand's 'brain drain' presents a problem as gifted, talented, and entrepreneurial young people travel overseas to take up lucrative professional positions, and scholarships. Thousands do not return, and any contribution they might have made to the welfare, prosperity and quality of life of their fellow citizens, is lost.

Conclusion

Any consideration of the gifted and talented among New Zealand's ethnic and cultural minorities involves dealing with, in Alexinia Baldwin's (1984) term, a 'minority's minority'. Probably with no other subpopulation are identification and nurturance more complexly interwoven with factors of educational environment, home circumstances, performance on tests and examinations, notions about giftedness, language, beliefs, deviation from mainstream culture, ambiguous attitudes regarding the intellectual and academic competencies of minority students, and differences in the manifestations of cultural behaviours. The problems, difficult as they are, are not going to go away. If New Zealand's predominantly dominant culture educators truly believe that it is the right of *every* child to be given a high-quality education that matches individual abilities and needs, then there is no time to lose in correcting the current chronic cultural myopia and in responding to the challenge.

Key questions

1   How do dominant culture teachers need to modify the existing education to meet the needs of gifted students for diverse populations?
2   Discuss the strategies that could be used to ensure that future diverse gifted adults remain in and contribute to their communities.
3   Analyse the advantages and disadvantages of different types of enrichment for diverse gifted New Zealand students.

References

Anae, M. (2003) O A'u/I – my identity journey, in P. Fairbairn-Dunlop and G. S. Makisi (eds) *Making our Place: Growing Up PI in New Zealand*. Palmerston North: Dunmore Press.

Baldwin, A. V. (1984) *Baldwin Identification Matrix 2 for the Identification of Gifted and Talented*. New York: Trillium Press.

Benton, R. A. (1986) Here today and gone tomorrow: talking and learning in New Zealand classrooms. Paper presented at the Twenty-first Regional Seminar, SEAMEO Regional Language Centre, Singapore, April.

Bevan-Brown, J. (1993) Special abilities: a Maori perspective, unpublished Master of Education thesis, Massey University, Palmerston North.

Bevan-Brown, J. (1996) Special abilities: a Maori perspective, in D. McAlpine and R. Moltzen (eds) *Gifted and Talented: New Zealand Perspectives.* Palmerston North: ERDC Press, Massey University.

Bevan-Brown, J. (2000) *Running the Gauntlet: A Gifted Maori Learner's Journey through Secondary School.* Retrieved 6 June 2003 and available online at: http://www.tki.org.nz/r/gifted/pedagogy/running_e.php

Bevan-Brown, J. (2002) Culturally appropriate, effective provision for Maori learners with special needs: He Waka Tino Whakarawea, unpublished doctoral thesis, Massey University, Palmerston North.

Brown, H. (2003) An Asian at my table, *North and South,* May: 46–58.

Cathcart, R. (1994) *They're Not Bringing my Brain out.* Auckland: REACH.

Cathcart, R. and Pou, N. (1992) The gifted child who is Maori. *NZAGC Gifted Children. Their Future: Our Challenge,* 17(3): 13–17.

Clay, M. M. (1985) Engaging with the school system: a study of interaction in new entrant classrooms. *New Zealand Journal of Educational Studies,* 20(1): 20–38.

Department of Education (1972) *Children with Special Abilities: Suggestions for Teaching Gifted Children in Primary Schools.* Wellington: Government Printer.

Doidge, G. (1990) Maori children, Maori studies: a special giftedness. *Apex,* 4(2): 36–39.

Doidge, G. and Leilua, L. (1992) Identifying and Catering for the Culturally Gifted. Report of a workshop, NZAGC Auckland Branch Teachers' Conference, March.

Fairbairn-Dunlop, P. and Makisi, G. S. (eds) (2003) *Making our Place: Growing Up PI in New Zealand.* Palmerston North: Dunmore Press.

Getzels, J. W. and Dillon, J. T. (1973) Giftedness and the education of the gifted, in R. M. Travers (ed.) *Second Handbook on Research on Teaching.* Chicago, IL: Rand McNally.

Hames, M. (2002) *The Crisis in New Zealand Schools.* Auckland: Education Forum.

Hill, C. G. N. (1977) Gifted is as gifted does. Address to NZAGC Annual General Meeting, Auckland, September.

Ioane, S. I. (1982) Cultural archiebunkerism in New Zealand schools. *Post Primary Teachers' Journal,* 2: 12–16.

Jones, A. (1987) What really happens in the classroom. *Set,* 2: item 7.

Kuo, Y-Y. (1992) Views of sagehood: the Chinese concept of genius. Paper presented at the Second Asian Conference on Giftedness, Taiwan, July.

McAlpine, D. and Reid, N. A. (1996) *Teacher Observation Scales for Children with Special Abilities.* Wellington: New Zealand Council for Educational Research and Palmerston North: ERDC Press, Massey University.

Metge, J. (1986) *In and Out of Touch: Whakama in Cross-cultural Context.* Wellington: Victoria University Press.

Metge, J. (1990) *Te Kohao O Te Ngira: Culture and Learning for a Multicultural Society.* Wellington: Learning Media, Ministry of Education.

Ministry of Education (2000) *Gifted and Talented Students: Meeting their Needs in New Zealand Schools.* Wellington: Learning Media, Ministry of Education.

Ministry of Education (2001) *New Zealand Schools/Nga Kura O Aotearoa: Annual Report on the Compulsory Schools Sector in New Zealand 2000.* Wellington: Ministry of Education.

Mitchell, B. M. (1988) A strategy for the identification of the culturally different gifted/talented child. *Roeper Review,* 10(3): 163–165.

Moltzen, R. (1999) Young, gifted and living in New Zealand. *Apex,* 12: 57–68.

Penetito, W. T. (1984) Taha Maori and the core curriculum. *Delta,* 34: 35–43.

Raven, J., Raven, J. C. and Court, J. H. (1991) *Manual for the Raven's Progressive Matrices and Vocabulary Scales: General Overview*. Oxford: Oxford Psychologists Press.

Reid, N. A. (1983) Polynesian conceptions of giftedness. Paper presented at the Fifth World Conference on Gifted and Talented Children, Manila, August.

Reid, N. A. (1985) Polynesian conceptions of giftedness, in A. H. Roldan (ed.) *Gifted and Talented Children, Youth and Adults: Their Social Perspectives and Culture*. Manila: World Council for Gifted and Talented Children.

Reid, N. A. (1989) Contemporary Polynesian conceptions of giftedness. *Gifted Education International*, 6(1): 30–38.

Reid, N. A. (1990) Identifying the culturally different gifted in New Zealand. *Apex*, 3(3): 3–10.

Reid, N. A. (1991) Gifted and disadvantaged in New Zealand, in B. Wallace and H. B. Adams (eds) *World Perspectives on the Gifted Disadvantaged*. Bicester: AB Academic.

Reid, N. A. (1992) Correcting cultural myopia, in E. Le Sueur (ed.) *Proceedings of the Guiding the Gifted Conference*, 6–7 July. Auckland: Conference Publishing Ltd.

Renzulli, J. S. (1973) Talent potential in minority group students. *Exceptional Children*, 39: 437–444.

Shepheard, N. (2003) The storyteller. *North and South*, November: 46–57.

Smith, G. H. (1990) Taha Maori: Pakeha capture, in J. Codd, R. Harker and R. Nash (eds) *Political Issues in New Zealand Education*, 2nd edn. Palmerston North: Dunmore Press.

Smith, G. H. and Smith, L. T. (1996) New mythologies in Maori education, in P. Spoonley, C. Macpherson and D. Pearson (eds) *Nga Patai: Racism and Ethnic Relations in Aotearoa / New Zealand*. Palmerston North: Dunmore Press.

Spoonley, P., Macpherson, C. and Pearson, D. (eds) (1996) *Nga Patai: Racism and Ethnic Relations in Aotearoa/New Zealand*. Palmerston North: Dunmore Press.

Sternberg, R. (1984) What should intelligence tests test: implications for the triarchic theory of intelligence testing. *Educational Researcher*, 13(1): 5–15.

Thakur, R. (1995) In defence of multiculturalism, in S. W. Greif (ed.) *Immigration and National Identity in New Zealand: One People, Two Peoples, Many Peoples?* Palmerston North: Dunmore Press.

Townsend, M. A. R. (1996) Enrichment and acceleration: lateral and vertical perspectives in provisions for gifted and talented children, in D. McAlpine and R. Moltzen (eds) *Gifted and Talented: New Zealand Perspectives*. Palmerston North: ERDC Press, Massey University.

Townsend, M. A. R. and Patrick, H. (1993) Academic and psychological apprehensions of teachers and teacher trainees toward the educational acceleration of gifted children. *New Zealand Journal of Educational Studies*, 28: 29–41.

Tsai, D. (1992) Family impact on high-achieving Chinese-American students: a qualitative analysis. Paper presented at the Second Asian Conference on Giftedness, Taiwan, July.

Walford, D. (1979) *Children with Special Abilities from Minority Cultures*. Paper presented at the First National Conference on Gifted and Talented Children, North Shore Teachers' College, Auckland, August.

Walker, R. J. (1985) Cultural domination of taha Maori: the potential for radical transformation, in J. Codd, D. Harker and R. Nash (eds) *Political Issues in New Zealand Education*. Palmerston North: Dunmore Press.

Walker, R. J. (1990) Korero: politics and performance. *New Zealand Listener*, 11 June: 98–99.

3.3   Case study: ethnicity – example of curricular intervention 'Quentin' (Excerpt from full case study)

Carole Ruth Harris

Quentin was a 7-year-old black male with a history of superior intellectual functioning; Quentin could read alone at age 4. His father was born in Haiti and his mother in the United States; both were highly educated. Although some French was spoken in the home, Quentin was not fluent in French. Quentin attended a prestigious private school at the time of evaluation. An outgoing, intense child, Quentin had an abundance of physical energy, coupled with some insecurity in social settings. During evaluation there was avoidance of immediate goals and frequent attempts to distract with extraneous matters. Quentin was distractible in the classroom with low self-esteem but had improved with a more demanding teacher. Although there were initial indications of attentional difficulty and impulsivity, these characteristics progressively diminished during the evaluation process, surfacing into evidence of a pervasive low frustration level coupled with low self-esteem. Quentin responded poorly to open-ended situations connected to his anxiety about being 'right' but demonstrated concentration when he did not perceive a threat.

A curriculum was designed for Quentin that attempted to strengthen Quentin's self-esteem and flexibility in thinking and to encourage tolerance for experimentation, divergent thinking, and trial and error, and maximize his creative approach while addressing weak areas in the type of insecurity that caused inappropriate responses and distortion of personal goal-setting (see Box 3.3.1).

At the last parental report, Quentin was being home-schooled and had been reading the curriculum materials with close attention. He experimented with new materials and exhibited good goal-orientation. Quentin had begun to run his own experiments on inventions of his own design, with plans to enter them in competitions. Quentin exhibited greater confidence in his ability and fewer patterns of low self-esteem and frustration. His behavior had improved and he was staying on task, with greater tolerance for his own mistakes and increased responsibility for carrying out independent study.

Box 3.3.1   Curriculum on inventions for Quentin

Activity	Rationale
A1. Watch *Edison the Man* (1940) [videotape]. MGM.	**Synthesizes** biographical concepts. **Utilizes** application of facts. **Stimulates** curiosity. **Introduces** Edison.
A2. Read Haskins, J. (1991) *Outward Dreams: Black Inventors and their Inventions*. New York: Walker. Add these great inventors to a timeline. Tell about their dreams and some of the obstacles they met, their mistakes and failures. How many inventions do you make use of that were invented by the people mentioned in this book?	**Introduces** new inventors. **Stimulates** identification. **Increases** awareness of overcoming obstacles. **Illustrates** examples and concepts. **Assists** introspection and awareness. **Provides** vehicle for thoughtful investigation and discussion. **Establishes** personal perspective.
A3. Read about Benjamin Banneker, p. 22, Norbert Rillieux, p. 50, Lewis Temple, p. 54, Jan Ernst Matzeliger, p. 85, Madame C. J. Walker, p. 102, Elijan McCoy, p. 106, Garrett Augustus Morgan, p. 124 and Percy Lavon Julian, p. 186, in Altman, S. (2001) *Extraordinary African-Americans*. New York: Children's Press. Read Parker, S. (1994) *Guglielmo Marconi and Radio*. New York: Chelsea Honse. Birch, B. and Corfield, R. B. (1995) *Marconi's Battle for Radio*. Hauppauge, NY: Barron's Educational Series; Skurzynski, G. (1996) *Waves: The Electromagnetic Universe*. Washington, DC: The National Geographic Society; and pp. 134–146 in Evans, I. O. (1962) *Inventors of the World*. London: Frederick Warne.	**Initiates** historical and scientific understanding. **Reinforces** studies. **Encourages** broadening of knowledge base. **Synthesizes** concrete thinking.
B1. Look at the directions for a 'wrench box' in Anderson, M. (1991) *Construction of the Classical Whanger and Other Lost Arts*.	**Assists** visualization. **Increases** breadth of interests.

Jacksonville, IL: Music Works. Music works and make a musical instrument from wrenches.	**Reinforces** unit goals. **Provides** connection to family background. **Encourages** creative productivity.
Play 'Brother John,' on p. 83 in Nelson, M. (1995) *You Can Teach Yourself to Make Music with Homemade Instruments.* Pacific, MO: Mel Bay.	
Ask your dad to teach you the French words to this song. See if you can make up a song about inventions.	
B2. Read about Thomas A. Dorsey on p. 50 Potter, J. and Claytor, C. (1997) *African Americans Who Were First.* New York: Cobblehill Books, Dutton.	**Introduces** gospel music form. **Initiates** music appreciation. **Encourages** aesthetic awareness.
Listen to the Gospel music CD, Ross, J. A. (1997) *Comin' Up Shouting!* Gospel music and spirituals, The New England Spiritual Ensemble. Revels Records [CD 1097].	**Provides** connection to family ethnicity/religion.
B3. Read Liddell, M. A. (2001). Roots of rhythm, *Smithsonian*, November 77–85 and study the photographs.	**Stimulates** musical activities. **Encourages** broadening of interests.
Watch the videotape, *Sousa to Satchmo* (1995). Sony Classical Film and Video.	**Provides** vehicle for understanding invention in music.
C1. Read Towle, W. (1995) *The Real McCoy: The Life of an African-American Inventor.* New York: Scholastic.	**Introduces** source of common expression from real life story. **Initiates** sharing of knowledge.
Not many people know what 'the real McCoy means', Write a biography of Elijah McCoy. Ask at least six other people what it means and show them your paragraph.	**Encourages** writing skills.
C2. Read Haskins, J. and Benson, K. (1991) *Space Challenger: The Story of Guion Bluford.* New York: Walker.	**Establishes** basis for new genre study. **Utilizes** comparison of genres.
This type of writing is called biography. What are some of its characteristics? How is this different from fiction writing? How does it get a message across to the reader?	**Provides** vehicle for literary analysis in nonfiction. **Assists** motivation for further research.
What made Bluford special?	

3.4   Conflict resolution 2: cultural prejudice

Suzanne Rawlins

The new principal of a large middle school in Florida planned initial parent conferences, as she had done previously in the Midwestern part of the United States. The conferences had been a wonderful and successful tradition there. So, individual appointments were made with the parents for each gifted student in the Florida school. The vision was to solicit goodwill and a team approach between the parent and the teacher for academic success. A small meeting room just large enough for the teacher, a parent and the student was designated. Difficulties arose immediately. As is the tradition in some Hispanic cultures, when parents arrived they were accompanied by sisters, brothers, aunts, grand-parents, and others. Each was proud to participate in the conference. However, there was no room! Having looked for other locations on a very crowded campus, it became apparent that this tradition might have to be abandoned. Office staff snickered and eyes rolled at the masses of people coming for the conferences. What should the new principal do? She knew that the conferences were worth the effort.

4 Socio-economic class issues

4.1 Beyond expectations: a new view of the gifted disadvantaged

Robert J. Sternberg and Carmen G. Arroyo

Disadvantaged children in the United States are from culturally diverse back-grounds. In general, they come from the most economically deprived sectors of American society, experience more psychological and physical difficulties, and face adverse conditions that hinder their education (Galley and Flanagan 2000; Payne 1998; US Department of Education 1993). These children reside within environments relatively devoid of challenges to *conventional* creativity and resourcefulness (Galley and Flanagan 2000); it is, therefore, difficult for these children to develop mastery of the various intellectual and artistic tasks traditionally associated with giftedness. Interestingly, their environments may provide substantially greater challenges to *unconventional* creativity and re-sourcefulness than do the environments of their advantaged peers. Indeed, the challenges to health, safety and well-being may so consume their time that they scarcely have the time, resources or desire to confront conventional academic tasks.

Because giftedness among the disadvantaged unfolds within the context of an economically deprived and socially distinct environment, it cannot be thought of as a stable unitary entity characterized by high IQ scores. Indeed, children high in practical intelligence may be relatively low in academic intelligence, and vice versa (Sternberg et al. 2000). Among disadvantaged children, giftedness is reflected in qualities in addition to, and sometimes other than, measurable intellectual capacity. It includes behaviors that allow disadvantaged students to cope with social and economic deprivation and a variety of stressful life events. Recent research on 'resilience' has identified a variety of behaviors and personal resources that disadvantaged children use to adapt to economic, social and educational poverty (Luthar 1999; Luthar et al. 2000). Because these adaptive behaviors are themselves governed by cognitive abilities that constitute intelligent behavior, it is reasonable to assume that the behavioral characteristics displayed by some disadvantaged children are reflective of giftedness.

Research on differences between gifted and non-gifted students has shown that gifted students are particularly sophisticated in their cognitive abilities (Steiner and Carr 2003), self-regulation (Shore and Kanevsky 1993) and strategic abilities (Coyle et al. 1999). Research also suggests that gifted disadvantaged students are highly conscious of the social constraints imposed by the environments in which they live, but they also actively strive to create lives that will ultimately provide them with success (Arroyo 1990; Arroyo and Zigler 1995). This evidence has led us to view the disadvantaged gifted and talented individual as one who maximizes his or her intellectual potential and transcends the impositions of a disadvantaged environment by creating alternative prospects that enrich both his or her personal life and the future lives of others. Gifted individuals transform the characteristics with which they enter schools into increasingly complex cognitive, behavioral, motivational and personal abilities that insure academic and personal achievement.

In this contribution, we present a conception that expands current conceptions of giftedness and describes the various ways in which the gifted disadvantaged attempt to transcend social constraints. One might ask whether yet another conception of giftedness is necessary, as Sternberg and Davidson (2005) have already reviewed different conceptions of giftedness. However, much of the research on academic performance among the disadvantaged has focused exclusively on low-achieving students and the detection of factors that contribute to school failure (Gibbs 1998). Little research has been conducted with disadvantaged students who are high-achieving and gifted; little is known about the intellectual abilities of these students. Consequently, many researchers simply propose that alternative culturally sensitive intelligence tests be constructed (Ford et al. 1990; Patton 1992). Other researchers argue that disadvantaged children have distinct cultural skills and styles that must be included in the repertoire of behaviors defined as characteristic of giftedness (Hilliard 1989). Social alertness, pragmatic alertness, confidence, humor, expressiveness, sensitivity to movement, risk-taking, linguistic creativity, field dependence and external locus of control are just a few of the variables associated with giftedness in disadvantaged children (Baldwin 1985; Evans and Quarterman 1983; Ford 1994).

Appeals for identification procedures that include alternative tests or that broaden the scope of abilities simply accommodate the existing definitions of giftedness. Because traditional theories of giftedness have assumed that giftedness is narrowly defined by intellectual exceptionality – any derivative of these purely abilities-based conceptions is inadequate. A meaningful definition of giftedness must also encompass behavior, motivation, and selected personality attributes.

We propose a broad-based conception of giftedness that focuses on four components: cognitive processes, social context, motivational factors and personality characteristics. We propose also to redefine the uses of the term 'gifted' in terms of highly purposive, goal-directed behavior, enacted within a real-world context (see Sternberg 1985a, 1997, 1999). We define as intellectually gifted those individuals who (a) are able effectively to adapt their behaviors and abilities to the demands of the particular environment, (b) actively alter the environment so that their unique abilities will receive higher value, and (c) are able to recognize insurmountable environmental constraints and move toward an alternative, more desirable environment (Sternberg 1985a, 1999).

Intelligence and self-management

The idea that intelligence entails adaptation to, shaping of, and selection of environments is reflected in the contextual subtheory of Sternberg's (1985a, 1999) triarchic theory of successful intelligence. This theory consists of three separate subtheories that describe the various aspects of intelligence. The first subtheory, the componential subtheory, specifies the internal mental structures that govern intelligent behavior. The second, the contextual subtheory, specifies how social structures define what is considered to be intelligent behavior. The third subtheory, an experiential one, specifies how the levels of experience with a task or situation influence the manifestation of intelligent behaviors.

According to Sternberg's contextual subtheory, intelligence is context-dependent, varying from person to person, and among different social groups. To illustrate this point, Sternberg and his colleagues have conducted studies which demonstrate that laypersons and experts in the field of intelligence differ with respect to the amount of importance they place on various behaviors characteristically deemed to be intelligent (Sternberg 1985b; Sternberg et al. 1981). In one study, Sternberg et al. (1981) presented subjects with a list of behaviors that characterized an intelligent, an academically intelligent or an everyday intelligent individual. Subjects were then asked to rate how characteristic each behavior was of an ideally intelligent person, an academically intelligent person, and an everyday intelligent person. Although the laypersons' view of intelligence generally corresponded with experts' views of intelligence, experts placed more emphasis on academic behaviors such as the abilities to read with high comprehension, show flexibility in thought and action, reason logically and well, display curiosity, learn rapidly, think deeply and solve problems well; laypersons placed greater emphasis on social aspects of intelligence such as politeness, patience with self and others, frankness and honesty with self and others, and the ability to get along well with others and to display emotions appropriate to the situation.

In the United States, similar differences may be seen in the conceptions of intelligence and the behavioral expectations held by members of distinct social groups (see Heath 1983, for example). These social differences in definitions of intelligence create discontinuities between the abilities individuals display within any given situation and the behavioral expectations imposed by that environment. Sternberg et al. (1993), for example, have shown that children who come from environments that stress the social aspects of intelligence are less likely to succeed in school than those children raised in environments that stress the academic aspect of intelligence valued by the school systems.

What is especially interesting is that lay conceptions of intelligence are quite a bit broader than ones of psychologists who believe in *g*, abroad as well as in the United States (Berry 1974; Sternberg and Kaufman 1998). For example, in a study of Taiwanese Chinese conceptions of intelligence (Yang and Sternberg 1997a, 1997b), it was found that although Taiwanese conceptions of intelligence included a cognitive factor, they also included factors of interpersonal competence, intrapersonal competence, intellectual self-assertion and intellectual self-effacement. In a study of Kenyan conceptions of intelligence (Grigorenko et al. 2001), it was found that there are four distinct terms constituting conceptions of intelligence among rural Kenyans – *rieko* (knowledge and skills), *luoro* (respect), *winjo* (comprehension of how to handle real-life problems), *paro* (initiative) – with only the first directly referring to knowledge-based skills (including but not limited to the academic). Even more importantly, perhaps, it was discovered in a study among different ethnic groups in San Jose, California, that although the 359 parents in different ethnic groups have different conceptions of intelligence, the more closely their conception matches that of their children's teachers, the better the children do in school (Okagaki and Sternberg 1993). In other words, teachers value students who do well on the kinds of attributes that the teachers associate with intelligence.

With respect to disadvantaged students, researchers have noted that disadvantaged students have less access to objects such as books, toys, puzzles, and pencils than non-disadvantaged children. Experience with such objects prior to school enrollment familiarizes children with essential information about the purpose and possible alternative uses of objects commonly used in schools. It also allows children to develop and practice basic cognitive skills. The absence of such materials in the home does not prepare children for their eventual confrontation with the behavioral requirements of the classroom (Payne 1998; Rodgers et al. 1994).

Verbal interactions among disadvantaged parent–infant dyads also do not fully foster the growth of cognitive abilities valued by the school (Heath 1983). Sociolinguists have detected considerable discrepancies between the communication patterns of parents and children from culturally diverse and socially disadvantaged backgrounds and the modes of communication most commonly valued in the schools (Erickson 1987; Labov 1972). Many disadvantaged children come from environments in which direct questions are avoided, eye-contact is considered to be impolite, and concepts of comparability and relativity are not taught (Boykin 1983; Erickson 1987; Heath 1983). Consequently, many disadvantaged children enter the school environment with a host of cognitive abilities and behavioral expectations they have learned at home, that are not necessarily valued by the school (Boykin 1983, 1984; Heath 1983; Sternberg 1986). Disadvantaged children avert their eyes when they are spoken to, they attend to several concepts at once and shift focus among them, they are emotionally expressive and they are spontaneous (Boykin 1983). All of these behaviors are discrepant with the school's emphasis on self-control, and its insistence that children attend to ideas in a focused and sequential manner, use direct questions and show their interest in instruction by maintaining direct eye-contact with teachers.

If disadvantaged students enter school equipped with inadequate cognitive skills or demonstrate abilities that are viewed as irrelevant to academic success, how can differences in achievement outcomes between two equally disadvantaged children be explained? What determines the academic success of one disadvantaged child versus the failure of another? The premises of the contextual subtheory of the triarchic theory of intelligence (Sternberg 1985a, 1999) and the existing body of research lead us to believe that such differences can be explained by the processes of self-management employed by children.

Empirical evidence suggests that children are capable of traversing the chasm between the cognitive abilities learned at home and the increasingly complex cognitive demands of school or other socializing agents through self-management skills that allow them to define problems, set goals, monitor their own success, and achieve mastery of required cognitive tasks (Campione et al. 1984; Diaz 1990; Diaz et al. 1990).

Self-management emerges primarily within mother–child social interactions. Initially, mothers provide the external structures that children learn and then later utilize to plan and monitor their behaviors independently (Diaz 1990; Diaz et al. 1990). In the absence of automatized cognitive abilities or external adult direction, children will attempt to define and solve problems on their own (Diaz 1990).

Because disadvantaged children's acquisition of cognitive abilities is not fully promoted by social interactions within their social environments, unless these children develop self-regulatory skills, their probability of attaining optimal intellectual development is quite low. We propose, therefore, that gifted disadvantaged children are capable of either finding alternative socializing agents to assist them, or of acquiring the necessary self-management abilities to facilitate achievement.

For disadvantaged children, teachers and other influential persons within the school can compensate for the lack of managerial abilities in disadvantaged mothers (Diaz et al. 1990). The structure of schools also imposes external regulations that some disadvantaged students may incorporate into their personal behavioral repertoires. Disadvantaged students demonstrate characteristics of exceptional intelligence in the ways in which they adapt their behaviors so that a good fit between their abilities and the expectations of the school environment can be achieved.

Self-management and adaptation among the disadvantaged

In order to elucidate the cognitive processes that enable disadvantaged students effectively to adapt their behavior to the requirements of the school, it is necessary that we return to the explanations of intelligence offered by the triarchic theory. We will present our theoretical notions regarding exceptional behavior in disadvantaged students.

The cognitive processes involved in exceptional behavior

As mentioned earlier, the experiential subtheory of the triarchic theory of intelligence defines the circumstances under which any behavior is representative of intelligence. According to this subtheory, intelligence is reflected in a person's ability to deal with novel kinds of tasks and situational demands and an individual's ability to automatize information processing. The experiential subtheory, however, makes a distinction between the cognitive processes needed to perform a novel task and those involved in understanding the nature of a novel task.

Individuals must be able to recognize that a novel situation requires mental processes or strategies different from those normally employed. The individual is said to have encoded an expectation of a change when he or she recognizes the need for a new conceptual framework. Because every situation can be managed in a variety of ways, an individual must determine which among the novel conceptual strategies is appropriate for the efficient and effective solution of the specific tasks to be performed. Sometimes, the most effective conceptual strategy may be one with which an individual is unfamiliar. Successful mastery of the task might then require an individual to acquire a new strategy.

Results from a study of high-achieving and low-achieving African-American students conducted by Arroyo and Zigler (1995) suggests that the cognitive processes Sternberg has associated with mastery of a novel task might be particularly useful to our understanding of self-management processes in the gifted disadvantaged student. In a study of students' school-related attitudes and beliefs, tenth-, eleventh- and twelfth-grade African-American students responded to a questionnaire that asked about various behaviors associated with achievement among African-Americans (Arroyo and Zigler 1995). The students were enrolled in a public high school in a lower middle-class urban school district, and had been identified as either high or low academic achievers on the basis of scores on the Metropolitan Achievement Test, school grades and teacher recommendations. The high-achieving students in this study had scored above the 95th percentile on the Metropolitan Achievement Test and had also participated in the school's educational programs for gifted and talented students.

The results of the study indicated that high-achieving African-American students were more likely than low-achieving African-American students to endorse items such as: 'The way I speak at home with my parents and brothers and sisters is different from the way I speak with my teachers', 'Blacks must change the way they act if they wish to succeed', 'Blacks should try their best to impress teachers, and other important people in our society' and 'I try to use proper English when speaking to my teachers and white friends'. We view these findings as suggestive of academically and intellectually gifted disadvantaged students' ability to identify the contrasting demands of social situations and of the abilities required to complete the academic tasks set by the school system. We believe the items endorsed by high-achieving African-American students are reflective of their comprehension of the novelty of the scholastic situation. For example, as indicated by the endorsed items, intellectually gifted disadvantaged students are capable of detecting differences in the required speech system of the school versus the home environment. They adapt their own speech in accordance with the behavioral expectations of these two contrasting environments. The adaptive behaviors employed by the intellectually gifted students in Arroyo and Zigler's (1995) study, therefore, reflect underlying processes entailed in encoding the expectation of a change, accessing alternative conceptual strategies, and adoption of effective strategies that lead to a successful solution of tasks.

Is it possible to assess diverse cognitive skills relevant to the disadvantaged? In a study supported by the College Board, Sternberg and his collaborators (2004) used an expanded set of tests on 1015 students at fifteen different institutions (thirteen colleges and two high schools). The goal was not to replace the Standard Attainment Test (SAT), but to devise tests that would supplement the SAT, measuring skills that this test does not measure. The study used both multiple-choice performance-based measures:

Consider first the multiple-choice measures:

1   *Analytical-verbal: figuring out meanings of neologisms (artificial words) from natural contexts:* students see a novel word embedded in a paragraph, and have to infer its meaning from the context.
2   *Analytical-quantitative: number series:* students have to say what number should come next in a series of numbers.
3   *Analytical-figural: matrices:* students see a figural matrix with the lower right entry missing. They have to say which of the options fits into the missing space.
4   *Practical-verbal: everyday reasoning:* students are presented with a set of everyday problems in the life of an adolescent and have to select the option that best solves each problem.
5   *Practical-quantitative: everyday math:* students are presented with scenarios requiring the use of math in everyday life (e.g. buying tickets for a ballgame), and have to solve math problems based on the scenarios.
6   *Practical-figural: route planning:* students are presented with a map of an area (e.g. an entertainment park) and have to answer questions about navigating effectively through the area depicted by the map.
7   *Creative-verbal: novel analogies:* students are presented with verbal analogies preceded by counterfactual premises (e.g. money falls off trees). They have to solve the analogies as though the counterfactual premises were true.
8   *Creative-quantitative: novel number operations:* students are presented with rules for novel number operations, for example, 'flix', which involves numerical manipulations that differ as a function of whether the first of two operands is greater than, equal to, or less than the second. Participants have to use the novel number operations to solve presented math problems.
9   *Creative-figural:* in each item, participants are first presented with a figural series that involves one or more transformations; they then have to apply the rule of the series to a new figure with a different appearance, and complete the new series.

In addition to the multiple-choice tests described above, we used three additional measures of creative skills and three of practical skills:

The three additional tests were as follows:

1   *Cartoons:* participants were given five cartoons purchased from the archives of the *New Yorker*, but with the caption removed. The participant's task was to choose three cartoons, and to provide a caption for each cartoon. Two trained judges rated all the cartoons for cleverness, humor and originality. A combined creativity score was formed by summing the individual ratings on each dimension.

2   *Written stories:* participants were asked to write two stories, spending about fifteen minutes on each, choosing from the following titles: 'A Fifth Chance', '2983', 'Beyond the Edge', 'The Octopus's Sneakers', 'It's Moving Backwards' and 'Not Enough Time'. A team of four judges was trained to rate the stories for originality, complexity, emotional evocativeness and descriptiveness.

3   *Oral stories:* participants were presented with five sheets of paper, each containing a set of pictures linked by a common theme. For example, participants might receive a sheet of paper with images of a musical theme, a money theme or a travel theme. The participant then chose one of the pages and was given fifteen minutes to formulate a short story and dictate it into a cassette recorder. The dictation period was not to be more than five minutes long. The process was then repeated with another sheet of images so that each participant dictated a total of two oral stories. Six judges were trained to rate the stories for originality, complexity, emotional evocativeness, and descriptiveness.

The additional tests were as follows:

1   *Everyday Situational Judgment Inventory (Movies):* this video-based inventory presents participants with seven brief vignettes that capture problems encountered in general, everyday life, such as determining what to do when one is asked to write a letter of recommendation for someone one does not know particularly well.

2   *Common Sense Questionnaire:* this written inventory presents participants with fifteen vignettes that capture problems encountered in general business-related situations, such as managing tedious tasks or handling a competitive work situation.

3   *College Life Questionnaire:* this written inventory presents participants with fifteen vignettes that capture problems encountered in general college-related situations, such as handling trips to the bursar's office or dealing with a difficult roommate.

The tests significantly and substantially improved upon the validity of the SAT for predicting first-year college grades. The test also improved equity: using the test to admit a class would result in greater ethnic diversity than would using just the SAT or just the SAT and grade-point average. Put another way, the assessment simultaneously *increased* predictive validity and *decreased* ethnic-group differences.

The social context of exceptional behavior

As we have reiterated throughout this chapter, our interest is in how intelligence manifests itself within real-world situations. We have emphasized the role of socialization in the development of intellect. Social anthropologists John Ogbu and Signithia Fordham have also emphasized the influences of social structures, particularly on disadvantaged African-American children (Fordham 1988; Fordham and Ogbu 1986; Ogbu 1978; Ogbu and Stern 2001).

According to Ogbu's social-structural explanation for school failure, poor academic performance among disadvantaged students is a result of the social stratification, marginality and racism experienced by socially and culturally distinct individuals in the society at large (Ogbu 1978; Ogbu and Stern 2001). Ogbu contends that inequalities in the social arid educational systems have led many disadvantaged individuals to reject academic competition and to perceive adaptation to the existing social structures as futile. Fordham, using Ogbu's social-structural model, has proposed that African-American students, and other disadvantaged students in the United States, guarantee their personal and academic success by adopting behavioral styles and attitudes that allow them to integrate the social demands of school and of their own culture.

In the previously mentioned study of academically gifted and non-gifted African-American students, Arroyo and Zigler (1995) sought to test Ogbu and Fordham's theory. Participants in the study were administered a questionnaire that assessed the attitudinal and behavioral elements of Ogbu and Fordham's theory. The items for the questionnaire were derived from the descriptions included in Fordham (1988) and Fordham and Ogbu's original papers (1986) detailing the characteristics of high-achieving African-American adolescents. Responses provided by gifted and non-gifted students revealed differences in students' perceptions of school. Gifted students were more likely than non-gifted students to perceive academic achievement within the existing school system as a viable means for social mobility.

Once disadvantaged children determine that schools are effective means for social mobility, they organize information about the demands and requirements of academic achievement according to a conceptual framework they have learned from experiences within a culturally distinct environment. This is evident, for example, in the speech patterns of high-achieving African-American adolescents.

In his analysis of the speech patterns of the high-achieving students in Fordham's study, Erickson (1987) discovered that although these students use grammatically correct English in the classroom, their pronunciation, voice pitch, stress patterns and diction were characteristic of Black English (Labov 1972). The speech system utilized by gifted disadvantaged adolescents represents an integration of their culturally distinct speech system and the standard speech systems endorsed in the schools.

The underlying motivational factors of exceptional behavior

Students' assessments of the school environment also have a great impact on their motivation to succeed (Lovaglia et al. 1998; Moyer and Motta 1982; Ogbu 1978). Consider a description of personal goals and future expectations offered by an African-American, female adolescent of 16 years of age. When asked to provide five self-descriptive sentences, she responded:

> Right now, I am a student under a lot of stress (my mother's in the hospital, I'm trying to keep my grades up, I'm the only child). I am a black child fighting off the evils in my neighborhood and of society (drugs and crime). I am a black child trying to succeed in my goals. I am a listener to other people's problems, but sometimes I need to listen to my own. I am unique.
>
> (quoted in Arroyo 1990)

When requested to describe the person she hoped to be in the future, this student's responses also reflected her desires to transcend the current limitations imposed by her environment:

> I'd like to feel comfortable (financially, socially). I'd like to be a successful CPA [Chartered Public Accountant]. I'd like to be a successful family woman. I'd like to be an active community leader. I'd like to be me.
>
> (quoted in Arroyo 1990)

Although the expressed goals and concerns of this individual student cannot be generalized to the rest of the population of gifted students, this case provides useful information. This student's responses address the question: 'Who are the gifted disadvantaged and what goals motivate their desires for achievement?' The responses offered by this gifted disadvantaged student reveal a sensitive individual with the capacity to consider the limitations of her environment and to establish goals that will allow her to transcend those limitations. In her desire to become 'an active community leader', she also demonstrates recognition of needed changes in the current circumstances of other disadvantaged individuals.

Other participants in Arroyo's study also expressed similar assessments of their current social environment and spoke of similar goals and expectations for their future. Apparently, social deprivation, stress, and impending danger motivate gifted disadvantaged children to manage their lives in ways that will lead to improved social conditions in their future. Once children are oriented toward specific achievement goals, they will structure their behaviors accordingly (Dweck 1999; Dweck and Elliot 1983). The motivational forces associated with goals can also activate and maintain the cognitive processes underlying the planning and execution of goal-directed behavior (Siegler 1996). Because we fully endorse this notion, we would also like to consider the personality characteristics of gifted disadvantaged students.

The personality characteristics of giftedness

Various studies have characterized high-achieving disadvantaged students as self-confident, industrious, tough-minded, individualistic and raceless (Allen 1985; Evans and Quarterman 1983; Fordham 1988; Fordham and Ogbu 1986; Foster and Seltzer 1986; Lee 1984, 1985; Sewell et al. 1982). In this section, we would like to examine the lack of black consciousness and characteristics of racelessness that many researchers have detected among high-achieving African-American students (Fordham 1988; Fordham and Ogbu 1986; Lee 1985).

Issues related to racial identification emerge within the context of the self; individuals' sense of belonging to a specific social group is one of the various components that constitute their conception of self (James 1890). From our perspective, people's notions about themselves are defined both by absences – by what they are not or do not possess (see McGuire 1984) – and by the things, qualities, or ways being fought against (see Sartre 1956). As such, individuals develop a sense of personal and collective identification, by remaining conscious of the possibilities available to them and to others, and by striving to transcend the limited possibilities imposed by the immediate social context. A personal sense of self is achieved through analysis of possibilities made available by the immediate environment and by alternative social contexts and systems (Lovaglia et al. 1998). As a consequence, gifted disadvantaged children cannot become raceless. Their inescapable notions of who they are and what it means to be of a distinct race and socioeconomic class are essential elements driving their motivations toward achievement. Gifted disadvantaged students often are highly cognizant of their racial identity and of the implications of their existence within socially deprived circumstances. They are also aware of the need for personal and social transformation.

Many of the gifted disadvantaged students we have spoken with have expressed a desire to become future community leaders and to help improve the current circumstances of disadvantaged persons. In other words, they wish to shape the very worlds from which they emerged. The gifted disadvantaged often believe that only time separates them from their ideals: they learn to live with ambiguity, and are able to delay gratification for abstract goals. They are willing to work toward the achievement of goals, sustain motivation to achieve, and do not succumb to the constraints of an environment inhospitable for the expression and development of their giftedness.

Conclusion

We have argued that gifted disadvantaged children utilize cognitive processes that determine how they interact with their environment. We have proposed that these children manage their lives in ways that allow them to function in diverse social systems. When disadvantaged children learn to adapt their behavior to the values and demands of school, they begin to accomplish required tasks successfully, their achievements attract the attention of teachers, and greater opportunities for success are made available to them. This 'snowball effect' carries crucial implications for the child's personal and motivational development. Alternative socialization agents expose disadvantaged children to wide-ranging experiences that impact their emerging views of themselves and the possibilities for their future.

The ability of gifted disadvantaged children to detect and benefit from circumstances that ensure achievement is profoundly influenced both by the social environments in which they are raised and by their use of self-management processes. Our conception of giftedness also implies a developmental perspective. The behaviors of the gifted disadvantaged are characteristically motivated by the desire to transform their own social and economic conditions, as well as those of other disadvantaged individuals. Because these goals require long-range planning and self-management, giftedness among the disadvantaged must be measured over time. Their giftedness is measured best by the various cognitive, motivational, and personal abilities they demonstrate throughout childhood and adolescence.

We believe ours is a conception of giftedness that not only accounts for the cognitive abilities of gifted students, but also addresses the other characteristics that together constitute the whole fabric of disadvantaged children.

Key questions

1   How can social deprivation and stress motivate disadvantaged students productively?
2   What adaptive behaviors do disadvantaged gifted students display in the home and school interface?
3   What is the relationship between economic identity and racial identity and how can a positive self-concept be developed in disadvantaged gifted students?

Acknowledgements

Preparation of this contribution was supported by Grant REC-9979843 from the National Science Foundation and by a government grant under the Javits Act Program (Grant no. R206R000001) as administered by the Office of Educational Research and Improvement, US Department of Education. Grantees undertaking such projects are encouraged to express freely their professional judgment. This contribution, therefore, does not necessarily represent the positions or the policies of the US government, and no official endorsement should be inferred.

References

Allen, W. R. (1985) Black students, white campus: structural, interpersonal, and psychological correlates of success. *Journal of Negro Education*, 54(2): 134–147.

Arroyo, C. G. (1990) A comparison of the real and ideal self conceptions of high- and low-achieving African-American students: their spontaneous responses. Unpublished raw data.

Arroyo, C. G. and Zigler, E. W. (1995) Racial identity, academic achievement, and the psychological well-being of economically disadvantaged adolescents. *Journal of Personality and Social Psychology*, 69: 903–914.

Baldwin, A. V. (1985) Programs for the gifted and talented: issues concerning minority populations, in F. D. Horowitz and M. O'Brien (eds) *The Gifted and Talented: Developmental Perspectives*. Washington, DC: American Psychological Association.

Berry, J. W. (1974) Radical cultural relativism and the concept of intelligence, in J. W. Berry and P. R. Dasen (eds) *Culture and Cognition: Readings in Cross-cultural Psychology*. London: Methuen.

Boykin, A. W. (1983) The academic performance of Afro-American children, in J. Spence (ed.), *Achievement and Achievement Motives: Psychological and Sociological Approaches*. San Francisco, CA: W. H. Freeman.

Boykin, A. W. (1984) Reading achievement and the social-cultural frame of reference of Afro-American children. *Journal of Negro Education*, 53(4): 464–473.

Campione, J. C., Brown, A. L., Ferrara, R. A. and Bryant, N. R. (1984) The zone of proximal development: implications for individual differences and learning, in B. Rogoff and J. Wertsch (eds) *Children's Learning in the 'Zone of Proximal Development', New Directions for Child Development*, no. 23. San Francisco, CA: Jossey-Bass.

Coyle, T. R., Read, L. E., Gaultney, J. F. and Bjorklund, D. F. (1999) Giftedness and variability in strategic processing on a multitrial memory task: evidence for stability in gifted cognition. *Learning and Individual Differences*, 10(4): 273–290.

Diaz, R. M. (1990) The social origins of self-regulation: a Vygotskian perspective. Paper presented at the meeting of the American Educational Research Association, Boston, MA, April.

Diaz, R. M., Neal, C. J. and Vachio, A. (1990) Maternal teaching in the zone of proximal development: a comparison of low and high risk dyads, unpublished manuscript, Stanford University, CA.

Dweck, C. S. (1999) *Self-theories: Their Role in Motivation, Personality, and Development*. Philadelphia, PA: Psychology Press.

Dweck, C. S. and Elliot, E. E. (1983) Achievement motivation, in P. H. Mussen and E. M. Hetherington (eds) *Handbook of Child Psychology*: Volume 4, *Socialization, Personality, and Social Development*. New York: John Wiley and Sons.

Erickson, F. (1987) Transformation and school success: the politics and culture of educational achievement. *Anthropology and Educational Quarterly*, 18: 335–356.

Evans, V. and Quarterman, J. (1983) Personality characteristics of successful and unsuccessful Black female basketball players. *International Journal of Sport Psychology*, 14(2): 105–115.

Ford, D. Y. (1994) Desegregation of gifted educational programs: the impact of Brown on underachieving children of color. *Journal of Negro Education*, 63(4): 358–374.

Ford, D. Y., Harris, J. J. and Winborne, D. G. (1990) The coloring of IQ testing: a new name for an old phenomenon. *The Urban League Review*, 13(2): 99–111.

Fordham, S. (1988) Racelessness as a factor in Black students' school success: pragmatic strategy or pyrrhic victory? *Harvard Educational Review*, 58(1): 54–84.

Fordham, S. and Ogbu, J. U. (1986) Black students' school success: 'Coping with the burden of "acting White."' *The Urban Review*, 18: 176–206.

Foster, W. and Seltzer, A. (1986) A portrayal of individual excellence in the urban ghetto. *Journal of Counseling and Development*, 64(9): 579–582.

Galley, L. S. and Flanagan, C. A. (2000) The well-being of children in a changing economy: time for a new social contract in America, in R. D. Taylor and M. C. Wang (eds), *Resilience across Contexts: Work, Family, Culture, and Community*. Mahwah, NJ: Erlbaum.

Gibbs, J. T. (1998) High-risk behaviors in African-American youth: conceptual and methodological issues in research, in V. C. McLoyd and L. Steinberg (eds) *Studying Minority Adolescents: Conceptual, Methodological, and Theoretical Issues*. Mahwah, NJ: Erlbaum.

Grigorenko, E. L., Geissler, P. W., Prince, R., Okatcha, F., Nokes, C., Kenny, D. A., Bundy, D. A. and Sternberg, R. J. (2001) The organisation of Luo conceptions of intelligence: a study of implicit theories in a Kenyan village. *International Journal of Behavioral Development*, 25(4): 367–378.

Heath, S. B. (1983) *Ways with Words*. New York: Cambridge University Press.

Hilliard, A. G. (1989) Cultural style in teaching and learning. *Education Digest*, 55(4): 21–23.

James, W. (1890) *The Principles of Psychology*, Volume 2. New York: H. Holt.

Labov, W. (1972) *Language in the Inner City: Studies in the Black English Vernacular*. Philadelphia, PA: University of Pennsylvania Press.

Lee, C. C. (1984) An investigation of psychosocial variables related to academic success from rural Black adolescents. *Journal of Negro Education*, 543(4): 424–434.

Lee, C. C. (1985) Successful rural Black adolescents: a psychosocial profile. *Adolescence*, 2Q: 131–142.

Lovaglia, M. J., Lucas, J. W., Houser, J. A., Thye, S. B. and Markovsky, B. (1998) Status processes and mental ability test scores. *American Journal of Sociology*, 104(1): 195–228.

Luthar, S. S. (1999) *Poverty and Children's Adjustment: Developmental Clinical Psychology and Psychiatry*. Thousand Oaks, CA: Sage.

Luthar, S. S., Cicchetti, D. and Becker, B. (2000) The construct of resilience: a critical evaluation and guidelines for future work. *Child Development*, 71: 543–562.

McGuire, W. J. (1984) Search for the self: going beyond self-esteem and the reactive self, in R. A. Zucker, J. Aronoff and A. I. Rabin (eds) *Personality and the Prediction of Behavior*. New York: Academic Press.

Moyer, T. R., and Motta, R. W. (1982) Alienation and school adjustment among Black and White adolescents. *Journal of Psychology*, 112: 21–28.

Ogbu, J. U. (1978) *Minority Education and Caste: The American System in Cross-cultural Perspectives*. New York: Academic Press.

Ogbu, J. U. and Stern, P. (2001) Case status and intellectual development, in R. J. Sternberg and E. L. Grigorenko (eds) *Environmental Effects on Cognitive Abilities*. Mahwah, NJ: Erlbaum.

Okagaki, L. and Sternberg, R. J. (1993) Parental beliefs and children's school performance. *Child Development*, 64(1): 36–56.

Patton, J. M. (1992) Assessment and identification of African-American learners with gifts and talents. *Exceptional Children*, 59(2): 150–159.

Payne, R. K. (1998) *A Framework for Understanding Poverty*. Boyton, TX: RFT.

Rodgers, J. L., Rowe, D. and May, K. (1994) DF analysis of the National Longitudinal Survey of Youth IQ/Achievement Data: Nonshared Environmental Influences. *Intelligence*, 19: 157–177.

Sartre, J. P. (1956) *Being and Nothingness*. New York: Philosophical Press.

Sewell, T. E., Farley, F. H., Manni, J. L. and Hunt, P. (1982) Motivation, social reinforcement, and intelligence as predictors of academic achievement in Black adolescents. *Adolescence*, 17(67): 647–656.

Shore, B. M. and Kanevsky, L. (1993) Thinking processes: being and becoming gifted, in K. A. Heller, J. Monks and A. H. Passow (eds) *International Handbook of Research and Development of Giftedness and Talent*. Oxford: Pergamon.

Siegler, R. S. (1996) *Emerging Minds: The Process of Change in Children's Thinking*. New York: Oxford University Press.

Steiner, H. H. and Carr, M. (2003) Cognitive development in gifted children: toward a more precise understanding of emerging differences in intelligence. *Educational Psychology Review*, 15(3): 215–246.

Sternberg, R. J. (1985a) *Beyond IQ: A Triarchic Theory of Human Intelligence*. New York: Cambridge University Press.

Sternberg, R. J. (1985b) Implicit theories of intelligence, creativity, and wisdom. *Journal of Personality and Social Psychology*, 49(3): 607–627.

Sternberg, R. J. (1986) *Intelligence Applied: Understanding and Increasing your Intelligence Skills*. San Diego, CA: Harcourt Brace Javonovich.

Sternberg, R. J. (1997) *Successful Intelligence*. New York: Plume.

Sternberg, R. J. (1999) The theory of successful intelligence. *Review of General Psychology*, 3: 292–316.

Sternberg, R. J. and Davidson, J. E. (2005) *Conceptions of Giftedness*, 2nd edn. New York: Cambridge University Press.

Sternberg, R. J. and Kaufman J. C. (1998) Human abilities. *Annual Review of Psychology*, 49: 479–502.

Sternberg, R. J., Conway, B. E., Ketron, J. L. and Bernstein, M. (1981) People's conceptions of intelligence. *Journal of Personality and Social Psychology*, 41: 37–55.

Sternberg, R. J., Wagner, R. K. and Okagaki, L. L. (1993) Practical intelligence: the nature and role of tacit knowledge in work and school, in H. Reese and J. Pucket (eds) *Advances in Life-span Development*. Hillsdale, NJ: Erlbaum.

Sternberg, R. J., Forsythe, G. B., Hedlund, J., Horvath, J., Snook, S., Williams, W. M., Wagner, R. K. and Grigorenko, E. L. (2000) *Practical Intelligence in Everyday Life*. New York: Cambridge University Press.

Sternberg, R. J., The Rainbow Project Collaborators and University of Michigan Business School Project Collaborators (2004) Theory based university admissions testing for a new millennium. *Educational Psychologist*, 39(3): 185–198.

US Department of Education (1993) *National Excellence: A Case for Developing America's Talent*. Washington, DC: Office of Educational Research and Improvement.

Yang, S-Y. and Sternberg, R. J. (1997a) Conceptions of intelligence in ancient Chinese philosophy. *Journal of Theoretical and Philosophical Psychology*, 17: 101–119.

Yang, S-Y. and Sternberg, R. J. (1997b) Taiwanese Chinese people's conceptions of intelligence. *Intelligence*, 25: 21–36.

4.2 Coolabah dynamic assessment: identifying high academic potential in at-risk populations

Graham W. Chaffey and Stan B. Bailey

Involuntary minority status

Minority students have to manage the values and attitudes of both their culture and the dominant culture. Those who fail to negotiate this often face school problems of underachievement (Ford 1996: 86–87). Ogbu (1994: 363), contrasts voluntary (immigrant) minorities, and involuntary (caste-like) minorities.

> Voluntary minorities have moved to a new society by choice, seeking opportunities and/or political freedom: while these children may have initial school problems due to language and cultural differences, this does not usually extend into school failure. Involuntary minorities have originally arrived through slavery or colonization.
>
> (Ogbu 1994: 9)

These people often experience caste-like conditions with poor education and life chances, for example African/Americans, Canadian First Nations peoples, New Zealand Maoris and Australian Aboriginal peoples.

Ogbu sees primary cultural differences as those existing before the two cultures came into contact (Ogbu 1994: 363), creating short-term difficulties within a society. It is the secondary cultural differences that lead to long-term difficulties for involuntary minority children when they enter schools controlled by the dominant society.

The secondary cultural differences that can affect schooling include different cognitive, communication, interaction and learning styles. Lack of teachers' understanding about these styles is an obvious impediment to learning, leading to the perception of deficit attitudes by the dominant society. Ogbu (1994) states:

> Involuntary minorities may consciously or unconsciously interpret school learning as a displacement process detrimental to their social identity, sense of security, and self-worth. They fear that learning the (dominant) cultural frame of reference, they will cease to act like minorities and lose their identity as minorities and their sense of community and self-worth.
>
> (Ogbu 1994: 364–369)

Current methods of identifying academic giftedness

IQ tests and teacher-centred processes (Davis and Rimm 1998) are potentially flawed with respect to children from cultural minorities and/or low socio-economic status groups. The ability of teachers to identify gifted students from these groups has also been questioned (Braggett 1985; Pendarvis 1990), the suggestion being that teachers are likely to overlook gifted students who display oppositional behaviours or are different in other ways (Davis and Rimm 1998; Pendarvis 1990).

Being identified publicly as highly able has both social and academic consequences for children. Gross (1989) suggests they face a 'forced-choice dilemma': peer friendship and acceptance or school achievement. Van Tassel-Baska et al. (1994) also note:

> Culturally diverse groups battle internally a dual value system message: . . . subgroup loyalty and adherence to tribal, family, and cultural traditions, (or) individual excellence in a mainstream world.
>
> (Van Tassel-Baska et al. 1994: 190)

Invisible underachievers

If gifted underachievers are not meaningfully accounted for in conceptions of giftedness and talent, then it is unlikely that gifted underachievers will be sought, especially in populations from cultural and social minority groups. That children may underperform both in the classroom and on commonly used measures of aptitude or potential has long been recognized (Butler-Por 1993; Reis and McCoach 2000; Whitmore 1987). However, a review of the literature reveals the absence of a consistent term for this type of underachievement, which can only lead to lack of recognition in the classroom, with low expectations, deficit assumptions and continued underperformance among the consequences. We, therefore, need a simple and consistent definition for this type of underachiever from 'at risk' populations. We use the term 'invisible underachievers' to denote individuals whose assessed potential determined by usual identification methods, is less than their actual potential.

Dynamic testing may provide a partial solution to the problem of assessment of invisible underachievers in at-risk populations (Grigorenko and Sternberg 1998). Dynamic testing is different from dynamic assessment in that it only seeks to determine the learning potential of an individual, rather than to establish long-term cognitive change (Grigorenko and Sternberg 1998). It follows the test–intervention–retest format of classic dynamic assessment, but involves a comparatively short intervention indicating ability to benefit from the intervention experience. After the initial pre-test, intervention is given to address the areas of under-performance; and then a post-test, given some time after the intervention, determines the extent of improvement, and thus establishes what is assumed to be a better indication of learning potential.

Coolabah Dynamic Assessment and Australian Aboriginal children

In 2002, the dynamic testing method was administered to 79 Aboriginal children in Grades 3 to 5 (aged 8 to 11) attending schools in a rural district in New South

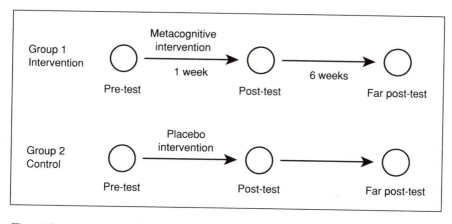

Figure 4.2.1 Experimental design used to investigate the principal research question.

Wales. Local Aboriginal communities were consulted, and they suggested working with small groups with a respected Aboriginal adult involved in each intervention. The Aboriginal communities' support for the project resulted in 90 percent of the target group participating.

The experimental design (see Figure 4.2.1) involved two groups (intervention and control) randomly matched on pre-test Raven's Standard Progressive Matrices (RSPM) scores. The intervention group received a metacognitive intervention designed to probe each child's cognitive potential (Vygotsky 1974), while the control group received a placebo intervention designed to appear the same as the metacognitive intervention. One week after the respective interventions, the RSPM was re-administered to both groups, thus concluding the formal dynamic testing process. A far post-test was administered to both groups six weeks after the post-test.

To maximize the test taking effort of the children and the effectiveness of the metacognitive intervention, we addressed socio-emotional and cultural factors that were possible inhibitors, such as the forced-choice dilemma (Gross 1989), self-efficacy (Bandura 1977), expectation issues (Lovaglia et al. 2000; Rosenthal and Jacobson 1968; Steele and Aronson 1995) and cultural differences. Thus the intervention had two components, the socio-emotional component giving access to the metacognitive one.

The dynamic testing metacognitive intervention was based on Vygotsky's (1974) notion that an individual's zone of proximal development (ZPD) can be explored by providing intervention to guide the individual's cognitive and metacognitive endeavours (Lidz 1997). The need to encourage the self-efficacy of the students was seen as pivotal to the procedure's ultimate success (Bandura 1977), and the gradual change from easier to harder cognitive tasks was scaffolded to ensure

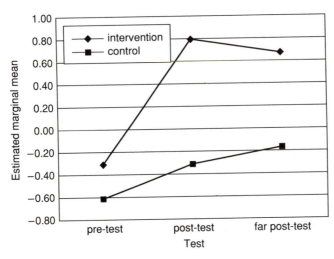

Figure 4.2.2 Comparison of RSPM of intervention and control group pre-test, post-test and far post-test mean scores presented as Rasch Analysis Case estimates.

this. Self-efficacy development was also supported with appropriate performance feedback and well-structured praise.

The results of the dynamic testing data analysis are presented as Rasch analysis case estimates (Figure 4.2.2). Any student who scored at or above the 85th percentile band in any of the three administrations of the RSPM was included in the 'Gifted Group'.

The dynamic testing procedure led to significant improvements in the intervention group's performance on the cognitive variable as measured by the RSPM, suggesting that dynamic testing would reveal invisible underachievement. The significant changes from pre-test to post-test were associated with using two approaches that addressed 'deficient learning habits, and motivational patterns that are responsible for the poor performance' (Tzuriel and Feuerstein 1992: 187–188). First, an overarching socio-emotional strategy was employed with both the control and intervention groups to help counter inhibitors to test performance and motivation. The second, and major, strategy used with the intervention group was the metacognitive intervention aimed at addressing inefficient learning habits.

The conclusion that the intervention group RSPM pre-test to post-test score gain was largely the result of the metacognitive intervention is congruent with the theoretical foundations of dynamic testing and cognitive modifiability. The significant increase in scores following intervention offers strong support for the conclusion that the participating children were performing below their potential at pre-test.

Table 4.2.1 Teacher expectations of academic performance and RSPM percentile band scores at pre-test, post-test and far post-test for case study children

Name	Teacher estimation of academic school performance	RSPM pre-test percentile band	RSPM post-test percentile band	RSPM far post-test percentile band
Jill	Just below average	2	80	52
Adam	Average	18	91	58
Nola	Slightly below average	43	81	83
Kate	Well above average	58	91	96
Sam*	Probably average	37	93	90
Ian	Average	86	97	93
Linda	Just below average	42	75	91
Claire	Average	28	81	72

Note: * Control group.

Identifying invisible underachievers

Eight case studies were developed of children who were found by dynamic testing to possess high academic potential. The dynamic testing outcomes were compared to teacher estimates of their classroom performance (see Table 4.2.1).

When school performances are compared with the RSPM pre-test scores only Ian was revealed as an underachiever. However, when school performance was compared to the RSPM post-test scores of the dynamic testing, the other seven children were revealed as invisible underachievers.

The literature, case studies and the dynamic testing outcomes have revealed an interaction of factors contributing to the school and test underachievement of the children in the present study (see Figure 4.2.3).

Conclusion

The dynamic testing method briefly outlined here was effective in identifying high academic potential in an encouraging proportion of the study children. The identification approach used in this study is known as Coolabah Dynamic Assessment.

The underachievement on the RSPM pre-test by the children in this study supports the finding by Lidz and Macrine (2001), Lovaglia et al. (1998), Skuy et al. (1988) and Tzuriel and Feuerstein (1992). One-off screening using relatively culture fair non-verbal standardized tests may not produce valid measures of learning potential for at-risk children. Indeed, their invisible underachievement on such tests reinforces deficit views and cultural stereotypes. The capacity of dynamic testing offers the hope of a more realistic, positive and just approach to the challenge of identifying potential in children from different cultural and social groups.

Here are two case studies highlighting 'invisible underachievement'.

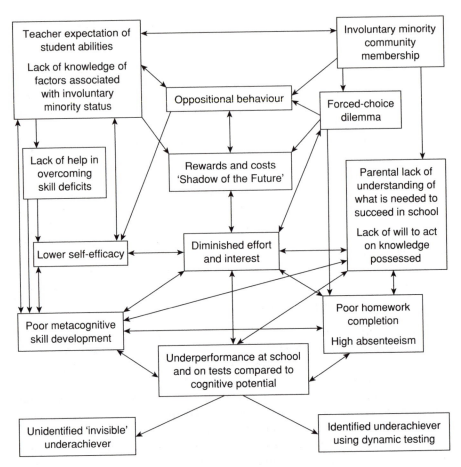

Figure 4.2.3 A model of the interacting factors leading to underachievement for the case study children.

Note: The arrows refer to all statements in any given box.

A snapshot of Kate

Kate, a shy 8-year-old, was described by her teacher as 'a very nice little girl'. She was proud of her Aboriginal heritage.

Kate was considered to be well above average in academic ability with an excellent attendance record. Kate was regularly given, and completed, homework – but not always to a good standard. She was considered to be working below her potential.

Kate's scores on the Grade 3 Basic Skills Test were a percentile rank of 68 percent for Literacy and 82 percent for Numeracy. Her dynamic testing percentile rank outcomes were 58 percent at pre-test, 91 percent at post-test and 96 percent at far post-test.

Kate and her mother both considered that she was clever at school.

A snapshot of Adam

Adam, 9 years old, was a gifted athlete and artist. Well liked by his teacher, he often helped his less able friends in class. He was proud of his Aboriginal heritage.

Adam was said to be average in his class although his teacher thought he had greater potential: his classroom performance was often negatively influenced by peer pressure.

On the Grade 3 Basic Skills Test Adam attained a percentile rank of 25 percent for Literacy and 10 percent for Numeracy. His dynamic testing percentile rank outcomes were 18 percent at pre-test, 91 percent at post-test and 58 percent at far post-test.

Adam was perceived to be coping and received no extra help from the school Aboriginal Education Assistant.

Adam and his mother both considered that he was clever at school.

Cross-cultural comparison: a Canadian pilot study

Seeking invisible underachievers among Canadian Indigenous children

Australian and Canadian Indigenous children share involuntary minority status with some common factors that contribute to academic underachievement. Therefore, it was thought that Coolabah Dynamic Assessment (CDA) could be used to identify invisible underachievers among Canadian Indigenous children. A pilot program was carried out in 2003, in partnership with Ken McCluskey, at the University of Winnipeg.

The pilot program comprised nineteen Indigenous children aged 8 to 10, from a generally low socioeconomic area. Approximately 67 percent of the school and 40 percent of the town population were Indigenous Canadians. The school was recognized as having a high percentage of at-risk children.

General comparisons

Comparisons will be made with the Australian intervention group only.

The overall CDA outcomes for the Australian and Canadian Indigenous children are presented in Table 4.2.2. A number of comparisons may be made. First, the pre-test mean score of the Australian children is considerably below (4.75 raw score points) that of the Canadian children. Second, following the intervention, there is only a small difference (of 1.26 raw score points) between the group means on the post-test. Hence, the overall mean gain scores of 8.39 for the Australian children and 4.90 for the Canadian children are strongly linked to the pre-test scores rather than the post-test outcomes. The Australian

Table 4.2.2 Pre-test mean raw scores and percentile bands for Australian and Canadian Indigenous children

	Australian raw scores	Australian percentile band*	Canadian raw scores	Canadian percentile band**
Pre-test mean	27.85	30.0%	32.60	41.9%
Post-test mean	36.24	54.5%	37.50	60.0%
Gain mean	8.39	N/A	4.90	N/A

Notes: * For uniformity the Australian norms have been used for both groups.
** The post-test percentile bands should not be considered in a psychometric sense and are only included to give an indication of change.

children scored a mean 30th percentile band at pre-test and a mean 55th percentile band at post-test, while the Canadian children achieved a mean 42nd percentile band at pre-test and a mean 60th percentile band at post-test.

These outcomes suggest that, generally, the Australian children have underachieved on the pre-test to a much greater extent than the Canadian children. Also the CDA intervention had a greater impact on the Australian children, supporting the notion that they were underachieving to a greater extent initially. Further, the closeness of the mean post-test scores suggests that the CDA intervention has advanced the children to approximately the same level of performance despite there being substantial differences in initial performance.

Individual CDA outcomes

The individual CDA outcomes for the Canadian children are especially revealing. Four of the high scoring children made either nil or only small gains from pre-test to post-test, suggesting that they had few impediments to optimal performance on the pre-test (Table 4.2.3). These high pre-test scores and small gains contrast sharply with the CDA outcomes of the Australian children, where

Table 4.2.3 High scoring Canadian children with minimal gains from pre-test to post-test

	Pre-test Raw Score	Pre-test Percentile Band	Post-test Raw Score	Post-test Percentile Band*	Raw Score Gain
Anne	43	80%	44	85%	1
Erin	45	88%	45	88%	0
Angie	46	91%	48	95%	2
Carmen	41	67%	43	73%	2
Toya	38	69%	42	83%	4

Note: * The post-test percentile bands should not be considered in a psychometric sense and are included only to give an indication of change.

Table 4.2.4 Canadian children with high gains from pre-test to post-test

	Pre-test raw score	Pre-test percentile band	Post-test raw score	Post-test percentile band*	Raw score gain
Susie	33	46%	46	95%	13
Dianne	30	38%	43	91%	13
Casey	39	75%	46	98%	7
Duke	32	43%	42	83%	10
Shaq	20	9%	37	44%	17
Ali	34	35%	43	80%	9
Kelly	30	23%	41	67%	11
Mary	29	14%	37	44%	8

Note: * The post-test percentile bands should not be considered in a psychometric sense and are only included to give an indication of change.

few children scored highly on the pre-test. The data for the Australian children suggest that the brightest children were underachieving to the greatest extent on the pre-test. The Canadian finding indicates that the Canadian children with high academic potential have largely benefited from special school support, and so were underachieving to a lesser extent than the Australian children at pre-test.

Eight children produced raw score gains ranging from 8 to 17 (see Table 4.2.4). These scores suggest that there was some degree of underachievement on the pre-test by these children. In the case of Susie, Dianne and Shaq the gains suggest that the pre-test represented a substantial underestimation of their academic potential. It was clear in Shaq's case that the pre-test was poorly attempted. Shaq, an outstanding athlete, rushed the whole pre-test to get to his gym practice. Consequently, the 17 point raw score gain at post-test was not a surprise. Dianne's teacher considered her to be a little below average in classroom performance but with the potential to do better, so the magnitude of her CDA post-test gain came as a surprise. Susie was performing a little above average in class but was considered to be capable of much better. Once again the CDA provided strong support for this view. Ali represents another situation, in that she was said to be working close to her potential near the middle of the class, so the CDA outcome came as a surprise to her teacher. The underperformance of these children on the pre-test, together with their high post-test scores above their level of classroom performance, suggest that these children are invisible underachievers.

Identifying gifted Indigenous children using the CDA

The similar mean post-test scores of the Australian and Canadian Indigenous children are noteworthy. This finding suggests that the CDA intervention scaffolded both groups to approximately the same performance level on the RSPM, despite the lower mean pre-test score of the Australian Indigenous children. This finding

strongly suggests that the CDA was successful in optimising the cognitive performance of a substantial proportion of the study children although there was
greater initial underachievement of the Australian Indigenous children.

The Wii Gaay project: potential to performance?

The Catholic Schools Office of Armidale, also in north rural New South Wales,
has established the Wii Gaay project to identify and develop the academic
potential of the greatest underachievers, the highly able Aboriginal children
(Chaffey 2002).

The Wii Gaay project has been developed using the following principles:

1   Children are identified using the Coolabah Dynamic Assessment method,
    and teacher and school assessment data in literacy and numeracy.
2   The children are identified at Grade 3 (8+ years).
3   Provision addresses children's low self-efficacy with respect to school, cognit-
    ive inefficiency and lack of appropriate skill levels in literacy and numeracy.
4   Aboriginal communities are included in the Wii Gaay project.
5   Teachers' low expectations of Aboriginal children are addressed (Chaffey
    2002).

Strategies

Identification

The CDA is used to identify the invisible underachievers, together with teacher
assessment on performance and potential, and mastery performance indicated
by NSW Basic Skills Tests.

Self-efficacy enhancement through mastery and vicarious experience

The Wii Gaay Aboriginal children participate in camps and are mentored by
Aboriginal role models, with additional peer and adult role modelling experiences provided through Internet mentoring. The curriculum focuses on literacy
and numeracy approached through appropriate context, a mastery focus and a
child-centred approach.

For example, the children researched an Aboriginal person they admired, and
then role-played this character to peers and staff. The numeracy component was
based on discovering real diprotodon bones 'planted' nearby. After a Dreamtime
story featuring the diprotodon, compass and distance coordinates were given
and the search was on. As the sun set in the Australian bush, the children were
immersed in an exercise where they 'encountered and hunted' a diprotodon of
10,000 years ago. The children then estimated the height and weight of the
animal from a skeletal diagram and bone fragments. The whole process produced intense engagement, and these highly able children were not fearful of
success, nor of standing out in their peer group.

Teacher education

All schools in the Wii Gaay project have been offered a full staff development day to discuss the factors contributing to the underachievement and motivation of Aboriginal children. The dynamic assessment research is also presented. An interactive workshop format enables teachers to feel that they are partners in developing a whole-school problem-solving approach. Moreover, there is inclusion of the community in the development of and feedback from the Wii Gaay project.

Conclusion

Not only does Coolabah Dynamic Assessment offer an effective alternative means of identifying high academic potential and invisible underachievers among at-risk populations, but also the principles on which it is based provide guidelines for how to plan appropriate curriculum to nurture these gifts into talents.

While the early applications of the CDA approach described above have been with Indigenous children, its rationale and processes are also pertinent for others whose customs and values differ from those of the mainstream culture. Indeed, it offers hope for achieving a more just and inclusive approach to talent development in our schools.

Key questions

1 What are some of the problems that involuntary minority children encounter when they enter schools controlled by the dominant society?
2 How is dynamic assessment different from other forms of assessment for identifying diverse gifted students?
3 What type of teacher training and collaboration is needed to implement dynamic assessment effectively?

References

Bandura, A. (1977) Self-efficacy: toward a unifying theory of behavioural change. *Psychological Review*, 84(2): 191–215.
Braggett, E. J. (1985) *Education of Gifted and Talented Children: Australian Provision*. Canberra: Commonwealth Schools Commission.
Butler-Por, N. (1993) Underachieving gifted students, in K. A. Heller, F. J. Monks and A. H. Passow (eds) *International Handbook of Research and Development of Giftedness and Talent*. Oxford: Pergamon.
Chaffey, G. W. (2002) Identifying Australian Aboriginal Children with high academic potential using dynamic testing, unpublished PhD thesis, University of New England, Australia.
Davis, G. A. and Rimm, S. B. (1998) *Education of the Gifted and Talented*, 4th edn. Needham Heights, MA: Allyn and Bacon.
Ford, D. Y. (1996) *Reversing Underachievement among Gifted Black Students*. New York: Teachers College Press.

Grigorenko, E. L. and Sternberg, R. J. (1998) Dynamic testing. *Psychological Bulletin*, 124(1): 75–111.

Gross, M. U. M. (1989) The pursuit of excellence or the search for intimacy? The forced-choice dilemma of gifted youth. *Roeper Review*, 11(4): 189–194.

Lidz, C. S. (1997) Dynamic assessment approaches, in D. S. Flanagan, J. L. Genshaft and P. L. Harrison (eds), *Contemporary Intellectual Assessment*. New York: Guilford Press.

Lidz, C. and Macrine, S. L. (2001) An alternative approach to the identification of culturally and linguistically diverse learners: the contribution of dynamic assessment. *School Psychology International*, 22: 74–96.

Lovaglia, M. J., Lucas, J. W., Houser, J. A., Thye, S. R. and Markovsky, B. (1998) Status processes and mental ability test scores. *American Journal of Sociology*, 104(1): 195–228.

Lovaglia, M. J., Thompkins, D., Lucas, J. and Thye, S. (2000) The shadow of the future: how negative expectations cloud test performance. Paper presented at the Fifth Biennial Wallace National Research Symposium on Talent Development, University of Iowa, Iowa City, IA, May 2000.

Ogbu, J. U. (1994) Understanding cultural diversity and learning. *Journal for the Education of the Gifted*, 17(4): 355–383.

Pendarvis, E. D. (1990) *The Abilities of Gifted Children*. Englewood Cliffs, NJ: Prentice Hall.

Reis, S. M. and McCoach, D. B. (2000) The underachievement of gifted students: what do we know and where do we go? *Gifted Child Quarterly*, 44(3): 152–170.

Rosenthal, R. and Jacobson, L. (1968) *Pygmalion in the Classroom: Teacher Expectation and Pupils' Intellectual Development*. New York: Holt, Rinehart and Winston.

Skuy, M., Kaniel, S. and Tzuriel, D. (1988) Dynamic assessment of intellectually superior Israeli children in a low socio-economic status community. *Gifted Education International*, 5: 90–96.

Steele, C. M. and Aronson, J. (1995) Stereotype threat and the intellectual test performance of African Americans. *Journal of Personality and Social Psychology*, 69(5): 797–811.

Tzuriel, D. and Feuerstein, R. (1992) Dynamic group assessment for prescriptive teaching: differential effects of treatments, in H. C. Haywood and D. Tzuriel (eds), *Interactive Assessment*. New York: Springer-Verlag.

Van Tassel-Baska, J., Olszewski-Kubilius, P. and Kulieke, M. (1994) A study of self-concept and social support in advantaged and disadvantaged seventh and eighth grade gifted students. *Roeper Review*, 16(3): 186–191.

Vygotsky, L. S. (1974) *Thought and Language*. Cambridge, MA: The MIT Press.

Whitmore, J. R. (1987) Conceptualizing the issues of underserved populations of gifted students. *Journal for the Education of the Gifted*, 10(3): 141–153.

4.3   A fairer deal for the gifted disadvantaged in rural areas in South Africa

Jacobus G. Maree

A broad definition of giftedness

There are a number of key concepts that are considered important in the definition of giftedness. Sternberg (1999) suggests that intelligent functioning revolves around problem-solving, and this generic ability can be taught and developed in all learners. Maker (1993) and Wallace et al. (2004), define problem-solving as the ability to solve complex problems efficiently, effectively, and economically. This view should be read in conjunction with the findings of Garrison (in Hall and Lin 1995), which show that 14-year-old children are as capable as adults in their ability to use competent reasoning skills in real-life dilemmas. Many writers emphasize the critical importance of creativity, and in the case of disadvantaged learners, using creative skills often means the difference between survival and non-survival. Sternberg suggests that disadvantaged learners who do manage to succeed 'against all odds' are unconventionally creative, and resourceful, and resilient in the face of seemingly debilitating adversity. Gardner (1993, 1999) first drew attention to the concept of multiple intelligences relevant to the full range of human endeavours, and Sisk (2002) has emphasized the role of spirituality in giftedness which is defined as 'a deep self-awareness in which one becomes more aware of the dimensions of self, not simply as a body, but a mind-body and spirit' (Sisk 2002: 209).

Sternberg (1999) argues that successful intelligence must embrace the concept of wisdom judged against the framework of a person's cultural context. He argues that wisdom can be developed in a number of ways, namely:

- Students need to be provided with problems that require negotiation, giving advice to others or dealing with ethical/moral dilemmas.
- Students need to be helped to think in terms of common good.
- In solving problems, students need to learn how to balance their own interests with those of others.
- Students need role models of wise thinkers.
- Students need to understand that what is right or wrong is a relative concept, varying with time, place and context.
- Both facilitators and students need to practise in reality what they have learned.

Passow and Schiff (1989) draw attention to 'another dimension of giftedness: the development of caring, concerned, compassionate, committed individuals who develop and use their giftedness for society's behalf as well as for self-fulfilment.'

Salovey and Mayer (1990) affirm that intelligence should be redefined in order to include a person's capacity to monitor his or her own and others' emotions, to discriminate among these emotions and to use this information to guide his or her thinking and actions.

BarOn elaborates on these views:

> Broadly speaking, emotional intelligence addresses the emotional, personal, social and survival dimensions of intelligence, vitally important in daily functioning. This less cognitive part of intelligence is concerned with understanding oneself and others, relating to people, and adapting to and coping with our immediate surroundings. These factors increase our ability to be

more successful in dealing with environmental demands. Emotional intelligence is tactical and immediate, and as such reflects a person's common sense and ability to get along with the world.

(BarOn in Van Rooyen 2002)

Disadvantage in South Africa

According to Eriksson (1993), the use of the term gifted 'disadvantaged' is defined from a socio-economic perspective. Although a significant percentage of urban children fall into this bracket, rural communities are hit particularly hard, are characterized by infant mortality, poverty, unemployment, inadequate housing, water and sanitation, and under-resourced educational facilities. The mental health effects of poverty on children are well documented, ranging from low birth weight, cognitive deficits to developmental problems (Pillay et al. 1999). Absence of fathers and mothers, large classes, and great distances that students travel to and from schools typify the rural situation. Pillay et al. (1999) draw attention to the fact that poverty is a regular concomitant in rural communities. This is especially due to lack of employment in rural areas. In South Africa, clearly, the term 'rural' almost inevitably implies major, subsistent socio-economic disadvantage.

It is not uncommon to see around a hundred learners crammed into a single classroom; learner support material is almost non-existent. Blackboards detached from the walls, broken classroom doors and windows are common. Clean water and toilets are non-existent. In this study, in-depth interviews were held with every headteacher whose school was visited, and their demotivation and sense of hopelessness were obvious.

It is, perhaps, understandable that 'deficit ideologies' have emerged in discussions on the situation in South Africa, deriving from the fact that black students, both urban and rural, grossly under-perform in schools. However, Ford and Harmon (2001) refer to the use of 'deficit ideologies' as failure to focus on individuals' strengths, focusing instead on their perceived shortcomings in order to explain the differences in students' achievements.

Against the reality of extreme poverty, inadequate schools and fragmented families, it is difficult to see how gifted disadvantaged learners can survive, let alone surmount the debilitating problems they face. Against this, however, we need to remember that the strengths in African culture revolve around the traditional wisdom of *Ubuntu*, an African word implying the spirit of fellowship, empathy, humanity and compassion, particularly encapsulating the concepts of emotional, social and spiritual intelligence in the service of the wider community. Together with the capacity for real and applied creative problem-solving for survival, these qualities still constitute the cultural capital or assets of many African communities (Hernandez 1998; McDonald 1997).

It is obvious that funding and local leadership which are focused on shared community action are urgently needed to improve school infrastructure, learning conditions and management. Then alongside this, relevant intervention programmes can be implemented. Passow and Schiff (1989) and Wallace (2004) propose a range of broad principles that should underpin intervention programmes for disadvantaged students: namely students should be involved in community development, making decisions and taking responsibility for implementing social action; they should debate local and national issues, drawing relevant parallels from the subject topics they study; they should seriously consider their life goals and how they will achieve these; and, wherever possible, be given the opportunity to network with other students nationally and internationally. Developing students' internal locus of control, empowering them through focused relevant action, is achieved through practical problem-solving of real life issues.

Herbert (1997) and Hayes et al. (1994) discuss the complexities of mentoring a gifted student from a disadvantaged background, and they stress the need for personalized school environments created by caring teachers who convey that they believe in the students' potential, and who teach with love and support.

Peterson (1997) points out that teachers often find it hard to distinguish between underachieving gifted students' outward appearance and behaviour and their true potential, mostly because they do not share personal information readily. Their school and life experiences may not have given them the vocabulary, intellectual enrichment, social experiences or behaviour models. They may be sullen and withdrawn, hostile and sensitive to slights and initially difficult to work with, yet usually respond to teachers who can become role-models and who engage in personal and meaningful dialogue about real life issues (Begoray and Slovinsky 1997).

With regard to training teachers, Ford and Harmon (2001) argue that it is essential to educate teachers with regard to multicultural and cross-cultural diversity, appreciating cultural strengths and infusing their teaching with understanding, acknowledgement and praise. In addition, teachers should build close contacts with the home, sharing aims and facilitating goal achievement. Benbow and Arjmand (1990) and Csikszentmihalyi et al. (1993) emphasize the positive role that social institutions can play in facilitating opportunities for growth and the realization of potential. Shumow's (1997) research shows that gifted students from low-income families, although in adverse circumstances, respond to mediation and support towards successful attainment.

Cosser (2002) highlights the motivating power of personal and career counselling. In Cosser's research in rural regions in South Africa, even the recognized gifted students are, by and large, left with little hope with regard to the future. As one gifted student said: 'There is simply no sense in working hard to achieve if you have no future whatsoever.' Thus, career guidance must run alongside any intervention programme, and these career counsellors would need the skills of other counsellors plus more – such as information about the workplace, employment trends, career assessments, bursaries and interventions. Casas (1997) and Hall and Lin (1995) make it clear, however, that children should retain a degree of decision-making responsibility and power in regard to their own counselling process.

Conclusion

Battling the poverty cycle, the escalating socio-economic deprivation, the lack of education, joblessness and spiralling crime levels, requires vision and wisdom from all concerned. We need to rekindle and nourish the African culture of *Ubuntu* through community leadership, involving people in their own growth and development using their strengths of emotional, social and spiritual intelligence, their creative and practical problem-solving ability. And the school should be at the centre of this dynamic development.

Sternberg's (2001) concept of wisdom, and specifically the supreme ideal of promoting the common good, needs to be grasped by all leaders and professionals. Passow and Schiff's (1989) dream of developing caring, concerned, compassionate, committed teachers who hold a passion for the common good should gradually become a reality for every gifted disadvantaged student. Investigation of world issues needs to appear in learning programmes with gifted disadvantaged leading the way in discussion in the light of their personal experiences. Sharing stories in order to create new and 'healing' stories is the right of every gifted disadvantaged student.

Focusing on and facilitating the strengths of our gifted disadvantaged are crucial cogs in the wheel we aim to set rolling. We need to alert the collective conscience of government, corporate business and educational-psychology fraternity at large, working for the common good and believing in what we are doing. Maybe, we can move closer to meeting the need for 'creative productive leaders who will engage in dynamic problem-solving at all levels' (Eriksson 1993: 108).

Key questions

1   Who will take the lead and facilitate a network of scholars with a keen interest in the field of the gifted disadvantaged in setting up working groups, facilitating exchange schemes?
2   Clearly, the gifted disadvantaged, everywhere, are currently not receiving a fair deal. How can we collectively create national and international awareness of their particular needs?
3   How do we facilitate an international study to investigate the comparative experiences of the gifted disadvantaged throughout the world?

References

Begoray, D. and Slovinsky, K. (1997) Pearls in shells. *Roeper Review*, 20(1): 45–49.
Benbow, C. and Arjmand, O. (1990) Predictors of high academic achievement in mathematics and science by mathematically talented students: a longitudinal study. *Journal of Educational Psychology*, 82: 430–431.
Casas, F. (1997) Children's rights and children's quality of life: conceptual and practical issues. *Social Indicators Research*, 42(3): 283–298.

Cosser, M. (2002) *Factors Affecting Student Choice Behaviour in the Course of Secondary Education with Particular Reference to Entry into Higher Education.* Pretoria: Human Sciences Research Council.

Csikszentmihalyi, M., Rathunde, K. and Whalen, S. (1993) *Talented Teenagers: The Roots of Success and Failure.* New York: Cambridge University Press.

Eriksson, G. I. (1993) The global village beyond 2000. Networking with the gifted disadvantaged, in B. Wallace and H. B. Adams (eds) *Worldwide Perspectives on the Gifted Disadvantaged.* Bicester, Oxon: AB Academic.

Ford, D. Y. and Harmon, D. A. (2001) Equity and excellence: providing access to gifted education for culturally diverse students. *Journal of Secondary Gifted Education*, 12(3): 141–150.

Gardner, H. (1993) *Frames of Mind: The Theory of Multiple Intelligences.* New York: Basic Books.

Gardner, H. (1999) *Intelligence Reframed: Multiple Intelligences for the 21st Century.* New York: Basic Books.

Garrison, E. G. (1991) Children's competence to participate in divorce custody decision making. *Journal of Clinical Child Psychology*, 20: 78–87.

Hall, A. S. and Lin, M-J. (1995) Theory and practice of children's rights: implications for mental health counselors. *Journal of Mental Health Counselling*, 17(1): 63–80.

Hayes, C. B., Ryan, A. and Zseller, E. B. (1994) The middle school child's perceptions of caring teachers. *American Journal of Education*, 103(1): 1–19.

Herbert, T. P. (1997) Jamison's story: talent nurtured in troubled times. *Roeper Review*, 19(3): 142–149.

Hernandez, E. (1998) Assets and obstacles in community leadership. *Journal of Community Psychology*, 26(3): 269–280.

McDonald, L. (1997) Building on the strengths and assets of families and communities. *Families and Societies*, 78(2): 115–116.

Maker, J. (1993) Creativity, intelligence, and problem-solving: a definition and design for cross-cultural research and measurement related to giftedness. *Gifted Education International*, 9: 68–77.

Passow, A. H. and Schiff, J. H. (1989) Educating gifted persons who are caring and concerned. *Gifted Education International*, 6: 5–7.

Peterson, J. S. (1997) Bright, tough, and resilient – and not in a gifted program. *Journal of Secondary Gifted Education*, 97(8): 121–137.

Pillay, A. L., Naidoo, P. and Lockhat, M. R. (1999) Psychopathology in urban and rural/peri-urban children seeking mental health care. *South African Journal of Psychology*, 29(4): 179–183.

Salovey, P. and Mayer, J. D. (1990) Emotional intelligence. *Imagination, Cognition and Personality*, 9: 185–211.

Shumow, L. (1997) Daily experiences and adjustment of gifted low-income urban children at home and school. *Roeper Review*, 20(1): 35–39.

Sisk, D. (2002) Spiritual intelligence: the tenth intelligence that integrates all other intelligences. *Gifted Education International*, 16(3): 208–213.

Sternberg, R. J. (1999) The theory of successful intelligence. *Review of General Psychology*, 3: 292–316.

Sternberg, R. J. (2001) Wisdom and education. *Perspectives in Education*, 19(4): 1–16.

Van Rooyen, J. (2002) *BarOn Emotional Quotient Inventory: Training Manual.* Randburg: Jopie van Rooyen and Partners.

Wallace, B. (2004) Lifting Underachievement. Keynote address, LEA Conference, London, June 2004.

Wallace, B., Maker, J., Cave, D. and Chandler, S. (2004) *Thinking Skills and Problem-Solving: An Inclusive Approach*. London: David Fulton.

4.4   Conflict resolution 3: classism

Suzanne Rawlins

The parents of gifted students in a large school district met once every six weeks. This 'Gifted Parent Network' heard presentations about topics relevant to their gifted learners, provided support with parenting tips and socialized. After several months of meeting, not-so-subtle complaints were voiced regarding the tardiness of certain parents. The meetings were held from 5:30 p.m. to about 7:15 p.m. so working parents could participate. Many attended on their way home from work, delaying their family dinner hour with their families. When members arrived late, information had to be repeated. Questions would be asked that had already been addressed. The group grew irritated with the latecomers. Rumblings began about creating two groups: the punctual and latecomers.

Within a short time, the late parents realized that the other parents were disgruntled. One very brave father asked to speak to the group. Time was running short, and the chairperson was concerned that openly addressing the issue might cause an immediate rift that could lead to lack of future participation. However, how could the chairperson deny a parent's right to speak?

5 Ethnic promise and prejudice

5.1 An Indian perspective on gifted education: the synergy of India

Krishna Maitra

India, the world's largest democracy, has a population expected to reach 1264 billion by 2016 (Bose 2000). Although the Indian Constitution directs all states to provide free and compulsory education up to age 14, with such population density, it is a challenging task to provide even minimum health, education and employment. India has expanded primary education, but the dropout rate is high, although impassioned debate has resulted in a universal urge to build a society of humane, committed, participative and productive citizens.

In 1985, the Indian government asked schools to nominate their 'meritorious' students with the aim of providing a boarding school in each district, allocating 75 percent of the places for rural children, and 33 percent of total students should be girls. The scheme has almost died under its financial weight, although 495 such schools are sparsely scattered across the different states of India, using the unitary IQ definition of 'intelligence' as the selection criterion.

The National Survey (1995–1996) reported that 31 percent of children in the age group 6–10 and 28 percent in the age group 11–13 were not in school (Bose 2000). The number of children who have never been to school is around 100 million, and many of these children belong to economically and educationally deprived families, although it is customary in India to involve all children in household and/or farm work:

- wage-earning child workers and bonded labourers approximate 44 million
- urban deprived children who live in slums, squatter colonies, streets and railway platforms include rag pickers, shoe shiners, hawkers and domestic servants, number 300,000 in Calcutta and Delhi alone

- migrant children number 30,000 in only one district of a state
- other victims of poverty are children of sex workers and primitive tribes.

(Jhingran 2003)

Contextual intricacies of development: social, economic, political and educational sub-cultural perspectives

Education for the adivasi (tribal) groups and the dalits (low caste)

India has a complex social profile representing various economic categories: adivasi who specialize in agriculture, carpentry, black-smithy, pottery and hunting. Each of these adivasi communities possess their own ways of knowledge acquisition and way of life.

Since the early 1990s, non-adivasi groups have moved into these formerly indigenous areas questioning the adivasi customs and ways of working, and introducing new methods of mass production. Many adivasi groups have lost ownership of land, skills and traditions, migrating to the cities in search of work. A jungle of slums has sprung up and children are left to fend for themselves while parents do menial, poorly paid jobs.

Dalits used to be the untouchables, and although the government has tried to bring about change, for example, by promoting their unique literature, the school dropout rate is high. Child labour is two to three times higher among dalits and adivasi groups than the rest of the population (Bose 2000). With regard to adult workers, 64 percent of dalits and 50 percent of adivasi people work as labourers compared with 30 percent of other groups. This, obviously, has serious implications for the educational development of their children.

Upper caste farmers have also been forced to migrate to different states in search of better prospects. However, some of the rich farmers can afford city education, or education abroad. Many youth belonging to farming families are away from their parents, and eventually help their families financially, buying land and building homes. But poor farmers cannot even retain their land. So, either they become agricultural labourers or migrate to cities for survival, and cannot afford education. Also, gender inequality results in girls, particularly Muslims, dropping out of schools.

Language: a vehicle of discrimination

India's multilingualism is reflected in nearly 3000 mother tongues: however, English is the dominant language of teaching and learning, with 'unofficial' indigenous languages facing extinction. As language and culture are closely related, restrictions in language choice can have serious emotional and educational effects. The scheduled castes and tribes, and the smaller ethnic and cultural groups, are not allowed to learn through their own language/dialect. Hindi is the national language, but many states maintain their state language as the official medium.

This means that a child must learn Hindi, English and the state language irrespective of his/her own mother tongue. In classroom transaction, an adivasi, dalit or minority child has no home language link with the curriculum. It is inevitable that the children belonging to these groups do not even start school (Pattanayak 1997).

Though researchers recommend that adivasi children should use their mother tongue for the first five years of schooling, adivasi schools primarily use regional language, often thrashing children for not using 'proper' tongue. Moreover, the child's inability to speak a standard language is usually considered as a lack of mental ability.

Access to school

There are many habitats in remote areas. For example, at least 700 families live on small phundis (floating bodies of soil and decaying matter), on the Loktak – a fresh water lake in north-east India. The children have no access to schools but are rich in native talents, smart enough to adapt to adverse situations, and to take care of their siblings.

The strengths of adivasi

Misra (1996) found adivasi students generally scored highly on flexibility and fluency measures of creativity, suggesting that adivasi place greater emphasis on independence and autonomy. Misra also found that forest children were also highly skilled in differentiation tasks, learning a wide range of skills contextually from observation and practice. In addition, children making and selling goods such as rope products and pottery were highly skilled in 'business' acumen and the contextual skills of number and market communication.

Parental support and individual resilience

Virja (1991) has shown that parental support is a more powerful correlate with positive development than socio-economic status or intelligence. This gives a clue to excellence found among poor and marginalized children when they are given opportunity for education. UNICEF (1994) reports that there are several million children who are deprived because of riots, wars, natural disasters, death of parents, disability or poverty, yet many not only survive but also surmount disadvantage. Verma (1999) argues that these children have a resilience developed through the necessity of having to survive deprivation and disadvantage.

Traditionally, the Indian family is not simply a social unit: it constitutes a value in itself (Misra 1996). The familial self or 'we self' is commonly present among Indians. Individual ambition and needs are sacrificed for the family, which is the outcome of an 'emotional-relationship-centred' culture, and good care centres for children are highly valued and esteemed. Aptekar and Stocklin (1997) note that the term 'children under difficult circumstances' is loaded with notions about children, childhood, cultures and coping from a dominant cultural perspective.

While 'middle class' children go to school understanding the concept of formal schooling, the same might not hold true for a child from a poor family. Aptekar and Stocklin (1997) urge for a more sensitive approach to 'culturally different' children who may have particular strengths such as coping under stress. In their view, children in 'deprived' circumstances tend to be active constructors of the coping mechanisms they need to survive their adverse circumstances. In addition, these children receive emotional support from the familial social network. Even children working away from home as rag-pickers, porters or domestic servants, often talk warmly about their families and send support money to their homes. The studies by Prasad (1993), Arora (1986) and Majumdar (1991) suggest that the sense of belonging to the family is responsible for helping these children survive through their difficult days.

Virja (1991) has reported that many poor families struggle to support an able child through school, but for a girl, this support is not generally available since she is perceived as a communal family member rather than as an individual. Indian girls, irrespective of social class, are trained to be good house makers, and even middle class urban girls compromise with their career for the sake of their prospective marital life. The western perspective of diversity is mainly based on personal identity, autonomy and individualism, but the Indian woman's identity is defined by her relationship to others. Nevertheless, India has produced many noted female writers, dancers and politicians, but all of these great women were alert to their familial responsibilities.

Government initiatives

> The development of our children is a true indicator of our progress, of the power of a vibrant democracy to fulfill its promises to people.
>
> (Murli Manohar Joshi, the then Minister of HRD,
> Government of India)

India is home to 21 percent of the developing world's young children with 170 million children under 6 years of age, making up 17.5 percent of India's population. UNICEF and World Bank support early years programmes in impoverished and remote areas, and the government has developed community programmes for early child care; this also enables young girls who previously looked after siblings to attend school and training centres focusing on vocational skills and self-esteem. CARE (USA Agency for International Development) helps to provide food to 12 million primary pupils and nearly 6 million pre-school children. In all endeavours, the community is closely involved, reflecting the community's concerns, setting the aims and monitoring the outcomes of such initiatives.

However, since survival depends on seasonal crops, parents often feel ambivalent towards the benefits of education since they migrate in search of jobs and are unwilling to leave the children behind. Another factor is that children themselves reject the schooling system since it is alien to their culture. Nevertheless, many parents are working long hours to save the money to send their children to school, and non-governmental organizations (NGOs) are working to achieve universal literacy.

At this point it is important to ask a number of questions:

- Does the Indian government really understand the complexity of educational need in the country?
- Do teachers understand how children in different cultures construct knowledge?
- Is there understanding of the importance of a child's sense of identity and self-esteem?
- In a country of such great diversity, should a majority perception of education and learning be imposed on vulnerable groups, particularly those who are scared to think 'what they think'?

The concept of giftedness

What does it mean to be gifted in a particular local culture?

Middle class parents have high career aspirations for their children since occupational status and power depend on academic achievement. Private expensive educational institutions are increasing exponentially as rich families pay high fees for their children's education, often sending them to western countries.

However, I would suggest that in an environment of extreme poverty, spiritual, emotional and social giftedness are shown by the sheer joy of living with dignity and self-esteem, showing love and affection to the family and others. You can walk through India's countless villages and hear natural untrained music which reflects purity of Sur, Taal and Dhun. I also suggest that Indian children possess an inherent sense of 'goodness' and 'brightness', their naive intelligence and intuitive sense are amazing.

> 'Marvelous children of the "City of Joy", Kovalski would say, 'little innocent beings nourished on poverty, from whom the life force never ceased to burst forth. Their freedom from care, their zest for life, their magical smiles and dark faces set off luminous gazes that colored the entire world in which they lived with beauty'.
>
> (Lapierre 1999: 399)

So, the concept of 'giftedness' varies greatly in India depending on the social and economic strata of people. 'When we talk of the unusual child, it has to be in a social context, not the established formal framework' (Chatopadhyay 1984). Academic brilliance is not understood by people who struggle for their daily bread. But that does not mean that children belonging to poor, marginalized families lack talent. Talent is caste free (Kunnunkal 1984).

Many children manage to earn a few extra rupees, a boy might learn tricks of daily survival and the nuances of family business at an early age. A girl learns to cook for the family and take care of her younger siblings. These are the traits, which are recognized and nurtured because they make the lives of poor people slightly better and happier. The indicator of 'giftedness' would be then be 'alert, quick and committed to the cause'.

A curriculum for the future

In India, there cannot be one definition of 'giftedness'. People who are educated in elite schools based on western concepts of excellence, consider high school achievement as the only criterion of 'giftedness'. To this elite group, poor people are as 'uncultured' as they are 'uneducated'. Since Indian independence, the 'elite' group has occupied the major positions in professions and bureaucracy: a 'superior' class has evolved who admire 'English' education and send their children abroad for higher education. English is the medium of instruction in these schools and the gateway to prestigious employment. In contrast, the government schools are for poor or lower middle class children, and Hindi is the medium of instruction.

Surely, a curriculum should take shape in the context of life and the child should be able to see her reflection in it. The child should have space to explore her emotional world and unrealized talent. Currently, we have a curriculum 'which is restrictive and irrelevant to the concerns of the majority of children' (Page 1996: 129).

In multicultural, multilingual India, we cannot have a national curriculum. We need to decentralize even the very process of curriculum development. In adivasi areas or remote hilly regions, district administration should evolve a curriculum framework based on local needs mediated through local dialects at least for primary children. Such a curriculum is born out of the soil one stands on: the child can then relate to meaningful learning experiences. Self-motivation and life skills need to drive a curriculum centred on learning how to learn.

The present curriculum is subject compartmentalized and examination-oriented with tests based on memory of facts and data. A curriculum of the future needs to be based on the principles of self-evaluation and self-monitoring, leading to autonomy so that individuals can shape their own learning (Page 1996: 131).

The curriculum should be driven by the community who express their needs, use their expertise and indigenous resources. Schooling needs to be flexible so that girls, when they are free from their domestic work, have time for learning.

The processes of interaction with the child should take into account different cultural backgrounds and different kinds of intelligence. Teachers need to be able to modify their content and pedagogy according to the particular context. In addition, teachers need to be proficient in local dialect/language and to belong to the same cultural community.

Indigenous ways of learning should be respected and should be made a part of 'teacher-education' curriculum. Most teacher-education institutions in India are based on western concepts: pupil-teachers are more fluent in theories propounded by foreigners rather than those of Indians.

A final reflection

'Disadvantage' has been coined to veil the true meaning of 'Diversity'. When we deconstruct the word 'disadvantage', we will reconstruct our understanding of the concept of 'diversity'.

Key questions

Today's world, despite differences in language, religion, culture, ethnicity and ecological diversity, is a global village: we need to celebrate difference and diversity. Globally we need also to reflect on the following questions:

1   Why do most curricula worldwide fail to reflect the cultural, historical contribution of the indigenous people of their country? How could schools incorporate multicultural issues into their curriculum?
2   Why do we negate diversity by propagating the concept of mainstreaming? Isn't the concept of a 'national curriculum' a rejection of diversity?
3   Why aren't we sensitive to issues of empowerment with regard to gender, race, and ethnic minorities? How could schools engender greater understanding?

References

Aptekar, L. and Stocklin, D. (1997) Children in particularly different circumstances: a cross-cultural perspective, in J. Berry, P. Das and T. S. Saraswathi (eds) *Handbook of Cross-Cultural Psychology*, 2nd edn, volume 2. Boston, MA: Allyn and Bacon.

Arora, S. (1986) Consequences of the child at work; cases of domestic servants and children working in the 'dhabas', unpublished master's thesis, Department of Home Science, University of Delhi, India.

Bose, A. B. (2000) *The State of Children in India: Promises to Keep*. New Delhi: MANOHAR.

Chattopadhyay, K. D. (1984) Inaugural Lecture on Gifted Children. *Report of the National Seminar on Identification and Development of Gifted Children*. New Delhi: National Institute of Public Cooperation and Child Development.

Jhingran, D. (2003) Universalization of elementary education: government policies and perspectives, in N. Kabeer, G. B. Nambissan and R. Subhramanian (eds) *Child Labour and the Rights to Education in South Asia: Needs versus Rights*. New Delhi: Sage.

Kunnunkal, T. V. (1984) Keynote address on gifted children. *Report of the National Seminar on Identification and Development of Gifted Children*. New Delhi: National Institute of Public Cooperation and Child Development.

Lapierre, D. (1999) *The City of Joy*. Delhi: Full Circle.

Majumdar, R. (1991) Profile of child workers in a 'Zardosi' workshop, unpublished master's thesis, Department of Home Science, University of Delhi.

Misra, R. C. (1996) Perceptual differentiation in relation to children's daily life activities. *Social Science International*, 12: 1–11.

Page, J. (1996) Education systems as agents of change: an overview of futures education, in R. A. Slaughter (ed.) *New Thinking for a New Millennium*. New York: Routledge.

Pattanayak, D. P. (1997) Language curriculum for teacher educators, in D. N. Khosla (ed.) *National Council for Teacher Education*, NCTE document 97/16 28–29. New Delhi: NCTE.

Prasad, A. (1993) Tender hands at work: a study of working children at market places, unpublished master's dissertation, Department of Home Science, University of Delhi.

UNICEF (1994) *The Right to be a Child*. New Delhi: India Country Office.

Verma, S. (1999) Socialization for survival: developmental issues among working street children in India, in M. Raffaelli and R. Larson (eds) *Developmental Issues among Homeless and Working Street Youth*. San Francisco, CA: Jossey-Bass.

Virja, A. (1991) Maternal literacy and school performance of girls in class II in a municipal corporation school, unpublished master's dissertation, Lady Irwin College, University of Delhi.

5.2   The development of creative talent: the Brazilian scenario

Eunice M. L. Soriano de Alencar and Denise de Souza Fleith

Since Guilford's seminal article in 1950, a substantial volume of studies on creativity have been developed, addressing personal attributes associated with creativity, as well as different aspects of the creative process and product. More recently, a resurgence of interest in creativity as a social, as well as an individual phenomenon, has been observed with an increasing number of studies on the influence of the social and historical context in creativity expression, development and recognition.

The complex interplay of interactions between the individual, social, cultural and historical variables is stressed in various recent theoretical perspectives, such as Sternberg and Lubart's (1993, 1995) investment theory of creativity, Amabile's (1983, 1990) componential model of creativity and Csikszentmihalyi's (1994, 1999) systems view of creativity. Such approaches emphasize distinct elements of the social context which nurture and recognize the creative expression.

One topic that has been addressed since Guilford's (1950) article, is the need for appropriate conditions to nurture creativity in schools. Torrance (1970, 1987, 1995), for example, called attention to the need to make elementary, secondary and higher education more creative. Torrance (1995) justified this by pointing to the demands of a highly changing world which requires abilities, skills, attitudes, and values to cope creatively with new problems. Other authors share his view: Cohen (1997), Tan (2001), Strom and Strom (2002) and Alencar (1995a, 1995b, 2000a) have described different countries' government interest in promoting educational policy and practice that assure the development of the students' creative abilities. The rationale for this interest is the recognition that the capacity for innovation and problem-solving is a requirement for success in this rapidly changing world, with its uncertainty, complexity and instability.

In spite of the increasing literature regarding the environmental influence on creativity, misconceptions on creativity occur that help to prevent the promotion of adequate conditions for the development and expression of creativity in the educational setting and in society. It is common, for example, to assume that creativity is a natural talent or gift which characterizes only a few individuals. There is also the belief that creative expression occurs independently of environmental conditions, suggesting a unilateral and individual conception of creativity, with an underestimation of the influence of school and society in its development and expression.

The purpose of this chapter is to describe some Brazilian studies on creativity, and how it has been implemented in programs for the gifted.

Characteristics of Brazil, its educational system and culture

Brazil is a country with a population of over 160 million (Alencar 1993; Fleith 2002). Most of the population inhabits the dense urban areas, while the vast rural areas are sparsely populated: there is unfair income distribution with a high incidence of poverty. Brazilian people generally are group-oriented, extroverted, inclined to be emotionally demonstrative (Fleith 1999), and usually flexible and optimistic that a solution can always be found.

The country faces many challenges: there are insufficient numbers of schools, and consequently, many children attend school for only two or three hours each day. School failure and truancy are common, and teachers' prejudices blame the children for their failures. Many teachers ignore the possibility that their teaching strategies, their low expectations of the poorest students, the number of hours a student attends school, poor conditions of the majority of schools with no equipment or libraries, account for the low achievement of pupils. In addition, the official curriculum is more appropriate for middle-class pupils.

There is a large number of elementary and secondary private schools catering for middle and upper-class children and they are, in general, better equipped, enrolling students from the fifth grade. Middle-class students are also likely to be enrolled in extra-curricular activities for part of the day, taking music or a second language classes, as well as sports. Most of these families are aware of the importance of schooling and try to offer the best to their children.

Middle-class children start school early in a kindergarten, and stay for three years, which gives them another advantage in relation to lower-class children. Due to the insufficient number of public kindergarten, many children from poor families start elementary school without the necessary skills to succeed in school.

The typical educational environment is not prepared to meet gifted students' needs. Misconceptions and lack of information regarding giftedness are still widespread: consequently, little attention is given to the affective and cognitive aspects of talent development. In addition, the Portuguese word for gifted, *superdotado*, conveys an image that giftedness is genius, or an exceptional all-rounder. Consequently the most talented and able students remain unnoticed, with no possibility of developing their talents more fully, nor with opportunities for discovering and nurturing multiple talents in schools.

Studies on creativity in the educational setting

Since the mid-1970s, our studies (Alencar 1995a, 1995b; Alencar and Fleith 2004; Fleith 2002) have suggested several inhibiting practices to creativity that are common in the Brazilian schools:

- emphasis on the correct response, reinforcing the fear of making errors and failing
- exaggerated emphasis on memorization and reproduction of often irrelevant knowledge
- low expectations of students' creative potential with emphasis on students' ignorance and incapacity, rather than on their competencies
- emphasis on students' obedience and passivity, rather than on their imaginative capacities.

To know more about the conditions for nurturing creativity, graduate students were requested to nominate from their present and past teachers, those who provided enabling conditions for creative development, and those who inhibited creativity (Alencar 2000b).

The facilitating teachers were described as those who provided opportunities for students to question, participate, criticize and reflect on the content discussed in class. Also, the teachers made use of a variety of activities, and were viewed as having an advanced competence in his/her field. They also developed a friendly relationship based on respect and cordiality, were open to divergent ideas, flexible, self-confident, punctual, responsible and enthusiastic.

The descriptions of the teachers who inhibited creativity featured: lectures centered on reproduction of knowledge, unmotivating didactics, content presented mechanically, monotonous classes. In the teacher–student relationship, students felt ignored, were fearful, anxious and embarrassed. The inhibiting teachers were described as authoritarian, arrogant, inflexible and excessively critical.

Cross-cultural studies on creativity

Brazilian researchers have investigated differences in creativity among cultures. Wechsler (1985), for instance, compared Brazilian and American elementary school children with respect to figural creativity using the Torrance Tests of Creative Thinking (TTCT). Regarding figural creativity, the findings indicated that Brazilian children presented more emotional expressiveness, unusual and internal visualization, and extended boundaries in their drawings when compared with American children. On the other hand, American children presented more humor and movement in their drawing compared to Brazilian students.

Fleith (1999) investigated the effects of a creativity training program on creative abilities and self-concept in elementary monolingual (American students) and bilingual (Brazilian immigrant students) classrooms. The creativity training program, 'New Directions in Creativity' (Renzulli 1986) slightly improved the creative abilities of students in the treatment group. However, placement in a monolingual or bilingual classroom was not found to affect students' creative abilities nor their self-concept. Moreover, the qualitative analysis suggested that a supportive and encouraging classroom in which the creativity training program was implemented, was an essential factor in the success of the program. Furthermore, the creativity training program had a positive impact on the self-concept of less academically able students from both monolingual and bilingual classrooms.

Obstacles to the expression of personal creativity were examined among 290 educators from Brazil, Cuba and Portugal by Alencar and Martínez (1998). The participants were requested to complete the following sentence: 'I would be more creative if . . .'. Responses were analysed through content analysis. While Brazilian and Portuguese educators indicated internal obstacles more frequently, Cuban educators pointed out social barriers. It was noticed that Brazilian and Portuguese professionals reported the fear of making mistakes, failure, and criticism as the most frequently occurring personal obstacles. On the other hand, the most common personal obstacles mentioned by Cubans were their insufficient observation, analysis and reflection.

In a cross-cultural study conducted by Alencar et al. (2003) personal obstacles to creativity between 385 Brazilian and 305 Mexican university students were investigated. The *Obstacles of Personal Creativity Inventory*, designed and validated by Alencar, was administered to these students. Significant differences were observed between Brazilian and Mexican students in the cluster of obstacles named Lack of Motivation. In this regard, Mexican students obtained higher scores compared to Brazilian students. Significant differences were also noticed between male and female students in the cluster of obstacles named Inhibition/Shyness. The mean of female students was higher than male students' mean on this factor. Differences between Mexicans and Brazilians were not found with respect to the factors Lack of Time/Opportunity and Social Repression.

The findings of the studies suggested that creativity may be fostered or hindered by cultural characteristics such as socialization, beliefs, values and traditions. Moreover, the socio-economic status and historical roots of a nation can also influence the development of the creative expression.

Creativity in Brazilian programs for the gifted

Gifted programs available in Brazil have used a multiplicity of criteria for the identification process: observation by teachers using a checklist, nomination by parents, and psychological assessment which includes intelligence, creativity and personality indicators.

In the enrichment program for gifted students implemented by the Secretary of Education of Federal District (SEFD), the Test for Creative Thinking – Drawing Production (TCT-DP: Urban and Jellen 1996) has been used to identify creative gifted students. Creativity activities are also used in the identification procedures to identify fluency, flexibility, originality, imagination and self-concept (Alencar 2000a; Virgolim et al. 2003). The Scales for Rating the Behavioral Characteristics of Superior Students-R (SRBCSS-R) (Renzulli et al. 2000) are also employed to identify talented students and to assess their strengths.

The Three-Ring Conception of Giftedness (Renzulli 1978) is the theoretical background supporting the SEFD program in which highly creative and productive individuals are characterized by three interlocking clusters: Above average ability, Task commitment and Creativity.

Furthermore, the program adopts the Enrichment Triad Model (Renzulli and Reis 1997) which develops Type I, II and III enrichment activities. In Type I, students are exposed to a wide variety of topics, themes, and disciplines that are not covered in the regular curriculum. Type II activities promote the development of the thinking and feeling processes and teachers are especially trained to carry out creativity techniques and activities with students. In Type III activities, students develop authentic products by acquiring advanced-level understanding of the knowledge and methodology.

Maia-Pinto (2002) investigated the effects of this program on students' creativity levels. Seventy-seven students from elementary and high schools attended the program: the students' report cards and the Creative Thinking Test – Drawing Production (Urban and Jellen 1996) were the instruments used to assess the impact on the students' academic and creative performance. The academically gifted students showed a better academic performance than artistic talented students, while the artistically talented students obtained a higher score in the creativity test.

Also Farias-Chagas (2003) investigated the relationship of gifted and non-gifted students' creativity level and their parents. The sample consisted of fourteen gifted students attending the SEDF program and their parents, and fourteen non-gifted students and their parents. The data was collected through the Test of Creative Thinking – Drawing Production (TCT-DP). No relationship was observed between creativity levels of parents and children. However, the gifted students obtained a higher performance on creativity tests when compared to non-gifted students. Likewise, Aspesi (2003) studied the standards occurring in the family processes relating to the development of gifted children at preschool age. The two variables investigated were non-verbal intelligence and creativity of parents, mothers and children. Twelve preschool age children, who attended the SEFD program, participated in this study, and their respective families composed of twelve mothers and nine fathers. A positive correlation was observed between non-verbal intelligence of both the father and his children. However, no relationship was noticed between children and parents with respect to creativity.

Virgolim and Gubbins (2001) found that gifted and talented students, from ages 9 to 17, who were attending this enrichment program, perceived themselves as both creative and intelligent. However, the ideal student profile described by those students was the schoolhouse type of giftedness (Renzulli 1986).

Conclusion

Recent trends in creativity research state that 'creativity is a systemic rather than an individual phenomenon' (Csikszentmihalyi 1996: 23). Therefore, creativity cannot be enhanced by isolating individuals from their context. According to Amabile (1995):

> It is obvious that there would be no creativity whatsoever without the person and his or her cognitive abilities, personality dispositions, and other personal resources; neither would there be any creativity whatsoever without a context in which to create – a context of resources, education, exposure, encouragement, stimulation, and appreciation.
>
> (Amabile 1995: 425)

Therefore, it is important to study and understand the emergence of creativity in different contexts in order to establish conditions that will maximize opportunities for the development of creative talents around the world. This plea is relevant especially in the case of developing countries like Brazil. As highlighted by Wechsler (2001), a Brazilian researcher,

> Although the international research has pointed out the wide range of traits and behaviors of the creative person that can be identified across cultures, there are preferences regarding behavioral and thinking styles in specific populations.
>
> (Wechsler 2001: 224)

Key questions

1   How important is the development of creativity in the curriculum? What teaching methodologies encourage creative thinking?
2   How should teachers be trained so that they are confident to develop children's creative questioning skills?
3   Design a series of lessons to develop children's creative thinking, and highlight the techniques you would use.

References

Alencar, E. M. L. S. (1993) Developing the potential of disadvantaged pupils in Brazil, in B. Wallace and H. B. Adams (eds) *Worldwide Perspectives on the Gifted Disadvantaged*. Bicester: AB Academic.

Alencar, E. M. L. S. (1995a) Challenges to the development of creative talent. *Gifted and Talented International*, 10: 5–8.

Alencar, E. M. L. S. (1995b) *Criatividade* [Creativity]. Brasília: Editora da Universidade de Brasília.

Alencar, E. M. L. S. (2000a) *Como desenvolver o potencial criador* [How to develop the creative potential], 8th edn. Petrópolis: Vozes.

Alencar, E. M. L. S. (2000b) O perfil do professor facilitador e do professor inibidor da criatividade segundo estudantes de pós-graduação [The profile of facilitating and inhibiting professor according to graduate students]. *Boletim da Academia Paulista de Psicologia*, 19: 84–94.

Alencar, E. M. L. S. and Fleith, D. S. (2004) Professors' and students' perceptions of incentive for creativity at university courses: a comparative study. *Gifted and Talented International*, 19: 24–28.

Alencar, E. M. L. S. and Martínez, A. M. (1998) *Barreiras a expressao da criatividade entre profissionais brasileiros, cubanos e portugueses* (Obstacles to the expression of creativity among Brazilian, Cuban and Portuguese educators). *Psicología Escolar e Educacional*, 2: 23–32.

Alencar, E. M. L. S., Fleith, D. S. and Martínez, A. M. (2003) Obstacles to personal creativity between Brazilian and Mexican university students: a comparative study. *Journal of Creative Behavior*, 37: 179–192.

Amabile, T. M. (1983) *The Social Psychology of Creativity*. New York: Springer.

Amabile, T. M. (1990) Within you, without you: the social psychology of creativity and beyond, in M. A. Runco (ed.) *Theories of Creativity*. Newbury Park, CA: Sage.

Amabile, T. M. (1995) Attributions of creativity: what are the consequences? *Creativity Research Journal*, 8: 423–426.

Aspesi, C. C. (2003) Processos familiares relacionados ao desenvolvimento de comportamentos de superdotação em crianças de idade pré-escolar [Family processes related to the development of gifted behaviors in preschool children], unpublished master's thesis, University of Brasilia, Brasilia, Brazil.

Cohen, D. (1997) Singapore wants its universities to encourage more creativity. *Chronicle of Higher Education*, 44(2): A71–A72.

Csikszentmihalyi, M. (1994) The domain of creativity, in D. H. Feldman, M. Csikszentmihalyi and H. Gardner (eds) *Changing the World: A Framework for the Study of Creativity*. Westport, CT: Praeger.

Csikszentmihalyi, M. (1996) *Creativity*. New York: HarperCollins.

Csikszentmihalyi, M. (1999) Implications of a system perspective for the study of creativity, in R. J. Sternberg (ed.) *Handbook of Creativity*. New York: Cambridge University Press.

Farias-Chagas, J. (2003) Características familiares relacionadas ao desenvolvimento de comportamentos de superdotação em alunos de nível sócio-econômico desfavorecido [Family characteristics related to the development of gifted behaviors in students from low socio-economic class], unpublished master's thesis, University of Brasilia, Brasilia, Brazil.

Fleith, D. S. (1999) The effects of a creativity training program on creative abilities and self-concept in monolingual and bilingual elementary classrooms, unpublished doctoral dissertation, University of Connecticut, Storrs, CT.

Fleith, D. S. (2002) Creativity in the Brazilian culture, in W. J. Lonner, D. L. Dinnel, S. A. Hayes and D. N. Sattler (eds) *Online Readings in Psychology and Culture*. Bellingham, WA: Western Washington University, Department of Psychology, Center for Cross-Cultural Research Website: http://www.wwu.edu/~culture

Guilford, J. P. (1950) Creativity. *American Psychologist*, 5: 444–454.

Maia-Pinto, R. R. (2002) Avaliação das práticas educacionais implementadas em um programa de atendimento a alunos superdotados e talentosos [Evaluation of the educational practices implemented in a program for gifted and talented students], unpublished master's thesis, University of Brasilia, Brasilia, Brazil.

Renzulli, J. S. (1978) What makes giftedness? Reexamining a definition. *Phi Delta Kappan*, 60: 180–184, 261.

Renzulli, J. S. (1986) *New Directions in Creativity*. Mansfield Center, CT: Creative Learning Press.

Renzulli, J. S. (1992) A general theory for the development of creative productivity in young people, in F. Monks and W. Peters (eds) *Talent for the Future*. Assen/Maastricht, The Netherlands: Van Gorcum.

Renzulli, J. S. and Reis, S. M. (1997) *The Schoolwide Enrichment Model*, 2nd edn. Mansfield Center, CT: Creative Learning Press.

Renzulli, J. S., Smith, L. H., White, A. J., Callahan, C. M., Hartman, R. K. and Westberg, K. L. (2000) *Scales for Rating the Behavior Characteristics of Superior Students. Revised edition (SRBCSS-R)*. Mansfield Center, CT: Creative Learning Press.

Sternberg, R. J. and Lubart, T. I. (1993) Creative giftedness: a multivariate investment approach. *Gifted Child Quarterly*, 37: 7–15.

Sternberg, R. J. and Lubart, T. I. (1995) *Defying the Crowd: Cultivating Creativity in a Culture of Conformity*. New York: The Free Press.

Strom, R. D. and Strom, P. S. (2002) Changing the rules: education for creative thinking. *Journal of Creative Behavior*, 36: 183–200.

Tan, A. G. (2001) Singaporean teachers' perception of activities useful for fostering creativity. *Journal of Creative Behavior*, 35: 131–148.

Torrance, E. P. (1970) *Encouraging Creativity in the Classroom*. Dubuque, IA: C. Brown.

Torrance, E. P. (1987) Teaching for creativity, in S. G. Isaksen (ed.) *Frontiers of Creativity Research: Beyond the Basics*. Buffalo, NY: Bearly.

Torrance, E. P. (1995) *Why Fly? A Philosophy of Creativity*. Norwood, NJ: Ablex.

Urban, K. K. and Jellen, H. G. (1996) *Test for Creative Thinking: Drawing Production Manual*. Frankfurt: Swets.

Virgolim, A. M. R. and Gubbins, E. J. (2001) Creativity and intelligence: a study of Brazilian gifted and talented students. Paper presented at the Fourteenth Biennial Conference of the World Council for Gifted and Talented Children, Barcelona, Spain, August.

Virgolim, A. M. R., Fleith, D. S. and Neves-Pereira, M. S. (2003) *Toc, Toc Plim, Plim! Lidando com as Emoções e Brincando com o Pensamento Através da Criatividade* [Knock, Knock Plim, Plim! Dealing with emotions and playing with thinking by creativity], 5th edn. Campinas: Papirus.

Wechsler, S. M. (1985) A identificaçao do talento criativo nos Estados Unidos e no Brasil [The identification of the creative talent in the United States and Brazil]. *Psicologia: Teoria e Pesquisa*, 1: 140–146.

Wechsler, S. M. (2001) Criatividade na cultura brasileira: uma década de estudos [Creativity in the Brazilian culture: a decade of studies]. *Teoria, Investigação e Prática*, 6: 215–226.

5.3   Diversity and gifted education: four Brazilian examples

Christina Cupertino, Zenita Guenther, Cristina Delou and Susana Pérez

Educators experience impasses when trying to transfer researchers' results into practice, since researchers often exclude the contexts due to the procedures considered scientifically reliable. This leads educators to a 'logic of experimentation, disappointment and abdication' because practice is much more complex than any theory (Hédoux 1994).

Educational studies based on qualitative methods are still submitted to criticism, because they are thought to be oriented to 'particular experiences', lacking objective validation. This divide between scientific and technologic development and those intended for education, severely affect general and special education programs (Ribeiro 2003).

However, the field of gifted education has gradually shown agreement that systematic intervention is necessary to encourage the development of ability in all children by individualizing the curriculum. Such concerns are reflected in educational legislation, but prejudices remain concerning the abilities of the disadvantaged majority of the population. Also, in Brazil, the need to reconstruct the meaning of 'citizenship' and 'equal opportunities' has been the priority concern after many years of dictatorship. However, the educational model adopted by the official institutions still alienates educators from any discussion or decision-making process.

Considering the above, we have decided to present some positive examples of gifted programmes in Brazil, rather than neutral reports distant from daily reality, hopefully offering readers the opportunity to find resonance with their practice.

Center for Potential and Talent Development – CEDET

CEDET's conception and organization are derived from humanistic education principles, committed to the development of highly able/gifted children. The project is not centered on specific talents but on the growth of personality, by strengthening the self, cultivating good relationships with others and building acceptable relationships with the world. Considering the self, besides studies focusing on motivation and task commitment, we focus on developing 'expertise in self-understanding, decision-making and self-regulation' (Moon 2003: 11), and on moral values, ethics and character building (Tirri 2003). Harmonious living with each other, leadership and social competence are dimensions that should be included in gifted education (Pyryt 2003). The third basis for CEDET's plan derives from working with scientific knowledge within the various fields of study.

CEDET's pedagogical organization encompasses three broad enrichment areas:

- *Communication, social organization and humanities:* where children can find enrichment through activities related to social life and human relationships, including groups and associations, languages, media communication, and ways of dealing with sharing, interacting and living together.
- *Research, science and technology:* which opens doors to the world of scientific knowledge, building relationships between people, and understanding the world around us.
- *Creativity, personal expressions and skills:* which explores the self, and personal feelings, cultivating one's own body and fostering the pursuit of common goals, such as in sports, recreation or performing arts.

CEDET provides educational support for talented children from elementary to high school level, working in cooperation with schools and the community, in a network formed by parent and friends affiliated to the Association for Supporting Talent (ASPAT). Both public and private schools support the Center by providing teachers and accommodation. Community involvement and participation is called upon according to the individual plans worked out with the children.

This complex network is regulated under ASPAT supervision. Once a child or a group shows a specific interest, we find someone suitable in the community to work with them. Each semester, about 60–70 volunteer instructors develop activities for 450–500 enrolled students. The children go to school for part of the day and attend CEDET at other times. The children's work is negotiated through an individual plan requiring about 10 hours a week.

The identification process (Guenther et al. 1998) relies on direct observation conducted in the following stages:

- At the end of the school year, classroom teachers from kindergarten to the fourth grade fill up a 26-item data sheet on the child's intelligence, creativity, and other areas of potential. The purpose of this is to place each child with classmates of similar ability.
- During the school year, the Center personnel develop continuous observation allowing a closer comparison of the child's ability within more demanding settings.
- An annual data collection by the classroom teachers is carried out, usually with a different teacher and a new comparison group of students.

When data from two of the three sets of observers agree that the child shows signs of high ability, he/she is enrolled at CEDET. From fifth grade on, when there is more than one teacher, the School Teacher Council appoints the child to be observed. Once identified and enrolled, the student stays in CEDET through high school.

Educational provision may include acceleration, and individual enrichment planning for each child according to specific need and learning style, and we encourage the children to choose their own activity to encourage internal locus of control. Interest groups are formed when five or more students show a common interest. Smaller groups develop a project, but each student is required to be sufficiently mature to work alone. General encounters for up to a hundred children are organized around multidimensional topics which aim to stimulate and provide new opportunities for making choices. The interaction network coordinated by facilitators, teachers and volunteer instructors is integrated to ensure that children meet a variety of mentors.

This type of community participation interwoven into our own methodology is certainly CEDET's most powerful feature since it assures diversity and variety activities, together with a high level of quality.

Objetivo Program for Fostering Talent: a private initiative

POIT (Programa Objetivo de Incentivo ao Talento – http://www.objetivo.br) is a cooperative program between Objetivo School and Paulista University (UNIP) in São Paulo, a city of 10 million inhabitants. Both these institutions form an educational conglomerate with 345,000 enrolled students, ranging from infant to postgraduate education (Cupertino 2000b).

POIT is the only Brazilian initiative developed within a private institution with autonomy to state its own agenda. Students come from middle-class and low middle-class families, and they expect an education oriented to university admittance examinations, so the school mainly offers standard curricula. Nevertheless, the school has created some space for the development of diversified talents. A large range of extra-curricular activities is offered especially for nurturing underachievers.

POIT provides advanced programs in topics the students are interested in: the Art and Culture Festival encourages artistic talent. POIT also cares for the affective development of highly able students, as well as fostering creativity and leadership, by providing a challenging environment while respecting youngsters' own rhythms (Landau 1987, 2002).

Services offered to Objetivo School

- Identification of talented students is based upon quantitative data obtained from tests, and qualitative data derived from direct observation of students. Creativity, motivation and/or high academic performance and artistic talent are considered (Cupertino and Sabatella 1998).
- The POIT extra-curricular program is different from typical gifted education programs, since it focuses on students' affective needs and relationships. Freeman (1992, 1995) states that the program design should depend closely on the conception of talent and high performance, and POIT's

intention is to foster development of current specific abilities without pre-judging eventual achievement. This means that we have to closely follow the students so that they establish their own development level according to their own criteria. Psychological work is integrated by teachers, psychologists and an educator. The activities are planned across a variety of themes that require the use of advanced technological tools, creativity development techniques, and ongoing emotional support.

• Counseling to school, families and staff, are included in the extracurricular program. Workshops are also offered, where parents and children work together in shared activities.

POIT emphasizes respect for differences and individuality, together with the capacity to relate with each other in a complex reality (Lévy 1995; Attali 1996); hence the activities encourage interpersonal exchange and collaborative work, aiming to avoid possible problems of isolation experienced by highly able/gifted children (Hickson 1992). The POIT program attempts to balance what students know with what they like and need to know, trying to avoid the pressure to maintain a constantly superior performance (Hannel 1991). The students are encouraged to make choices, identifying areas of preference, devoting energy to them, but also spending time in leisure and entertainment.

Services at UNIP Applied Psychology Centers

The Applied Psychology Centers of UNIP offers diagnostic counselling to individuals families and schools (Ancona-Lopez et al. 1995). The POIT services are increasingly being offered to at-risk children and adolescents living in the poor communities of the city (Cupertino 2000a, 2001). Training of specialized professionals and resources are generated and shared between universities and schools to ensure coherence, reliability and sustainability.

Gifted education under Brazilian southern winds

Gifted educational services have recently increased in Rio Grande do Sul state. FADERS (Fundação de Articulação e Desenvolvimento de Políticas Públicas para Pessoas Portadoras de Deficiência e de Altas Habilidades no Estado do Rio Grande do Sul) maintains a small department (Centro de Desenvolvimento, Estudos e Pesquisas sobre Altas Habilidades/Superdotação: CEDEPAH) solely responsible for gifted screening and counseling, human resources training and research; the Education Center of the Federal University of Santa Maria promotes discussion on Giftedness and enrichment classes; and the Military School of Porto Alegre offers tutored projects to eighth graders and secondary students.

AGAAHSD (Associação Gaúcha de Apoio às Altas Habilidades/Superdotação http://www.agaahsd.pop.com.br), is a statewide non-profit NGO supporting and advocating for gifted people, and is a co-founder of the Brazilian Council for the Gifted. AGAAHSD, run by gifted people and parents, has adopted Renzulli's

(1986) Three-Ring conception of giftedness, and believes that education is a social concern, with enrichment opportunities offered to all children within an inclusive approach. The core activities focus on the following:

- Counseling and advising with regard to giftedness generally.
- Public advocacy and promotion of gifted people's rights in governmental and community committees: during 2001, AGAAHSD demanded that the State Education Department sponsor a high abilities course for representatives from the 30 educational districts. In 2005, 30 resource rooms will be established within the state.
- Encouragement of research: using a wider concept of giftedness based on the work of Renzulli (1986) and Gardner (1983, 2000), a recent survey (AGAAHSD 2001) suggests that approximately 272,300 students, and almost 800,000 people in Rio Grande do Sul, have giftedness indicators, thus deserving gifted education.
- Awareness promotion and information: public lectures reaching thousands of people have provided increasing awareness on giftedness. AGAAHSD maintains one of the few libraries in the country, and published a manual for parents and teachers in 2000 (AGAAHSD 2000). Since 1997, hundreds of children have attended the free scientific, artistic and leisure workshops offered by association. AGAAHSD also organizes free registrations at professional lectures for low income attendees, and scholarships to universities.

Therefore, although only a few gifted students are catered for, our collective efforts are allowing us to make significant progress.

The project to serve highly able children in Rio de Janeiro: PAAAHSD

Delou (2001) shows that in Rio de Janeiro, those public school gifted students who attended specialized resource rooms, still ended up conforming to the minimum standards necessary to pass to the next grade, believing that the difficulties they encountered in school were a result of their own lack of intelligence. As a result of this, since 2002, the Education School of the Universidade Federal Fluminense has developed a project whose main objective is to develop pedagogy that will nurture gifted students in creative thinking (Projeto de Atendimento a Alunos com Altas Habilidades/Superdotação: PAAAHSD. http://www.paaahsd.hpg.ig.com.br/index.htm). The pedagogy is based on the work of Vygotsky who said that 'if inheritance makes genius possible, only the social environment realizes this potential, and creates the genius' (cited in Delou and Bueno 2001; see also Alencar 2001; Novaes 1999; Sternberg and Lubart 1999; Sternberg 2000; Sternberg and Grigorenko 2003).

Gifted students of 10 to 20 years old were selected on free diagnostic assessment using House-Tree-Person Projective Technique (HTP), ideative production (My Hands) and Intelligence (Raven's Progressive Matrices and Koh's

Block Design). In addition students submitted a descriptive life-story about their interests and achievements. All students were then interviewed. At two-hour weekly meetings, the students experienced activities to encourage creative thinking and computing (Virgolim et al. 1999; Sternberg 2000; Sternberg and Grigorenko 2003). Project evaluation considered: regularity of attendance, quality of student participation, and analysis of the pre-existing competences with follow-up of the acquirement and sustainment of new competencies in collective work. The final results showed many students achieving highly across a range of creative projects. In addition, many students showed significant growth in social communication.

Conclusion

The initiatives briefly presented here suggest that, to build a bridge between cumulative knowledge and practice, it is necessary to analyse, deconstruct and adapt the frameworks supporting the actions. The scientific community is no longer solely committed to the classic scientific model, grounded in rational logic and the search for a single truth. On the contrary, there is increasing awareness of, and involvement in, the trend towards global realization of ethical respect for individuality and cultural diversity. To link traditional scientific discourse to practice, it is important to build contextualized understanding of human groups, and to the social and physical contexts. The purpose is to build up knowledge of a world, not with a single meaning for everyone, but with many meanings that can be understood from the standpoint of a micro-political approach. Practice then becomes the locus for research and a source of contextualized knowledge, leading to creative discovery rather than replication of research routines.

Special programs for talented people in Brazil have proved inestimably valuable in increasing society's awareness of the need to accept and nurture difference. As an inclusive education is established, the pilot programmes demonstrate alternatives to the traditional education.

Key questions

1   What are the arguments for and against developing after school special enrichment activities for very able children?
2   What principles should underpin programmes that are developed for enhancing pupils' opportunities to extend their repertoire of activities?
3   Outline an enrichment programme that provides opportunities for all children to discover their particular strengths.

References

AGAAHSD (Associação gaúcha de apoio às altas habilidades/superdotação) [Rio Grande do Sul state Association for Gifted Support] (2000) *Manual de orientação para pais e professores* [Guiding manual for parents and teachers]. Porto Alegre: AGAAHSD.

AGAAHSD (2001) *Relatório Final. Pesquisa sobre Portadores de altas habilidades. Região Metropolitana de Porto Alegre* [Final Report. Survey on gifted. Metropolitan Region of Porto Alegre]. Porto Alegre: AGAAHSD.

Alencar, E. M. L. S. (2001) *Criatividade e educação de superdotados* [Creativity and Gifted Education]. Petrópolis: Vozes.

Ancona-Lopez (ed.) (1995) *Psicodiagnóstico: processo de intervenção* [Psychological assessment: an intervention process]. São Paulo: Cortez.

Attali, J. (1996) *Chemins de sagesse* [Pathways to knowledge]. Paris: Fayard.

Cupertino, C. M. B. (2000a) The limits of traditional evaluation and the identification of gifted children in a Brazilian favela. *Gifted Education International*, 15(1): 71–79.

Cupertino, C. M. B. (2000b) Practicas educativas: la universidad y la escuela cooperan para ayudar a los potenciales diferenciados [Educational practices: university and school cooperate to help differentiated potentials], in Y. Benito (ed.) *Ideacción, Special Issue*, pp. 135–46.

Cupertino, C. M. B. (2001) *Identificação de potenciais diferenciados: encontros e desencontros de uma equipe de pesquisa em uma comunidade de periferia de São Paulo* [Identification of differentiated potentials in an underpriviledged community in the boundaries of São Paulo]. Boletim da Associação Portuguesa para Estudos da Inteligência, da Criatividade e do Talento APEPICTa, pp. 30–39.

Cupertino, C. and Sabatella, M. L. (1998) *Identificação de talentos: fundamentos e limites* [Identification of talent: foundations and limits]. Anais do Congresso Internacional sobre Superdotação, 3°. Congresso Iberoamericano sobre superdotação, 12°. Seminário Nacional da Associação Brasileira para Superdotados, p. 89.

Delou, C. M. C. (2001) *Sucesso e fracasso escolar de alunos considerados superdotados: um estudo sobre a trajetória escolar de alunos que receberam atendimento em salas de recursos de escolas da rede pública de ensino* (Tese de Doutorado) [School success and failure of student considered as gifted: a study on the school path of students who were served in resource rooms of public schools (Doctoral dissertation)]. São Paulo: Programa de Estudos Pós-Graduados em Educação: História e Filosofia da Educação. Pontifícia Universidade Católica – PUC/SP.

Delou, C. M. C. and Bueno, J. G. S. (2001) *O que Vigotski pensava sobre genialidade* [What Vygotsky thought about geniality]. Sobredotação. Braga, Portugal: ANEIS.

Freeman, J. (1992) *Quality Basic Education: The Development of Competence.* Paris: UNESCO.

Freeman, J. (1995) Review of current thinking on the development of talent, in J. Freeman, P. Span and H. Wagner (eds) *Actualizing Talent.* London: Cassell.

Gardner, H. (1983) *Frames of Mind: The Theory of Multiple Intelligences.* New York: Basic Books.

Gardner, H. (2000) *Inteligência: um conceito reformulado* [Intelligence reframed: multiple intelligences for the 21st century]. Rio de Janeiro: Objetiva.

Guenther, Z., Barrozo, E., Bezerra, I. and Veiga, D. (1998) *Identificação do talento pela observação direta* [Assessment of talent through direct observation], Research report. Lavras, MG, Brazil: UFLA-FAPEMIG-CEDET.

Hannel, G. (1991) The complications of being gifted, *Gifted Education International*, 7(3): 126–128.

Hédoux, J. (1994) Sciences humaines, pratiques de formation et praticiens: des rapports complexes [Human sciences, education practices and practitioners: complex relationships]. *Revue Contradictions*, 76: 3–37 (Brussels, Belgium).

Hickson, J. (1992) A framework for guidance and counselling of the gifted in a school setting. *Gifted Education International*, 8(2): 92–95.

Landau, E. (1987) *El vivir creativo* [The creative living]. Barcelona: Herder.

Landau, E. (2002) *A coragem de ser superdotado* [The courage to be gifted]. São Paulo: Arte e Ciência.

Lévy, P. (1995) *L'Intelligence collective* [Collective intelligence]. Paris: La Découverte.

Ministério Da Educação E Do Desporto (MEC) – Secretaria de Educação Especial [Ministry of Education and Sports – Special Education Department] (1994) Política Nacional de Educação Especial [Special Education National Policy]. Brasilia: MEC.

Moon, S. (2003) Developing personal talent, in F. Monks and H. Wagner (eds) *Development of Human Potential: Investment into our Future.* Proceedings of the 8th ECHA Conference. Bad Honnef, Germany: ECHA/K. H. Bock.

Novaes, M. H. (1999) *Compromisso ou alienação frente ao próximo século* [Commitment and alienation in the next century]. Rio de Janeiro: Nau.

Pyryt, M. C. (2003) Social giftedness: historical, psychometric and educational perspectives, in F. Monks and H. Wagner (eds) *Development of Human Potential: Investment into our Future.* Proceedings of the 8th ECHA Conference. Bad Honnef, Germany: ECHA/K. H. Bock.

Renzulli, J. S. (1986) The three-ring conception of giftedness: a developmental Model for Creative Productivity. *The Triad Reader.* Mansfield Center, CT: Creative Learning Press.

Ribeiro, R. J. (2003) *A Universidade e a vida atual* [University and current life]. Rio de Janeiro: Campus.

Sternberg, R. J. (2000) Creativity and giftedness: identifying and developing creative giftedness. *Roeper Review* 23(2): 60–64.

Sternberg, R. J. and Grigorenko, E. L. (2003) *Inteligência Plena: ensinando e incentivando a aprendizagem e a realização dos alunos* [Teaching for successful intelligence: to increase students learning and achievement]. Porto Alegre: Artmed.

Sternberg, R. J. and Lubart, T. I. (1999) The concept of creativity: prospects and paradigms, in R. J. Sternberg (ed.) *Handbook of Creativity.* New York: Cambridge University Press.

Tirri, K. (2003) Morality and high ability, in F. Monks and H. Wagner (eds) *Development of Human Potential: Investment into our Future.* Proceedings of the 8th ECHA Conference. Bad Honnef, Germany: ECHA/K. H. Bock.

Virgolim, A. M. R., Fleith, D. S. and Neves-Pereira, M. S. (1999) *Toc, Toc, Plim, Plim. Lidando com as Emoções, Brincando com o Pensamento Através da Criatividade* [Toc, Toc, Plim, Plim – Dealing with emotions, playing with thoughts through creativity]. São Paulo: Papirus.

Vygotsky, L. S. (1929) *Genial'nost* [Genius]. Bol'shaja Medicinskaja Enciklopedija. Moscow 6, col. 612–613.

5.4 Personal perspective: Kimeru gifted (Afrocentrism) – from a village in Kenya

Prudence Mutuma

'When I grow up, I want to be a driver,' all the children in my village would say. They admired the bus driver for he seemed knowledgeable, although the nearest highway was seven miles from my remote village. Twenty years later, the difference is minimal.

I loved my primary school life because we played. At home, a girl of 7 was expected to do chores. Boys could be rough and play. They couldn't take care of their baby sisters and brothers or fetch firewood or draw water. They grew up slower and could go on with school when we were ready to be 'sold' out to suitors.

The language of instruction in lower primary was Kimeru (my first language). In Class 4 some of us were forced into 'dumbness' because we had to use the 'Queen's tongue', English. If you uttered a word in Kimeru, you were caned. Faking dumbness was a brilliant idea! The Anglo-European hangover was pervasive in our curriculum. I remember a history question that asked the name of the first person to see Mount Kenya. The answer was Dr Krapf! Instruction meant we listened and the teacher talked; we had no reference books and the teacher was never wrong. The biggest challenge in upper primary was to understand English written tests.

Sounds gloomy? Not in the least! There was great excitement in simple things: chasing birds and squirrels and collecting wild fruits in the nearby hills. We sang and danced at festivals like weddings, child naming ceremonies and yes, at circumcision ceremonies. One sad memory is that some of us were excluded from learning purely because we were uncircumcised: female circumcision was traditional. When reproduction was taught in Class 7, we would be ordered to leave; still considered children even though we were over 13. I want to applaud my parents for not letting me go through the ritual.

I went to a girl's secondary boarding school in nearby Maua and the English that I had so painfully learnt came in handy. We were not allowed to use Swahili except in the Swahili lesson. My joy came from debating, cultural clubs and school teams because I could travel to performances, which we could seldom afford. In high school, a desire came into me to join the Catholic sisterhood. An old Indian nun, Sister Christine, talked to me about waiting and searching – I owe her! After high school she sent me to work as a catechist in Consolata Girls Secondary School where I was inspired by young women fresh from university who still wanted to be nuns. My parents struggled to send me to Catholic university, a very expensive institution, organizing two 'Harambees'. For a man from my dad's setting, selling land to educate a girl was a big undertaking. After all, girls belong to another clan upon marriage. They were overwhelmed many times; my four siblings were still in school and needed tuition. We lived on Dad's salary and ate the food Mommy got from the fields. During the dry seasons, we actually had to live on relief food.

After four years at university, I decided not to become a nun. My first teaching assignment was at a Catholic high school in Isiolo, a semi-arid region of Kenya inhabited mainly by the Turkanas Boranas Somalis and the Merus. It is an area of tribal conflicts and lives were at stake. I realized that I could strongly impact the lives of young people. I began dreaming of making the curriculum more relevant for the people, of working with the UN, of speaking for the voiceless. I thought about ways that could develop my village.

At this time, a friend moved to America to study and I thought about going too. Soon I was at the University of Central Florida, but with no family, no scholarship and only this one friend: life was unbearable. The savings I had from teaching and my family's Harambee collection were soon gone. Even though I got a little money working for the university dining services, life was so tough that with bread and milk in my fridge, I was at least fed. The folks back home could not understand why I was lazy at harvesting dollars like everyone else in America. I had helpful professors but when I was finally cleared to work off campus at a daycare, I worked myself to death! My grades were still straight As. Since scholarships for international students are few, I never won one. When I was almost dropping out, the international students' office gave me a grant based on my excellent grades.

When I graduated it was such a great achievement! Although still heavily in debt, I am so proud I fought to earn a master's degree in curriculum and instruction. I might not be able to change any curriculum right now, I might even be jobless, but my passion for gender, education and development in Africa still drives me. Being accepted is a battle one has to fight. My dreams kept growing bigger the more challenges I met. Some days I felt like I would never achieve them. Other nights, I felt like they were above my head and all I needed was to just stretch out my hands. I am still on my journey and I will find fulfillment one day.

5.5   Conflict resolution 4: racism

Suzanne Rawlins

Students in a rural, Midwestern part of the United States lived in a community that literally had only white Americans. The teacher was completing a unit about the Civil Rights Movement of the 1960s. She spoke with passion about the leadership of Dr. Martin Luther King. The students listened politely, but it was obvious that they did not comprehend the issues. They had virtually no frame of reference. Most of the students had been to the 'big city' only once or twice. They had never encountered or known anyone of a different race. What difference could it make? Why would anyone get upset about being treated differently because of color? Couldn't they just ignore it? Isn't everyone just the same?

6 Ethical perspectives

6.1 Developing spiritual intelligence and higher consciousness

Dorothy Sisk

Addressing spiritual intelligence provides opportunities for students to honor life's most meaningful questions: How can I make a difference? Why am I here? Does my life have meaning? Discussing such questions engages students with something larger than their ego; connecting to the lives of others, to nature and to the mystery of being alive. In this chapter, spiritual intelligence is defined as the capacity to use a multi-sensory approach, including intuition, meditation and visualization to tap one's inner knowledge to solve problems of a global nature (Sisk and Torrance 2001).

The psychological base for spiritual intelligence

Carl Jung was convinced that myths represent what is universally known by everybody, linking us with our past and to contemporary human society (Campbell 1971). Jung's four functions of consciousness are *sensing* and *intuition* by which facts and the fact-world are apprehended; *feeling* and *thinking* involved in judging and evaluation. Feeling and intuition are essential to the development and use of spiritual intelligence. Jung (1969) described the theory of synchronicity, as an inner psychic condition and an external event coming together in a way that can be perceived as having a meaningful coincidence.

Dabrowski (1967) divided his theory of disintegration into two parts: Over-excitabilities (Oes) which interact with special talents and abilities of the individual. He identified five over-excitabilities (Oes) – psychomotor, sensual, imaginational, intellectual and emotional – which interact and manifest in capacity to care, insatiable love of learning, vivid imagination and endless energy. These capacities form the core of spiritual intelligence (Sisk and Torrance 2001). Individual development comes through a process of lower cognitive-

Table 6.1.1 Dabrowski levels of positive disintegration

Level I (Primary Integration)	Individuals at this level are described as being primarily egocentric, rigid and stereotypical.
	Level I individuals lack empathy and self-examination, and they tend to blame others when something goes wrong.
Level II (Unilevel Disintegration)	Individuals are influenced by their social groups, and they are moral relativists with no clear-cut set of self-determined values.
	Level II individuals display the beginning of shame, and extreme or changeable identification with others.
Level III (Spontaneous Multilevel Disintegration)	Individuals have developed a hierarchical sense of values, and their inner conflict is made up of a struggle to live up to their higher standards.
	Level III individuals can become depressed and anxious with their perceived lack of achieving these established goals.
Level IV (Organized Multilevel Disintegration)	Individuals are well on the way to self-actualization, and they have figured out how to reach their ideal goals.
	Level IV individuals manifest high levels of responsibility, reflective judgement, empathy and authenticity.
Level V (Secondary Integration)	Individuals have mastered their personal struggle regarding self, and disintegration has been transcended by the integration of their values and ideals.
	Level V individuals live a life in service to humanity, and according to the highest universal principles of love and compassion; manifest dynamisms of responsibility, autonomy, empathy, and perfection.
	Level V individuals are committed to universal principles; identify with humanity; and their lives reflect the compassion and forgiveness that represent the core of their being.

Source: Dabrowski and Piechowski 1977.

emotional structures being disintegrated and replaced by higher level structures (Table 6.1.1).

Carl Rogers (1980) had a deep trust in human nature, and said people have an internal biological drive to fully develop their capacities and talents, which he called the actualizing tendency. Rogers, like Jung, suggested that people are influenced by feeling-experiencing processes, and information processing which may be akin to dream-states and meditation. Rogers proposed the *Qualities of the Person of Tomorrow* (Rogers 1980), and Table 6.1.2 includes many of the qualities of spiritual intelligence (nos. 1, 3, 4, 5, 6, 7, 8, 10 and 12).

Table 6.1.2 Qualities of the Person of Tomorrow, by Rogers

1	Openness (open to new experience and ways of seeing and being)
2	Desire for authenticity (value of open communication)
3	Skepticism regarding science and technology (distrust of science used to conquer nature and people; sees science used to enhance self awareness)
4	Desire for wholeness of life, body, mind and spirit
5	Wish for intimacy, new forms of communication and closeness
6	Process person (aware that life is change, welcomes risk-taking and the change process)
7	Caring (eager to help, nonjudgemental)
8	Symbiotic attitude toward nature (ecologically minded, feels alliance with nature)
9	Anti-institutional (antipathy for highly structured, bureaucratic institutions)
10	Authority within (trusts own experiences and moral judgements)
11	Unimportance of material things (money and material status symbols not main goal)
12	Yearning for the spiritual (wish to find meaning and purpose in life that is greater than the individual)

Source: Rogers 1980: 350–351.

Maslow (1968) described human evolvement through five basic categories of needs: physiological, safety, love, esteem, all leading towards self-actualization. Maslow said that satisfaction of lower needs (Deficit values), allows higher needs (Being values) to be fulfilled. Being values are associated with growth motivation and expanded horizons, and include wholeness, perfection, justice, beauty, uniqueness, creativity – all important aspects of spiritual behavior. Maslow also developed his concept of peak experiences as movement toward perfect values, and he described self-actualized people as individuals who manifest the positive qualities of self-awareness, creativity, spontaneity, openness to experience, self-acceptance, and the special qualities of democratic character and social interest.

From this brief summary of the key tenets of Jung, Dabrowski, Rogers, and Maslow, several concepts of spiritual intelligence emerge. Dabrowski's Level V of development in which individuals live a life in service to humanity with love and compassion, represent the core behaviors of spiritual intelligence (Sisk and Torrance 2001). Individuals with the capacity to care, and insatiable love are individuals who manifest spiritual intelligence or self-actualization as described by Maslow (1968). They demonstrate the *Qualities of the Person of Tomorrow* as described by Rogers (1980). People manifesting spiritual intelligence are open to a multisensory way of knowing, using the core capacities of meditation, intuition, and visualization as proposed by Jung (1969).

The scientific base for spiritual intelligence

Science as a search for truth

Neuroscientist Candace Pert (1997) describes science as a spiritual endeavor that explores the linked system of 'bodymind'. Pert concludes that neuropeptides (strings of amino acids) are responsible for emotions, not just anger and fear, but also awe and bliss. Pert (1997) emphasizes the important role of intuition in her scientific discoveries and says that a higher intelligence comes to us via our molecules and cannot be received from the five senses alone.

Consciousness in the brain

The brain research conducted by Rodolfo Llinas and Urs (1993) suggests that consciousness or mind is a state of the brain that is intrinsic, rather than the result of sensory experiences, and that when we dream, the brain switches off the outer world and attends to its inner processes. Zohar and Marshall (2000) report that the brain appears to have a transcendent dimension, and the brain can synthesize perceptual and cognitive events into a larger more meaningful whole.

Energetic network

Caroline Myss (1996) suggests that the human body can be viewed as a vast energetic network where spirit, matter, and power intersect. Myss has studied this energy system and its link to consciousness and spiritual traditions, demonstrating how the body encodes thought, converts it into matter, and stores it within specific areas of the body.

Greg Braden (1997) also discusses the interconnectedness of the body with energy. Magnetite can be found in the brains of birds and mammals, including humans, and it allows us to tune into, and to respond to, the magnetic field of the earth. Braden reports that previous cultures were sensitive to this and built temples or used natural sites which exhibited the requisite geographical cyclic conditions to tap altered states of consciousness.

Everything in the universe is connected

Fritjof Capra (1991) says that the image of the universe is that of an interconnected, dynamic whole whose parts are interdependent and need to be understood as patterns.

From this exploration of science, there emerges a concept of a conscious universe in which we interact as part of a continuous connected process of unity. The brain research of Llinas (1987) and Ramachandran and Blakeslee (1998) suggests that there may be an intrinsic area of the brain, the temporal lobe, that can be included as a brain state of spiritual intelligence.

The basis for spiritual intelligence derived from ancient wisdom and eastern mysticism

Thoth, an ancient Egyptian sage, is credited with the invention of sacred hieroglyphic writing, and he is portrayed as a scribe with the head of an ibis. The ancient Greeks identified Thoth with their god Hermes, the guide of souls in the realm of the dead. Hermes promoted reflection and meditation, and taught that an enlightened being belongs to nature, and feels unity with everything.

The ancient Essenes were communal agriculturists living in harmony with nature: a simple, peaceful life with a pure tradition of eating no meat or drinking alcohol. The Essenes' practice of the 'communions' expressed an exceptional knowledge of psychology: the morning communion opened the mind to harmonious forms of energy and brought them into the physical body, the evening communion put the subconscious into contact with the superior cosmic forces, and the storehouse of information so that problems can be solved during sleep. The Essenes linked body and the mind to form a dynamic unit: they believed love to be the primordial source of energy, harmony and knowledge, providing dynamic harmony to all cells, organs, and senses. They believed 'will' to be the key to the manifestation of this great source of energy through creative imagination.

There are three central concepts in the Sufi tradition: the heart, the self, and the soul. Heart refers to the spiritual heart that contains our intelligence, wisdom, and power to love. In western culture, logical reasoning is considered the highest human skill; the Sufi tradition calls this the lower intellect, useful in schooling, and in learning skills related to worldly success. The Sufi's higher intellect enables understanding of spiritual truths and the meaning of life. Abstract intellect, according to the Sufi tradition, must have the light and wisdom of the heart.

The essence of Hinduism is found in *Moksha* or liberation. When one experiences concretely and personally that everything is Brahman (the inner essence of all things), then one becomes liberated and recognizes that everything is connected, sensing the unity and harmony of all nature, including ourselves.

Buddhism enshrines four Noble Truths. The first truth accepts that the human situation is suffering; the second truth attributes the cause of all suffering to our clinging and grasping; the third truth states that suffering can be ended when we reach a state of liberation called Nirvana. The fourth truth points to an eightfold path: Right Belief, Resolve, Speech, Right Conduct, Daily Occupation, Effort, Alertness, and finally the ecstasy of Selfless Meditation.

Zen teaches that words cannot express ultimate truth: Zen Enlightenment is active participation in everyday life, not withdrawal from it, and when Enlightenment is attained, there is wonder and mystery in every single act. Zen stresses naturalness and spontaneity to focus on the process of Enlightenment, to realize that we become what we already are from the beginning.

The major purpose of Confucianism is to provide an ethical basis for the traditional Chinese family system, life in society and ancestral worship. Taoism is concerned with observing nature and discovering the way or 'Tao'. Human happiness in Taoism is achieved by following the natural order, acting spontaneously and trusting intuitive knowledge. The Chinese believe in an ultimate reality that underlines and unifies all things, and is an all-embracing whole.

Confucianism is rational, masculine, active and dominating, whereas Taoism is intuitive, feminine, mystical, and yielding, and the contrast of yin and yang is reflected in these two dominant trends of thought.

Jewish Kabbalah teaches that the human being consists of a spirit that represents the highest degree of existence, a soul which is the seat of good and evil attributes, and a coarser spirit or life of the senses that is closely related to the instincts of animal life. Above the life of the senses soars the soul, and above the soul soars the spirit which is ruled and illuminated by the light of the life.

The Native American philosophy is earth-centered, and the creator is manifested in every bush and tree, in the gifts of food and shelter, in nurturing, and in the fulfillment of the everyday needs of life. Native Americans believe in the interconnectedness of all things, the circular nature of the universe, and the rightness of both birth and death in the overall scheme of creation. Eastman (1980) said everything has a soul, the rocks, the seven directions, the wind and water, the earth and fire, the plants and animals, the sun, the moon and stars. The Sioux Native American tradition teaches that spirits can step out of the body, and spirit travel. Mails (1991) says that in the old days, people did not separate daily life from spiritual life: when Fools Crow was asked to describe spiritual power, he said that it felt like energy or electricity when it moves through you.

Native American people tapped their intuition through visions, and they believed one gains wisdom by visualizing. They believed in the intuitive way of knowing, and preferred innermost thoughts over learning through the senses.

The ancient wisdom and eastern mysticism, and the wisdom and traditions of Native American and indigenous people share a common strand for building a concept of spiritual intelligence: the concern for unity, and the interrelation or connectedness of all things, with all things viewed as interdependent and inseparable from the cosmic whole, the Creator and Creative force. Ultimate reality is called 'Brahman' in Hinduism, 'Dharmakaya' in Buddhism, 'Tao' in Taoism and 'Wakan-Tanka,' by the Native American. These common elements are similar to the fundamental feature of the world-view of a conscious universe that emerges from science.

The role of education in developing spiritual intelligence

Support is growing for home schooling in the United States, and for the use of federal funds for private religious schools: some individuals are reacting to perceived hostility toward their views; some resent the neutrality of the schools; and others feel that schools are ignoring the central aspect of living a meaningful life. With the growing cultural diversity in schools all over the world, and more children representing Islamic, Hindu and Buddhist traditions in their families – learning about other religious traditions may help to prevent cultural wars in our schools. Palmer (1999) describes the current challenge to education:

> Fear is everywhere – in our culture, in our institutions, in our students, in ourselves – and it cuts us off from everything. Surrounded and invaded by fear, how can we transcend it and reconnect with reality for the sake of

teaching and learning? The only path I know that might take us in that direction is the one marked spiritual.

(Palmer 1999: 6)

Palmer (1999) says the price that has been paid for a system of education so fearful of things spiritual is that it fails to address the real issues of life – dispensing facts at the expense of meaning, and information at the expense of wisdom. Such schooling alienates and dulls, and he defines 'spiritual' as a quest for connectedness with self, with others, with the worlds of history and nature, and with the mystery of being alive. This definition represents spiritual intelligence as proposed by Sisk and Torrance (2001). The disciplines of history, physics, psychology and literature can be taught using connectedness as an organizing theme. Teachers can focus on the big picture, and provide students opportunities to explore how connectedness applies to them as individuals.

Palmer (1999) has created a teacher training program *The Courage to Teach* during which teachers examine the spiritual questions that are at the heart of the season in which they attend. Teachers report several outcomes; for example, feeling more grounded and flourishing in their selfhood and home lives, and less likely to burn out, and feeling that they are better teachers, able to deal with conflict and change peacefully and with hope.

Educators want to address the broader implications of Gardner's (1983) interpersonal and intrapersonal intelligences, Goleman's (1995) emotional intelligence, and the interconnectedness of learner and teacher, local and global communities, and the cosmic world which represent the core of spiritual intelligence (Sisk and Torrance 2001). Suhor (1999) says that the current diversity in schools provides access to many traditions and strategies including writing from the inner self: he forecasts greater recognition of methods like imaging and meditation saying spirituality grows in classrooms when teachers view themselves as agents of joy and conduits for transcendence, rather than merely as licensed trainers or promoters of measurable growth.

Noddings (2000), at Teachers College, Columbia University, has developed curriculum to address spiritual questions, suggesting that teachers address the existential questions of 'How should we live?' 'Is there meaning to life?' 'Why is there something, rather than nothing?' She also recommends that schools have gardens and animals so that students experience and build a strong awareness of, and connection with, nature.

Sisk and Torrance (2001) stress that spiritual intelligence develops through compassion, interconnectedness with self and others. Students need to solve real ethical dilemmas of today: they need to explore the core values underlying compassion, honesty, fairness, responsibility and respect, and applying these core values in education will

- build a common language
- help define a common purpose
- develop and maintain trust

- influence the school climate to enhance the teaching and learning goals
- provide the basis on which to nurture the spirit, and create a deeper sense of meaningfulness.

Wesley (1999), a principal in New York, says education is about content and theme, full of energy and pathos, and master teachers give themselves fully and selflessly to their art. He emphasizes that most students have little identity beyond home and school, and feel they are anonymous nobodies, but through the way teachers treat, challenge, and coach students, they can become somebodies. He stresses that believing in students is not only good for them, but is a powerful ennobling experience for teachers.

Miller (1999), a professor at the University of Toronto in Ontario, says holistic, connected learning can provide a broader vision of education, as well as improve academic ability and performance. He suggests a balance between individual and group learning, analytic and intuitive thinking, content and process, and learning and assessment. He stresses the need for classrooms to become learning communities, places where people know one another, and feel responsibility toward the total environment.

Many educators are aware that students are seeking answers to questions about the meaning of life, and there is a need to encourage spirituality in the classroom. The Passages Program (Kessler 1999) addresses six interrelated yearnings: the search for meaning and purpose, the longing for silence and solitude, the urge for transcendence, the hunger for joy and delight, the creative drive and the need for initiation. She stresses that if we are educating for wholeness, citizenship and leadership in a democracy, spiritual development belongs in school.

Many school districts have added service learning projects to their gifted programs, and to requirements for graduation. Krystal (1999) says that service learning should be at the core of every curriculum because it provides purpose for students, and nurtures their spirit as few experiences can. Students report that service learning helps them to know they can make a difference in someone's life, and in their community.

Earth Force in Alexandria, Virginia, is a service learning program that can be integrated into science or social studies, and it follows a six-step process:

- take a community environment inventory
- select a problem
- research the problem and investigate the cause
- identify options for influencing policy and practice, and look for ways to define a course of action
- plan and take action in the civic arena
- celebrate and assess the completion of the project.

Boston (1999) calls this a transforming experience in the lives of students.

Brown (1999) says that spiritual education is not about creating some kind of educational Nirvana, it is about waking up to the sacredness of everyday

Table 6.1.3 Likely traits of spiritual intelligence and ways to strengthen for learning

Likely traits	Ways to strengthen for learning
• Uses inner knowing • Seeks to understand self • Uses metaphor and parables to communicate • Uses intuition • Sensitive to social problems • Sensitive to their purpose in life • Concerned about inequity and injustice • Enjoys big questions • Sense of Gestalt (the big picture) • Wants to make a difference • Capacity to care • Curious about how the world works/ functions • Values love, compassion, concern for others • Close to nature • Uses visualization and mental imaging • Reflective, self-observing and self-aware • Seeks balance • Concerned about right conduct • Seeks to understand self • Feels connected with others, the earth, and the universe • Wants to make a difference • Peacemaker • Concerned with human suffering	• Provide time for reflective thinking • Use journal writing and processing • Study lives/works of spiritual pathfinders • Use problem-solving (predicting) • Conduct service learning projects • Use personal growth activities • Use problem-based learning on real problems • Provide time for open-ended discussion • Use mapping to integrate studies/big themes • Develop personal growth activities • Service learning projects • Integrate science/social science • Use affirmations/think-about-thinking • Employ eco-environmental approach • Read stories and myths • Use role playing/sociodrama • Goal setting activities • Process discussions • Trust intuition and inner voice • Stress unity in studies • Use what, so what, now what model • Negotiation-conflict sessions • Study lives of eminent people

learning. He stresses by separating the intellect from the other senses and from the body itself, all of our intelligence suffers.

Educating for spiritual development embodies the goal of developing students capable of discovering what is essential in life; and ways to strengthen spiritual intelligence for learning are listed in Table 6.1.3.

Conclusion

Inherent in the seven ways of developing your spiritual intelligence is finding a sense of purpose, and creating a vision (Table 6.1.4). Once the vision of your goals is created, then you will need to make a commitment to these goals, followed by an intention to carry through toward your identified goals. It is essential for the development of your spiritual intelligence that you sense the connectedness of everything-to-everything, and to shift your locus of authority and perception in your life from external to internal. Equally essential to the development of your spiritual intelligence is for you to recognize and to honor your relationship to the earth.

Table 6.1.4 Seven ways to develop or raise your spiritual intelligence

1	Think about your goals, desires, and wants in order to bring your life into perspective and balance, and identify your values
2	Access your inner processes and use your vision to see your goals, desires, wants fulfilled, and experience the emotion connected with this fulfillment
3	Integrate your personal and universal vision, and recognize your connectedness
4	Take responsibility for your goals, desires and wants
5	Develop a sense of community by inviting more people into your life
6	Focus on love and compassion
7	When chance knocks at your door, invite it in, and take advantage of coincidences

Key questions

1   How are the principles of global education connected to the development of spiritual intelligence?
2   What role does locus of control play in the development of spiritual intelligence?
3   How can teachers of diverse gifted students develop their ethical perspectives while celebrating their ethnic diversity?

References

Boston, B. (1999) If the water is nasty, fix it. *Educational Leadership*, 56(4): 66–69.

Braden, G. (1997) *Awakening to Zero Point*. Bellevue, WA: Radio Bookstore Press.

Brown, R. (1999) The teacher as contemplative observer. *Educational Leadership*, 56(4): 70–73.

Campbell, J. (1971) *The Portable Jung*. New York: Penguin.

Capra, F. (1991) *The Tao of Physics*. Boston, MA: Shambahla.

Dabrowski, K. (1967) *Personality Shaping through Positive Disintegration*. Boston, MA: Little Brown.

Dabrowski, K. and Piechowski, M. M. (1977) *Theory of Levels of Emotional Development: Volume I, Multilevelness and Positive Disintegration*. Oceanside, NY: Dabor Science.

Eastman, C. (1980) *The Soul of the Indian*. Lincoln, NE: University of Nebraska.

Gardner, H. (1983) *Frames of Mind*. New York: Basic Books.

Goleman, D. (1995) *Emotional Intelligence*. New York: Bantam.

Jung, C. (1969) *Collected Works*. Translated by R. F. C. Huyll, Bollingen Series XX. Princeton, NJ: Princeton University Press.

Kessler, R. (1999) Nourishing students in secular schools. *Educational Leadership*, 56(4): 49–52.

Krystal, S. (1999) The nurturing potential of service learning. *Educational Leadership*, 56(4): 58–61.

Llinas, R. (1987) Mindfuluess as a functional state of the brain, in C. Blakemore and S. Greenfield (eds) *Mindwaves*. Oxford: Basil Blackwell.

Llinas, R. and Urs, R. (1993) Coherent 40-Hz oscillation characterizes dream state in humans. *Proceedings of the National Academy of Science*, 90: 2078–2081.

Mails, T. (1991) *Fools Crow, Wisdom and Power*. Tulsa, OK: Council Oaks Books.

Maslow, A. (1968) *Toward a Psychology of Being*. Princeton, NJ: Van Nostrand.

Miller, J. (1999) Making connections through holistic learning. *Educational Leadership*, 56(4): 46–48.

Myss, C. (1996) *Anatomy of the Spirit*. New York: Crown.

Noddings, N. (2000) *Educating for Intelligent Belief or Unbelief*. New York: Teachers College Press.

Palmer, P. (1999) Evoking the spirit in public education. *Educational Leadership*, 56(4): 6–11.

Pert, C. (1997) *Molecules of Emotion*. New York: Scribner.

Ramachandran, V. S. and Blakeslee, S. (1998) *Phantoms in the Brain*. New York: William Morrow.

Rogers, C. (1980) *A Way of Being*. Boston, MA: Houghton Mifflin.

Sisk, D. A. and Torrance, E. P. (2001) *Spiritual Intelligence: Developing Higher Consciousness*. Buffalo, NY: Creative Education Foundation Press.

Suhor, C. (1999) Spirituality: letting it grow in the classroom. *Educational Leadership*, 56(4): 12–16.

Wesley, D. (1999) Believing in our students. *Educational Leadership*, 56(4): 42–45.

Zohar, D. and Marshall, I. (2000) *Connecting with our Spiritual Intelligence*. New York: Bloomsbury Publishing.

6.2 Reclaiming soul in gifted education: the academic caste system in Asian schools

Mary Anne Heng and Kai Yung Brian Tam

In Singapore, as in other Asia-Pacific countries such as Hong Kong, Korea and Japan, intense academic competition pervades schools. Although Singapore has impressive performance in international mathematics and science competitions (Keys et al. 1996), a recent poll of at least twenty countries reported that Asian students scored second-lowest in *enjoyment* of math and science (School daze 2002).

The academic caste system

Academic success in a school culture of ruthless academic competition leaves many students increasingly dissatisfied with themselves, as pointed out by a 14-year-old student: 'In some ways, school encourages superficial success, because society encourages this' (Heng 1999). A number of fundamental questions follow: Do schools educate for life? Is there meaning to school beyond the academic 'A'? Roeper (1995: 142) cautions: 'education has become a one-sided (academic) instrument. . . . it does not stress the development and the growth of the self. Yet it is this inner self . . . that is the central point of their lives'.

In a twelve-nation survey in 1998, Singaporean youth rated goals of 'getting rich and having social position' as a major aspiration. A subsequent study (Wake-up call for Singapore youths 2000) indicated that Singaporean teenagers exhibit narrow-mindedness, tend to be smug and egocentric, and see the paper chase as the means to a good life. Hong Kong conducted a similar youth survey in 1998, and the results revealed that 30 percent of respondents equated success with good academic results, 25 percent rated 'fulfillment of goals' and 15 percent rated 'having a prosperous career' as measures of success (Commission on Youth 2002). The then Acting Education Minister, Tharman Shanmugaratnam, pointed out that Singaporeans make good employees but few can think out-of-the-box, much less lead. Furthermore, Singaporeans tend to be more interested in sustaining their current lifestyle rather than pursuing their dreams (Changing in time for the future 2003).

In Hong Kong, admission to prestigious kindergartens and primary schools is competitive, often requiring interviews and examinations. Parents begin planning by relocating their homes near the preferred school; children are prepared for entry examination(s) two to three years in advance with interview skills, musical skills and knowledge, language proficiency in Mandarin and English, and problem-solving skills. Parents invest tremendous time and resources believing that a good primary school ensures better secondary and university education.

The competitive Asia-Pacific economies have long experienced a school culture that engenders an academic caste system and correspondingly high levels of stress. A survey of 500 students aged between 13 and 19 from Hong Kong, Shanghai and Taiwan found that nearly 40 percent of teenagers polled in Shanghai and Taiwan, and more than 20 percent of those polled in Hong Kong rated study fears as the foremost factor in suicidal thoughts (Teens crushed by study pressure 2003). The survey also reported tremendous pressure from intense competition among peers, high expectations and copious school assignments. In Singapore, one in three primary school children finds life not worth living; nearly four out of five spend as many as three hours daily on homework; and seven out of ten receive extra classes after school (Gregory and Clarke 2003).

Table 6.2.1 is a typical daily schedule for high school students in Korea (School daze 2002). Korean parents typically send their children to 'cram school' by age 7 to give their children a headstart on the academic track. Notoriously known for contributing to a childhood of 'examination hell', East Asian schools generate an elite of 'winners' and an underclass of 'losers'. The biggest problem with Asia's schools today is the cumulative, detrimental effects of high-stakes

Table 6.2.1 A typical daily schedule for high school students in Korea

6:50 a.m.	Wakes, gets dressed for school and eats some toast
7:40 a.m.	Walks to school
8:10 a.m.	Attends a 40-minute English comprehension lesson
8:50 a.m. – 4:30 p.m.	Classes
5:00 p.m.	Eats some rice cakes, starts homework
6:00 p.m.	Private math tutorial
8:00 p.m.	More homework
8:50 p.m.	Leaves home for cram school
9:20 p.m.	Attends English lesson at cram school
Midnight	Teacher drives student home
12:30 a.m.	Arrives home, takes a shower, does more homework, has a snack, plays computer games
2:00 a.m.	Time for sleep – for less than five hours

assessment and an unhealthy focus on school grades: children no longer link substantive learning with schooling as they struggle to cope with relentless, almost crushing, school pressure (Gregory and Clarke 2003).

Reflective of a more pervasive problem of all developed economies, in recent interviews conducted by the *New York Times*, sixth graders showed intense pre-occupation with getting into the right college to gain access to good jobs (Newman 2000). A college freshman survey by the Higher Education Research Institute, University of California, Los Angeles (2004) reported only a small number of college freshmen said it was important to 'develop a meaningful philosophy of life', while interest in being 'well-off financially' was rated the most important.

> Many young people today do not have any understanding that their lives have a higher purpose. . . . from the poorest to the most affluent, (they) are imprisoned by our culture's obsession with material things. . . . Instead of fostering meaningful discourse, tolerance of divergent thinking, and the opportunity to get to know ourselves and each other, schools today look more like huge centers for testing preparation.
>
> (Lantieri 2001: 2–3)

Failure to nurture soul in schools: half-sighted versus whole-sighted vision

Webster's (1971: 2176) definition of soul reads: 'the immaterial essence or substance, animating principle, or actuating cause of life or of the individual life'. Kessler (2000: x) refers to soul as the 'inner life – the depth dimension of human experience – a student's longing for something more than material, fragmented existence'. The notion of soul in education does not concern issues of religion, but life philosophy, a more penetrating attempt at 'seeing' and 'knowing.' Western ways of knowing and understanding reality often center on the observable, on perceiving reality as divorced from an understanding of self and others.

The Chinese characters for 'busy' and 'blindness' have the same pronunciation, suggesting figuratively that incessant activity could render people blind to the realities around them. P. Palmer (1993) refers to this as 'half-sightedness', seeing things with only one eye: the other eye, representing spirit or soul, offers another lens to seeing and understanding reality. Palmer argues for 'whole-sighted' education that should reappraise the fundamental assumptions underlying educational policies and practices and the impact they have on children's learning.

In Asia and elsewhere, competitive learning environments are typically characterized by a narrow focus on right answers and test outcomes – half-sighted education. Whole-sighted education encourages learners to question, take risks and pursue passions, looking beyond academic excellence and nudging the learner in pursuit of meaning and purpose.

Most modern teaching, even at university level, is about facts disconnected from a philosophy of the whole (Martin 2000). Thomas S. Popkewitz in Rogers (2000: 269) cautions that a major contradiction exists in which the 'good intentions of teachers, manifested through their university-certified pedagogical practices, limit the possibilities for genuine intellectual experiences for all children in schools, particularly children of color and poverty'.

Borland (1996: 134) urges educators to question the extent to which we are dealing with something real when we talk about 'gifted' and 'average' children as if those labels referred to discrete categories of human beings. In our half-sighted classification of children as gifted or learning-disabled, we are grossly simplifying the complexities of learner needs and capabilities.

Education *is* about teaching individuals to read and write, and to acquire skills to earn a living, and grade standards matter; but what about children's spirit, vision, curiosity and imagination? Should education not also be about celebrating diversity and talents, respect and perseverance? Most importantly, should education not also be about helping children discover meaning, purpose, compassion and joy in life?

The changing nature of community points towards more globalized economies and cosmopolitan living with young people in search of new cultural contexts and identities. Although educators and policy-makers proclaim the importance of education that maximizes children's potential, the system usually establishes 'one-size-fits-all' standard tests to judge success or academic potential. Our world children need an education grounded in a sense of self-realization for living and being.

Reclaiming soul in education through the Evolving Self Model

The Evolving Self Model stems from the authors' search for meaning and mission, as they sought to understand themselves and aspire to be of service to community. The Evolving Self Model (Figure 6.2.1) delineates four broad philosophical beliefs that guide the individual's search for self-understanding in relation to family and peers, and the wider perspective of service to the community.

The Evolving Self Model has its conceptual roots in the thoughts and ideas of Confucius and Dewey who embrace the widest perspectives that illuminate 'soul' in education. Confucius believed in *living an experience*, and Dewey conceived of experience as the *touchstone of life*.

Confucius charted a developmental path for his students, beginning with the growth of self, then self in relation to achieving family harmony, and then self in relation to peace and order in the empire (J. Palmer 2001). He perceived learning as the foundation of self-development:

> If one loves humaneness but does not love learning, the consequence of this is folly; if one loves understanding but does not love learning, the consequence of this is unorthodoxy; if one loves good faith but does not love learning, the consequence of this is damaging behaviour; if one loves straightforwardness but does not love learning, the consequence of this is rudeness; if one loves courage but does not love learning, the consequence of this is

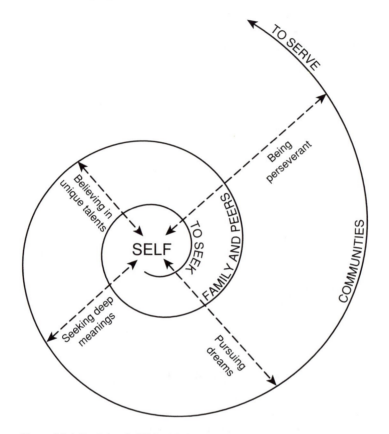

Figure 6.2.1 Evolving Self Model: from seeking self to serving communities.

rebelliousness; if one loves strength but does not love learning, the consequence of this is violence.

(J. Palmer 2001: 1)

Confucius was concerned with finding the right way or *dao* to handle a situation.
This involves finding the developmental path that begins with the self, as shown
in Figure 6.2.1. The journey begins with a deep understanding of the uniqueness
and talents of self. For educators, this means valuing children for their unique
talents, striving to understand the whole child. We need to help children answer
questions such as: Who am I? What is the meaning and purpose of life?

The second philosophical belief is seeking deep meanings to unite thought and
action, morality and fact, body and mind, individual and community (Grange
2003: 15–16). Dao seeks real balance, not harmony achieved at the expense of
others. Good teachers help students find connection and purposeful direction
in their learning, encouraging meta-understanding of self, family, peers and
communities.

The third philosophical belief concerns helping children pursue dreams by developing the life of the mind and the spirit: helping children ask big, transcendent questions, developing courage to find a vocation that brings meaning and self-fulfillment.

The fourth philosophical belief highlights the importance of perseverance in pursuing the best for all, and enduring personal hardships.

Resonant with Confucian beliefs, Dewey (1916) was concerned with the enhancement of democratic community together with developing the concept of the unique self. He viewed schools as life itself, rather than a preparation for life.

> [We must] make each one of our schools an embryonic community life, active with types of occupations that reflect the life of the larger society, and throughout permeated with the spirit of art, history, and science. When the school introduces and trains each child of society into membership within such a little community, saturating him with the spirit of service, and providing him with the instruments of effective self-direction, we shall have the deepest and best guarantor of a larger society which is worthy, lovely, and harmonious.
>
> (J. Palmer 2001: 177)

In summary, we believe that a school culture should be guided by four philosophical beliefs:

- individuals are uniquely talented
- education should seek deep meaning, and help children discover connection and purpose
- children should be encouraged to pursue dreams
- children should develop perseverance through adversity.

What can teachers do?

John Gardner (1984 [1961]: 144) asks if it is possible for people to achieve excellence if they don't believe in anything. He argues that talent in the service of beauty or justice is one thing; talent in the service of greed or tyranny is quite another. Roeper (1997) philosophizes:

> True success in teaching gifted children can only be achieved when the passions of the child – her soul and mind – are accepted as the foundations upon which we bridge society's expectations as well as our own.
>
> (Roeper 1997: 166)

She strongly urges educators to nurture the psyche of the child towards self-actualization, while developing understanding of the wider world.

A young Singaporean teacher with a personal record of high achievement, and a recent award acknowledging him as an outstanding educator, says:

> I used to cry myself to sleep in secondary school. I needed reassurance that it was okay to question and to search. My parents felt that I had found my path, but I couldn't really communicate with them, in a deep sense. . . . A teacher could have helped to push boundaries to help me find *me*.

Tharman Shanmugaratnam (2004) emphasizes that the greatest challenge in Singapore education is to 'provide more space for kids to pursue their passion . . . [t]o create a culture of intellectual curiosity in children . . . and a spirit of initiative to try something different, even if one might fail'.

Handy (1998) uses the *hungry spirit* as a metaphor for the emptiness people feel after the quest for material and academic success to the exclusion of anything else. He writes:

> I am angered by the waste of so many people's lives, dragged down by poverty in the midst of riches. I am concerned by the absence of a more transcendent view of life . . . and by the prevalence of the economic myth which colours all that we do. Money [and traditional conceptions of success] is the means of life and not the point of it. There must be something that we can do to restore the balance.
>
> (Handy 1998: 3)

P. Palmer (1997) writes that we teach who we are: he emphasizes that good teaching cannot be reduced to a technique; good teaching comes from the identity and integrity of the teacher. Good teachers join self, subject and students in the fabric of life because they teach from an integral and undivided self; they manifest in their own lives, and evoke in their students, the quest to develop the intellect, to realize the self and to search for meaning.

McLeod (1996) describes deep learning as having shifts in cognitions, attitudes, emotions and values. Grauerholz (2001) proposes that teachers use pedagogical approaches that consciously promote student learning on levels beyond the cognitive, incorporate diverse methods that engage students in personal exploration, relate course material to their own lives and help students clarify their own values and responsibilities to others. Teachers need to love questions and to live in search of answers. Pleiss and Feldhusen (1995) emphasize the critical role of a teacher/mentor who not only contributes knowledge and expertise, but also models the self, providing values, vision and life goals.

Csikszentmihalyi and Larson (1997: 179) identify the development of a personal *life theme* as the ultimate achievement in the path of personal growth. This refers to a process of 'transforming misfortune in one's life – or in the wider social environment – into a goal that gives direction and meaning to a whole life'. This puts the individual on a path of determined perseverance, enabling significant self-growth despite the presence of major obstacles. In their work with adolescent populations, Csikszentmihalyi and Larson (1997) note that only a small number of adolescents actually develop authentic life goals. The majority are content to pursue life themes scripted by society, namely, getting a degree, a good job, marriage and children.

Conclusion

Confucius and Dewey viewed education as thinking about life. Writing this chapter has given us an opportunity to look back to our own education and the cultures we grew up with, seeking to understand self in the larger context of humanity beyond self.

Key questions

1   Academic biases in the education of children with high ability exist, despite encouraging educational reform efforts on many fronts. Identify possible sources of academic biases in your country. What can be done to minimize or eliminate these biases?
2   'Half-sightedness' refers to seeing things with only one eye, with the other eye, representing spirit or soul, offering another lens to seeing and understanding reality (P. Palmer 1993). What are some examples of a half-sighted vision of education? How would perspectives differ with a more whole-sighted vision of education?
3   To develop a life or depth dimension in the education of the gifted, the Evolving Self Model put forward in this chapter highlights a culture of school that: (a) believes in the unique talents of all children, (b) seeks deep meaning and helps children discover connection and purpose, (c) encourages children to pursue dreams, and (d) encourages children to be perseverant in times of adversity. What are some specific ways in which teachers could play a part in helping their children?

References

Borland, J. B. (1996) Gifted education and the threat of irrelevance. *Journal for the Education of the Gifted*, 19: 129–147.

Changing in time for the future (2003) *The Singapore Straits Times*, 4 October: 26.

Commission on Youth (2002) *Youth in Hong Kong: A Statistical Profile 2002*. Retrieved 10 November 2003 from http://www.info.gov.hk/coy/text/eng/report/youth_statistical2002full. htm

Csikszentmihalyi, M. and Larson, R. (1997) The growth of complexity: shaping meaningful lives. *NAMTA Journal*, 22(2): 177–195.

Dewey, J. (1916) *Democracy and Education: An Introduction to the Philosophy of Education*. New York: The Free Press.

Gardner, J. W. (1984 [1961]) *Excellence: Can We be Equal and Excellent Too?* New York: W. W. Norton.

Grange, J. (2003) John Dewey and Confucius: ecological philosophers. *Journal of Chinese Philosophy*, 30: 419–431.

Grauerholz, L. (2001) Teaching holistically to achieve deep learning. *College Teaching*, 49(2): 44–50.

Gregory, K. and Clarke, M. (2003) High-stakes assessment in England and Singapore. *Theory into Practice*, 42: 66–78.

Handy, C. (1998) *The Hungry Spirit*. London: Arrow.

Heng, M. A. (1999) Scrutinizing common sense: the role of practical intelligence in intellectual giftedness, unpublished doctoral dissertation, Teachers College, Columbia University, New York.

Higher Education Research Institute, University of California, Los Angeles (2004) *The American Freshman: National Norms for Fall 2003*. Retrieved 1 March 2004 from http://www.gseis.ucla.edu/heri/news_freshman.html

Kessler, R. (2000) *The Soul of Education: Helping Students Find Connection, Compassion, and Character at School*. Alexandria, VA: ASCD (Association for Supervision and Curriculum Development).

Keys, W., Harris, S. and Fernandes, C. (1996) *Third International Mathematics and Science Study: First National Report (Part 1)*. Slough, UK: National Foundation for Educational Research.

Lantieri, L. (2001) Why we need schools with heart and soul. *Reclaiming Children and Youth*, 10(1): 2–4.

McLeod, A. (1996) Discovering and facilitating deep learning states. *National Teaching and Learning Forum*, 5: 1–7.

Martin, T. (2000) Man is a misshapen monster: G. K. Chesterton. *Vital Speeches of the Day*, 66(21): 659–664.

Newman, F. (2000) Saving higher education's soul. *Change*, 32(5): 16–23.

Palmer, J. A. (ed.) (2001) *Fifty Major Thinkers on Education: From Confucius to Dewey*. New York: Routledge.

Palmer, P. J. (1993) *To Know as We are Known: Education as a Spiritual Journey*. New York: HarperCollins.

Palmer, P. J. (1997) The heart of a teacher. *Change*, 29(6): 14–21.

Pleiss, M. K. and Feldhusen, J. F. (1995) Mentors, role models, and heroes in the lives of gifted children. *Educational Psychologist*, 30(3): 159–169.

Roeper, A. (1995) *Annemarie Roeper: Selective Writing and Speeches*. Minneapolis, MN: Free Spirit.

Roeper, A. (1997) Listen to the gifted child. *Roeper Review*, 19: 166–167.

Rogers, D. L. (2000) [Review of Thomas S. Popkewitz's book *Struggling for the Soul: The Politics of Schooling and the Construction of the Teacher*]. *Contemporary Sociology*, 29(1): 269–270.

School daze (2002) *Time*, 15 April: 46–51.

Teens crushed by study pressures (2003) *The Singapore Straits Times*, 28 November: A8.

Shanmugaratnam, T. (2004) Tharman's greatest challenge, *Today*, 18 February: 1–2.

Wake-up call for Singapore youths (2000) *The Singapore Straits Times*, 24 February: 1.

Webster (1971) *Webster's Third New International Dictionary*. Springfield, MA: G&C Merriam.

6.3 Personal perspective: Muslim gifted – religious education in Saudi Arabia

Aisha Arshad

I am originally from Pakistan, but I lived in a two-bedroom apartment in Al-khobar, Saudi Arabia for sixteen years. The laws are strictly according to Islam, the major religion; crime is rare. We felt lucky living in Saudi Arabia because we could go on a Haj pilgrimage to visit the two holy mosques, Masjod Al-Itaram (Mecca) and Masjod-e-Nabwi (Medina), the location of prophet Muhammad's tomb.

As well as learning English, I learnt the official language, Arabic. The men in Saudi Arabia wear a long white shirt called a *tumb* and a headdress, a *gutrah*. The women have to cover themselves with a black veil called an *abaaya* when they are outside their homes. I started wearing the *abaaya* when I was 10 years old. The Arab women in Saudi Arabia wear long straight dresses that may have embroidery or beads on them and gold jewelry. Women decorate their hands, feet and fingertips with henna. I love decorating my hands with henna for Eid.

Eid is the name of the two Muslim festivals. We celebrate Eid-Al a Fitr, after the month of Ramadhan, by praying, dressing up, giving gifts and visiting family and friends. The second festival, Eidal-Adha, takes place after Haj. Middle Eastern food is light and healthy, consisting of lots of fresh vegetables, rice, chicken, lamb, grains, yogurt sauces and dips, pita bread and cheese. Alcohol is prohibited in Saudi Arabia; there are no illegal drugs there such as heroin because of severe punishment. Women are not allowed to drive in Saudi Arabia and the only jobs they can hold are teacher, doctor or nurse.

In first grade I attended Manarat, a small private Muslim school, and had to wear a uniform: a white blouse under a blue pinafore. We started the day with an assembly reciting the holy Quran, and singing the Saudi national anthem. Based on the British system, we were taught reading, English, Math as well as Arabic and Islamic studies, physical education and art. The younger classes such as kindergarten were coeducational, but from first grade, the class was all girls or all boys.

Up until the ninth grade I attended Dhahran Academy, a coeducational American-based international school. Other than the general subjects, we also had extracurricular courses such as art, music, band, home economics, French, Spanish, Arabic and various sports. Methods of instruction and assessment were varied and included a blend of interesting projects, hands-on activities and field trips. We attended school from Saturday to Wednesday with Thursday and Friday being the weekend. The students could wear anything they wanted within the school dress code. Most of my teachers were from the United States, but the student body was ethnically diverse, and throughout the year this diversity was celebrated. Dhahran Academy was not a religious school, but the various holidays were recognized. After graduating in ninth grade, many of the students went to the United States or different boarding schools around the world.

After completing the ninth grade, I attended Manarat-Al-Sharkia, an all-girls Islamic school, and being used to the American system of education, studies in Manarat, although in English, were at times a challenge for me. Although the majority of the students and teachers were Muslim, they came from various parts of the world such as Asia, North America and Africa. In Manarat, we were required to wear a uniform, and had to cover ourselves with the veil and cover our faces when entering and leaving the school. As Muslims, everyday we had break so that we could observe the afternoon prayer, and that gradually got me to try to pray five times a day facing Mecca. Other than the general education subjects, extracurricular education included arts and crafts, home economics, various sciences, and different clubs that students could join based on their interests. Islamic studies were part of the curriculum and a Quran and Arabic class.

After completing the tenth grade my family and I moved to Orlando, Florida where I completed my education at University High School, pretty easy for me because it was just like Dhahran Academy including American history. I bought jeans and T-shirts to fit in: it would be awkward to walk around in a *shalwar qamiz* at school! There were hardly any Pakistani students and I really missed that because there are so many Pakistanis in Saudi Arabia. I received my bachelor's degree from University of Central Florida in elementary education, and am currently taking courses towards a master's degree in reading education. What I really like about moving to Florida was that there is more independence and job opportunities. So being independent, such as getting my first job teaching at the Muslim Academy, and driving was something I had to get used to. I love it here. I do really miss Mecca and Medina in Saudi Arabia and being able to go on a pilgrimage. What I miss most, however, is the peace in Saudi Arabia.

6.4   Conflict resolution 5: religious intolerance

Gillian Eriksson

A student, who was an immigrant from China, had been attending an American elementary school in fifth grade for a few months. This student had a fluency in English, and had demonstrated a keen interest in American culture and history. Much to the dismay of her traditional Chinese parents, she had striven to dress, talk and behave like her American peers. She was very advanced in technology and mathematics and had been referred to the gifted program. The family had lived in a system that had provided no exposure to religion. One day after recess, the student arrived in class very upset and politely asked to speak privately to the teacher. She said that she had met some other students on the playground, who had told her that if she did not believe in Jesus that she would be 'condemned to Hell' when she died. 'Is this really true?' the student asked the teacher.

7 Gender issues

7.1 Winning girls, winning women

Sylvia Rimm

Counseling gifted girls for successful careers in our society takes planning for a generation of counselors that was itself raised by families where a mother's only role was typically homemaker. Barbara Kerr (1985) did a ten-year follow-up study of twenty-four of her classmates who had been identified as gifted in the post-Sputnik (1957) era. Their school had been provided with a seven-year curriculum designed to foster leadership and success. She compared her female classmates to males in the same program, and her findings were not surprising for the times. Six (25 percent) hadn't completed their bachelor's degrees. Twelve (50 percent) had earned only bachelor's degrees, six in education. Three had master's degrees, one had a medical degree and one had a law degree. Among the men who had graduated from the same school gifted program, all had at least bachelor's degrees, three also had master's degrees, two had doctorates, two had law degrees and one had a medical degree. Even more relevant, all the men were employed in professions. While one-third of the women were homemakers with children, four were employed as medical technicians or nurses and four were teachers. Two women were employed in the arts and crafts field, two were graduate assistants, one was a physician, one an attorney and two were business women. This was progress compared to early generations, but the gender differences were nevertheless dramatic.

When our own children were growing up, there were no female physicians or attorneys in our community. There were almost no women executives in business, and absolutely none were elected to government office. Although our children had heard of scientist Marie Curie, she represented all women in science, because no other women scientists were apparent. Even in the media, successful women role models were sparse. Women could be in glamorous roles or act as mothers or nurses on the screen, but serious news journalists on radio, TV or in the press were rare. Nor were the arts a safe haven for women. Symphony orchestras rarely included women, and almost no women had their work exhibited in serious art galleries. Nurturing careers, including teacher, social worker or nurse, invited women, but only if those careers didn't interfere with mothering, their primary role.

The women's movement initiated changes that accessed new and dramatic opportunities for girls. My daughters, Sara and Ilonna, assisted me in researching the childhood environments that lead girls to becoming pioneering successful women. We published that research in our book *See Jane Win: The Rimm Report on How 1000 Girls Became Successful Women* (Rimm et al. 1999). This describes how parents, educators and counselors can nurture the talents of gifted girls based on what we learned about how gifted women were nurtured toward success. We shared these findings further in story book form in *How Jane Won: 55 Successful Women Share How They Grew from Ordinary Girls to Extraordinary Women* (Rimm and Rimm-Kaufman 2001) and also translated those findings to advice directly for middle school girls in *See Jane Win for Girls* (Rimm 2003) which contains quizzes and exercises that girls can use on their own but would be more effective if counselors used them with groups of girls.

Themes for developing successful women

Before reviewing the themes that most frequently emerged in the lives of the 1236 successful women in our research study, I'll emphasize how we defined success, and recruited the women we surveyed and interviewed. In order for women to be included in the study, they had to be in one of twelve arbitrarily selected high-status careers. The eight non-traditional careers included law, government, business, medicine, science, media, orchestral music and visual art. Four additional categories included the traditional nurturant careers of home-maker, teacher, nurse and mental health professional. Other criteria for inclusion were that the women had to consider themselves reasonably happy in their career, family and relationship lives. Women interviewed typically closed their interviews with a statement similar to, 'I'm so fortunate to find work that's so fulfilling and permits me to make a positive difference', so it was truly a fulfillment definition of success that we used. We gathered our candidates through national advertising, letters to women in professional groups and through word-of-mouth communication. Analysis of the questionnaire and interviews led us to the main themes, described next.

Competition

When asked about these women's most positive experiences in childhood, more women included winning in competition than any other experience. Apparently, winning was both exhilarating and motivating to these girls. The form of competition varied and included everything from sports or music contests, having an essay accepted for publication or getting an all-A report card. Some women described themselves as highly competitive, for example, environmental engineer

Teresa Culver, who couldn't imagine playing a game without keeping score; gifted educator Frances Karnes described her victories as gains she made compared to her own past experiences. When news journalist Jane Pauley became a winning debater in high school, she thanked her teacher, Harry Wilfong, for introducing her to winning in competition for the first time. Jane attributes her career in television to the excitement that came from winning in debate, which for the first time cast her in the role of an excellent speaker. Many other women credited winning in speech or debate competition to their attraction to government, law or the media where they could continue their successful oratory.

> A major milestone for me was winning a speaking tournament at Ball State University. Before that, I didn't know the feeling of being number one. I really liked it. I kept at it for three years, ultimately becoming a state champion and competing in the national tournament.

The successful women in our research didn't always win. Their stories of resilience or recovering after failure were inspiring and will help girls understand how winning builds confidence and losing builds resilience. Their optimism that emerged despite losses was energizing. Martha Lindner, a dyslexic child who eventually became a successful attorney, asked us to remind girls that when you think the worst has happened to you, it often turns out to be the best. Although Martha graduated at the top of her law school class, she was unable to get a job in a law firm because they were hiring only men. Instead, she formed her own firm and became more successful than her fellow graduates, despite their abundance of job offers. Being her own boss also allowed the flexibility to continue her mothering responsibilities because she could control her own schedule. Her resilience was impressive.

Smart, hardworking and independent

The women were asked to check characteristics that described them in childhood, and the most frequently checked were descriptors such as smart, hardworking and independent. Quite a few described themselves as good little girls, 30 percent as shy and a similar percentage as perfectionistic. There were also quite a few bookworms and tomboys, but very few described themselves as troublemakers or fashion leaders in their middle and high school years.

The women attributed their feelings of intelligence to a variety of strengths. A love of reading often built intellectual confidence. African-American neurosurgeon Alexa Canady remembers reading ten to twelve little blue biographies a week, and Senator Kay Bailey Hutchison had read all the biographies in her school library. Being highly verbal was also viewed as a basis for feeling highly intelligent. The women in law most frequently reported they were early talkers, followed by the women in media. Perhaps that's not a surprising finding.

Astronaut Cady Coleman attributed her feelings of being gifted to her being included in gifted programming. She concluded that her intelligence was valued if schools were willing to invest money in special programs for gifted kids. Environmental engineer Teresa Culver remembered herself as the 'nerdy little kid who finished the math book early and taught the other kids' and Red Cross President Martha Evans recalled her family celebrations of her excellent report cards as proof of her high intelligence. As to hard work and independence, Lesley Seymour, editor of *Marie Claire* magazine, recalls that she was a worker bee and always had creative ideas. Being a hard worker was a repeated theme for many of these women as girls, an example of independence came from former Governor of New Jersey Christie Whitman who was a loner as a child, which she said prepared her well for politics.

Television news journalist Deborah Roberts found integration to be pivotal in proving her intellectual confidence. She, like many of her friends, was worried about whether she would be successful when African-Americans and whites were integrated in the small Georgian town where she grew up.

> My earliest memories of deciding who I was and what I wanted to do with my life go back to the fourth grade. I lived in Georgia and distinctly remember segregation, colored waiting rooms, and a colored school. When I moved to an integrated school, it was a time of nervousness, but also a time of wonder and exploration. I made friends with white children for the first time and realized that the big scary world wasn't as scary as I'd thought. I tried out for cheerleading in seventh grade and was upset because I didn't make it, so I tried again the next year and did. My activities emboldened me to feel like I could do well in the world.
>
> (Deborah Roberts, ABC's 20/20 Newsmagazine)

Active and interested

The successful women were actively involved in extracurricular activities like music, art, sports, drama, Girl Scouts and religious activities. They seemed to be honing their skills, inasmuch as their areas of interest often led them toward future careers. For example, women in government were typically in student government or active in politics, and women in law were often debaters. Business women showed entrepreneurial activities early. They often talked about selling the most Girl Scout cookies or created little business enterprises of their own. Scientists and physicians typically became interested in science and math as youngsters, and the artists and musicians practiced their talents early. They won contests or were known among peers for their talents. Active involvement helped girls cope with social issues such as feeling different, not considering themselves popular or pretty enough, feeling left out of cliques or not being confident enough. Most girls experience self-esteem and peer pressure problems during the middle and high school years, but successful women seemed to know how to escape those pressures positively.

> I wasn't the prettiest or the most popular. I was very gawky, with curly dark hair that I went out of my way to iron and straighten at a time when

having straight blond was in. But I was very active in student government and Jewish youth groups. I was committed to standing up for what I believed in.

(Shelly Berkley, US Congresswoman from Nevada)

Among the successful women, only 25 percent considered themselves very social, while 40 percent considered themselves less social than typical and the remaining 35 percent described their sociability as average. Perhaps their interests gave them less time for partying, or their lesser social life provided more time for their learning and involvement in their interests.

Role models and mentors

At least one parent, and often both, tended to have expectations of their daughters. About half of the successful women identified mainly with their mothers, and about a quarter of the successful women identified with their fathers. Also, grandparents, teachers and other adults were often inspirational to them. Many thanked their teachers for inspiring them.

> My seventh-grade English teacher was Mrs. Hardy. Her expectations were very high. Everyone was terrified of her, but I always wanted to please her. She introduced me to poetry, to speaking grammatically and to striving to do more. She was hard but fair, and it meant so much to me to do well in her class. She was responsible for my yearning to want to be the best.
>
> (Deborah Roberts, ABC's 20/20 news journalist)

Most of the women thanked multiple mentors, both male and female, for their continued inspiration. Personally, it was my guidance counselor, Henrietta Herbert, who inspired me to go on with my education beyond high school, and I will appreciate her forever.

Counseling activities

The purpose of counseling girls is to build sufficient confidence and resilience so that they may successfully contribute to our society and fulfill themselves. By any comparative standard, women continue to lag behind men in almost all professional career fields, but as Reis and Moon (2002) point out, that isn't the only standard of assessing women's underachievement. More pertinent are women's lost opportunities. Too many talented women look back at their lives with feelings of regret because family responsibilities and societal pressures have prevented them from developing and applying their talents. Counseling girls so that they will achieve to their potential in life is the motivation for teaching Jane to want to be a winner.

Although *See Jane Win for Girls* (Rimm 2003) provides many counseling activities to encourage these themes, I share a few here. The first is the development of a strengths and weaknesses chart for building self-esteem (see Box 7.1.1).

Box 7.1.1   Strengths, weaknesses and changes

My own strengths, weaknesses and changes chart

Strengths	Things to improve	Changes to make	Things to accept

From Rimm, S. (2003) *See Jane Win for Girls: A Smart Girl's Guide to Success.* Minneapolis, MN: Free Spirit. 866.703–7322 (This page may be photocopied for individual, classroom or small group work only. Used with permission.)

We first ask the girls to list their strengths or the qualities they like about themselves. Some girls will develop long lists while those with less confidence may need encouragement for finding their positive characteristics. The next column allows girls to list their characteristics that they aren't happy about. Sometimes, girls find too many negative characteristics about themselves while others have a hard time admitting any problems. It helps to explain to the girls that sometimes weaknesses are related to strengths. For example, a person who perseveres (a good quality) may sometimes be considered stubborn, a not-so-positive trait. A generous girl may also find she does so much for others that she doesn't get her own work done. Viewing weaknesses on a continuum with strengths often helps girls accept that they have problems and prevents them from becoming defensive about admitting them. The last two columns can help girls to set goals for doing something about their weaknesses, or if indeed there are problems they can't change, learning to at least accept these problems they can learn to live with. For example, a girl who's taller or bigger than she'd like to be will have to accept that shrinking herself isn't possible. She can eat healthfully and exercise to have a healthy body but may never be petite. Sharing discussions about strengths and weaknesses can help girls feel good about themselves while realizing that no one else is perfect either.

The discussion of strengths and problems provides opportunities to talk about perfectionism and coping with competition as well. Some suggestions to help girls cope with perfectionism:

- Take pride in your efforts. When you've completed a project that you've worked hard on, give yourself credit for what you've done.

- Learn to see your mistakes and other people's criticism as proof that you're challenging yourself. Tell yourself, 'I made a mistake, but that's okay. What lessons can I learn from this?'
- If you're studying more than anyone else in your class, try cutting back your study time by ten minutes a day. If it doesn't lower your grade, cut your study time ten minutes more until you find the right balance between study time and good grades. If your grades go down while you're experimenting, add back some study time. Be proud of your good study habits, but leave yourself time for fun, too!
- Enter a contest or try an activity that you may not be very good at. Take a chance! Don't even think about being the best. Record your progress as you go along, and compare it to where you started. For example, if you try running, keep track of how much your speed or distance improves. If you try music, play an easy song every so often and remember how hard it once was.
- Read stories about successful women. Notice how many times they learned from their failures and mistakes, and how they coped with hard times.
- Compliment a friend, sister or brother about something they've done – especially something that you wish you could do. You'll be amazed how good it feels to help someone else feel good about their strengths, and it will help you accept that you don't have to be the best at everything.
- Ask a parent or teacher to make written suggestions about how you can improve a project. Thank her for the ideas. Then decide which pieces of advice (if any) you want to take. Remind yourself that it's okay to have different opinions, and the suggestions were meant to help you, not criticize you.
- When you need a topic for an essay, a research report or a science project, quickly jot down as many ideas as you can. Don't criticize any of them until you have a long list. Then whittle down the ideas until you're left with the ones you feel are the best.
- If you see yourself becoming too serious about things, try laughing at your own mistakes.

Because developing interests is so important for building confidence, I've included *My Interest Inventory Chart* (Box 7.1.2).

Girls can list their activities in the first column and take time to think about rating those interests for their feelings about them, their level of skills and what they think they derive from the activities. When they've completed their list, they can decide whether they need to explore further activities or consider dropping some because they're too busy or not enjoying them. This is an activity you may want girls to review with their parents. A girl may not particularly enjoy her religious instruction or her Greek lessons, but parents may be prioritizing them for good reason. The last column that permits them to describe the benefits they derive from activities may even help them to understand why they should continue their Greek lessons even if they happen not to be enjoying them.

Additional counseling activities include ideas for enhancing feelings of intelligence, improving social skills, learning from travel, coping with changes in lives,

Box 7.1.2   Interest inventory

My interest inventory chart

Activity	How I feel about it (Rate 1–5)	My talent/skill level (Rate 1–5)	What I get from it

From Rimm, S. (2003) *See Jane Win for Girls: A Smart Girl's Guide to Success*. Minneapolis, MN: Free Spirit. 866.703–7322 (This page may be photocopied for individual, classroom or small group work only. Used with permission.)

finding role models and mentors, managing family relationship and sibling rivalry, planning their dreams for their future and finally, making the world a better place.

> Everything I've done that led me on the path to being chief was motivated by passion and by the issues. I saw needs and felt moved to try to do something about them. For example, I became director of the Cherokee Nation's Community Development Department because some of our people really needed housing, so I felt I could do something about that. Even if I'd lacked the self-confidence to run for office, my feelings about the issues at hand would have overcome that because I felt so strongly about them.
> (Wilma P. Mankiller, Former Principal Chief, Cherokee Nation)

Key questions

1   How could the activities in the book be used with coeducational groups or be adapted for boys?
2   What do the findings of this research demonstrate about the specific needs of girls from minority backgrounds?
3   How should the curriculum be modified to infuse the needs of girls?

Acknowledgements

The essence of this chapter has appeared in *Gifted Education International* 19(3). AB Academic Publishers (used with permission).

References

Kerr, B. (1985) *Smart Girls, Gifted Women*. Dayton, OH: Ohio Psychology Press.

Reis, S. M. and Moon, S. (2002) Models and strategies for counselling, guidance and emotional support of gifted and talented students, in M. Niehart, S. M. Reis, N. M. Robinson and S. Moon (eds) *The Social and Emotional Development of Gifted Children: What do we Know?* Washington DC: National Association for Gifted Children.

Rimm, S. (2003) *See Jane Win for Girls*. Minneapolis, MN: Free Spirit.

Rimm, S. and Rimm-Kaufman, S. (2001) *How Jane Won: 55 Successful Women Share How They Grew from Ordinary Girls to Extraordinary Women*. New York: Crown.

Rimm, S., Rimm-Kaufman, S. and Rimm, I. (1999) *See Jane Win: The Rimm Report on How 1000 Girls Became Successful Women*. New York: Crown.

7.2   Young gifted women in Taiwan: barriers or supports?

Ching-Chih Kuo

In 2002, we began to trace female students who graduated from gifted classes in senior high schools from 1986 to 1998 in Taiwan. The purpose of this research was to understand their career progress and self-evaluation of the development of their potential; 840 subjects participated and returned their questionnaires: 'The Career Development Questionnaire for Gifted Female Students'.

The questionnaire included three open-ended questions:

1   To what extent have you developed your potential up to now?
2   What are the significant factors that have impacted your self-fulfillment?
3   What are the primary barriers that might hinder your potential actualization?

The following, collated from the feedback of questionnaires, are the supporting and obstructive factors that have influenced career development. We intend to use the findings to help young gifted women to fulfill their potential.

For 199 young gifted women talented in science, 68 percent of the subgroup said that they had failed to develop their potential or had developed very little and 28 percent said that they had developed their potential to some extent. No members of the subgroup said that they had fully developed their potential. Encouragement from family, discussion with peers, and warm friendship were the primary supporting factors.

> It depended on whether I was ambitious and active, how much my family gave emotional and financial support, and whether I was the person with the ability to endure the frustration or pressure.

Barriers included mismatch between educational experience and work, and personal factors, such as poor time management, financial pressure, lack of recognition of self-ability, interests, or potential.

Regarding 108 young gifted women talented in language arts, nearly 70 percent of them said that they had seldom developed their potential or had developed to a limited extent. Almost 30 percent of this subgroup said that they developed their potential as far as they could.

'Full support from family, the sense of achievement from working or studying, challenging work, and positive attitudes toward working from colleagues' allowed verbally young gifted women freedom to develop their talents.

As to barriers, most verbally young gifted women complained that they dealt with trivial, messy, routine work, and 'busyness with laborious tasks.' Some answered that they chose jobs that met parental expectations, and not in accord with interests or talents, owing to financial difficulties.

As to 209 young gifted women talented in music, 60 percent of this group stopped developing or developed their potential to a limited extent, while 36 percent of this group developed their potential frequently or constantly.

Doing tasks or researches in accord with interests or talents, receiving appropriate support from family, and keeping learning were significant for self-fulfillment.

'But I did believe that it was my interests that made me keep self-actualizing.' Limitation of the working environment, lack of career counseling and opportunities to perform, and financial burdens were the main barriers.

Concerning 241 young gifted women talented in visual art, 72 percent developed their potential to a little extent, but there were 25 percent who were developing their potential to a great extent. Encouragement and assistance from family were the essential factors. Linking work or study with talents was also helpful. Pressure for money was the main limiting factor: 'It was impossible for us to earn a living simply by selling our paintings.' Mismatch between talents and work and limitation of working conditions were apparent: 'The principal of my working school asked me to be the tutor for lower classes. My talents in visual arts were seriously ignored.'

For 83 young gifted women talented in dance, nearly 60 percent of the subgroup did not, or barely, developed their potential, and 37 percent developed their potential reasonably well. Training exercises, self-expectation, appropriate pressure from employers, correspondence of talents or interests with work, assistance and support from colleagues were the significant elements. For instance: 'Gifted education made me know what my talents were and I had chances to explore and to enjoy my giftedness.'

Financial burdens were the main barriers, together with self-doubt, uncertain career planning, mismatch between talent and work, and lack of opportunity: 'I just graduated this year. I thought I had better earn my living firstly and delay the schedule to study further.'

We analysed external/internal supports and barriers from the answers given to the three open-ended questions. Internal supports included self-identification and expectation, positive life values, professional educational background, insistence on research, correspondence of talents and interests with work or study. External supports included encouragement from employers, family, peers, and tutors. Internal barriers included lack of ambition, unsettled state of mind or life, poor health, poor time and pressure management, negative female stereotypes, mismatch between talent and work, and self-doubt. External barriers included lack of family support, limitation of opportunity, restriction in working environment, financial considerations, social values, and jealousy from peers. Some of the findings with regard to supporting factors correlate with Fleming and Hollinger (1994). Most interpretations relating to internal/external barriers are in accord with the findings of Farmer (1976, 1997).

From the feedback derived from questionnaires, we find that more than 60 percent of young gifted women evaluated the development of their potential as very limited. As Reis (1991) has shown, gifted women spend too much time on their work occupation, family and children. They may abandon their career expectations or personal needs to meet social expectations. How to assist gifted women to reconcile their self-actualization with social roles is a major issue.

Key questions

1   Discuss any issues in the above chapter that are paralleled in the context of your own society.
2   How would you encourage girls to develop the self-confidence to challenge any prejudice they encounter in pursuing career opportunities?
3   How would you develop a careers curriculum that would promote equality of opportunity?

References

Farmer, H. S. (ed.) (1976) What inhibits achievement and career motivation in women? *The Counseling Psychologist*, 6: 12–14.

Farmer, H. S. (ed.) (1997) *Diversity and Women's Career Development.* London: Sage.

Fleming, E. S. and Hollinger, C. L. (1994) Project choice: a longitudinal study of the career development of gifted and talented young women, in R. F. Subotnik and K. D. Arnold (eds) *Beyond Terman: Contemporary Longitudinal Studies of Giftedness and Talent.* Norwood, NJ: Ablex.

Reis, S. (1991) The need for clarification in research designed to examine gender differences in achievement and accomplishment. *Roeper Review*, 13: 193–198.

7.3　Contemporary issues impacting gifted boys

Gil Caudill

Issues of security and tradition make it difficult for societies to adjust their perspectives regarding gender roles and functioning. Societies are more comfortable when things remain the same but if they are to realize their greatest potential, both genders should be given equal opportunities. The field of boys' studies is an increasing trend, and this contribution presents some of the subtle and underlying issues specifically affecting gifted boys in multicultural settings.

We, in gifted education, probably pay too much attention to gender differences. The abilities of gifted girls and gifted boys are quite similar, if not intellectually identical. However, our societies place varying importance on gender. Consequently, we must deal with the discrepant values and expectations taught to each gender. Educationally, we must deal with interests and abilities of our students, regardless of gender. Psychologically, we would be remiss were we not to understand and explain to our charges the overt and covert pressures and expectations our societies imbue, and the short and long term consequences for ignoring or combating those pressures.

Throughout the research it is assumed that gifted boys have the 'best deal'. While there are areas and instances where this may be true, there are significant gender specific issues with which gifted boys must deal.

Expectations for males may be subtler than for females

Many societies expect males to be strong, assertive, decisive and economically functional. Although these expectations may never be voiced, the role models admired by many young males, and the societal feedback, epitomize these expectations. Some believe that males demonstrate a tendency to avoid introspection. They can see that others such as minorities, females or socioeconomic groups have problems, but that their own socialized masculinity may be confining or in need of reexamination does not occur to them (Farrell 1973).

Male peers often denigrate high academic achievement or intellectual function

There is significantly more pressure on boys to be virile than to be academically and/or intellectually functional. This may have a bearing on dropout rates and underachievement. Underachievement may also be an attempt to assert masculinity in some gifted males (Kerr and Foley Nicpon 2003). These pressures can intensify feelings of estrangement leading to asocial or antisocial behavior. A high degree of intelligence does not guarantee a high degree of social awareness nor responsibility for high social values, high moral character or a social conscience. When gifted individuals feel estranged, they may use their intelligence to combat rather than complement the society in which they live. Each society has an obligation to try to nurture their children to make a positive contribution to the world.

Gifted males often react more emotionally to situations than do their intellectually average male peers

This, as well as high achievement, often helps to alienate them from their peers. Male peers are often not very accepting of gifted males who react emotionally, or who exhibit behaviors usually attributed to girls. Female peers, however, are more accepting of girls who exhibit behaviors usually attributed to males (Caudill and Croteau 1993). If it were not for societal pressures on both males and females, would children's behavior be androgynous? Probably not, but they would certainly be more free to behave in ways other than expected societal norms.

Many gifted males, and many societies, attribute the failures of males to exogenous factors, and males' successes to endogenous factors

Research suggests that this allows males to retain their confidence (Pipher 1994). This may be correct in many instances, but it is hardly an accurate perception of self. If our goal is to help gifted males toward self-actualization, we must help them to be accurate assessors of their abilities and functions. Confidence and high expectations are paramount for success. False confidence and unrealistic expectations are harbingers of failure.

Because in many societies gifted females have not been afforded the same opportunities as males, there is a 'backlash' which is intended to rectify history, but which may also handicap males

Correcting inequitable history with inequitable policies is just as unjust. Programs that target females, while positive in intent, may deny those opportunities to males.

There is significantly more research concerning females than males

Research is intended to shed light and to give focus to the problems and needs of diverse groups. The more we know, the better we can ameliorate problems and set realistic goals. It is interesting to observe in the research that expected gender differences in ability often did not exist. What did exist were perception and expectation differences. There is still much needed research about both gifted males and females, and the expectations of their societies. Gowan et al. (1979) suggested a need for research in the area of gender discrimination. Were there other reasons for women not being as successful as men besides discrimination? Perhaps discrimination is equally applied to males and females, but in different ways.

Whatever pressures and expectations are placed on males, twice exceptional, minority, or highly gifted males have increased pressures and expectations

Twice-exceptional have the conflicting messages that they have great abilities but at the same time they have limitations. Until these limitations and abilities are well understood, confusion and frustration can interfere with functioning and adjustment. Gifted minority males appear to be especially influenced by cultural pressures and expectations, sometimes in anti-academic or antisocial ways. The social isolation felt by many gifted individuals appears to be magnified in the highly gifted population.

Conclusion

Somewhat justifiably, gender research since the mid-1970s has focused on females. In many cultures females have not been afforded opportunities that were available for males. Since the mid-1990s the need to focus gender research on males has manifested itself. Societal discriminations are focused on both genders. Those discriminations for males appear to be subtler than those for females. Because of this the need for attention and research regarding males has often gone unnoticed. Male peers are less accepting of androgynous or female-like behaviors in gifted males. The pressures on gifted males to be like other males are significantly greater than pressures on females to be like other females. In attempts to help females bridge the gaps in educational and occupational opportunities, males may have been denied those opportunities. Research in this and other areas should be focused equally on males and females.

Key questions

1   What impact does a female dominated teacher work-force in gifted education have on the development of gifted males?
2   Complete a review of current research on gifted males. What areas of research still need to be developed?
3   Profoundly gifted students who have made headlines tend to be males – why do you think that is? What changes need to take place to address this issue?

References

Caudill, G. and Croteau, J. (1993) *Guiding Images: Helping Gifted and Talented and Creative Children*. New York: Trillium Press.
Farrell, W. (1973) *The Liberated Man*. New York: Random House.

Gowan, J., Khatena, J. and Torrance, E. P. (1979) *Educating the Ablest*. Itasca, IL: Peacock.

Kerr, B. and Foley Nicpon, M. (2003) Gender and giftedness, in N. Colangelo and G. Davis (eds) *Handbook of Gifted Education*. Needham Heights, MA: Allyn and Bacon.

Pipher, M. (1994) *Reviving Ophelia: Saving the Selves of Adolescent Girls*. New York: Ballantine.

7.4   Defensive masquerading for inclusion and survival among gifted lesbian, gay, bisexual and transgender (LGBT) students

Trae Stewart

Contrary to the predominant history of denial of homosexuality in the 1900s, the twenty-first century has evidenced a flood of events related to diverse sexual orientations. However, with increased visibility has come great resistance. For example, in response to state and federal judiciary activity in the United States, the Bush administration proposed a constitutional amendment to ban marriage between same-sex peoples. Although the amendment was not accepted, in November 2004 elections voters in almost a dozen states decided to 'protect' marriage by defining it as an act between a man and a woman.

The media also endured recoil. Both publicized commentary and social discourse have pointedly critiqued the stereotypical light in which LGBT characters have been depicted – overly effeminate, epicurean and unable to maintain a monogamous relationship. For every progressive step forward, there seems to have been an equal or greater reactive one backwards, creating an ostensibly dichotomous social agenda vis-à-vis sexual orientation.

For educators, helping young adults to make sense of these contradictory messages is difficult. For adolescents struggling with their own identity formation, mixed messages can be both a blessing, as well as an invisible force, advocating that they continue to ignore their true selves or be subjected to bitter repercussions. The struggle often becomes overbearing, insurmountable and, in some cases, life-threatening especially for adolescents that belong to multiple minority groups. Insight is needed into the experiences of one of these groups that is often 'invisible' and not accounted for in methods, curricula or school services – gifted LGBT.

Brief history of homosexuality

At one time or another, homosexuality has been accepted by about two-thirds of human societies (Zeldin 1994). Non-western cultures, in particular, have a history of accepting sexual variation in human beings (Herdt 1997; Williams 1992). Some Native American cultures believe that a homosexual is a special being with androgynous powers – a 'two-spirited person' (Wilson 1996). In contrast, contemporary western Puritan-based cultural attitudes assume heterosexuality, which has led to the marginalization of homosexuality as 'deviant'.

From the beginning of its academic discussions in the late nineteenth century, homosexuality was seen as a mental defect for which physicians and psychologists suggested 'cures' like castration, sterilization and electric shock (Halperin 1989; Katz 1976). Homosexual-associated pathologies continued until the late 1940s when Alfred Kinsey proposed that sexual orientation was not a monolithic phenomenon, but entails a range of sexual orientations (e.g., Level 0 – exclusive heterosexuality, Level 6 – exclusive homosexuality; Kinsey et al. 1948). Despite Kinsey's efforts, it was not until 1973 that the American Psychological Association (APA) removed homosexuality from its list of mental illnesses. The American Medical Association (AMA) has since joined the APA in affirming that homosexuals are just as healthy, competent, and able to function in society as heterosexuals (Koppelman and Goodhart 2004). Researchers widely agree that there is no single cause for the sexual orientation of an individual, but that multiple biological and cultural factors are responsible (Stein 1999; Pillard 1997; Le Vay 1996).

Realities of gifted LGBT

In today's schools social pressures and academic expectations are often overwhelming; increased division of the nuclear family unit, and one's multiple roles therein, add to the pressures. Nonetheless, some populations consistently suffer more unwelcoming and sometimes hostile educational experiences than their peers. Due to their continuous marginalization, it is not surprising that LGBT peoples are the most frequent targets of discriminatory acts by both fellow students and the adults charged with their protection.

Harassment and violence

Homosexuals have received the dubious honor of being the most frequent victims of hate crimes in the United States (US Department of Justice 1987). The National Gay and Lesbian Task Force (1984) found that 45 percent of gay males and 20 percent of lesbians experienced sexual orientation-linked verbal harassment and/or physical violence during high school. For the 19 percent of LGBT youth that suffered physical attacks, roughly 24 percent of them each year require medical attention (Massachusetts Department of Education 1998). Such feelings of disrepute are intensified when teachers often punish students who make racist remarks, but evade homophobic comments, which indirectly legitimize the attacks (Herek and Berrill 1992).

Missing adult role models

LGBT students can expect little empathy, support or solutions from school faculty and staff: 77 percent of prospective teachers would not encourage a class discussion on homosexuality and 52 percent would feel uncomfortable working with an openly gay/lesbian colleague (Sears 1992). Such reluctance is predict-able when 80 percent of tomorrow's teachers self-report negative attitudes toward gay and lesbian people. Sears (1992) has found that one-third of them can be classified as 'high-grade homophobes'. Similarly, two-thirds of guidance counselors harbor homophobic feelings – attributable, in part, to only 20 percent having received any training about LGBT issues (Sears 1992).

Unlike school staff who can serve as role models to minority youth, gay and lesbian teachers, in particular, must hide their sexual identity and even distance themselves from LGBT youth, decreasing the opportunity to provide guidance out of fear similar to that experienced by their students (Jennings 1994; Litton 2001). Emotional isolation results from feeling alone, without role models, and without anyone with whom to share information (Martin and Hetrick 1988; Krivascka et al. 1992). During adolescence, these feelings are commonplace, as heterosexual and homosexual teenagers alike frequently believe that no one under-stands them or can empathize with their experiences. This isolation, though, is exacerbated for gay and lesbian youth, not only because they do not benefit from the array of key social allegiances, specific educational resources, or cultural support routinely established for other youth subcultures (Martin 1982), but also because they have an inability to recognize others of their group because sexual orientation is not phenotypically apparent. Cohn (2003) postulates that in a large urban high school of 3000 students, 3 to 9 students might be both gifted and LGBT, which significantly limits the probability that these individuals ever connect with one another.

Juggling dual personas

Like other minority groups in schools, all LGBT students do not experience the same levels of overt discrimination. Reasons for this differentiation include geographic location, socio-economic status of school populations, religious ideo-logies of surrounding communities, and how well an individual conforms to normative gender types. More covert institutionalized heterosexism, such as that in textbooks, dating norms and school policies, indirectly and often more deeply affect these students. For many gay and lesbian adolescents, these moments are particularly painful and give youth a distinct impression that their sexual identity is not typical, ideal or acceptable.

Homosexual adolescents initially make one of three choices in dealing with their newly acknowledged feelings: (a) try to change them, (b) continue to hide them, or (c) accept them (Martin 1982). Often individuals consciously create private and public personas (Krivascka et al. 1992), which are quite disparate. For example, some adolescents engage in heterosexual behavior in order to affirm a heterosexual identity, even though they self-identify as homosexuals (Dunham 1989). On the other hand, their private self is characterized by silence, secrecy and restraint (Stewart 2005).

For the adolescent, a crisis of self-concept occurs from the juxtaposition of the negative ideas about homosexuality learned throughout childhood, their own newly deepened awareness of homosexual attractions, and their simultaneous involuntary association with a stigmatized group. Gifted LGBT students may experience identity struggles at an even earlier age because of their relatively accelerated cognitive development. For gifted students, especially boys, pressures to conform to rigid stereotypes of masculinity are more often expected than for non-gifted peers (Kerr and Cohn 2001). The energy spent on maintaining a mask of gender-conforming behavior is energy that is not spent on the tasks of positive cognitive and social development. In addition to social isolation (Stewart 2005), the distinction between the public and private personas can strengthen and persist to such a degree that serious psychological disorders develop.

Missed developmental opportunities

In order for adolescents to develop a healthy sense of identity they must have opportunities to grow in confidence, self-reliance and self-understanding (Mitchell 1986; Erikson 1968). Covert and explicit societal restrictions on the expression of homoerotic feelings result in a loss of developmental opportunities. Impressionable LGBT youth, in particular, lose opportunities to explore relationships and experience intimacy (D'Augelli 1998). A strong sense of 'otherness' results and, in response, they attempt to deny their true selves.

Since the mid-1990s, numerous models of LGBT identity development have been offered. These multi-stage models demonstrate that sexual orientation is a complex psychological construct (Walling 1997). When these models of identity development for LGBT youth are considered, it becomes evident that harmful treatment of, and internalization of self-hate by, LGBT youth can retard their development (Table 7.4.1).

Developmental opportunities are further reduced for gifted LGBT students even though they begin to question at a very young age. When juxtaposed with Dabrowski's (1964) model of development for the gifted and talented, LGBT students can become petrified at the primary levels of survival and self-protection. Cohn (2003) has warned that gay gifted boys, in particular, will struggle with the double stigma of being gifted and gay, often losing part of themselves in their attempt to ignore or hide one or both of these socially stigmatized identities. One explanation espouses that gifted LGBT identities are often reduced to their cognitive abilities. The limited empirical work on gifted LGBT students has focused on spatial-visual reasoning (Halperin and Wright 1996), mathematical reasoning (Benbow 1988) and verbal fluency (Stanley 1993).

Table 7.4.1 Key stages in LGBT identity development

1	Awareness of sexual 'otherness' and associated social stigma
2	Denial of and resistance to sexual identity
3	Acceptance of sexual identity
4	Disclosure and exploration of sexual self
5	Self-integration of sexual identity

'Besides emphasizing the cognitive, it also is essential to include emotional and social development' (Betts 1991: 143).

Underachievement and diminished aspirations

Many LGBT students associate school with pain and suffering, and do not attempt their studies to their fullest potential, resulting in poor performance, diminished aspirations and lessened opportunities for academic attainment. When the special needs of gifted students are not recognized and addressed, these students, especially male gifted students, underachieve (Colangelo et al. 1993; Whitmore 1980). Underachievement has been postulated as a means by which gifted boys define their masculinity, avoiding yet another identity stigma, especially one that will put them at a higher statistical chance for harassment and attack (Colangelo et al. 1993).

LGBT youth that report significant verbal harassment are twice as likely to report no intent of seeking postsecondary education. Such diminished aspirations have causal links to the students' truant behavior: 22 percent of LGBT students skipped school at least once in any given month (Kosciw 2003).

Substance abuse and suicide

LGBT youth are at higher risk for substance abuse, depression, prostitution, AIDS, running away, truancy, underachievement and dropping out of school, than their peers. For example, 68 percent of adolescent gay males use alcohol, 26 percent or more at least once a week, and 44 percent use other drugs; 83 percent of adolescent lesbians use alcohol and 56 percent use other drugs, specifically 11 percent using either crack or cocaine (Hunter et al. 1992). Gay and lesbian youth are also more likely to attempt suicide than their heterosexual counterparts. A study by the US Department of Health and Human Services reported that gay and lesbian youth represent about 30 percent of all teen suicides, and the incidence of suicide among gay subjects has been reported as high as six times than found for straight youths (Gibson 1989).

The Harvey Milk School: one successful educational Model

Schools that have successfully met the needs of their LGBT students are relatively few and are not easily replicable. One characteristic shared by successful programs is that they were started through the initiative of professionals who decided to create schools where youth could experience a safe high school community, validate their sexual orientation, develop a social support network, earn their diploma and learn collaborative skills necessary for navigating situations dominated by heterosexuals (Campos 2003).

One particular school has earned the attention of educators worldwide due to its distinctiveness. Founded in 1978, the Harvey Milk School (www.harveymilkschool.org) is the world's first and only public high school dedicated solely to serving the unique needs of gay, lesbian, bisexual and transgender students. The currently enrolled 100 students follow the core curriculum designated by the New York City Board of Education, with refinements to reflect their interests and needs. Fred Goldharber, the first faculty member at the Harvey Milk School reflects:

> Working at the school has made me realize what awful lives many of our kids have had as gay and lesbian youths. They're unwilling to trust, unwilling to believe in themselves or that anyone could give a damn about them without trying to use them. We stress responsibility, self-empowerment, commitment to self-learning, and the development of social skills.
>
> (cited in Woog 1995: 239, 241)

Over 90 percent of students that attend Harvey Milk School graduate, and about 80 percent of students pursue higher education (Campos 2003). Although its impact is well documented and the school's notoriety has reached global audiences, the Harvey Milk School remains the only one of its kind in the world.

Meeting the needs of gifted LGBT students

Table 7.4.2. summarizes the pressures placed on gifted, LGBT and gifted LGBT students who cope with dual minority status, and whose gifted characteristics intensify their reactions to stereotyping and prejudice.

Creating safe spaces

Students who feel isolated, alienated and victimized must feel comfortable and safe at school. To achieve this, changes in school policies to reflect a more diverse student population, the development and implementation of a curriculum that actually educates students about all issues, and the creation of a support system where students can express themselves without fear of harassment and/or violence are requisite. The end result, therefore, would be that students, who previously focused their energy on defensive masquerades, could redirect their efforts toward their healthy cognitive and psychosocial development.

The typical first strategy to creating a safe space in high schools is the establishment of a Gay/Straight Alliance (GSA). GSAs (www.gsanetwork.org) are student-run school-based support groups 'designed to meet the needs of students who are interested in addressing issues related to sexual orientation and anti-gay prejudice and to address the concerns of lesbian and gay students and their friends' (Gay/Straight Alliance 2005). Size, frequency of meeting, agenda topics and names of GSAs differ among schools depending on the needs of their participants. Most GSAs try to strike a balance between social, consciousness raising and political events, while simultaneously offering emotional support to members.

Table 7.4.2 Characteristics of gifted LGBT students

Gifted students	LGBT students	Gifted LGBT students
Heightened sensitivity to social issues	Protection from discrimination, sanctions and violence	Intense awareness and personal ethics
Peer pressure to hide giftedness	Peer pressure to remain 'in the closet'	Highly developed system of masks and scenarios to protect self
Need for intellectual challenge	Need for tolerance and acceptance	Knowledge of contributions of great leaders and achievers who were/are gifted and LGBT
Need for normalizing social experiences	Positive peer relationships	Need to be supported by other gifted and LGBT students
Examination of social/ cultural systems	Awareness of being a discriminated minority	Acceptance of diverse family and social structures: documentation in literature
Creative productivity in interest area	Self-esteem and creative expression	Acceptance of diverse forms of creative productivity specific to gay community
Modification to regular curriculum: acceleration, enrichment	Positive contributions of gay achievers	Incorporation of orientation into curriculum study
Mentoring and internships	Gay mentors	Heroes who are gay and gifted

Source: Eriksson and Stewart 2005.

Culturally responsive teacher training

Teachers should be trained in 'gifting' (Schultz and Delisle 2002) or helping individuals to recognize and celebrate the differences among one another, and how these fit into a seemingly uncaring society. More critically, these discussions should center on why certain tendencies, lifestyles and differences are less accepted than others. Unlike other minorities, members of this group remain 'invisible' until they exhibit some out-of-the-ordinary or stereotypical behavior. Their identification becomes difficult for educators who have not been trained about, and therefore are not sensitive to, the unique needs of this dual minority population (Ford 1994; Rhodes 1992). Teacher preparation programs must provide training about diversity while focusing on the individual as the unit of learning. Gay (2000) refers to the use of students' cultural knowledge, prior experiences, frames of reference, and performance styles to make learning more relevant and effective as 'culturally responsive'. Through a curriculum of tolerance, homophobic teachers will be discouraged from expressing anti-gay prejudices (Kissen 1996; Harbeck 1992) and closeted LGBT faculty and staff will become more comfortable disclosing their identities and acting as indirect role models to students.

Gifted LGBT research

The field of gifted education itself must make ardent and conscious strides to 'queer' research, practice, and policy discussions. To date, studies on gifted LGBT, while few in number, consistently involve small samples due to the difficulty in identifying willing subjects. Although it is virtually impossible to determine the demographic characteristics of the gifted LGBT student population to establish a representative sample (Walling 1997), even when identified some are still fearful of participation in that they might be labeled and subsequently attacked. Issues of anonymity are further exacerbated when research focuses on teenagers under the age of 18, whose participation would require parental consent. Admittedly the 'queering' of gifted education is difficult given that LGBT issues are culturally taboo in many environments internationally. However, without a better understanding and/or explanation of the experiences of gifted LGBT students, we will not be able to recommend proactive solutions to the problems or replicate practices that are working.

Key questions

1 How should teacher and guidance counselor training programs be restructured to ensure a cohort of educational personnel more sensitive to the needs of multiple minority students, specifically gifted LGBT teens? Should certain classes/internships be required? If so, which ones? Why?

2 The cognitive domain receives the most attention in schools worldwide. Why is this the case, particularly when there is abundant research showing a causal connection between a student's affective well-being and academic success? What can we honestly hope for in terms of addressing the needs of gifted LGBT students then?

3 Consider the concept of overexcitabilities. How is this concept also applicable to LGBT students? What does this mean for LGBT students who are also members of other minority groups (e.g., African American, the poor, gifted, Muslim)?

4 What are your personal feelings about LGBT peoples? How do you think that your feelings (whether positive or negative) will affect your treatment of LGBT students or colleagues? How can you work to control these biases, especially if you are an employee of a government education system?

References

Benbow, C. (1988) Sex differences in mathematical reasoning ability in intellectually talented preadolescents: their nature, effects, and possible causes. *Behavioral and Brain Sciences*, 11: 169–232.

Betts, G. T. (1991) The autonomous learner model for the gifted and talented, in N. Colangelo and G. A. Davis (eds) *Handbook of Gifted Education*. Boston, MA: Allyn and Bacon.

Campos, D. (2003) *Diverse Sexuality and Schools: A Reference Handbook*. Oxford: ABC-Clio.

Cohn, S. (2003) The gay gifted learner: facing the challenge of homophobia and antihomosexual bias in schools, in J. A. Castellano (ed.) *Special Populations in Gifted Education: Working with Diverse Gifted Learners.* Boston, MA: Allyn and Bacon.

Colangelo, N., Kerr, B., Christensen, P. and Maxey, J. (1993) A comparison of gifted underachievers and gifted high achievers. *Gifted Child Quarterly*, 37: 155–160.

Dabrowski, K. (1964) *Positive Disintegration.* Boston, MA: Little, Brown.

D'Augelli, A. (1998) Developmental implications of victimization of lesbian, gay, and bisexual youths, in G. Herek (ed.) *Stigma and Sexual Orientation: Understanding Prejudice against Lesbians, Gay Men, and Bisexuals,* Volume 4. Thousand Oaks, CA: Sage.

Dunham, K. L. (1989) *Educated to be invisible: The Gay and Lesbian Adolescent.* East Lansing, MI: National Center for Research on Teacher Learning. (ERIC Document Reproduction Service No. ED 3366 76.)

Erikson, E. H. (1968) *Identity: Youth and Crisis.* New York: W. W. Norton.

Eriksson, G. I. and Stewart, T. (2005) Gifted and gay (G^2): the characteristics and educational needs of a dual minority group. Unpublished MS, University of Central Florida at Orlando.

Ford, D. Y. (1994) *The Recruitment and Retention of African-American Students in Gifted Education Programs: Implications and Recommendations.* Storrs, CT: National Research Center on the Gifted and Talented.

Gay, G. (2000) *Culturally Responsive Teaching: Theory, Research, and Practice.* New York: Teachers College Press.

Gay/Straight Alliance (2005) *Gay/straight Alliance: A Student Guide.* Retrieved 11 February 2005 from http://www.doe.mass.edu/hssss/GSA/Intro.html

Gibson, P. (1989) Gay male and lesbian youth suicide, in *Report of the Secretary's Task Force on Youth Suicide.* Washington, DC: US Department of Health and Human Services.

Halperin, D. and Wright, T. (1996) A process-oriented model of sex differences in cognitive sex differences. *Learning and Individual Differences*, 8: 3–24.

Halperin, D. M. (1989) Sex before sexuality: pederasty, politics, and power in classical Athens, in M. Duberman, M. Vicinus and G. Chauncey, Jr. (eds) *Hidden from History: Reclaiming the Gay and Lesbian Past.* New York: Meridian.

Harbeck, K. M. (ed.) (1992) *Coming Out of the Classroom Closet: Gay and Lesbian Students, Teachers and Curricula.* New York: Harrington Park Press.

Herdt, G. (1997) *Same Sex, Different Cultures: Exploring Gay and Lesbian Lives.* Boulder, CO: Westview.

Herek, G. M. and Berrill, K. T. (eds) (1992) *Hate Crimes: Confronting Violence against Lesbians and Gay Men.* Newbury Park, CA: Sage.

Hetrick-Martin Institute (1988) *Hetrick-Martin Institute Violence Report.* New York: Hetrick-Martin Institute.

Hunter, J. and Associates (1992) Unpublished research, Columbia University HIV Center for Clinical and Behavior Studies.

Jennings, K. (ed.) (1994) *One Teacher in 10: Gay and Lesbian Educators Tell their Stories.* New York: Alyson.

Katz, J. (1976) *Gay American History: Lesbians and Gay Men in the USA.* New York: Harper Colophon.

Kerr, B. and Cohn, S. (2001) *Smart Boys: Talent, Manhood, and the Search for Meaning.* Scottsdale, AZ: Great Potential Press.

Kinsey, A. C., Pomeroy, W. B. and Martin, C. E. (1948) *Sexual Behavior in the Human Male.* Philadelphia, PA: W. B. Saunders.

Kissen, R. M. (1996) *The Last Closet: The Real Lives of Lesbian and Gay Teachers*. Portsmouth, NH: Heinemann.

Koppelman, K. and Goodhart, L. (2004) *Understanding Human Differences: Multicultural Education for a Diverse America*. Boston, MA: Allyn and Bacon.

Kosciw, J. G. (2003) *National School Climate Survey: The School-related Experiences of our Nation's Lesbian, Gay, Bisexual, and Transgender Youth*. New York: Gay, Lesbian and Straight Education Network.

Krivascka, J. J., Savin-Williams, R. C. and Slater, B. R. (1992) Background paper for the resolution on lesbian, gay, and bisexual youths in schools, unpublished manuscript for the American Psychological Association and the National Association of School Psychologists.

LeVay, S. (1996) *Queer Science: The Use and Abuse of Research into Homosexuality*. Cambridge, MA: Massachusetts University Press.

Litton, E. F. (2001) Voices of courage and hope: gay and lesbian Catholic elementary school teachers. *International Journal of Sexuality and Gender Studies*, 6(3): 193–205.

Martin, A. D. (1982) Learning to hide: the socialization of the gay adolescent. *Adolescent Psychiatry*, 10: 52–65.

Martin, A. D. and Hetrick, E. S. (1988) The stigmatization of the gay and lesbian adolescent. *Journal of Homosexuality*, 15(1–2): 163–183.

Massachusetts Department of Education (1998) *Massachusetts Youth Risk Behavior Survey Results*. Malden, MA: Massachusetts Department of Education.

Mitchell, J. J. (1986) *The Nature of Adolescence*. Calgary, Alta: University of Alberta.

National Gay and Lesbian Task Force (NGLTF) (1984) *Antigay/Lesbian Victimization*. Washington, DC: NGLTF.

Pillard, R. C. (1997) The search for a genetic influence on sexual orientation, in V. Rosario (ed.) *Science and Homosexualities*. New York: Routledge.

Rhodes, L. (1992) Focusing attention on the individual in identification of gifted black students. *Roeper Review*, 14(3): 108–110.

Schultz, R. A. and Delisle, J. R. (2002) Gifted adolescents, in N. Colangelo and G. A. Davis (eds) *Handbook of Gifted Education*, 3rd edn. Boston, MA: Allyn and Bacon.

Sears, J. (1992) Educators, homosexuality, and homosexual students: Are personal feelings related to professional beliefs?, in K. Harbeck (ed.) *Coming Out of the Classroom Closet: Gay and Lesbian Students, Teachers, and Curricula*. New York: Haworth Press.

Stanley, J. (1993) Boys and girls who reason well mathematically, in G. R. Bock and K. Ackrill (eds) *The Origins and Development of High Ability*. Chichester: John Wiley and Sons.

Stein, E. (1999) *The Mismeasure of Desire: The Science, Theory, and Ethics of Sexual Orientation*. Oxford: Oxford University Press.

Stewart, T. (2005) Limits in discourse in high schools: effects on sexual minority adolescents, in T. Stewart and A. Munroe (eds) *Transmission and Transformation in Education: Analytic Inquiries through Social Theory*. Boston, MA: Pearson.

US Department of Justice (1987) *The Response of the Criminal Justice System to Bias Crime: An Exploratory View*. Washington, DC: US Department of Justice.

Walling, D. R. (ed.) (1997) *Hot Buttons: Unraveling 10 Controversial Issues in Education*. Bloomington, IN: Phi Delta Kappa.

Whitmore, J. (1980) *Giftedness, Conflict and Underachievement*. Boston, MA: Allyn and Bacon.

Williams, W. L. (1992) Benefits for non-homophobic societies: an anthropological perspective, in W. Blummenfield (ed.) *Homophobia: How We All Pay the Price*. Boston, MA: Beacon.

Wilson, A. (1996) How we find ourselves: identity development and two-spirit people. *Harvard Educational Review*, 66(2): 303–317.

Woog, D. (1995) *School's Out: The Impact of Gay and Lesbian on America's Schools*. Boston, MA: Alyson.

Zeldin, T. (1994) *An Intimate History of Humanity*. New York: HarperCollins.

7.5   Personal perspective: lesbian gifted – what your students may be thinking

Grace Moskola

As a teacher, you may be wondering what your students are really thinking. You seldom get a chance to read their minds, especially if they happen to be diverse in at least two ways, both gifted and lesbian. This piece was written during a class and gives you insight into my interpretation of your well-planned lesson on gender.

'. . . Seven, eight, nine, ten . . .'

I wonder if I'm the only one who sits in psychology class trying desperately to keep my sanity by counting heads and silently pondering if the statistic that states that one out of every ten people is gay could possibly be true. I thumb through my textbook past the Kinsey Report and grimace as I look up to see my class, every seat occupied by a Barbie or Ken clone, and that little voice in the back of my mind laments, 'No, probably not.'

In this class, we've spent the last two weeks covering a unit on love, sex and relationships. So far, it has played out much like a non-existent 1950s sitcom entitled, 'How to be Straight'. I'm just waiting for Donna Reed to float in and take a seat next to me. Today, as my class becomes immersed in a discussion on what makes a perfect marriage, and if that doesn't work, a crash course in Divorce 101, I muse to myself if anyone in the room had ever considered what it would be like if they couldn't get married? This thought is pushed aside as the subject matter shifts to 'How to put on a condom', and I feel the urge to bang my head repeatedly against my desktop until the fluorescent lights glaring down at me would all fade to black.

Being in this class is vaguely reminiscent of high school for me. High school is a mixture of Purgatory and Hell for most gay students, where we learn how to play a game called 'Passing as Straight'. The rules of this game call for fake boyfriends, fake crushes and a good imagination. Luckily, I had all three. I figured, everyone puts on roles and masks in high school, even more so if you are identified as gifted. We learn to adapt to survive, much like being small prey on the African Serengeti. In such a social situation, there are two choices really: to either blend in as well as possible with your surroundings, or be able to run fast. I never was much of a runner, so I chose the former approach, and in a way, I guess I still do.

They say that coming out is a process, but no one tells you what steps there are to follow or how long this ordeal takes. No one tells you that when you are gay, you are forced to make decisions everyday that no one else has to think twice about. And now I'm coming to realize that this 'Coming out' business never really ends.

So here I am, in psychology class, listening to my teacher read a passage out of John Gray's delightful book, *Men are from Mars, Women are from Venus*. I'm biting my tongue, wondering what might happen if I stood up right in the middle of her sentence and say, 'Hello. I am a lesbian. Now how does this subject matter apply to me?' I imagine a hush falling over the room as all eyes turn to me in anticipation to see what a real, live lesbian looks like. It just doesn't seem worth it, so I continue to sit quietly and redirect my attention to this psychology class of the damned.

Thirty minutes into the class, we are broken off into small groups to discuss the differences between men's and women's needs in a relationship. The woman I'm sitting next to begins going into fits over the whole Mars and Venus thing, claiming that she swears by the book, and thanks to John Gray, is just inches away from reaching some sort of spiritual enlightenment on what makes her husband tick. The fellow next to her starts to chuckle and offers his opinion on the matter, 'Sex and food, lady, you don't need to bring astronomy into the equation!'

I can't help but laugh out loud, and this gives me an idea. Maybe I'll start my own line of self-help books. I could call them *Mars and Venus Gone Wrong*, or *Jupiter and Saturn at the Gay Bar*, just to throw them off.

I watch as the second hand appears to be moving backwards on the clock and gnaw absent-mindedly on my pen cap, waiting for the hour to be over. So maybe I don't quite fit in with this group of hyper-heterosexuals, but as I sit here quietly nodding and smiling, I think maybe that's a blessing after all.

References

Gray, J. (1993) *Men are from Mars, Women are from Venus*. New York: HarperCollins.

Moskolo, G. (2004) Mars and Venus gone wrong. *Discovering Diversity*, Volume 4. Office of Global and Multicultural Education, University of Central Florida.

7.6   Conflict resolution 6: sexism

Suzanne Rawlins

Registration for the fall term began as each high school student completed course requests for the following year. Celeste completed her preferred selections: Honors Geometry, Chemistry I Honors, Honors English II, Western Civilizations,

Chorus and Physical Education. When the fall arrived, her schedule reflected: Geometry, Honors English II, Western Civilizations, Chorus, Physical Education, Home Economics and Typing. She met with the guidance counselor. She was told that the master schedule would not permit her to register for Honors Geometry and Chemistry I Honors. She was informed that all girls must take Home Economics and that the Home Economics course was offered at the same time as Chemistry I Honors, currently all boys. She did not need this to graduate. Typing was a much better selection because many women have supported their families on a secretarial salary. When she explained that she had no interest in Home Economics, but preferred Chemistry I and Honors Geometry, the counselor politely explained that the master schedule could not be changed for just one girl and those were the rules.

8   Exceptionality issues

8.1   Double exceptionality: gifted children with special educational needs in ordinary schools

Diane Montgomery

Two traditions have grown up in the education of the gifted. The first, particularly in the United States, is educating them as 'special' and selecting them for 'pull-out' programmes, special schools, acceleration and enrichment classes. The second may be seen in *inclusive* schooling where teachers are expected to cope with the diverse range of abilities and needs of mixed ability classes. Teaching such a wide range of abilities involves increasing the autonomy of learners and engaging them in problem-based learning and collaborative educational activities.

I will focus here on inclusive education as a means by which schools can make good provision for pupils who not only are gifted, but also have some form of special need. There are many more gifted and talented pupils than teachers and administrators think and 'creaming off' a few for special education can have counterproductive effects. Often the most able are missed, and those receiving the special provision, which may not always be so special, become socially segregated and can despise their less fortunate non-selected peers. In the United Kingdom up to the 1970s, when there was universal selection of the top 20 percent for grammar school education at the age of 11, all of these disadvantages were experienced, and children who failed to obtain a grammar school place regarded themselves as second class citizens, life's failures.

Who are the more able?

Two-thirds of the population are in the average range of ability according to psychometric IQ tests. This puts them between 85 and 115 IQ. With IQs between 116 and 130 the children are said to be highly able, and 130–145 very highly able, and at 146 and beyond 'gifted'. But these labels like the tests are arbitrary. Built in test errors mean that an IQ of 115 may really be anywhere between 112 and 119 so cut-off points for selection are crude devices. Moreover, children with very high IQs may never contribute anything significant in life, whereas one with an average IQ may. IQ is thus only one indication of potential for achievement; there are many others such as creativity, persistence, chance, mentors, facilitating home background, schooling experiences and so on.

High ability refers not to intelligence alone but to many other aspects such as talent in social perceptions, social communication, leadership, problem-solving, creativity or performance arts. Some of these talents require a significant amount of practice and some students find the practice too boring to maintain. Thus it is that the teacher of a class of thirty children may imagine only one or two are more able and none are gifted or talented, when in fact half the class might be regarded as more able and practically every child has some talent/ability if only it can be identified and nurtured. This is the diverse nature of humanity. We also need to remember that the human brain has an enormous capacity to learn and we only use it in a very small measure.

What kinds of special educational needs (SEN) are there?

The more able with SEN may have:

* SpLD – specific learning difficulties (learning disabilities in USA) such as dyslexia, dyspraxia (movement difficulties), ADHD (attention deficit hyper-activity disorder)
* PSM – physical, sensory (vision and hearing) and medical difficulties
* SEBD – social, emotional and behavioural difficulties
* Special populations/disorders – ASD (autistic spectrum disorders); DS (Down syndrome); CCD (central communicative disorders – severe speech and language difficulties).

Children with SpLD and SEBD are found in the largest numbers and are significant for their underachievement. Suffice it to say that in the case of children with PSM once their special need is catered for, e.g. in visual impairment low vision aids or Braille, concept teaching and aural strategies, then they need the same kind of provision as any other more able child.

Among the children with ASD there will be those who are high functioning with Asperger syndrome and their needs can be met with individualized social skills training, highly structured teaching settings, behaviour training and an understanding of the literal nature of their comprehension and lack of 'theory of mind' (Montgomery 2003).

What is double exceptionality (2E)?

Pupils with different types of special need and who are also highly able may be regarded as doubly exceptional. Often their special needs will be met and their giftedness ignored: it is unusual for them to be given provision for both, but in inclusive settings it is feasible.

In the case of pupils with SpLD and SEBD the profile seen most often is one of underachievement. There seem to be three groups of doubly exceptional underachievers:

- those identifiable by *discrepancies* between and within test scores and school attainments – an uneven pattern of abilities
- those unidentified because abilities are masked by *deficits*
- those unidentified because social, emotional and behaviour (SEBD) problems become the focus or because using persistence and compensatory strategies they hide their difficulties – *deceptive.*

Potential numbers of 'gifted' underachievers

If a wide range of attributes are considered as indicators of giftedness, 15–50 percent of the gifted are underachievers according to Gagné (1995). Lupart (1992) uses a discrepancy definition between IQ and school attainments and finds 21 percent underfunction, and Whitmore (1980) found 70 percent of gifted students were underfunctioning – having attainments at least one standard deviation below IQ. Most recently Stamm (2003) found 25 percent of her very highly gifted group were underfunctioning in maths and/or literacy, and the more able they were the more likely they were to be underfunctioning.

The profile of typical underachievers (Whitmore 1980; Silverman 1989; Butler-Por 1987) was found to be as follows:

- large gap between oral and written work
- failure to complete school work
- poor execution of work
- persistent dissatisfaction with achievements
- avoidance of trying new activities
- does not function well in groups
- lacks concentration
- poor attitudes to school
- dislikes drill and memorization
- difficulties with peers
- low self-image
- sets unrealistic goals.

The underlying theme is an inability to produce written work of a suitable quality.

Identification of underachievers

To a large extent the methods used are those which are appropriate for all learners, but just using an IQ test only gives a small part of the picture. Schools should use a range of methods including diagnostic testing, awareness checklists, sensitive observation, parental referral and, importantly, self-referral.

External barriers to learning for 'gifted' underachievers

Some children learn to underperform to conform to the peer group or to avoid teacher praise. Very quickly they may adopt a daydreaming attitude, quietly gazing at the teacher but with their minds elsewhere. Such habits become chronic over time, and if the teaching is geared to the average, it fails to challenge the more able, who fill 'dead time' with manifold opportunities to misbehave. Unnecessary repetition and practice for able pupils exacerbates the problem, resulting in minimum effort.

Schools need to audit the kind of provision they provide: one kind may be *structural* and may involve setting, compacting and accelerating; and the other may be *integral* or *developmental* involving enrichment or extension within the classroom. Getting the mix of these strategies right for individual learners is a vital school achievement.

Developmental differentiation requires the teacher to encourage the pupils to contribute their own knowledge to a topic before they engage in individual or group-work: this involves a modest change in the teaching methods, and involves the cognitive curriculum.

The cognitive curriculum

The cognitive curriculum should be taught in all subjects across all age groups, not as bolt-on provision, and should include the following:

- developmental positive cognitive intervention (PCI) positive comments, spoken or written on all work with suggestions on how it could be developed or improved
- cognitively challenging questioning – 'why' questions which cause the pupils to reason about what they hear and see and experience
- deliberate teaching of thinking skills and protocols, making use of problem based learning and investigative techniques in all subject areas
- creativity training, allowing time and opportunities for creative responses
- reflective learning and teaching, making reflections upon what has been learned and how it was learned
- cognitive process teaching methods e.g.
  - experiential learning
  - games and simulations
  - language experience methods
  - cognitive study skills – higher order learning strategies and research skills
  - collaborative learning and team building.

The cognitive process teaching methods create a therapeutic democratic educational environment rather than a coercive one (Montgomery 1998, 2000).

Working in mixed ability groups does not lower the attainments of the more able, it raises the attainments of all the pupils. Teachers also need to provide for a wider range of pupil response especially as underachievers find written methods so difficult. These different methods I have called the *Talking Curriculum*, which provides a range of opportunities to record ideas and experiences other than in writing, such as cartooning, drawing, mapping, taping, videoing, photographing, exhibiting. Pupils can also use different methods for exploring ideas such as: 'Think–Pair–Share', mime, formal and informal discussions, plenaries, poster presentations, microteaching, peer tutoring and so on.

In order to support extended writing the pupils need to be introduced to different types of cognitive study skills and research skills. Scaffolding structures for written work can help with organizational difficulties. Assessment methods also need to allow for principles and practices to be shared: through formative, constructive, supportive and diagnostic feedback so that individuals have goals and purposes to achieve and know how to get there.

Internal barriers to learning

'Gifted' pupils with SpLD and SEBD who have undetected literacy difficulties will underfunction not only in school subjects, but also on IQ test items involving verbal processing, verbal memory (auditory digit span and mental arithmetic) and coding (Montgomery 1997a).

Types of specific learning difficulties (SpLD) can be divided into two main subsections: first, *verbal learning difficulties such as dyslexia* (reading *and* spelling difficulties) and *dysorthographia* (spelling difficulties alone) and mild *dysphasia* (mild speech and language difficulties, word finding and naming difficulties); second, *non-verbal learning difficulties such as dyspraxia*, i.e. general motor coordination difficulties, also often called *developmental coordination difficulties* (*DCD*) and *dysgraphia* (fine motor coordination difficulties particularly affecting handwriting).

ADHD (Attention Deficit Hyperactivity Disorder) and ADD

There is also what clinicians call co-morbidity between each of these conditions so that some unlucky children have dyslexia, dyspraxia and ADHD and may have immune disorders as well. However, the most frequent problems of gifted underachievers in schools refers to their written language difficulties, and these result from hidden difficulties.

Dyslexic spectrum difficulties (DSD)

This condition is a severe difficulty in learning to read *and* spell. Just 10 percent of the population are thought to have dyslexia and 4 percent have the severe condition (British Dyslexia Association 2004); 10 percent of dyslexics are also in the gifted range or doubly exceptional. In research terms this means they have at least one IQ score at 130 and above (Montgomery 1997a, 1997b). However,

Silverman (1989) recommended that in selection processes for special provision, students with learning disabilities should have at least ten points added to their IQ scores. In my studies this would mean that 34 percent of the dyslexic groups were gifted (at least one IQ score of 120 or above). Usually a discrepancy of 20 percent, roughly two years between ability and attainment in literacy, is the trigger for 'specialist' help. Unfortunately, this training is not always with specialist APSL dyslexia programmes. The earlier the intervention the more effective it can be, and should begin in Reception or Year 1 (Montgomery 1997a, 1997b, 2000).

Dysorthographia: a hidden barrier

This is a severe difficulty in learning to spell in the presence of average or even very good reading skills. Some highly able pupils with verbal processing difficulties frequently learn to read self-taught before entering school, or overcome their difficulties once in school because of their high ability and individual persistence. Spelling is a more difficult skill to develop than reading. Reading involves recognition in the presence of the syntactic and semantic contexts. Thus a photographic memory can conceal a dyslexic difficulty for several years. Spelling is a recall skill and much more difficult to learn, relying on phonology and linguistics as well cues gained from reading.

Dysorthographia is mainly an unrecognized specific verbal learning difficulty. It consists of mild to severe spelling problems but in the presence of average or even excellent ability to read. Mispellings of easy words makes people underestimate the child's ability: however, the problem may go deeper than this, and may affect not only spelling but also the ability to organize and create a coherent account or argument in text.

Many pupils are very clever at concealing their problems for they use proof readers and spell checkers. The barrier is often reached only at high school exams and undergraduate level, when they meet new technical vocabulary or have to write rapidly in examinations.

Here are two examples of gifted children's spelling. Maria (5 years 10 months) with spelling problems wrote: 'I wnt to the Titic Esbtnn I swo srm thes fom the Titic and srm thes war reil' (Translation – 'I went to the Titanic Exhibition. I saw some things from the Titanic and some of these were real'.) Maria began reading self-taught at 4 years. She is a good reader now, highly verbal and bilingual in German and English. Gifted children writing like Maria will be overlooked in busy classrooms and will be considered low average in ability on the basis of the standard of the writing.

Annette (5 years 11 months) without spelling problems wrote: 'Wild animals often live in woodland, the fox, the squirrel, the woodmouse and the shrew, the largest of these animals is the fox, the fox is carnivorous which means he eats meat.'

While most gifted DSD students will read adequately, a spelling test will identify most of them. If only reading is taken as an indication of literacy skills, then these children will get no extra learning support. The spelling problems are frequently blamed upon the child's carelessness and stupidity.

To overcome dysorthography, an analysis of the errors needs to be made then cognitive strategies need to be taught to override the error. Briefly the cognitive strategies include: articulation; over articulation; cue articulation; syllabification; phonics; origin; rule; linguistics; family; meaning; analogy; funnies (Montgomery 1997b).

Developmental coordination difficulties (DCD)

Some types of difficulty such as in handwriting (dysgraphia) and in gross motor coordination (developmental dyspraxia or DCD) attract a great deal of criticism and bullying. The pupil is blamed for carelessness and little help is given. This is very demotivating and undermines the self-concept and progress in school: any giftedness and talent is then masked. This can lead to disaffection and exclusion because pupils are regarded as lazy, defiant, awkward and problematic.

Dyspraxia

This is a difficulty with or an inability to motor plan, or put such a plan into fluent operation after a reasonable period of skill acquisition. There are a range of dyspraxic difficulties from gross motor coordination difficulties – a general clumsiness in running and walking – to specific fine motor coordination difficulties in handwriting, bead threading, shoe-lace tying and buttoning. A dyspraxic pupil might lurch out of the classroom door, speed down the corridor veering to one side and grazing the wall, losing books and pens on the way, burst into the next classroom and send desks and others' property flying: exercise books are filled with scrappy work loaded with crossings out and erasures.

Such pupils are not picked in team games and are frequently seriously bullied. The difficulties may affect not only general coordination but also deeper neuro-cerebral levels and pathways. Despite a range of seemingly stupid behaviours, and perhaps a lack of control of emotional responses, the individual may be highly intelligent trapped in a body which will not do as instructed.

Dysgraphia

A significant number of pupils have handwriting coordination difficulties without any other motor difficulties. Estimates vary from Sassoon's (1989) report of 40 percent of boys and 25 percent of girls at age 15, stating that they found writing painful, to 10 percent in other studies where the fine motor control itself was examined (Gubbay 1975; Laszlo et al. 1988) and 48 percent in my studies of Year 7 boys' writing was 10–15 percent poorer than girls.

When speed was investigated by Roaf (1998), she found that 25 percent of pupils were unable to write faster than 15 words per minute and were struggling in lessons where a lot of writing was required. She found a close link between self-concept and handwriting presentation. The majority of the slow writers showed difficulties with motor coordination, spelling and letter formation. She regarded a speed of

25 words per minute as a successful rate for coping with secondary education. In my Year 7 samples, only 5 percent were capable of achieving this speed and 26 percent were writing at speeds slower than the mean for their age group.

Handwriting difficulties are distributed across the ability range, but wherever they occur there is little sympathy. Gifted children's thoughts may run much faster than their writing skills can cope with, and so they will also be criticized and the content ignored. It is only when a piece of work arrives word processed and deeply thoughtful that the busy teacher may realize the potential. A speed of only 12 words per minute or less at GCSE (Year 10 examinations) should be the diagnosis for awarding 25 percent extra time in exams (Allcock 2001).

Diagnosing writing difficulties

To diagnose writing difficulties four types of analysis are needed:

- a fluency and speed test
- a letter formation analysis for fluency and economy
- analysis of penhold, paper and body position
- a diagnostic motor coordination analysis such as the following:

Signs of motor coordination difficulties in handwriting

- writing pulling in from the margin towards the midline
- 'rivers' of spaces running down through the writing
- apparent capital letters spotted about but which are really large forms of the lower case letters out of control, especially of s, w, k and t
- writing which looks scribbly or spiky
- shaky and wobbly strokes on letters
- writing which varies in 'colour' sometimes dark and in other places very faint indicating variation in pressure and fatigue
- writing which produces ridges on the reverse of the paper and even holes in it due to pressure exerted
- inability to maintain the writing on the line
- difficulties in making letters and syllables in one fluid movement.

All the above may be in addition to poor formation of the letters themselves with changes in style, slope and body size usually due to lack of consistent and coherent teaching, a common problem in the United Kingdom.

Roger (10 years)

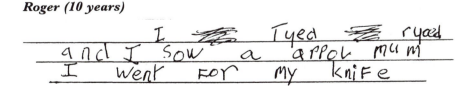

Roger after 12 short lessons

jumped on the two men and the scratched and scratched them the policemen rewarded the cats.

Handwriting interventions

The most important intervention a school can make is to develop a school policy which requires all teachers to teach and encourage a fluent joined hand – cursive writing – from reception, as is done in many countries and was done in the UK in the early twentieth century.

Conclusion

Two major factors have been discussed which form significant barriers to learning in 2E and contribute widely to underachievement. The first was the problem of teaching methods. To overcome this, schools need to implement the cognitive curriculum in all subject areas and ensure that it is accompanied by more participative assessment and a talking curriculum to cut down the amount of writing pupils are required to do.

The second factor is that created by internal barriers. These were called the 'hidden handicaps' not because they are hidden from view but because we regard them as faults, and fail to recognize them as barriers to learning. These can be overcome by up-skilling the teaching of spelling, handwriting and organizing writing.

Key questions

1   What strategies can teachers of 2E students use in the regular curriculum that will be appropriate for these diverse gifted students?
2   How can these types of disabilities result in prejudice by teachers and peers and what can be done to prevent this?
3   How can teachers give gifted students insight into their own exceptionalities that will develop positive self-concepts?

References

Allcock, P. (2001) The testing of handwriting speed. *PATOSS Bulletin*, November: 23–6.
British Dyslexia Association (BDA) (2004) *Characteristics*. Reading, UK: BDA. Available online: http://www.bda-dyslexia.org.uk/main/information/adults/a01what.asp (accessed January 2004).
Butler-Por, N. (1987) *Underachievers in Schools: Issues and Interventions*. Chichester: John Wiley and Sons.

Gagné, F. (1995) Learning about gifts and talents through peer and teacher nomination, in M. W. Katzko and F. J. Monks (eds) *Nurturing Talent: Individual Needs and Social Ability Proceedings of the 4th ECHA Conference*. Assen, The Netherlands: Van Gorcum.

Gubbay, S. S. (1975) *The Clumsy Child*. London: W. B. Saunders.

Laszlo, M., Bairstow, P. and Bartrip, P. (1988) A new approach to perceptuomotor dysfunction: previously called clumsiness. *Support for Learning*, 3: 33–40.

Lupart, J. L. (1992) The hidden gifted: current state of knowledge and future research directions, in F. Monks and W. Peters (eds) *Talent for the Future*. Assen, The Netherlands: Van Gorcum.

Montgomery, D. (1997a) *Spelling: Remedial Strategies*. London: Cassell.

Montgomery, D. (1997b) *Developmental Spelling: A Handbook*. Maldon: Learning Difficulties Research Project.

Montgomery, D. (1998) *Reversing Lower Attainment*. London: David Fulton.

Montgomery, D. (ed.) (2000) *Able Underachievers*. London: Whurr.

Montgomery, D. (ed.) (2003) *Gifted and Talented Children with Special Educational Needs: Double Exceptionality*. London: David Fulton.

Roaf, C. (1998) Slow hand: a secondary school survey of handwriting speed and legibility. *Support for Learning*, 13(1): 39–42.

Sassoon, R. (1989) *Handwriting: A New Perspective*. Cheltenham: Stanley Thornes.

Silverman, L. K. (1989) Invisible gifts, invisible handicaps. *Roeper Review*, 12(1): 37–42.

Stamm, M. (2003) Looking at long term effects of early reading and numeracy ability: a glance at the phenomenon of giftedness. *Gifted and Talented International*, 18(1): 7–16.

Whitmore, J. R. (1980) *Giftedness, Conflict and Underachievement*. Boston, MA: Allyn and Bacon.

8.2 Overcoming barriers to learning in gifted children: a neuro-developmental approach

Shirley J. Kokot

'I simply don't understand John,' said his mother despairingly.

He is always in trouble for forgetting things, for work not handed in, for being disruptive in class. Even I can't get him to take responsibility for a few simple chores or making sure his homework is done. They say that he has a very high IQ but has attention problems and may need medication. I don't like the idea of Ritalin. How can I help him?

John is one of many gifted children who struggles with attentional issues, including the ability to concentrate, focus on tasks and general organization.

Attention problems and the gifted child

There seems to be a consensus that referrals for attention problems among gifted children have been growing at a rapid and unexpected rate (Baum et al. 1998;

Webb and Latimer 1993). Many researchers (e.g. Webb and Latimer 1993; Tucker and Hafenstein 1997; Baum et al. 1998; Leroux and Levitt-Perlman 2000; Reis and McCoach 2000) believe that a diagnosis of ADD is incorrect in many instances and due to characteristics of giftedness being mistaken for neurobiological weaknesses. Poor compatibility between the educational needs or learning style of the child and the school environment may also play a role (Whitmore 1989; Baker et al. 1998). Indeed, the frustrations of a gifted child in an inappropriate educational environment cannot be ignored as many do lose interest in schoolwork (Winner 2000). But there are gifted learners who do not complain of boredom but continue to display difficulties with focusing, sustaining attention, remembering equipment, completing tasks, organization of thoughts, time and work, and dislike of handwriting.

These characteristics may lead to the diagnosis of ADHD with stimulant medication as the treatment. In many cases this does not prove exceptionally helpful, and neither does behaviour modification nor counseling bring about significant or long-term change. However, neurodevelopmental therapies have been successful in helping such children and warrant closer investigation.

A neurodevelopmental basis for therapy

The search for a neurophysiological basis to, and therapy for, attentional and/or learning difficulties finds support in the work of Blyth and McGlown (1978, 1979), Dennison (1981), Field and Blythe (1989), Bireley (1992), Goddard (1990, 1996) and Cheatum and Hammond (2000). For example, if the premotor cortex is malfunctioning, children at rest may not know the exact position of their body (proprioceptive sense) and so constantly move to get input from their muscles in order to know their exact spatial position (Gold 1997). This manifests as symptoms of hyperactivity and an inability to attend to a teacher. Another low functioning area in many children diagnosed with attentional difficulties may be the prefrontal cortex, which acts as an inhibitor of inappropriate responses. Children who cannot easily access information stored in this area to judge whether or not to embark on a certain action, may show the impulsivity so frequently associated with ADHD. Neurodevelopmental therapists are using movement therapy to restructure such irregularly functioning areas of the brain.

The role of movement

The role of movement in helping to overcome neurobiological inefficiencies is becoming clearer. The importance placed on physical movement stems from earlier theorists such as Kephart (1975), Ayres (1979), Cratty (1972, 1973) and Delacato (1959, 1974), who realized the importance of neural organization to successful learning and linked movement to brain structure. Movement reflects neural organization and provides the stimulation to neurological systems that is necessary for their development and optimal functioning.

Lack of good empirical research to substantiate their views has led to a division of opinion between practitioners and researchers regarding the validity of their theories. Since the mid-1970s, however, theoretical brain research has shown quite conclusively that the brain is 'plastic' in that it can adapt continuously, and its structure can be changed by certain kinds of stimulation (Thompson 1996; Gold 1997; Robertson 2000; Stiles 2001).

Furthermore, work has been done that establishes movement as a form of stimulation that creates the neural pathways making up the structure of the brain (Berthoz 2000). Examples include the work with nerve growth factor for which Rita Levi-Montcalcini won the Nobel prize in 1986, Changeux and Conic (1987), whose work proved that movement is necessary for neural growth, and Ito (1984, 1987), who found that stimulation of the vestibulo-ocular reflex arc resulted in changes in the structure of the cerebellum. This is leading to significant support for movement therapies, and recognition of the value of movement for helping children with problems interfering with school performance. Many of these therapies rely on anecdotal reports of success, but well designed research is beginning to emerge. Longhurst (2003) compared the result of different kinds of movement programmes on the motor efficiency and learning of children with learning problems and found that while the 'normal' physical education programme had little effect, programmes based on sensory-motor and perceptual-motor activities were responsible for significant gains in the children's ability to attend and cope with classroom tasks.

Putting theory into practice

One approach that uses movement as a therapeutic intervention is that of The HANDLE® Institute. This name is an acronym for a Holistic Approach to Neuro-Development and Learning Efficiency. The approach, used with clients with a wide variety of functional difficulties, is appropriate for children in need of therapeutic aid to overcome problems causing attentional difficulties. Assessment involves examination of possibly dominant subcortical systems that are interfering with cortical functioning, such as aberrant primitive reflexes, dysfunctions in tactile, olfactory, gustatory and vestibular functioning, as well as processing of visual and auditory information.

HANDLE sees neurodevelopment not as a given sequence of accrued skills but as an interactive hierarchy of brain functions, with a vestibular foundation for skills presumed to be isolated in particular sites in the brain. This interactive and interdependent hierarchy is schematically illustrated in Figure 8.2.1.

The arrows indicate the interdependent and interactive nature of the different subsystems. The relative position of each subsystem on the chart is indicative of the hierarchical nature of the neurological system, and illustrates how higher level functions depend on those at a lower level. For example, problems with reading or math may be traced all the way back to a dysfunctional vestibular system.

Practitioners drafting a therapy programme would sequence and prioritize exercise activities according to where an individual's weaknesses would appear on

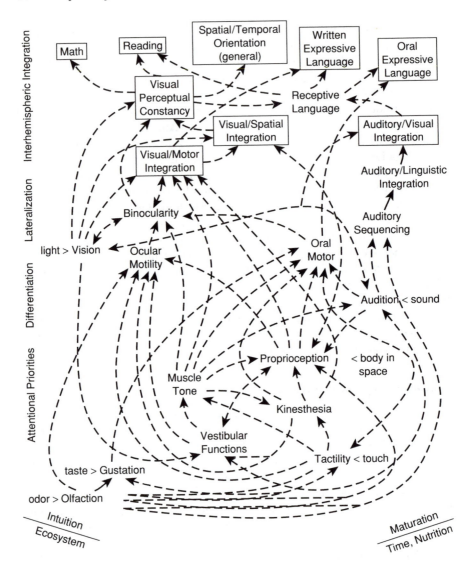

Figure 8.2.1 Affected systems chart.

the hierarchy. Lowest level systems would be addressed first so that, strengthened, they may support the functions of higher level systems, which could then benefit optimally from corrective therapeutic activities. To address 'higher level' functions, which amount to splinter skills in this paradigm, before strengthening the weakened foundational systems, is an exercise in futility: frustrating to the child and the teacher or therapist because such an approach achieves at best minimal gain, and serves only a stop-gap purpose. While possibly improving the splinter skill at issue at the time, because this approach does not resolve the causal issue, it leaves the weakness to affect other skills. In addition, even if higher level functions are relatively intact, until the lower system functions have been addressed, the 'energies' of the higher level function may be used to compensate for a weakness in a more foundational system. For example, if a child's visual system is well-developed, but her tactile system is hypersensitive, she may use her vision to remain hyper-vigilant of her surroundings rather than to use it freely for tasks of visual discrimination.

The holistic nature of this approach also requires recognition of internal and external influences. This means acknowledging possible causal roles of chemicals, allergens, nutritional deficits (especially the absence of essential fatty acids, dehydration and toxins of any kind). In addition, it includes the individual's social environment, such as the increasing cocooning lifestyle that keeps children indoors and inactive, and the decreased demand on their creativity as a result of TV and computers (Suliteanu 2001).

Each individual and each problem has unique aspects but the trained observer can determine patterns of dysfunction in the neurological subsystems required to support learning. These patterns then suggest how to resolve the problem with gentle, progressive strengthening of the weak areas.

While movement is central to HANDLE therapy, the concept of 'gentle enhancement' forms a cornerstone of the approach. This concept means the process of introducing therapeutic activities on a regular, consistent basis strictly according to how much the individual tolerates before that activity induces stress. For therapeutic benefit, individuals must be carefully monitored during exercises and encouraged to stop if any stress is noticed. Such signs include change of facial colour, reddening of the ears, change in visual focus, change in breathing or muscle tone, feelings of nausea or dizziness, or a general discomfort while performing an activity. This is a reason why HANDLE practitioners do not rely on therapeutic equipment. Rolling a child over a ball may be a specific vestibular exercise but will obscure the child's unwillingness to move beyond a certain point because of experiencing stress.

Repetitions of certain activities are thus limited to those that will ensure that the Sympathetic Nervous System is not activated, with resulting flight or fight symptoms. Treatment must be limited to as much input as their systems can use. Bluestone (2004) explains that an irregularly functioning neurological system must not be put under stress, because stress causes the system to shut down. Part of the reported success of this approach is based on clients being taught not to overwork systems that are not supporting higher level functioning (D. Frishkoff, personal communication, 1998). To achieve maximum benefit from regular but relatively brief periods of treatment, the programme is carried out at home, for between 15 and 20 minutes per day, rather than for longer, more intense sessions at a therapist's venue.

Many clients see significant results within the first few months (Reed 1996) but each client is encouraged to benefit from six months of fine-tuning at programme review sessions every six weeks.

'Attention deficit disorder' (ADHD) renamed

Implied in the diagnosis of ADHD is a 'lack' of attention. Bluestone (2004) contends that no one has an attention deficit. Rather, everyone is always attending to something, and individuals who show difficulties in sustaining attention may be blocking certain types of stimulation and seeking others; they may have difficulties adjusting attention flexibly to meet varying demands from the environment. Therefore, a more accurate name for this set of behaviours is attentional priority disorder (APD), and the condition is neither hereditary nor irreversible. By resolving issues that focus the individual's attention to more basic and pressing needs in underlying neurological subsystems, the individual can be freed to attend to social, academic, and other demands from the environment.

Common patterns of APD

Most people who have difficulty sustaining their attention and/or adjusting easily to the demands of changing situations show irregularities in specific neurodevelopmental functions on both input and output levels.

On an input level, there are frequently signs of:

- hypersensitivity to at least one modality such as touch, vision and/or sound
- weakness in the vestibular system which supports and regulates such functions as listening, eye functions, balance, knowledge of where our bodies are in space, muscle tone.

On an output level, individuals with APD may demonstrate:

- insufficient integration between the two sides of the body and brain
- immature reflex integration and irregularity in differentiation of movement/response.

The case of Alexis: a gifted child with diagnosed ADHD

Alexis was 7 years and 10 months old when she was referred for help. She had been diagnosed with ADHD as well as auditory and visual-motor perceptual dysfunctioning by a psychologist, neurologist and occupational therapist. She had also received vision therapy. In spite of some scatter among the scores of an IQ test, she still managed to fall within the superior range of intelligence. The school described her as a strong-willed child with a very short concentration span, who was unable to sit still and listen or focus on her work due to distractibility. On a modified Conner's Rating Scale, her teacher gave her the highest rating of 3 ('Very much') for restless/overactive; excitable/impulsive; disturbing other children; failing to finish things/daydreaming; constant fidgeting;

temper outbursts/unpredictable behaviour; and a rating of 2 ('Substantial') for quick and drastic mood swings and frustration if demands are not instantly met. The neurologist had prescribed Ritalin and her teacher was very supportive of this.

Background information

After an easy pregnancy, Alexis' birth had some complications. She was a big baby, weighing 4.21 kg. After three hours in labour, she showed signs of distress so was delivered with the help of forceps. Her APGAR scores were 8 and subsequent development was incident free, except that she did not have much movement stimulation as a baby. Her mother was able to leave her in her cot or carry her around in a baby chair for most of the early months. As long as there was something to look at, Alexis seemed to be happy to be mainly immobile. She achieved normal motor milestones (crawling and walking) and early language development. After experiencing colic during the first three months, she was a healthy child with no ear infections or other significant illnesses.

From toddler days, she showed an ever-increasing liking for constant activity. She enjoyed wild roundabout rides as well as running and jumping and spent long times walking on her hands, which she mastered at 5 years. She also liked rocking on her school chair – backwards, forwards and sideways and occasionally fell over. She went through phases of being clumsy, and bruised her legs by bumping into chairs, walls, doors and even people. However, she was a slow starter in the mornings, showing little urgency to begin the day and often spent a long time just gazing at herself in the bathroom mirror. She was not an extremely restless sleeper but liked company in bed. She covered her head with her blankets when she slept. She was very sensitive to light and disliked sunlight, torchlight or waking up in the morning with her bedroom light burning. She had a very sensitive scalp and thought that her finger tips were also very sensitive to touch – hating having her fingernails trimmed. She was extremely ticklish. Her favourite foods were salads and french fries or fish. She was not very fond of meat and particularly disliked the texture of chicken and some vegetables. She was very conscious of smells and seemed to be more sensitive to odours than most of her friends and family members.

Observations

Alexis did not move very much during the evaluation. She soon expressed a liking for eyes-closed activities because she said that her eyes get tired very quickly. She showed some uneven saccadic movements when asked to follow a moving object with her eyes and also said that it made her dizzy. Her eyes could not converge easily at close distances. Low muscle tone was suspected when she displayed untidy handwriting and also showed a preference for having her body supported by the chair or the desk. Her mother confirmed this by commenting that she is often rebuked for 'slouching'. She showed a dominant right hand and right eye and it seemed that her left brain hemisphere processed information more rapidly than the right. She used a technique known as 'cognitive override' to cope with demanding tasks. For example, she quickly used counting to help her master a finger tapping task. She was also found to have some primitive reflexes present.

When given a series of nonsense syllables to repeat, Alexis had some difficulty accurately recalling syllables with the plosive 'K' sound and she also forgot some details from a sentence read out to her.

Deductions

Alexis' sensitivity on her scalp and fingers and her ticklishness are indications that her sense of touch is irregular. This, coupled with a hypersensitivity to smell and light, can be very distracting to a child in a classroom. Her need to move, difficulty processing the plosive 'K' sound, issues with visual tracking as well as her lowered muscle tone showed that her vestibular system was weak and unable to support the many functions for which it is responsible. Her slow adjustment to the morning and her tendency to bump into things pointed to a weak proprioception. Alexis' vision was still compromised in spite of vision therapy. Her light sensitivity and problems with tracking and convergence caused her to experience dizziness and headaches, and she preferred eyes-closed activities because they give her eyes a chance to rest. Because of poor proprioception, however, she found it necessary to depend on her eyes, which became increasingly strained. Alexis needed a great amount of energy to sustain her weakened systems during the day, and her short temper and frustrations were making it hard for her to maintain interpersonal relationships.

Alexis had been compensating well for the difficulties she experienced with immature or underdeveloped systems. She was using her superior intellect to her advantage, but she did not have the underlying support systems for focusing, sustaining her attention flexibly and for completing tasks.

Recommendations

The programme designed for Alexis included several activities to strengthen her vestibular system. These, as well as the special massage that was recommended to reduce Alexis' hypersensitivity to touch, were also targeting her muscle tone issues to help strengthen this crucial function.

Other simple, non-taxing activities were suggested to strengthen her visual functions and reduce her light sensitivity, without stressing her weak vestibular system or relying on muscle tone and differentiation of eye movements from head movements. Drinking through a 'crazy straw' was one of these. The rationale for this simple activity is outlined in the appendix at the end of this contribution. Alexis was also encouraged to supplement her diet with omega-3 fatty acids, to ensure myelination of those neural pathways which the exercises were creating and strengthening.

Follow-up

Alexis' initial assessment took place in September. By late in November, her mother reported much progress. According to reports from the school, she was sitting still and finishing her work, and this improvement was substantiated by the school awarding her certificates of excellence. They no longer thought Ritalin was necessary.

Conclusion

The novel work of neurodevelopmental approaches which rely on movement to restructure areas of the brain has not yet been empirically proven. This means that the validity of this approach remains untested and therefore, in the eyes of many cautious scientists, suspect. However, the anecdotal reports of success are sufficient to warrant further research into the role of movement as a therapeutic intervention. These reports suggest that a wide range of behavioural and learning difficulties may be helped by applying the knowledge emerging from the field of neuroscience. Ongoing brain research that is revealing how the body structures the brain, rather than the brain being all-important for the functioning of the body, is a compelling argument for revisiting the views of earlier theorists as well as taking cognisance of emerging new knowledge. We need to learn to recognize the signs of neurodevelopmental roots of learning and behaviour problems; we need to restrain ourselves from labelling children with disorders too quickly; we need to know what movements are crucial to restructuring the brain and so help many children overcome their barriers to learning success. And lastly, we need to design good research to explore the physiological changes that seem to be brought about by movement to better understand the brain–body unity.

Key questions

1   How accurate is the diagnosis of ADHD in gifted children who appear to pay adequate attention to matters of personal interest?
2   Does the labelling of learning disorders and behaviour mask the root cause of a child's difficulties?
3   How does a neurodevelopmental approach differ from that of remedial therapy?
4   What are the advantages of a therapeutic approach that considers the physiological response of the body to stress?

Appendix: example of a simple therapeutic activity

This and other activities as listed on the website of the HANDLE® Institute, www.handle.org, do not require training to use. Other exercises and techniques referred to in the case studies cannot be implemented without training.

The crazy straw

Drinking through a crazy straw can help to improve many functions frequently found to be irregular.

1   We integrate the two sides of our mouth and cheeks while sucking and thereby stimulate the two cerebral hemispheres in a coordinated rhythmic fashion. This enhances our interhemispheric integration.
2   As we suck, our trigeminal nerves are stimulated and they in turn help regulate many aspects of our vision, including the ability of our eyes to converge.
3   One reason that people become more light sensitive is that the two eyes do not team in their processing of the visual images, which is based on perception of light and darkness. Another is that the pupils have a reduced degree of reactivity to light. Drinking through the straw enhances these functions.
4   Stimulation of the trigeminal nerve directly stimulates the nerves that service the ear. We are all familiar with how chewing gum helps people tolerate the pressure change in their ears during take-off and landing on flights.
5   Tongue and lip control and coordinated breathing, all of which support our ability to speak with good articulation, are aided by sucking.

The procedure is to encourage the child to hold the straw in the centre of his/her mouth and to drink one or two drinks each day slowly, relaxing between sips. Make sure that all drinking is done with eyes closed.

Useful websites

The HANDLE Institute, USA: http://www.handle.org
Shirley Kokot, at Integrated Learning Therapy, South Africa: http://www.ilt.co.za
For contact numbers or emails in the UK and Europe, contact: support@handle.org

References

Ayres, A. J. (1979) *Sensory Integration and the Child*. Los Angeles, CA: Western Psychological Services.

Baker, J. A., Bridger, R. and Evans, K. (1998) Models of underachievement among gifted preadolescents: the role of personal, family and school factors. *Gifted Child Quarterly*, 42(1): 5–15.

Baum, S. M., Olenchak, F. R. and Owen, S. V. (1998) Gifted students with attention deficits: fact and/or fiction? Or, can we see the forest for the trees? *Gifted Child Quarterly*, 42(2): 96–104.

Berthoz, A. (2000) *The Brain's Sense of Movement*. Cambridge, MA: Harvard University Press.

Bireley, M. (1992) Physiological uniqueness: a new perspective on the learning disabled/gifted child. *Roeper Review*, 15(2): 101–107.

Bluestone, J. (2004) *The Fabric of Autism: Weaving the Threads into Cogent Theory*. Seattle, WA: The HANDLE Institute.

Blythe, P. and McGlown, D. J. (1978) *Neurological Disorganization, Dyslexia and Learning Disabilities*. Chester, UK: Institute for Neuro-Physiological Psychology.

Blythe, P. and McGlown, D. J. (1979) *An Organic Basis for Neuroses and Educational Difficulties*. 4 Stanley Place, Chester, UK: Insight.

Changeux, J-P. and Conic, M. (eds) (1987) *The Neural and Molecular Bases of Learning*. Report on the Dahlem Workshop. Berlin: John Wiley and Sons.

Cheatum, B. A. and Hammond, A. A. (2000) *Physical Activities for Improving Children's Learning and Behaviour: A Guide to Sensory Motor Development*. Champaign, IL: Human Kinetics.

Cratty, B. J. (1972) *Physical Expressions of Intelligence*. Englewood Cliffs, NJ: Prentice Hall.

Cratty, B. J. (1973) *Movement, Behaviour and Motor Learning*. London: Henry Kimpton.

Delacato, C. H. (1959) *The Treatment and Prevention of Reading Problems*. Springfield, IL: Charles C. Thomas.

Delacato, C. H. (1974) *The Ultimate Stranger, the Autistic Child*. Novato, CA: Academic Therapy.

Dennison, P. E. (1981) *Switching On: A guide to Edu-Kinesthetics*, 3rd edn. Glendale, CA: Edu-Kinesthetics.

Field, J. and Blythe, P. D. (1989) *Towards Developmental Re-education*. Chester, UK: Institute for Neuro-Physiological Psychology.

Goddard, S. (1990) Developmental milestones: a blueprint for survival. Paper presented to the Institute for Neuro-Physiological Psychology, November, Sheffield.

Goddard, S. (1996) *A Teacher's Window into the Child's Mind: And Papers from the Institute for Neuro-Physiological Psychology*. Eugene, OR: Fern Ridge Press.

Gold, S. J. (1997) *If Kids Just Came with Instruction Sheets! Creating a World without Child Abuse*. Eugene, OR: Fern Ridge Press.

Ito, M. (1984) *The Cerebellum and Neural Control*. New York: Raven Press.

Ito, M. (1987) Characterization of synaptic plasticity in the cerebellar and cerebral cortex, in J-P. Changeux and M. Conic (eds) *The Neural and Molecular Bases of Learning: Report on the Dahlem Workshop*. Berlin: John Wiley and Sons.

Kephart, N. C. (1975) *The Slow Learner in the Classroom*. Columbus, OH: Merrill.

Leroux, J. A. and Levitt-Perlman, M. (2000) The gifted child with Attention Deficit Disorder: an identification and intervention challenge. *Roeper Review*, 22(3): 171–176.

Longhurst, G. (2003) The effects of different physical education programmes on the motor proficiency of children with learning difficulties, unpublished PhD thesis, KwaZulu Natal, University of Zululand.

Reed, G. (1996) HANDLE Institute's back-to-basics approach successful. *The Seattle Press*, X(25), 29 February–12 March 5, 9.

Reis, S. M. and McCoach, D. B. (2000) The underachievement of gifted students: what do we know and where do we go? *Gifted Child Quarterly*, 44(3): 152–170.

Robertson, I. H. (2000) Compensations for brain deficits: 'Every cloud . . .'. *British Journal of Psychiatry*, 176: 412–413.

Stiles, J. (2001) Neural plasticity and cognitive development. *Developmental Neuropsychology*, 18(2): 237–272.

Suliteanu, M. (2001) Outcomes are in the eye of the beholder. *ADVANCE Newsmagazine*, 6 August: 33–34.

Thompson, R. F. (1996) Motor learning and synaptic plasticity in the cerebellum. *Behavioral and Brain Sciences*, 19(3): 475–477, 503–527.

Tucker, B. and Hafenstein, N. L. (1997) Psychological intensities in young gifted children. *Gifted Child Quarterly*, 42(3): 66–75.

Webb, J. T. and Latimer, D. (1993) *ADHD and Children Who are Gifted* (ERIC Document no. EDO-EC-93-5). Reston, VA: Council for Exceptional Children.

Whitmore, J. R. (1989) Understanding a lack of motivation to excel. *Gifted Child Quarterly*, 30(2): 66–69.

Winner, E. (2000) The origins and ends of giftedness. *American Psychologist*, 55(1): 159–169.

8.3   Personal perspective: cerebral palsy gifted – unlimited possibilities of the physically challenged

Coury M. Knowles

Dreams define people. Achieving them takes discipline, determination, and a 'winner' attitude. I was born with Cerebral Palsy. Cerebral Palsy has not been a handicap, but a challenge I have used in character building. I am aware of my limitations – that I won't set any records in 50-meter sprint – but I *am* a doctoral student at a state university.

My early years can be described as a fight to be normal. I wanted to do everything my friends did. If they rode skateboards, I would take mine up my street (which was on a hill) and sit down on the board and ride it! Of course, I have many scars but I earned the respect of my friends quickly through this fearless attitude. As a result, they adapted all games for me. I played basketball, football, soccer, baseball and many unorganized games. Despite this, I was always picked last in PE class. About the age of 10, I realized I was different; I came home wishing I could run, jump and throw like everyone else and many nights I cried myself to sleep. My mother told me that I could contribute to sports without being an active player. A retired PE teacher, she allowed me to referee and coach. From these times, I learned how important positive people are. My father made me do laps around my house to gain strength and did not put up with excuses. I hated him then for his expectations, but I love and cherish him now for his 'tough love'. This helped me overcome five surgeries, the last at 12 involved cutting nerve endings in my spinal cord which send incorrect signals to my muscles that make up my scissor-like gait. I had to learn to walk again, again, and again on five separate occasions. Each occasion showed me the value of humility and courage not only in myself, but also in my parents. They allowed me to fall and get up again on my own. My dad always told me: 'You can do anything, but you are going to have to work harder than everyone else.'

Middle and high school were tough times as I sought acceptance. I had many friends at school, but girls did not give me the time of day. I used this as a motivating factor for succeeding in school, athletically and academically. I began managing the basketball and baseball teams at my schools. When I would 'walk-in-the-mall', I would notice how people, especially girls, would seem to be afraid to walk next to me. It crushed me. As a junior in high school, I worked hard and ran for student government offices (student body vice-president my senior year). I graduated well and earned several academic scholarships to the University of Florida.

Life got harder in college as I lost one of my scholarships in my first semester. Athletically I was told I could not be a student-manager due to my physical disability, and socially I had lots of friends, but few were girls. Academically, I took out a student loan so I could 'volunteer' my spare time with the baseball team. I worked on my major coursework (exercise and sport sciences) earned straight 'As' and found myself on the president's honor role. On the baseball field, I was given more responsibilities, attended team workouts, worked out and 'shagged' baseball balls during batting practice. My goal was to catch a live fly ball. The team knew it. Lot of days after practice I would be dirtier than some of the players. This effort made me a leader in the locker room. I was treated as a player. In 1998, we (the Gators) went back to the College World Series and I was part of the traveling party. I had finally achieved the dream of being a part of a team.

In 1999, I also had my first girlfriend, Elke. Two years later, I was hurt by our breakup, but Elke put me on the path to accept my disability as strength and not a weakness. I graduated from the University of Florida (UF) with a bachelors of science with a specialization in sport management (1999) and a master's in exercise and sport sciences, with emphasis in adapted physical education/physical education (2001). In 1999, I had two graduate assistant positions at UF: teaching adapted physical education at local schools, and supervising fifteen student-managers for five different intercollegiate sports within the athletic department. This was ironic because five years prior I was told I could not manage due to my disabilities and now I was leading student-managers due to my abilities! I was voted in the Student Hall of Fame 2001.

I am currently in my fourth year as a specially designed physical education teacher in Seminole County, Florida. My job responsibilities involve teaching students with various disabilities, such as the physically impaired (PI), the trainable mentally disabled (TMD), profoundly mentally disabled (PMD) and autistic. I have also been a varsity assistant baseball coach at Lake Brantley High. I have been a guest speaker on disability awareness at many universities. Furthermore, I am pursuing my doctorate degree at the University of Central Florida in education. I aspire to become a head baseball coach and a professor.

At 27 years old, I drive my car, have learned to swim and have completed three 5-kilometer road races as well as win several teaching and coaching awards. More importantly, I am blessed to have many friends who love me for me. In the end, 'To believe you can is everything!'

Remember, dreams define you regardless of your physical strength, physical speed and physical size.

8.4   Conflict resolution 7: twice exceptional

Suzanne Rawlins

Raymond is a highly gifted middle school student, with a severe attention deficit (ADHD), emotionally handicapped and health-impaired due to early childhood brain injury. His father was recently released from prison on drug charges and is restricted from seeing him; his mother is fighting her own addiction. Raymond is Black like his mother, and is uncomfortable with his White father not respecting his desire to be with his Black friends. His gifted classes are almost entirely filled with White and Asian students. Raymond's behaviors demonstrate frustration and anger toward all the teachers, except the band instructor. Music is 'his thing'. Raymond is failing all his gifted classes on purpose. He wants to 'hang with the boys'. His teachers, believing in his abilities, tried interventions that included the band teacher in a positive behavior plan. That worked for three days. The father threatened military school, 'boot-camp' and removal of all privileges. Raymond just grinned. He was winning. Schedules were rearranged to permit Raymond to mix his classes: some with gifted students, some with general education students. Nothing changed. Raymond was placed on a less crowded school bus to lessen the opportunities for confrontation. He started walking the three miles home, leaving school any time he chose. What should be done?

9 Developmental and age issues

9.1 The fragility of the faceted child: gifted, culturally conflicted, isolated

Carole Ruth Harris

Any working definition of diversity must take into account that every individual has complex facets formed by family structure and personal attributes which combine with ethnicity in a unique manner. Added to this are changing perceptions that are developmental – the way in which the child is viewed by parents, teachers and schoolmates, and the way in which the child interprets experiences to form self-concept and self-esteem. This chapter offers ideas for the planning and organization of ethnographically derived techniques for accurate identification that recognizes the problem areas of the faceted child.

Problem areas in faceted children

Single parents, blended families, same sex parents

The children of single parents, blended families and same sex parents obviously play several roles, but the children within these families also assume roles that are differentiated from the mainstream family. The outgrowth from these 'different' family structures may be positive or negative, depending upon the climate of the home, the particular personal relationships, and the stage of development of the individual child. The security level of the child also varies, sometimes due to maturity expectations that may be beyond the child's capability or developmental stage. Fantasy life is often active in a child of a single parent (M. Morelock, personal communication, 1995), with a dichotomy between increased responsibility and self-concept that may be tempered with a sense of isolation and difference. If the child is gifted, the child may delay creative or intellectual development until later in life when conventionality does not loom as large within the school or peer setting (Gardner 1993).

Intergenerational conflict

Intergenerational conflict occurs across ethnic groups, from the placing of responsibility on gifted young children who act as interpreters for immigrant families to multigeneration households, with a shift in cultural values within generations. The newly acculturated children and youth may resent the dependence of the elders, who may perceive the younger generation as disassociating itself with the old traditions. This produces stress that has a negative effect on self-concept, on family relationships, and on manifestation of accepted gifted characteristics: moreover, seemingly 'new' ideas in the school setting may seem offensive to traditional cultural values. Some gifted children assume counterbalancing roles reflecting values of peers and teachers on the one hand, and family members among three generations on the other. Furthermore, when there are more than two generations in a household, the expectations of the parents and the grandparents are likely to differ markedly, resulting in misunderstandings and wide communication gaps. Where there are different languages in each generation, the perception by parents, caught between the generations, is tempered by conflict and respect patterns and desire for assimilation. According to Coll (2003), in a study of Portuguese, Dominican and Cambodian children, pupils who accept their diversity and differences, and are supported by home environment, have higher academic success, but may sacrifice social ease within the culture of the school, fostering isolation (Gruenwald 2003).

Economic pressure

Societal economic conditions are linked to a pattern of educational inequity that causes masking of ability coupled with low self-esteem, making it extremely difficult to identify giftedness (Vanderslice 1999). In 1988, policy makers (Commission on National Challenges in Higher Education) reported that 20 percent of the American school age population were from ethnic minorities of low economic status. By 2000, it was accurately predicted that this would rise to one-third of the nation with 'herculean social and economic costs' (Lindsay 1990: 200). That few children of poverty are recommended to gifted programs remains an unfortunate fact (Ford and Harmon 2001; Harris in press) and is a problem that requires strong efforts to break this self-perpetuating cycle.

Refugee problems and illegal immigration

Many immigrants feel they do not belong in their new country (National Coalition of Advocates for Students 1988). Many experience emotional problems, including symptoms of depression, periods of disorientation, separation anxiety and isolation (National Coalition of Advocates for Students 1988: 24). This is heightened by guilt over survival when members of the family have been killed, or when members remain in the endangered area. Often there is fear of authority when a near relative is an illegal immigrant (Gratz and Pulley 1984; Portes et al.

1978; Vasquez 1988), thus preventing close relationships with teachers. This mistrust of authority results in a syndrome associated with exhaustion of coping behavior (L. Clark 1988). According to Clark (1988), frustration often turns to self-hatred and extends to hatred of school and family, constantly aggravated by a feeling of not belonging.

Isolation

When a minority culture comes into conflict with the power structure of the dominant culture, perception of diminished strength produces deterioration of the culture's own value system (Marsella 1979) and can lead to a feeling of isolation (Adams 1975). Within the classroom, the gifted child is the minority culture and often feels isolated and symptoms of cultural conflict precipitate the same forms of isolation that occur in the culturally conflicted individual (Harris 2003a). If we substitute the school society for the term *dominant society*, the problem is more clearly seen. In a follow-up study of the Hollingworth group (Harris 1992), adults who were identified as gifted when children and placed in a special program revealed numerous instances of isolating factors, with substantial similarity to cultural conflict areas outlined by Ogbu (1978), Sugai and Maheady (1988) and Trueba (1988). The culturally diverse gifted child is *twice isolated*, with associated difficulty in sorting out constantly shifting conflict situations.

Masking talent

Stereotypes are frequently imposed upon bicultural families. Asian children, for example, are expected to excel in mathematics (Harris in press) and to succeed academically. In trying to live up to expectations, they often mask other abilities. In cases where children have advanced moral development and social sensitivity, this can be so different from other children's awareness that it creates a dichotomy between the inner experience and the practical world that is difficult to balance (Harris 2003b). When the child does not feel able to cope with the inner and outer conflicts, the frequent perception that the child is not well adjusted often leads to masking giftedness, propelled by the instinct to protect the vulnerable inner self from possible ridicule.

Shifting cultural adjustment and value systems

Western theories of creativity were modeled on patriarchal western societies, but what if we were to take these theories and apply them to a different type of society, a matriarchal society, a less developed society, or a society that finds itself with large numbers of immigrant and refugee families? Would they operate in the same way?

Within the classroom and the general school society, cultural conflict exacerbates the isolation that occurs when the child experiences cultural erosion and is also negotiating assimilation within the 'new' culture. Maretzki (1983) related strategies for adults of different cultural backgrounds to the presence or absence of conflict as follows:

- *Strategy A:* a person could eradicate completely all traces of her ethnic cultural background and merge into the larger society, or she may become a purist who sees herself entirely as a person of her ethnic ancestry.
- *Strategy B:* a person may select ethnic alternation in which he is sometimes one or the other in terms of cultural identity and actions. The switches are situationally determined and may be so difficult to carry through that personal discomfort and disorientation may occur.
- *Strategy C:* a person may blend two cultures as a mutual enrichment in which neither cultural background is negative in its effect in a behavioral or psychological sense.

(Maretzki 1983: 46)

Children do not have the maturity and sophistication to employ these strategies, and conflict arises that affects those internal and external perspectives essential to strong locus of control, good self-concept, balance and wholeness as they grow and mature within the family, school and dominant culture. Marsella and Leong (1995) maintain that cross-cultural assessment needs to take a cross-cultural perspective, and maintains that ethnocentrism plays a part in any conceptualization of culture.

Parent perceptions of giftedness and school achievement

Although giftedness has global characteristics, parent perceptions of giftedness and school achievement differ among cultural groups (Reid 1992). Planners of gifted programs frequently seek broad definitions and then present these definitions to the community (Gallagher 1985; Chapey et al. 1986). When screening procedures fail to take into account parental comprehension of giftedness and talent, a potential problem area is created (Harris 1998a). In a study utilizing six schools with low socio-economic status, questionnaires, distributed to a number of other cultures, including Micronesian, Filipino, Japanese, Chinese, Marshallese and Hawaiian, reflected concepts of giftedness among parents, and whether the special programs in the schools met the needs of their children (Harris 1998b). Many parents, especially those with Asian backgrounds, related concepts of giftedness to competence, industry and family involvement: while others, especially parents of younger children, felt that giftedness was bestowed by fortune and enabled the child to do academic work with ease. There were also parents whose concepts of giftedness were related to family involvement rather than cultural factors. The element of blessing, or religious association, was raised repeatedly. A few of the parents stated that some of the characteristics by which their children were identified were not what they had considered 'gifted', and were surprised to have their children thus identified. These parents had considered giftedness associated with activities such as music, art, science or mathematics. The group was culturally different but not culturally cohesive: that is, the group was in varying degrees of cultural conflict, with traditional values and concepts of giftedness clashing with western concepts of giftedness. Some parents said their children were *only smart in school* and had no special gifts, while others stated that they were gifted but not good at schoolwork (Harris 1987).

Leadership roles

Findings emerging from the study cited earlier (Harris 1998b) indicated that leadership is an aspect of great importance to giftedness, especially in the Marshallese culture. This was complicated by the problems in those aspects of the culture that had undergone change as a result of cultural conflict. Although humility and gentleness, especially in males, is highly valued, the presence of the US military had created an altered view of leadership ability. In Marshallese society, women are highly regarded and girls are highly valued; thus, many leadership roles in the community were carried out by females. Because of the presence of the US military and some US–Marshallese intermarriage, traditional Marshallese male leadership styles had become confused and the progress reports in the implemented curriculum of groups with male leaders were frequently not positive. Nevertheless, the community concept of giftedness was strongly connected with the idea of leadership.

The conclusions from Harris's (1998b) study reflected giftedness defined as environmentally and familial-influenced achievement in one culture, and gender-driven leadership in another culture. This raises the issue of who defines concepts of giftedness in a community, and continuing parent-educator communication would do much to avoid an ethnocentric and distorted lens when giftedness is examined in the light of parental definitions that stem from cultural association.

Self-esteem and self-concept issues

Gifted children are often also *asynchronous*, that is, strong in one area and weaker in another, for example, socially immature and intellectually advanced. The child may misinterpret this uneven learning pattern as being 'dumb' in a given subject, or unpopular with peers. The gaps between maturity level and intellectual functioning are sometimes great, with skill development sharply contrasted across curriculum areas. A teacher may address the weak areas and let the child find his/her own way in the strong area, and the child absorbs the obvious mixed messages. In addition, gifted children who are asynchronous, with developmental attributes at age level and intellectual capability at an advanced level, are 'shape shifters', with behavioral attributes shifting rapidly from young developmental stage to adult verbalization (Duncan 1999). The result is confusion about the child's actual potential, for both the child and the caretaker.

Cultural erosion, assimilation and role conflict

Cultural erosion can include rejection of the originating culture by extended family, as well as confusion of personal identity, thus multiplying the fragility of the faceted gifted child. Cultural erosion and cultural assimilation are closely related factors influenced by geographical area, proximity of the dominant and subdominant cultures, and immigrant status, and overlap so closely as to make separation of influencing factors difficult. These factors, however, are often seen in layers. Cultural erosion takes place in a contained environment with a strong existing culture with its own traditions, with superimposed factors creating an influence on traditional values. Cultural assimilation places the individual in an environment dominated by a culture that either integrates with the originating culture or displaces it. In high ability children, cultural shifts occur within asynchronous behaviors and adaptation techniques utilize advanced perceptivity alongside development, and intellectual and creative capability.

According to Zhou and Bankston (1998), Vietnamese immigrant families in the United States experience conflict that is counterproductive to generational consonance in areas of authority, views of US culture and gender roles. This applies to other cultures in the context of academic achievement (Hunsaker 1995), with families who have high expectations, but who frown upon adapting American ways that reflect instant gratification or materialistic values, and reject traditional ways. Conflicts are also likely to occur in the social arena with patterns of obedience, appropriate clothing and gender roles. Differences between modes of discipline within American culture and the originating culture are readily perceived by high ability children who tend to gravitate to older children as intellectual peers. Stress specifically related to cultural isolation is manifested in role conflict stress. This is exhibited by individuals who assume multiple and conflicting roles (Harris 1991). Because gifted children are frequently doubly isolated (Harris 1998a), both by ability and by culture, social conflicts are often multiplied and tangled in mixed perceptions of values in the country of settlement and values from the originating culture.

Neglect of creativity and creative potential

Misplacement in schools, when placements are made according to chronological age rather than level of education, causes severe problems in the identification of creativity in culturally diverse gifted children (Harris 2001). Culturally diverse immigrant students may have had little or sporadic schooling, or possibly no schooling, prior to coming to the new country and misplacement is aggravated by the lack of school records. Wei (1983) also reports the frequency of the wrong date of birth in school records. The problem is often not solely attributable to school authorities because many children hide facts about years spent in the former school to save face (Center for Educational Research and Innovation 1987; Vuong 1988).

Poor motivation for creative endeavor in school and clashes with school personnel can be put down to low sensitivity of teaching personnel coupled with misconceptions about the originating culture. Goldberg (National Coalition of Advocates for Students 1988: 52) relates the practice of superficial treatment of the originating culture, 'two foods and three old heroes' as a source of conflict. Overcrowded classrooms and schools, opposition from staff to curricular alteration, and inappropriate use of standardized tests often preclude entrance to any enrichment activities that might stimulate creativity in this population. According to testimony by Steinberg and Halsted (National Coalition of Advocates for Students 1988) immigrant children are frequently tracked into second language classes, and then encouraged to take vocational courses or academic subjects that do not require verbal skills (Romo 1993). Frequently there is a complete neglect of art which the family might perceive as non-serious study. Absurdities also result in ethnocentric misplacement, such as placing a rigorously trained Japanese 14 year old in need of calculus with a Laotian 14 year old who had but two years of schooling, because they were both Asian (Vuong 1988). In both cases, creative activities were eliminated entirely. In addition, a very high barrier to proper placement can be erected by the parents of creatively gifted diverse children who mistrust any kind of enrichment and regard it as trivial (Wei 1983; Harris 2001).

Many cultures, especially those that originate in less developed countries, do not foster independent work but emphasize group cooperation, team effort and obedience.

Field-dependent learning styles foster a dynamic exchange of ideas and broaden understanding of other cultures, but the field-dependent learning style, which depends upon group interaction and cooperative effort, is frequently open to misunderstanding and may be interpreted as 'cheating' rather than idea exchange.

Methodological approaches

Methodological approaches include planning, organization and implementation of ethnographically derived techniques for accurate identification and offer effective program design and evaluation in practice.

Ethnographically derived techniques

A first step in ethnographic study for diverse populations must be a study of demographics about the multiple facets of the community and include review of current census data on new immigrants, district or school information on personnel background, issues related to health and psychological services, including guidance and professional development given to staff. A second step consists of theoretical sampling coupled with observation and involves time spent in classrooms observing, interviewing and analysing videotaped interviews conducted with individual children and families.

Interviewing

An initial interview should be conducted with both parents if possible, and the individual child. Prior to the interview, family background should include education of the parents, birthplace, languages spoken in the home and other relatives living with the family. A statement of goals for the child, such as intellectual and creative development, self-esteem and commitment, should be shared and discussed with the parents. In addition, parents should be asked to provide their assessment of the child's personality characteristics along with any perceived learning problems such as ADHD and dyslexia. Parental anecdotal records should describe the child from the time of birth, including any previous testing results, school records and products such as the child's drawings, paintings, stories, hobbies, computer-related activities and types of books read. All such records and products assist analysis and insight into the family dynamic by providing a fuller picture for the assessment profile and subsequent curricular intervention. It also gives the parents the opportunity to formulate a multifaceted portrait of the child's attributes. As the process evolves, parents should be encouraged to add to the portfolio. The interview itself should consist of a combination of discussion, observation, problem-solving, drawing and age-appropriate manipulatives.

During the interview, the interaction between parent and child should be closely observed, with parents encouraged to participate in the activities, but not to interfere. While the approach is flexible, the interactions should also be within a reasonable time frame depending on the age of the child. Creative follow-up exercises to do at home should also be given.

Video analysis

Although the process is time consuming, videotaping the interview allows detailed review of the session (Harris and Ratcliff, in process). Used with background information and assessment, the videotape provides a basis from which curricular planning, design and application can be derived.

Utilizing a clinical case study approach

Videotape provides another perspective because it assists the researcher to process significant actions and reactions that are significant: the videotape is then coded for ethnographic patterns (Becker and Geer 1960; Wolcott 1974). Typical coding includes aspects of motor coordination, dependence–independence, self-esteem, frustration patterns, imagination, linguistic skills, reasoning in mathematics, ability to problem-solve and flexibility (Harris 1999). Clinical case study analysis should include the tape analysis and review of all available records.

Phenomenological assessment analysis

Although tests may be given and scores produced, phenomenological assessment depends upon observation and synthesis of all information. Additionally, all assessment instruments should be coded for the purpose of phenomenological curriculum design, along with observation notes. Osborn (1998: 9), who views assessment as 'part science and part art', recommends a comprehensive assessment evaluation and learning profile of the individual child's blend of gifts and talents through the use of instrumentation, behavioral observation, records and research.

Assessment

Assessment should develop a child's learning profile to design curriculum experiences that strengthen weakness by using the child's strengths and particular learning style. B. Clark (1991) concludes that there is a genetic-environmental factor that promotes accelerated development, with the quality of stimulation and quality of interaction directly related to increase in the development of potential. The answer to the question 'Who is Gifted?', however, is usually an operational response and schools frequently define giftedness in terms of state-mandated giftedness, thus narrowing the definition to exclude genetic-environmental factors, quality of stimulation and quality of interaction.

Curriculum is a plan for instruction, but the interaction itself, the implementation of that plan, depends upon what is taught, and by whom, and whether it can be evaluated as effective (Harris 2002). Differentiation for the gifted and talented depends upon content, teaching strategies, resources, personnel and evaluation, with attention to the formal and informal factors involved.

Conclusion

Realization of potential in diverse families requires a differentiated approach to identification and curricular planning that takes into account ways to surmount the obstacles to recognizing and servicing children from diverse families. Accurate identification and curricular intervention needs to address the multiple facets of the child's life beyond the classroom, and to incorporate locus of control and self-esteem issues. Methods of profiling differences in family dynamics are an essential first step towards acceptance and understanding, validating, and planning for giftedness in home situations that are as diverse as our multifaceted, ever-changing society. The gifted need an education that is prepared to understand and speak to their fragility and the multiple facets of their increasingly complex lives.

Key questions

1 When considering diversity, what are some of the issues that go beyond ethnicity?

2 What are some of the problems that must be considered when identifying diverse gifted students?

3 What are the advantages of a clinical case study approach to designing curricula for the diverse gifted student?

References

Adams, B. (1975) *Rust in Peace*. Sydney: Antipodean.

Becker, H. S. and Geer, B. (1960) Participant observation: the analysis of qualitative field data, in R. Adams and J. Preiss (eds) *Human Organizational Research*. Homewood, IL: Dorsey Press.

Center for Educational Research and Innovation (CERI) (1987) *Immigrant Children at School*. Organization for Economic Cooperation and Development (OECD). Paris: CERI.

Chapey, G. D., Trimarco, T. A., Crisci, P. E. and Capobianco, M. G. (1986) Gifted and talented education: parents and the schools in Cleveland and New York, in A. J. Cropley, K. K. Urban, H. Wagner and W. Wieczerkowski (eds) *Giftedness: A Continuing Worldwide Challenge*. New York: Trillium Press.

Clark, B. (1991) Growing Up Gifted, 4th edn. New York: Macmillan.

Clark, L. (1988) *Early Warning of Refugee Flows*. Washington, DC: Center for Policy Analysis and Research on Refugee Issues (available from Refugee Policy Group, Suite 401, 1424 16th Street, Washington, DC 20036).

Coll, C. G. (2003) Academic pathways through middle childhood, in T. Antonucci (Chair) *Development in Immigrants*. Symposium conducted at the Third Biennial Meeting of the Society for the Study of Human Development, Harvard University, Cambridge, MA, November.

Duncan, K. (1999) Homeschooling with an individualized curriculum. Paper presented at the Annual Hollingworth Conference for Highly Gifted Children, Manchester, NH, May.

Ford, D. Y. and Harmon, D. A. (2001) Equity and excellence: providing access to gifted education for culturally diverse students. *Journal of Secondary Gifted Education*, 12(3): 141–147.

Gallagher, J. J. (1985) *Teaching the Gifted Child*, 3rd edn. Boston, MA: Allyn and Bacon.

Gardner, H. (1993) *Creating Minds: An Anatomy of Creativity Seen through the Lives of Freud, Einstein, Picasso, Stravinsky, Eliot, Graham, and Gandhi*. New York: Basic Books.

Gratz, E. and Pulley, J. L. (1984) A gifted and talented program for migrant students. *Roeper Review*, 6(3): 147–149.

Gruenwald, D. A. (2003) *American Educational Research Journal*, 40(3): 619–654.

Harris, C. R. (1987) An ethnographically derived curriculum for culturally different gifted students, doctoral dissertation, Teachers College, Columbia University, University Microfilms International 8721119.

Harris, C. R. (1991) Identifying and serving the gifted new immigrant: problems, strategies, implications. *Teaching Exceptional Children*, 23(4): 16–30.

Harris, C. R. (1992) The fruits of early intervention: the Hollingworth group today. *Advanced Development: A Journal on Adult Giftedness*, 4: 91–104.

Harris, C. R. (1998a) Social and intellectual isolation of the gifted: causal factors and strategic intervention. Paper presented at the meeting of the Hollingworth Center for Highly Gifted Children, Cambridge, MA, May.

Harris, C. R. (1998b) Micronesian and Hawaiian parent perceptions of giftedness and achievement. Paper presented at the meeting of the Comparative and International Education Society, Buffalo, NY, March.

Harris, C. R. (1999) Deriving curricular Design from phenomenological observation: videotaping, instrumentation. Paper presented at the meeting of the National Association for Gifted Children, Albuquerque, NM, November.

Harris, C. R. (2001) Fostering creativity in the Asian-Pacific child, K–8: identification, strategies, implications, in M. D. Lynch and C. R. Harris, *Fostering Creativity in Children, K–8: Theory and Practice*. Boston, MA: Allyn and Bacon.

Harris, C. R. (2002) Passow's four curricula: designing for gifted applied practice. Paper presented at the annual meeting of the National Association for Gifted Children, Denver, CO, November.

Harris, C. R. (2003a) Cultural erosion, assimilation, and the high ability student: a clinical case study approach. Paper presented at the Western Regional Meeting of the Comparative and International Education Society. Honolulu, HI, January.

Harris, C. R. (2003b) Child-centered identification and the hidden child. *Understanding Our Gifted*, 15(3): 6–9.

Harris, C. R. (in press) *How Can Gifted Asian-Pacific Students be Identified and Served? (FAQ)*. Washington, DC: National Association for Gifted Children.

Harris, C. R. (in process) Differences in parent perceptions of giftedness using the Rimm AIM.

Harris, C. R. and Ratcliff, D. (in process) Video analysis in qualitative research.

Hunsaker, S. L. (1995) *Family Influences on the Achievement of Economically Disadvantaged Students: Implications for Gifted Identification and Programming* (Research Monograph 95206). Storrs, CT: National Research Center on the Gifted and Talented.

Lindsay, B. (1990) Educational equity in cross-national settings, in R. M. Thomas (ed.) *International Comparative Education: Practices, Issues, and Prospects*. New York: Pergamon.

Maretzki, M. (1983) *Native Hawaiian Educational Assessment Project*. Kamehameha Schools, Bernice Pauaki Bishop Estate, Honolulu, HI.

Marsella, A. J. (1979) Cross-cultural studies of mental disorders, in A. J. Marsella, R. G. Tharp and T. J. Cibarowski, *Perspectives on Cross-cultural Psychology*. New York: Academic Press.

Marsella, A. J. and Leong, F. T. L. (1995) Cross-cultural issues in personality and career assessment. *Journal of Career Assessment*, 3(2): 202–218.

National Coalition of Advocates for Students (NCAS) (1988) *New Voices, Immigrant Voices in US Public Schools* (Research Report 1988–1). Boston, MA: NCAS.

Ogbu. K. I. (1978) *Minority Education and Caste: The American System in Cross-cultural Perspective*. New York: Academic Press.

Osborn, J. (1998) Intelligence revisited. *Understanding Our Gifted*. 10(2): 9–12.

Portes, A., McLeod, S. A., Jr., and Parker, R. N. (1978) Immigrant aspirations. *Sociology of Education*, 51 (October): 241–260.

Reid, N. (1992) Correcting cultural myopia: the discovery and nurturance of the culturally different gifted and talented in New Zealand. Paper presented at the Second Asian Conference on Giftedness, Taipei, Taiwan, July.

Romo, H. (1993) *Mexican Immigrants in High Schools: Meeting their Needs. ERIC Digest* ED357905. Reston, VA: ERIC.

Sugai, G. and Maheady, L. (1988) Cultural diversity and individual assessment for behavior disorders. *Teaching Exceptional Children*, 21(1): 28–31.

Trueba, H. T. (1988) Culturally based explanations of minority students' academic achievement. *Anthropology and Education Quarterly*, 19: 270–287.

Vanderslice, R. (1999) Rural Hispanic children and giftedness: why the difficulty in identification?, in *Rural Special Education for the New Millennium: Proceedings of the 19th American Council on Rural Special Education* ED4289752 (Microfiche). Albuquerque, NM: ERIC Clearinghouse.

Vasquez, J. A. (1988) Contexts of learning for minority students. *Educational Forum*, 6(3): 243–253.

Vuong, V. (1988) Finding solutions, in National Coalition of Advocates for Students, *New Voices, Immigrant Voices in US Public Schools*. (Research Report 1988–1). Boston, MA: NCAS.

Wei, T. (1983) The Vietnamese refugee child: understanding cultural differences, in D. Omark and J. Erickson (eds) *The Bilingual Exceptional Child*. San Diego, CA: College-Hill Press.

Wolcott, H. F. (1974) Criteria for an ethnographic approach to research in schools. *Human Organization*, 34: 111–24.

Zhou, M. and Bankston, C. L. (1998) The biculturation of the Vietnamese student. *ERIC/CUE Digest 152*. Reston, VA: ERIC.

9.2   Counseling: grief and the culturally diverse gifted student

Montserrat Casado-Kehoe and Ximena E. Mejia

Defining giftedness as a cultural concept

From a dominant cultural perspective that values high intellectual ability in order to better society, giftedness includes intelligence, creativity and social concern. Greenlaw and McIntosh (1988: 33) define a gifted child as possessing 'cognitive ability that is noticeably superior to that of age mates. This cognitive superiority is coupled with a propensity for creative action in any of a multitude of areas'. Thus, giftedness includes not only high cognitive ability, but also other talents and capabilities such as creativity, rapid learning, high curiosity, motivation and advanced thinking.

Issues in mental health for diverse gifted students: being 'different'

Each gifted child is different with respect to his or her need for counseling. Depending on the level and type of a child's giftedness, and depending on the children with whom the gifted child is associating, the difference may be blatant or less noticeable. Gifted children need to be helped to accept their uniqueness, not deny it. Upon entering school, children may perceive that 'sameness' and conformity are rewarded and being 'different' or diverse is sanctioned. A counselor should work with gifted children and their families to help them understand their uniqueness as both acceptable and valuable. Knowing *how* they are unique is much more helpful for extraordinary young people than just knowing that they are gifted.

Giftedness in the psychological well-being of diverse students

Gifted students from diverse cultural backgrounds have unique issues that must be addressed early and consistently in counseling. Counselors may represent the only or primary source of professional support for students who underachieve, have poor self-perceptions and face social barriers such as ethnic injustices and low expectations.

Underachievement

Gifted students are likely to be our most severely underachieving population. According to Barnette (1989), individuals underachieve either because they cannot or will not utilize their inner resources. Ford (1995) suggests that gifted diverse children may be underachieving because their inner resources

- have atrophied due to disuse
- have been numbed by expectations of convergent production
- have been squelched by uninformed teachers or parents
- have been blocked because all attention and energy have been diverted to handle a tough situation.

Also, gifted individuals may choose to underachieve in order to

- better 'fit in' with their age-mates
- meet family expectations
- rebel against the achievement emphasis of our culture.

Whitmore (1980, 1986) included the failure to perform basic academic tasks in the prescribed manner.

Grieving 'being normal'

Children's social-emotional and educational problems often relate to an inability to fulfill their basic needs (Maslow 1968) including the desire to belong and to feel loved. Whitmore (1980, 1986) noted the feelings of alienation and isolation gifted children experience due to their unique abilities. These feelings of not belonging and isolation bring up grief and loss for gifted students. A new identity is developed when one is labeled as 'gifted'. It is not uncommon to see signs of depression as a result of having to let go of the notion of 'being normal'. Counseling can provide a safe place in which children can learn more about the grief and loss cycle and its impact on emotional health. Diaz (1998) found that social factors significantly and negatively impact achievement among talented Puerto Rican students. Being placed in a situation with students and teachers who look, speak and behave differently can negatively influence one's social self-concept (Coleman and Fults 1985). Davis and Rimm (2004) note that the self is multi-faceted with many parts such as social, emotional, physical and academic. Gifted students may feel confident about their academic self but may not feel good about the other self facets. Thus, issues that may be helpful to address in counseling are personal adjustment of gifted students in a variety of settings, social skills, emotional understanding, as well as social self-concept.

Understanding cultural factors in the gifted self-concept

Students from different backgrounds may exhibit giftedness differently (Siegel 2001). Thus, understanding the culture of the gifted student is a crucial factor in recognizing and fostering the gifts and talents of students. Minority students are socially and community oriented, as reflected by strong kinship networks and large extended families. Traditional theories of self-concept have yet to include ethnic self-concept, despite the reality that ethnicity is central to self-concept of many people of color who confront issues of race on a daily basis (Cross 1995). For instance, Lee's (1996) qualitative research highlighted the ethnic dilemmas facing some Koreans, Diaz (1998) studied Puerto Rican students and Ford (1993) discussed the identity confusion faced by some African-American students. Ponterotto and Pedersen (1993) noted that ethnic understanding and appreciation are lifelong developmental processes that begin with a healthy sense of one's own ethnic identity. Siegel (2001) points out that those who make student recommendations should be knowledgeable of how talents are presented in various cultures and that the socioeconomic status of the student can influence teacher ratings.

Social injustices and discrimination

Minority students may experience discrimination on a daily basis, a problem that students bring into the classroom. Students who are unable to cope with injustices or prejudice (of any kind), also pervasive in our schools, are unable to work or learn effectively. Many minority students receive negative input about their ability to achieve academically. In addition, peers may promote anti-academic views. Such low expectations may come directly from teachers, parents, or peers and weaken an important facet of self-concept in minority students.

Ethnic identity

Ethnic identity concerns one's self-concept as a person, as well as one's beliefs, attitudes, and values relative to other ethnic groups (Cross 1995). By age 3 or 4, children know their race, and by the time they enter school, the implications of ethnic group membership and status become even more salient (Helms 1994). Few empirical studies on self-concept have been conducted using gifted minority students as the primary subject group and school counseling approaches rarely operate from a multicultural orientation; thus, counselors may find it difficult to promote positive ethnic identities among minority children.

Creative therapies: self-understanding for gifted diverse children

Bibliotherapy

One approach to counseling gifted students is bibliotherapy, the use of literature to promote self-understanding and awareness (ethnic pride), persistence, resilience, and social relations. Bibliotherapy for gifted students has been recommended in several publications (Herbert 1991; Kyung-Wong 1992; Reis and Dobyns 1991). Halsted (1994), for instance, reviewed approximately 300 books with gifted characters or with issues common to students identified as gifted. While bibliotherapy represents a potentially powerful tool for counseling students, few efforts have used bibliotherapy as an intervention with gifted minority students. Kyung-Wong (1992) noted that bibliotherapy has four stages:

- *identification:* the reader sees similarities between him/herself and the character in the literature
- *catharsis:* the reader allows emotions and internal conflict to surface
- *insight:* the reader makes connections with the characters and issues
- *universalization:* the reader understands that he/she is not alone, that his/her problems are not unique.

Ford and Harris (1991) suggest a fifth stage in addition to the four that Kyung-Wong presents:

- *action:* this represents the essence of bibliotherapy – behavioral and cognitive change.

In this final stage, readers are able to act upon this newfound insight. Long-term effectiveness of the intervention is a question for future research.

Reality therapy

Reality therapy can be valuable for addressing issues surrounding self-direction and independence and can teach gifted minority students to take increased responsibility for their behaviors. It asserts that all behavior is internally motivated, and that individuals must learn to take responsibility for their choices and behaviors. Reality therapy, therefore, reeducates and empowers students to identify their needs, wants and goals, to establish realistic behaviors necessary to attain these goals, and, to explore negative school experiences. It can help gifted minority students to explore the need to belong and be loved, the need for power and control, and the need for freedom. Counselors can help gifted minority students to establish and evaluate their present behaviors, to develop a plan of action to cope effectively with specific situations and immediate concerns, and to make a commitment to take action.

Prevention and intervention strategies

Although counselors recognize the interrelation of the social-emotional and cognitive domains of development, programs for gifted students appear to have largely neglected this area of development (Barnette 1989: 525).

Individual counseling

An appropriate counseling approach must take into consideration the uniqueness of each gifted student's personality. For instance, some students encounter problems establishing relationships and lack self-esteem while others are self-confident and gregarious. The primary goal of developmental counseling is to help each gifted student develop a holistic self-understanding and a strong personal identity as a way to ensure academic success, and should be an integral part of the services offered to gifted students. Crisis-centered counseling is indeed very necessary and appropriate, but preventative and developmental counseling promote self-actualization. Gifted children need more intensive guidance in order to be mentally healthy enough to be creative. Counselors can help gifted students learn about their strengths and special characteristics, as well as learn coping skills to address feelings of being different, alienated and inferior. In schools, counselors need to be advocates in creating a support system not only for gifted students, but also for teachers and parents. Counselors should focus on validating the personal story of each unique gifted child in a cultural context. The main goal of counseling is to empower each gifted child as a whole person and normalize his or her experiences.

Group counseling

Group counseling for gifted students is often recommended: one of the goals in group counseling is to build a safe, trusting, accepting environment to allow the students to establish interpersonal communications and build interpersonal relationships, as well as provide permission to feel normal. Gifted students also need to have a forum in which they can express emotions with others their age particularly concerning expectations of teachers and parents. A group experience will assist in relieving some of the emotional isolation gifted students tend to feel at times and will fulfill their need to belong.

Family counseling

When working with families, counselors need to help them identify what stressors each family member may be facing and the impact of giftedness on the family as a whole. As such, the counselor needs to explore how parents foster and nurture their notion of giftedness in their children. Parents may have goals for their children that the school may not offer nor identify with. It is also important to examine family values in relation to achievement and self-concept. Parents may feel that giving their child their best may not be enough. Thus, counselors may need to give parents permission to be imperfect and help them acknowledge that they have limitations. Parents need to understand that doing their best in terms of supporting their children's goals and talents *is* enough.

Conclusion and recommendations

It was not until the 1950s that counseling scholars began to target gifted students in such issues as suicide, depression, perfectionism, self-concept, self-esteem, anxiety and poor peer relations among gifted students (Colangelo 1991). It is not surprising, then, that few scholarly articles focus exclusively on counseling gifted students from diverse backgrounds (Ford 1993).

Diverse gifted students and their families have specific counseling needs that must be recognized by counselors and they place certain demands on the practitioner. Counselors of gifted children should be open, caring, warm, intelligent, non-authoritarian, not biased toward one field of study, not prejudiced, experienced and able to communicate effectively with students, teachers, parents and other professionals. One should never forget that all children, gifted or otherwise, have a need for acceptance, friendship, belonging, self-understanding and love.

Key questions

1   How can strategies aimed at preventing prejudice about diverse gifted students reduce the impact of grief?
2   What type of curriculum would be appropriate to address issues of grief in diverse gifted students?
3   How can the understanding of ethnic preferences and perspectives be incorporated into counseling strategies?

References

Barnette, E. L. (1989) A program to meet the emotional and social needs of gifted and talented adolescents. *Journal of Counseling and Development*, 67: 525–528.
Colangelo, N. (1991) Counseling gifted students, in N. Colangelo and G. A. Davis (eds) *Handbook of Gifted Education*. Needham Heights, MA: Allyn and Bacon.
Coleman, M. J. and Fults, B. A. (1985) Special-class placement, level of intelligence, and the self-concepts of gifted children: a social comparison perspective. *Remedial and Special Education*, 6(1): 7–11.
Cross, W. E., Jr. (1995) The psychology of Nigrescence: revising the Cross model, in J. G. Ponterotto, J. M. Casa, L. A. Suzuki and C. M. Alexander (eds) *Handbook of Multicultural Counseling*. Thousand Oaks, CA: Sage.
Davis, G. A. and Rimm, S. R. (2004) *Education of the Gifted and Talented*, 5th edn. Boston, MA: Pearson Education.
Diaz, E. (1998) Perceived factors influencing the academic underachievement of talented students of Puerto Rican descent. *Gifted Child Quarterly*, 12(2): 105–122.

Ford, D. Y. (1993) An investigation into the paradox of underachievement among gifted Black students. *Roeper Review*, 16(2): 78–84.

Ford, D. Y. (1995) *Counseling Gifted Black Students: Underachievement, Identity, and Social and Emotional Well-being* (Research-Based Decision Making Series). Storrs, CT: National Research Center on the Gifted and Talented.

Ford, D. Y. and Harris, J., III. (1999) *Multicultural Gifted Education*. New York: Teachers College Press.

Greenlaw, M. J. and McIntosh, M. E. (1988) *Educating the Gifted: A Sourcebook*. Chicago, IL: American Library Association.

Halsted, J. W. (1994) *Some of My Best Friends Are Books: Guiding Gifted Readers from Pre-School through High School*. Dayton, OH: Ohio Psychology Press.

Helms, J. E. (1994) Racial identity in the school environment, in P. Pedersen and J. C. Carey (eds) *Multicultural Counseling in Schools: A Practical Handbook*. Boston, MA: Allyn and Bacon.

Herbert, T. (1991) Meeting the affective needs of bright boys through bibliotherapy. *Roeper Review*, 13: 207–212.

Kyung-Wong, J. (1992) Bibliotherapy for gifted children. *Gifted Child Quarterly*, 15(6): 16–19.

Lee, S. J. (1996) *Unraveling the 'Model Minority' Stereotype: Listening to Asian American Youth*. New York: Teachers College Press.

Maslow, A. H. (1968) *Toward a Psychology of Being*, 2nd edn. Princeton, NJ: Van Nostrand.

Ponterotto, J. G. and Pedersen, P. B. (1993) *Preventing Prejudice: A Guide for Counselor and Educators*. Newbury Park, CA: Sage.

Reis, S. M. and Dobyns, S. M. (1991) An annotated bibliography of nonfictional books and curricular materials to encourage gifted females. *Roeper Review*, 13: 129–134.

Siegel, D. (2001) Overcoming bias in gifted and talented referrals. *Gifted Education Communicator*, 32: 22–25.

Whitmore, J. R. (1980) *Giftedness, Conflict, and Underachievement*. Boston, MA: Allyn and Bacon.

Whitmore, J. R. (1986) Understanding a lack of motivation to excel. *Gifted Child Quarterly*, 30(2): 66–69.

9.3 Personal perspective: homeschooling gifted children

Susan Sikes

After my children were born and I began to look into my various options, I sensed that the institutional school experiences available to us would not serve them well. As I read the available research, homeschooling came to my attention. My son was a gifted child in his development: he began to teach himself to read the words he saw on signs around the age of 2½. I also read to him daily, at least half an hour at a time and at least twice daily. Around age 4, I spent a few days showing him the basic rules of phonics. After a week in his room, very busy with books, he proceeded to read a book to me, including '-ough' and '-tion' words, pronounced correctly. Fluency and comprehension increased rapidly, reading at a sixth grade level in his kindergarten year, and by the end of his second grade year, at a twelfth grade level. This was with no more formal training.

In much the same way, my daughter began to learn about the world around her. Her strengths were in her interpersonal skills, a natural athleticism and analytical thinking. As my son and I discussed how to add three plus three, she chimed in at 2 years old with a loud, proud proclamation of 'six'! Again, much like her brother, she had listened as we talked about the things we saw as we walked, played and dealt with life.

As most homeschoolers do, I began my children's 'formal' education with curricula for each major subject. Certain trends began to develop; primarily that any learning experience – with the exception of any kind of pencil and paper work – was greeted with enthusiasm. Often they would develop their own learning activities out of an interest. However, the papers from curricula seemed to become less and less enticing, to the point that I would find them under beds and in closets. Their standardized test scores showed that their most exceptional scores were in the subject areas that they learned without the assistance of a curriculum of any kind, usually by reading literature or through experiential learning.

About that same time, I was hearing more about unschooling – an approach to homeschooling that had come to mean learner-led education, using the learner's interests to provide meaningful educational moments. I realized that my children were doing this naturally, simply because they loved to learn. I also realized that their enthusiasm for learning was rapidly dwindling in the subject areas they had experienced through a formal curriculum. Over the next year or two we gradually weeded out all formal curricula and implemented numerous real-life experiences to take their place – museums, public speaking clubs, lemonade stands, and later as they got older, building computers, repairing cars and starting businesses. Through these experiences, and many others, my children seemed to naturally fill in any gaps in their information base. Moreover, they learned how to learn. I never needed to test because I was with them, discussing topics in depth. I became their facilitator, mentor, guide and door-opener. As they reached for new experiences or expressed an interest, I provided options and opportunities, always deferring to their final decision to learn or not to learn about a topic – with two exceptions: safety rules and respectful behavior were not optional. My experience has taught me to trust my children's natural interests, provide opportunities and treat them with respect.

My children, now in their late teens, understand that they have been given a childhood and learning experience like few others and they have always appreciated it. When asked whether they would like to attend an institutional school, they repeatedly decline, stating they would have to give up too many activities, too many friends and too much freedom. There have been pitfalls, of course, also approached as learning experiences. But they have been able to focus on the areas in which they are highly talented and interested. More importantly, they have come to trust and respect themselves, and ultimately have taken responsibility for achieving those goals that they have created themselves. How many adults can say the same?

9.4   Conflict resolution 8: ageism

Gillian Eriksson

Kumalo was a gifted student who had amazed his elementary school teachers in his rural African village. At 7 years old, he was confident, eloquent and friendly and got on very well with his peers, indeed he was often chosen as a leader in games and sports teams, which he enjoyed. He came from a poor family, but his mother, who worked as a domestic maid, had encouraged him to read and learn from a very early age. His father worked in another town in the mines, and came home only on weekends. Kumalo loved to do tricks, act and show-off in front of his friends, and he was the 'class clown'. He had rapidly mastered the curriculum in writing, reading and mathematics; he easily achieved As without much effort. He had been accelerated to third grade, but had rapidly outstripped the standards and often disrupted the classroom with his antics. There were no programmes for gifted students in his school, which had no library, nor in any local area schools. The teachers were worried that if they put him up another grade again that he would cause more disruption, but knew that he was very bored with his schoolwork. With few resources, what were they to do?

10 Global education issues

10.1 Gifted world citizens and global nomads: developing intercultural excellence

Gillian Eriksson

This chapter points out the need for global perspectives in gifted education; to recognize that concepts of giftedness are cultural, that international provisions for gifted students are impacted by trends and advocacy. It describes the nature of intercultural competence, so necessary to support the needs of a diverse gifted community, and the skills that can be developed into intercultural excellence. It defines and supports the nature of gifted world citizens and gifted global nomads, whose learning is the world forum, and whose skills need to be validated and celebrated in a global community. It points out the important role these students play in going beyond tolerance to productively serving the needs of diverse, unique individuals in the global village. Finally, it presents a curriculum from a global perspective that serves the needs of gifted students as world citizens.

Global trends

We live in an international society with global trends that impact us all in the global village. We bear global responsibility for events, seen in glaring detail on our television and computer screens, where we identify with the plights, fears, challenges and wonders of global changes. Voices that bounce off our satellites cross all languages, cultures, genders, classes, ages and religions. Our lifestyles are interdependent, our living spaces replicated through media in architecture, design, and engineering around the world. The air we breathe and the water we drink is impacted by local and international pollution; standards of food and health around the world become relevant locally as we consume foods grown and produced in far off countries.

In addition, the trend to unify large areas, shown in the European Union and the African Union, has created a forum for larger democratic, social and economic systems, wherein citizenship crosses previously ethnic and national boundaries, creating a sense of ownership and more economic interdependence. This has great impact on education; teachers are being recruited from around the world for industrialized nations (for example, South African teachers for New Zealand; Indian and Asian teachers for England; Asian teachers for the United States). In any metropolitan US community you can expect to find teachers from Russia, Germany, France, Kenya, China, Taiwan, India, Philippines, Middle East, Australia, to name a few. The reflection of diversity and internationalism is echoed in the student body; we are an ever changing, mobile world. Teachers need to be globally literate, according to Swiniarski and Breitborde (2003: 17), meaning that they use international perspectives and make universal connections, know about and be active in social and world issues and events, be open to new ideas and willing to share, and use critical thinking and creative problem solving.

The need for global education

This is becoming increasingly important, particularly post September 11th, 2001, with the threat of international terrorism and the subsequent stereotyping and victimization of those who practice diverse religions. Swiniarski and Breitborde (2003: 5) have identified twelve principles: global education is basic education; lifelong learning; cooperative learning; inclusive of all; education for social action; economic education; involves technology; requires critical and creative thinking; is multicultural; is moral education; supports a sustainable environment; and enhances the spirit of teaching and learning.

> A child's community at the turn of the 21st century is the world. . . . We believe that young children are by nature tolerant human beings, curious about and accepting of differences. We suggest teachers build on these natural impulses and fuel them with experiences that support children's uniqueness and local lives while linking them to the wonderful diversity of human and physical life on the planet.
>
> (Swiniarski and Breitborde 2003: 214)

UNICEF's 2005 State of the World's Children Report focuses on how poverty, conflict and HIV/AIDS threaten children around the globe. The United Nations Convention of the Rights of the Child (UNHCHR 1990: 182), ratified by 192 countries, includes: 'the right to survival; to develop to the fullest; to protection from harmful influences, abuse and exploitation; and to participate fully in family, cultural and social life'. It supports non-discrimination and global ownership; equity and social justice; world responsibility for the highest standards of health and education and personal dignity. The rights of gifted and talented children, from the most affluent to those in extreme poverty, to an appropriate education are therefore a part of the right to 'develop to the fullest', abilities recognized as being vital to the future leadership of the world.

Global perspectives in gifted education

Global and International Education has been implemented in several organiza-
tions that support gifted students, among them: The Council for Exceptional
Children (CEC), the National Association for Gifted Children (NAGC-USA),
European Council for High Ability (ECHA), National Association for Able
Children in Education (NACE). The conferences and activities of the World
Council for Gifted and Talented Children (WCGTC) aim to:

> Create a climate of acceptance and recognition that gifted and talented
> children are a valuable global asset whether disabled or able bodied, from
> advantaged or disadvantaged backgrounds, or from developing or developed
> countries.
>
> (WCGTC 2004)

Gifted immigrants

Students who have been identified as gifted in one country who immigrate to
another, go through stages of acculturation. Cushner et al. (2003) describes these
in the U-Curve Hypothesis as honeymoon (excitement, optimistic, novelty),
hostility (alienation, prejudice, ignorance of home country, lack of knowledge of
local conditions), humor (enjoyment of differences) and home (self-acceptance,
sense of local community belonging, local competence, frame of reference). These
processes may be exacerbated for gifted students by educational misplacement
in inappropriate programs and incomplete and discriminatory identification
methods. In addition, the very talents recognized in their original culture may
not be valued or recognized in the new setting. This includes those abilities often
ignored in narrow definitions, such as visual and performing arts, psycho-motor
abilities, creativity, and interpersonal and leadership abilities.

Gifted Global Nomads (GGN)

Global Nomads have been defined as those children who have lived and studied
in a country other than their birth or citizenship. The Global Nomad Profile, as
formulated by David Pollock, includes eight dimensions of life experience:
mobility (migratory), leave-taking (empathy), relationships (multiple), cultural
balance (diverse cultural identities), world-view (broad knowledge base), cross-
cultural skills (flexible, less prejudiced, suspends judgement), linguistic (multilingual), development (autonomy, multifaceted) (Pollock and Van Reken 2001;
Useem 1999; Schaetti 2004). Norma McCaig (1994) has identified the challenges
these students may face: 'rootlessness', indecision, unstable relationships, delayed
adolescence, unresolved family tension, independence, different academic standards, learning styles, cultural norms and patterns of thinking. She suggests four-
tiered coping strategies: communication (parent–child discussion of issues),
collaboration (choices and responsibilities), continuity (family traditions), and

Table 10.1.1 Characteristics of gifted global nomads (GGN)

Characteristics	Possible areas of frustration
• Multiple relationships	• Leave-taking, different youth interests and sports in other countries
• Transitions between countries generates knowledge of global issues • Transitions between school systems who have a different concept of giftedness • Knowledge of world economies • High technology competence	• Re-entry into major originating country, feeling alienated, left out • Conflicting standards and demands, giftedness not recognized without curriculum modifications • Adapting to different standards of living • Weak or no access or outdated equipment
• Intense interest in diverse viewpoints and international media literacy • Multicultural perspective of tolerance for diverse individuals • Develops bilingualism or a multilingual competence	• Being overwhelmed with conflicting views and loyalties • Enduring intolerance and ignorance about major originating country • Not valued in a monolingual society; may be forced into language immersion without continued intellectual challenge

closure (grief and loss). Global Nomads can react to their perceived marginality in two ways, as clarified by Bennett (1993): *encapsulated marginality*, they feel alienated, depressed, indecisive and have conflicting loyalties, or *constructive marginality*, they develop an integrated multicultural self with a sense of personal truth and easy transition between cultures. Support groups such as Global Nomad International and Third Culture Kids provide a basis of validation and celebration of their skills.

The lifestyle of the global nomad is one that appeals to many gifted students; GGNs can be found in many international schools (Association for the Advancement of International Education (AAIE), Department of Defense Schools (DODS)) and diverse communities. They develop effective multicultural and multilingual skills: a heightened sense of world issues, an empathy with the suffering of those who are poor, diseased, victimized and oppressed, and a commitment to addressing world problems. As a result of their intense interests, wide research and reading, they are more subject to future and cultural shock, as they perceive diverse perspectives, balance alternate viewpoints, understand media from international sources that span multiple countries, cultures, religions and political structures. Theirs is a lifestyle where mobility is the norm; they are familiar with international currency, economies and resources, duality in families and communities, long distance relationships, diverse norms and standards, and changing cultural roles (see Table 10.1.1).

Gifted world citizens (GWC)

The definition of world citizens includes the establishment of a global identity where the rights of all people in the world are respected and celebrated; where the state of the planet for life sustainability is valued; and where loyalties are to humanity and values are universal.

> The goal is working with people, progressive governments, and international institutions to create a Global Village of lasting peace, social and economic justice, and the foundation for a new civilization based on respect for life and the environment. The key to achieve this goal is for people to think and act as responsible Citizens of the World. World Citizenship is not a replacement for national citizenship, but rather a new responsibility in this interdependent world to work together across national boundaries to secure our common fate.
>
> (Association of World Citizens 2004)

The transformation of gifted students into world citizens requires visionary teachers, who have global perspectives (see Table 10.1.2).

Table 10.1.2 Characteristics of gifted world citizens (GWC)

- They have developed effective skills of communicating on an international basis
- They have multicultural skills that allow them to switch frames of reference according to country and culture
- They have a commitment to addressing critical world issues that affect people all over the world
- They have a profound sense of mission to serve the underprivileged, uneducated, exploited and victimized
- They have a knowledge of world trends to pose alternative possible futures
- They explore future scenarios and employ creative problem-solving
- They use critical thinking and conflict resolution strategies to negotiate changes and transform schools, institutions, non-government and government legislation
- They foster a sense of global community, engaging in social action, often creating their own foundations
- They have a working knowledge of political, social and economic systems and their interdependence
- They value first-hand interaction with people at all social levels, empathizing and validating their personal stories and experiences
- They expect to learn new traditions, customs, and values and reflect on their own global identity and value system
- They have a strong sense of personal truth, positive and humble self-concept that can face suffering of others constructively
- They have developed an appreciation of cultural arts, music, dance
- They have an effective system for evaluating local and international media
- They know how to manage international foreign exchange and travel
- They have effective leave-taking and re-entry skills
- They are usually multilingual, switching languages and frames of reference from one country and culture to the next
- They are competent with new technologies that allow international asynchronous communication and learning
- They have made effective personal choices about their own education and their future career options from a moral global viewpoint

The profoundly gifted: world citizens

The concept of identifying a continuum of advanced giftedness into highly and profoundly gifted has been criticized as artificial and discriminatory as it includes only those who have economic advantages and a privileged education. Morse and Meckstroth (2003) clarify the challenges of highly gifted students: a complicated enigma, intensity, craving complexity, creating chaos in search for truth, multiple focusing, insatiable fervor for intellectual stimulation and learning, relentless curiosity and hunger for novelty, a challenge to authority, poor handwriting, immersion in area of interest, empathy and energy, and a tendency to introversion. Irrespective of the undeniable abilities these children demonstrate, the use of the word 'profound' herein, implies that it inspires, illuminates, enriches and transforms into deep universal meaning. There are wonderful examples of the profoundly gifted, exhibiting characteristics of gifted world citizens, who have established international foundations.

International Youth Advocates

Gregory Smith, a profoundly gifted student raised mostly in Jacksonville, Florida, United States, started high school at 7 years old, graduated high school at 10, graduated with a B. Science in mathematics from Randolph-Macon College, and at 13 was admitted as a doctoral candidate to the University of Virginia. At 14 years old, he has traveled the world seeking attention to children's rights and been nominated for the 2004 Nobel Peace Prize. He founded International Youth Advocates, in Virginia, whose mission is to:

> Promote principles of peace and understanding among young people throughout the world with the objective of instilling enlightened attitudes that will ultimately advance education, improve families, influence world events and provide hope for the neglected, abused and disenfranchised.

He has established many international and global projects, including the Amani Peace schools in Kenya. Many years later, he is fulfilling his vision.

> I try my best to be the best world citizen I can be and help others through my words and work to believe that they can achieve their dreams too.
>
> (Smith 2004)

Free the Children

Craig Kielburger, from Toronto, Canada, was concerned about children's rights and world issues at the age of 12 when he read an article about a young boy sold into bondage as a carpet weaver in Pakistan. He founded Free the Children with friends and family, campaigning for children's rights and child labor laws, developing petitions and raising funds with car washes, walk-a-thons, garage sales, speeches to local schools and organizations. Their mission is an international network of children helping children at a local, national and international level through representation, leadership and action . . . The primary goal of the organization is not only to free children from poverty and exploitation, but to also free children and young people from the idea that they are powerless to bring about positive social change and to improve the lives of their peers.

(Kielburger 2004)

Inspired by meeting and negotiating with many world political leaders, in 1999 he and his brother founded Leaders Today, a leadership development program (Kielburger 2004).

Heartsongs

Matthew (Mattie) Stepanek became well known internationally as a young poet and philosopher promoting world peace and global tolerance. He was physically disabled but profoundly gifted spiritually and linguistically, and his intrapersonal and interpersonal skills were evident to the many leaders he met, including his hero, past US President, Jimmy Carter. He suffered from muscular dystrophy and died at the age of 13 on 22 June 2004. Mattie was the author of five 'Heartsong' books of poetry. As a result of all that he achieved, he became the Muscular Dystrophy Association's National Goodwill Ambassador. His optimism, global vision, and champion of children's rights were an inspiration, as shown in the poem entitled 'For our World': 'And now, let us pray, differently, yet together . . .' (Stepanek 2002)

The Nkosi AIDS Foundation

Xolani N'kosi Johnson (1989–2001) gained world attention at the age of 11 in a speech at the UN Conference about his struggle with AIDS and the tragic plight of AIDS patients in South Africa (UNHCHR 2001). He was one of 200 babies born in South Africa daily who are HIV-positive and was adopted by Gail Johnson when he was 2 years old after the death of his Zulu mother of AIDS. His case attracted media attention when a school in Johannesburg, Melpark Primary, refused him admission. Gail Johnson founded a centre for the treatment and care of AIDS children and their mothers, Nkosi's Haven, which evolved into The Nkosi AIDS Foundation. He was nominated posthumously for the World's Children's Prize and the Global Friends' Award 2002. His interaction with world leaders, such as Nelson Mandela, showed him to be an exceptionally gifted individual, a charismatic personality with a profound moral duty coupled with a child-like humility.

I want people to understand about Aids – to be careful and respect Aids – you can't get Aids if you touch, hug, kiss, hold hands with someone who is infected. Care for us and accept us – we are all human beings.

(Johnson 2001)

A curriculum for gifted world citizens: key components

This curriculum should support their socio-emotional needs addressing travel, transitions, diverse educational adjustments, relationship upheavals, and cultural adaptation while providing an appropriately challenging and individualized academic, creative, intellectual, and heightened moral education. A central objective is to create opportunities and choices that will also foster normalizing experiences with other gifted students (GWCs and GGNs).

Developing intercultural excellence (the DICE model)

Developing a global perspective encompasses the development of teaching and learning skills, so that gifted students are challenged to develop excellence in relating to people from diverse cultures and countries. Developing a global perspective, defined by the National Council for the Social Studies, emphasizes human experience influenced by transnational and cross-cultural interaction, the wide variety of actors on the world stage, the state of the global environment, realities and alternative futures, citizen participation, interconnectedness (Swiniarski and Breitborde 2003) (see Table 10.1.3).

Table 10.1.3 Developing intercultural excellence (the DICE model)

Intercultural competence	*Intercultural excellence*
• Examines own stereotyping and prejudices to develop tolerance of those who differ • Recognizes that there are diverse cultural interpretations of behavior just as valid • Knows how to mediate conflicts by suspending criticism and supporting diverse views • Understands and supports diverse cultural ways of thinking • Develops skills in communicating with diverse cultures effectively • Behaves in culturally sensitive and responsive ways • Is open to new experiences about diverse cultures • Realizes and supports diverse perspectives about cultural and historical events	• Thinking skills from ethnorelative perspectives, that each human has a unique perspective • Knowledge of global dynamics and world systems • Addresses global issues using dynamic problem-solving strategies • Effective human choice and decision making • Alternative futures speculated • Global communications interconnectedness, interdependence • Examines self prejudice and active social actions against discrimination • Constructivist approach to knowledge; state of planet awareness • Cross cultural awareness of interdependence, fosters global peace

Sources: adapted from Cushner et al. 2003; Diller and Moule 2005; National Council for the Social Studies, in Swiniarski and Breitborde 2003).

Issue-based education

The intense focus on critical issues by GWCs demand a curriculum with an extensive knowledge of global systems. This should not only be interdisciplinary, but also centered on higher-level thinking with the aim of creative productivity that has worldwide impact. Students need opportunities to speculate about alternative futures; with knowledge of existing and emerging technologies that will dramatically change the world we live in, and therefore the actions that need to be taken today to create alternative possible futures (The Futurist Society). Issues that address prejudice and discrimination need to be a focus (Teaching Tolerance Group). A teacher of the gifted developed a multicultural, issue-based program: elementary gifted students identified the problem of prejudice against autistic children in their school; researched the nature of autism; focused the problem by each student becoming a buddy of an autistic child; analysed their first-hand observations, documented the knowledge they obtained; presented an educational program to classes throughout the school; and then presented the project on a website (Rollins 2004). Moral and ethical education for a higher calling for community problem-solving is a key principle in issue-based global education: programs that support this component and have international participation include: The Future Problem-Solving Program (FPS) created by E. Paul Torrance, Oddysey of the Mind created by C. Samuel Micklus, and Philosophy for Children (P4C) created by Matthew Lipman.

Cultural relativity: first hand experiences

The development of empathy for the life experiences of others, to view their experiences from within or from another's perspective, is known as cultural relativity. The reflection on one's own stereotypes and prejudices about others is challenged when we encounter those who differ in terms of gender, ethnicity, language, religion and ability. We begin to understand their personal stories, struggles and possibilities. Much of the knowledge of the world of affluent children is mediated and interpreted by someone else; they need to have first-hand experiences to see, talk and engage, to fully understand diverse life experiences. Most highly gifted students who have received recognition come from affluent communities. This will prepare them for their altruistic role and meet their needs, not only in terms of a constructivist perspective on knowledge, but also as a creative producer. Opportunities to work first-hand in the field with experts through mentorships and internships provide knowledge of their concerns, skills, project management, networking with agencies and key individuals and lifestyle choices. The development of service-learning on a global stage for these students offers the opportunity to research critical issues of social justice and equity and empathic learning while providing service to the multicultural community. The attitude of 'doing charity or community service' must be avoided to prevent perpetuating elitist, racist, classist, and sexist prejudices. Using a multicultural objective, the aim is to empower others in the interests of social justice, overcoming stereotyping and prejudice (Wade et al. 2001).

Collaborative international projects

The strong interpersonal skills of GWCs make them active in social action groups. Diverse gifted students from oppressed groups prefer cooperative settings that validate their perspectives. Global education projects where students from different countries work on interdisciplinary group problem solving are most relevant. The Multicultural Stories Project links students from different parts of the world in addressing critical incidents related to issues of gender, race, language, age and class; and Computer Pals Around the World is a global network of students, teachers and educators who develop projects and reach out for productive contributions, such as the International Writers Project (IMAGE 2004). Several global interactive education projects have been developed to empower students and teachers on a range of interdisciplinary themes, issues and problems, such as the International Education and Resource Network (iEARN); The International Activities Committee of National Council of Social Science; The Global Schoolhouse; International Schools CyberFair; Kidlink; and UNICEF's The Meeting Place. Several organizations provide for global volunteer projects that teachers and senior students can participate in, such as The Coordinating Committee for International Voluntary Service (UNESCO); International Cultural Youth Exchange; and Global Volunteers.

Unschooling and homeschooling

The complexities of switching education systems, with resulting gaps in knowledge, makes homeschooling relevant. Homeschooling appeals to diverse students, particularly from religious minorities: local school districts maintain registration and assessment (Griffith 1998). This allows gifted students to work individually at their own pace and depth, to compact the curriculum, and study independently. Unschooling maintains that the students can set their own goals, develop their own curriculum and evaluate their own progress, with minimal parental facilitation. John Holt, critical of institutional systems that imposed discrete and artificial units of learning, competitiveness and external motivations on children, formulated a concept of education, 'Growing Without Schooling', that was rooted in the child's natural instinct to learn (Farenga 1999). Griffith (1998) uses a global perspective in unschooling with activities that cover a range of subject areas through real life experiences tailored to each child's abilities, needs and interests.

Technology skills: asynchronous distributed learning

In the global classroom new technologies are emerging and transforming teaching roles and learning outcomes (Oblinger and Maruyame 1996). The Internet allows immediate and flexible access to vast resources, materials and experts, and has changed the concept of knowledge from stable forms (textbooks and materials) to fluid and fast changing (modules, websites, movies, discussions, videoconferencing). New roles for the teacher of the gifted beyond the classroom facilitator encompass the monitoring, management and creative use of online formats in virtual environments accessible at any time, anywhere.

Global mobility and accessibility

The Florida Virtual School (FLVS) provides a full schooling experience online free for any state residents, but is available to all. It also provides a FLVS Virtual Leadership Training Institute for teachers in creating their own virtual schools. The Virtual School for the Gifted (VSG), based in Australia but accessible to international students, offers online learning that enriches and extends the regular curriculum but is differentiated for gifted students in areas of their interest. Many communities offer study abroad or international student exchange projects.

Educating global teachers of the gifted

There is a great need to provide for the education of teachers of gifted students that is applicable and accountable internationally. This type of training in a virtual environment using distributed learning is available at the University of Central Florida (UCF), that offers an opportunity to earn a master's degree and certification in gifted education online with an international and multicultural perspective. Opportunities for teachers of the gifted to work internationally, and become global nomads themselves, are available through several agencies, such as the The Peace Corps, Department of Defense Schools and AAIE.

Summary and conclusion

As the world adapts to emerging technologies, it becomes more mobile and more globally interdependent, crossing continents, transcending time and space. The attraction for learning 'on the go' will increase, and the number of gifted global nomads will increase, as will the need for meaningful education from a global and multicultural perspective. For global nomads who are gifted, the experience can be intense, disorienting and alienating as they react with a heightened sensitivity to issues and divided loyalties that affect their search for a national and intercultural identity. The media attention given to gifted world citizens makes it appear that their achievements are nothing short of miraculous, and belies an elaborate system of facilitation and support by parents, teachers, mentors and activist communities. We can admire their achievements from afar, but as teachers of diverse populations of gifted students, we need to emulate their optimism and strive to develop our own intercultural excellence.

Key questions

1   How will emerging technologies impact the classrooms of the future for gifted global nomads?
2   What teaching strategies are most appropriate to implement the 'least restrictive environment' for gifted global nomads?

3   What great leaders exhibited the characteristics of gifted world citizens during their childhood and education? What does this tell us about the type of education they needed to face world problems?

References

Association of World Citizens (2004) *Goals of the AWC*. Retrieved 10 January 2005 at http://www.worldcitizens.org/

Bennett, J. (1993) Cultural marginality: identity issues in intercultural training, in E. M. Paige (ed.) *Education for the Intercultural Experience*. Yarmouth, ME: Intercultural Press.

Cushner, K., McClelland, J. and Safford, P. (2003) *Human Diversity in Education: An Integrative Approach*, 4th edn. New York: McGraw-Hill.

Diller, J. V. and Moule, J. (2005) *Cultural Competence: A Primer for Educators*. Belmont, CA: Thomson Wadsworth.

Farenga, P. (1999) *Growing without Schooling: A Record of a Grassroots Movement* (Vol. 1, August 1977 Newsletter). Cambridge, MA: Holt Associates.

Griffith, M. (1998) *The Unschooling Handbook: How to Use the Whole World as your Child's Classroom*. Rocklin, CA: Prima.

IMAGE (2004) *The Multicultural Stories Project*. Orlando, FL: Office of International, Multicultural and Global Education, University of Central Florida. Available online: http://pegasus.cc.ucf.edu/~multicul

Johnson, N. (2001) Care for us and accept us, we are all human beings. Speech delivered at Thirteenth International AIDS Conference, Durban, South Africa, January. Retrieved at http://nkosi.iafrica.com/nkosi_aidsfoundation/

Kielburger, C. (2004) *Free the Children*. New York: HarperCollins.

McCaig, N. M. (1994) Growing up with a world view: nomad children develop multicultural skills. *Foreign Service Journal*, September: 32–41. Retrieved 10 November 2004 at http://www.kaiku.com/nomads.html

Morse, K. and Meckstroth, E. (2003) Expanding horizons of highly gifted children, in J. F. Smutny (ed.) *Underserved Gifted Populations*. Cresskill, NJ: Hampton Press.

Oblinger, D. G. and Maruyama, M. K. (1996) *Distributed Learning*. Professional Paper Series 14. Boulder, CO: CAUSE Association for Managing and Using Information Resources in Higher Education.

Pollock, D. and Van Reken, R. E. (2001) *Third Culture Kids: The Experience of Growing Up among Worlds*. Yarmouth, ME: Intercultural Press.

Rollins, Z. (2004) Gifted students work with autistic students to overcome prejudice. Personal interview, University of Central Florida, Orlando, June.

Schaetti, B. F. (2004) *Phoenix Rising: A Question of Cultural Identity*. Worldweave website. Retrieved 10 December 2004 from http://www.worldweave.com/BSidentity.html

Smith, G. (2004) *A Vision: International Youth Advocates*. Retrieved 10 December 2004 from http://www. gregoryrsmith.com

Stepanek, M. J. T. (2002) *Heartsongs; Celebrate through Heartsongs; Loving through Heartsongs; Journey through Heartsongs; Hope through Heartsongs*. Hyperion. http://www.mattieonline. com/

Swiniarski, L. B. and Breitborde, M. (2003) *Educating the Global Village: Including the Child in the World*, 2nd edn. Upper Saddle River, NJ: Pearson Education.

UNHCHR (1990) *Convention of the Rights of the Child*. Geneva: Office of the United Nations High Commissioner for Human Rights.

UNHCHR (2001) World Conference against Racism, Racial Discrimination, Xenophobia and Related Intolerance. Durban, South Africa, 31 August–7 September 2001. Retrieved 10 February 2005 at: http://www.un-org/WCAR/

UNICEF (2005) *State of the World's Children Report for 2005*. United Nations Children's Fund. Retrieved 1 March 2005 at http://www.unicef.org/sowc05/english/index.html

Useem, R. H. (1999) *Third Culture Kids: Focus of Major Study – TCK 'Mother' Pens History of Field*. Available at: http://www.tckworld.com/

Wade, R. C., Boyle-Baise, M. and O'Grady, C. (2001) Multicultural service learning in teacher education, J. B. Anderson, K. J. Swick and J. Yff (eds) in *Service-Learning in Teacher Education*. Washington, DC: AACTE.

WCGTC (2004) *Mission of the World Council for Gifted and Talented Children*. Retrieved 15 February 2005 at http://www.worldgifted.org

Advocacy groups

(These websites were retrieved 15 January 2005.)

Global nomads

The Global Nomads Group http://www.gng.org/
Global Nomads Virtual Village http://www.gnvv.org/
TCK World (Third Culture Kids) http://www.tckworld.com/

World citizens / global education

Coordinating Committee for International Voluntary Service (UNESCO) http://www.unesco.org/ccivs/
Free the Children (Craig Kielburger) http://www.freethechildren.org/
Global Education (Australia) AUSAID http://www.globaleducation.edna.edu.au/globaled/page1.html
The Global Schoolhouse (International Schools Cyber Fair) http://www.gsn.org/
International Cultural Youth Exchange http://www.icye.org/
The Peace Corps http://www.peacecorp.gov
Kidlink http://www.kidlink.org/
The National Council for the Social Studies (NCSS) http://databank.ncss.org/article.php?story=20020402120154452
The Nkosi AIDS Foundation, Melville, Johannesburg http://nkosi.iafrica.com/nkosi_aidsfoundation/

International education

Association for the Advancement of International Education (AAIE) http://www.aaie.org/
Computer Pals Around the World (CPAW) http://reach.ucf.edu/~cpaw
Department of Defense Schools http://www.odedodea.com/pers/
Florida Virtual School (FVS) http://www.flvs.net/
International Education and Resource Network iEARN http://www.iearn.org/
Virtual School for the Gifted (VSG Australia) http://www.vsg.edu.au/

Gifted education

World Council for Gifted and Talented Children http://www.worldgifted.org
Gifted Certification, University of Central Florida (UCF) http://pegasus.cc.ucf.edu/~gifted

Multicultural education

IMAGE – University of Central Florida http://pegasus.cc.ucf.edu/~multicul
Teaching for Tolerance http://www.tolerance.org

Futures/problem solving

The Future Problem-Solving Program (FPS) http://www.fpsp.org/
Odyssey of the Mind http://www.odysseyofthemind.com/
Philosophy for Children (P4C – New Zealand) http://www.p4c.org.nz/
The World Future Society, 2004 http://www.wfs.org

10.2 Diversity: perceptions of pre-service teachers – a cause for concern for gifted minorities

Alexinia Baldwin

The United States with its extensively diverse population needs to seek ways to enrol and train teachers who are prepared to work with children from diverse backgrounds, helping all children to develop an appreciation and tolerance for others who may be different. This means looking beyond the traditional examples of giftedness to include students who are woefully missing in programs for the gifted. From its earliest history, the United States has always promised opportunities for education to all, thus supporting its democratic principles. Now the American education system is challenged not only to offer the opportunity of education for all, but also to raise each child to a certain level of mastery, no matter what cultural, intra-cultural, socio-economic, geographic, generational, gender, sexual orientation, disability or individuality factors are present. This also means looking for those diverse students who might be gifted.

However, the growing multicultural composition in classrooms set against the steady influx of monocultural pre-service teachers completing degrees, places pressure on teacher educators to equip graduates with the attitudes, skills and experiences necessary to be successful in these multicultured classes. One of the most difficult obstacles to overcome is the lack of commonality, awareness and understanding between the increasing population of European-American, middle-class, young, female teachers, and the increasing racial and ethnic diversity of the school population. Demographic data estimates that by 2020, 40 percent of the nation's school-age population will be students of color, yet American

Association of Colleges for Teacher Education (1995) reported that 80 percent of pre-service teachers are white females who are unfamiliar with the cultural experiences of their diverse students.

Diversity as an issue in teacher training

Fuller (1994) investigated three areas: poverty, cultural diversity and diversity in family structure, and she showed that although pre-service teachers were caring, intelligent people, they failed to understand the issues of ethnicity, culture, race and family structure that affected their students.

The Personal and Professional Beliefs about Diversity Scales (Pohan and Aguilar 1999) was used to determine the professional and personal attitudes of pre-service teachers in several institutions. They found that pre-service teachers' personal and professional beliefs were related to age, with experienced teachers having a more constant belief system regarding diversity. Also, females were more accepting of diversity in their personal and professional beliefs. Further, the study showed that multicultural coursework changed personal and professional beliefs.

In an attempt to seek further information about the attitudes and beliefs of pre-service teachers, Baldwin (2001) used the scales of Pohan and Aguilar (1999) with a small group of students. It was found that students of color had varying degrees of awareness of diversity issues, although overall, they had a higher awareness of diversity issues than white middle and upper class males. White males who considered their families poor or working class in general had a better understanding of diversity issues. It was also clear in this study, and one by Fuller (1999), that newly graduated teachers were more sensitive to Hispanic than African-Americans of limited resources.

Myths and realities that encompass the issue of diversity

According to Fuller (1999) and Baldwin (2001), many teachers hold stereotypes of low-income families: they offer simplistic solutions, like finding better living conditions, getting a job or going back to school. These are good suggestions, but they do not address the learning needs that many of these students have. Pre-service teachers were impatient with the students' parents as evidenced by their if-they-would-only-work-harder attitude.

It is very easy to group children of a particular ethnic group together, and to judge them on the basis of news reports and other myths. However, Banks (1989) has illustrated how the variations of interests, abilities, cultural attributes, and behaviors are interlocking within and between groups even though all the groups have some basic similarity in culture. He explains that

> [a] nation as culturally diverse as the United States consists of a common-overarching culture, as well as a series of micro-cultures. These micro-cultures

share most of the core values of the nation-state, but these values are often mediated by the various micro-cultures and interpreted differently within them. Afro-Americans and Hispanic Americans who have not experienced high levels of cultural assimilation into the mainstream culture are much more group-oriented than are mainstream Americans. These students experience problems in the highly individualistic learning environment of the school.

(Banks 1989: 10)

Identification of students for gifted programs often relies on those teachers who understand the environment, home situations, and the indicators of giftedness in minority students. Borland and Wright (1994), cited in Baldwin (1999), discussed a three-stage identification procedure which was a screening, assessment and placement decision. In phases one and two of the study, standardized, non-traditional assessment, teacher nominations and parent input were used as indicators of giftedness. With practicing teachers, trained to understand the differences in needs for students among this group, they were able to create a first step toward recognizing gifted students. Similar courses and field experiences for pre-service teachers are urgently needed.

There is a lack of statistics in the studies of Asian Americans:

The use of averages to represent the social and economic characteristics of diverse groups of Asians in the United States . . . masks the significantly different levels of social attainment experienced by subgroups of Asian Americans, thereby furthering the myth, . . . that Asians are a 'model minority'.

(Liu and Yu 1995: 263)

Defining multicultural education for a diverse educational community

Teacher education programs need to prepare pre-service teachers for diverse classrooms of children who have varying learning styles and ability levels, extending from the earliest primary school to the university, and to include information on education of the gifted. Multicultural education is not just addressing cultural backgrounds, it also directs attention to a range of differences, including ethnicity, race, gender, social class, culture, income level, special needs and familial structure. These factors sculpt the identity of a person and their place in the world, influencing the ways people treat, interact and communicate with one another. Mono-cultural pre-service teachers have trouble sorting out the effects of poverty and familial structure from cultural characteristics, and that confusion determines the decisions they make about the students' instruction. They need knowledge and skills to be able to interact beneficially, design curriculum, and formulate instruction. As stated earlier by Liu and Yu (1995) and reaffirmed by Fuller (1999):

[Any] discussion focusing on . . . cultural backgrounds risks stereotyping and over-dependence on generalizations. The many differences resulting from cultural, intra-cultural, socioeconomic, geographic, generations, gender, sexual orientation, and individuality factors among people contribute to their diversity . . . it remains crucial for educators to understand individual children and adolescents within a culture through conscientious study and firsthand contact. . . . failing to consider crucial differences may result in assuming too much cultural homogeneity – for example, that all Hispanic cultural groups share identical values, problems, and cultural expectations or that all Asian Americans [are highly intelligent].

(Manning and Baruth 2000: xvii)

For pre-service teachers to shed their mono-cultural orientations, both teacher and student need to go through stages of development (Fuller and Ahler 1991). This process helps the teacher of pre-service teachers to understand better how . . . students learn and the manner in which they incorporate those learnings into their identities as pre-service and practicing teachers. Teaching must address the students' 'immediate psychological needs such as security, affiliation, self-esteem, as well as developmentally appropriate needs such as allowing students to develop their emerging professional identities' (Fuller 1999: 253).

Effective pedagogy for pre-service teachers regarding diversity

Middle class pre-service teachers need to be better prepared to work with diverse children, and, essentially, more teachers are needed from diverse ethnic, racial, economic and other backgrounds, particularly to provide role models. They are a vital influence on students' values and norms (Bandura and Walters 1963). Not only do they allow minority children to reproduce attitudes, emotional responses and actions exhibited by real people, but also students of majority populations have an opportunity to interact with them. In addition to this, the school environment should, with a plurality of staff and students, serve as a model of a community where people with differences work and play together successfully.

Multicultural education has started in the school systems but policy makers need to look at the college and university levels also. A survey of the faculty of education departments representational of public universities of the Midwest United States showed that 82 to 100 percent of the faculties were of European descent. Of that group, 36 to 70 percent were tenured European-American male professors (Fuller 1992). Recommendations stemming from the survey included field experiences, including internships, should be established in more diverse racial, ethnic, gender and class settings; more minority teachers and those from inner city schools should be recruited for teacher education; and professorships should be demographically representative of society.

Models of attitudes

Educators perceive diversity in three broad categories (Manning and Baruth 2000):

- *Cultural deficit model:* students from other cultures are viewed as 'disadvantaged' and 'socially deprived' because their behaviors, language and customs reflect different standards and values from the middle class. The individual is blamed for not being socially and educationally successful. The crux of this model is that society has failed to address cultural biases that shape these negative perceptions, and inhibit the understanding of the roles of socio-political forces.
- *Cultural mismatch model:* this implies that the learning styles of students from different cultural backgrounds are incompatible with teaching practices and thus they fail. It assumes that cultural traits of minorities do not match the dominant culture reflected in schools. Success is measured by a degree of congruence between group values and traits and those of the educational system. Efforts to improve success aim at increasing congruence between schools and various cultures. Perhaps a more constructive attitude is that one culture is not necessarily superior or inferior to the other.
- *Culturally different model:* this implies that a source of enrichment in the classroom comes from the differences that make individuals unique. Although students need to learn cultural values and knowledge of the mainstream, differences are valued and seen as strengths enriching both the schools and society. Differences are not perceived as deficiencies: a variety of learning styles and language expression can facilitate learning.

Developing teacher awareness of the forms of prejudice and stereotyping can help to promote more flexible attitudes. The common patterns of racism are hostile and insensitive acts toward others, bias in the use of punishment and in giving attention to students, bias in curriculum materials, inequality in the amount of instruction, bias in attitudes toward students, failure to employ educational professionals from various cultural backgrounds and denial of racist acts (Manning and Baruth 2000: 52). Other subtle forms of prejudice are interpreting the same behavior in different ways: for example, a white student asking for help is seen as a motivated student while an African American or Hispanic student is considered lacking confidence or skill.

Stereotyping emphasizes differences, and often these perceptions of a few are generalized to the many. Since educators make numerous professional decisions based upon observations, it is important that these observations do not result in judgements that are negative about a group or culture. Learners' perceptions of cultural differences and their opinions of others' perceptions, play significant roles in their degree of self-worth and self-image. Educators can help learners recognize how culture affects people's lives, and understand that different cultures hold different values. Providing all children and adolescents with accurate and objective materials, and leading discussions of culture and cultural differences can remove many myths and stereotypes (Manning and Baruth 2000: 54).

Pre-service and in-service activities should provide opportunities for professional reflection and assessment of attitudes: teachers need opportunities to identify with their own cultural beliefs, values and expectations, as well as learning about these in other cultures. Many in the teaching field today have taught at a time when values and beliefs were taken from the school and left to the domain of the home and church. Now the curriculum is filled with instruction that must be handled with an open mind because of the values imbedded.

Within the *cultural responsibility model*, policy-makers and decision-makers consider the schools one of the best sources to repair and change the ills of society. However, while much of the multicultural approach discusses the responsibility of the teacher, little is said about the rest of the community and nation. Decision-makers from school boards to legislatures, need to define the policy and fund programs involving the whole of society.

Teachers and/or curriculum planners could alleviate some of the cultural misconceptions held by the students by using three curriculum models suggested by Baldwin (1999). The three models provide a way to incorporate materials that help diminish stereotypes and gain effective knowledge about different groups. These models are:

- *Sensitivity enhancement model:* activities such as role-playing and simulations place individuals in crucial decision-making positions, or take them out of their usual culture and role. Unfinished stories or debates can challenge concepts or stereotypes. Peter Yarrow (2000) has developed a program called 'Don't Laugh at Me' which helps the students use various scenarios to come to mutual agreement that ridicule, bullying and disrespect are not allowed and alternative ways of addressing conflict are encouraged.
- *Information processing model:* this provides facts about various events (historical and contemporary). Activities would include research using the National Archives, field trips, local historians, time capsule strategies and role assumptions.
- *Concept development model:* content from various cultures and ethnic information are used to teach a concept. Activities include rhetoric analysis, use of poetry from various cultures to teach form or other concepts, socio-political parallels found in various cultures, graphic and performing arts of the world and concept of family life in various cultures.

Delineating good pedagogy

The role that school personnel play is a major factor. It is ineffective to provide worksheets and drill times without a meaningful purpose, use European-oriented textbooks and materials, and base academic and behavior standards and expectations on stereotypical expectations. Manning and Baruth (2000) delineate three principles underlying multicultural curricula: pre-service teachers need to

Table 10.2.1 Comparison of assimilationist teaching and culturally relevant teaching

Conditions	Assimilationist teaching	Culturally relevant teaching
Others	Ethnic groups should change and adopt the values, beliefs and behaviors of the dominant culture and not preserve their own cultural groups	Attend to the needs, values, beliefs and behaviors of all students
Self	Failure is inevitable for some	All students can succeed
Social relations	Encourage competitive achievement	Encourage community building
Knowledge	Knowledge	Viewed critically

become aware of materials that enhance students' self-concept, engage student interest, and provide examples, vocabulary and models that relate to students' cultural backgrounds. Skills in analysis and critical thinking should be a major focus of instruction and ethnic differences and cultural diversity should be taught using authentic and multidimensional materials, activities, and experiences. Irvine and Armento (2001) made a distinction between assimilationist teaching and culturally responsive pedagogy. Table 10.2.1 summarizes the two forms of teaching.

The responsive teacher is sensitive to the needs, interests, learning preferences and abilities of their students, uses a variety of teaching methods and materials, pays attention to classroom context using peer tutoring and cooperative learning, provides appropriate structure, concrete models and manipulatives and develops personal relationships with students (Irvine 1990). Teaching is seen as a social action and involves activities such as sharing personal stories and encouraging students to express themselves openly. In addition, the teacher integrates diversity into the curriculum each day and discusses issues and ways in which to change society (King 1991).

The culturally responsive pedagogy

Irvine and Armento (2001) give four critical elements that support the development of a culturally responsive pedagogy:

- Culture is a powerful variable that influences teaching and learning.
- Effective teaching research is compatible with the principles of culturally responsive pedagogy.
- Teacher knowledge and reflection are important considerations when designing and implementing a culturally responsive lesson.
- High standards and high expectations are important components of culturally responsive pedagogy.

(Irvine and Armento 2001: 6)

The inclusion of these elements not only assists teachers to view culturally responsive pedagogy in non-stereotypic ways, but also is a foundation for best practice for all students.

The first element: culture

From a cultural identity both teacher and learner develop a concept of self and their capabilities: this dual sense of positive self-worth is the foundation of an effective classroom. Teachers need to understand that diverse learners

- respond to things in terms of the whole instead of isolated parts
- prefer group learning situations
- prefer inferential reasoning
- approximate space and numbers rather than adhere to exactness or accuracy
- focus on people rather than things
- prefer learning by doing
- are more proficient in non-verbal than verbal communications
- prefer learning characterized by variation in activities.

'All students have an incredible capacity for developing the ability to use multiple learning styles, in much the same way that multiple language competency can be accomplished' (Hillard 1992: 373). Teachers who understand the preferred style of a student can design and plan instruction that encourages their students to experiment with a wider repertoire of learning approaches.

The second element: effective teaching research

Cruickshank (1990) indicates that effective teachers are identified by what they know, what they teach, how they teach, what they expect from their students, how their students react to them and how they manage the classroom. Examples of some of these effective instructional strategies include the following:

- connecting students' prior knowledge and cultural experiences with new concepts by using relevant cultural metaphors and images
- designing appropriate transfer devices
- setting high expectations
- instituting positive classroom climates and relationships with parents and community
- understanding students' cultural knowledge and experiences and selecting appropriate materials
- helping students find meaning and purpose in what is to be learned
- using interactive teaching strategies
- seizing the 'teachable moment'
- allowing students to participate in planning activities
- using culturally familiar speeches and events

- preparing students to effect changes in society
- helping learners construct meaning by organizing, elaborating and representing knowledge in their own way
- using primary sources of data and manipulative materials
- aligning assessment with teaching through activities such as teacher observations, student exhibitions and portfolios.

The third element: teacher knowledge and reflection

Teacher knowledge and reflection are important considerations when designing and implementing a culturally responsive lesson. From an ethnologist standpoint, Kahaney and Liu (2001) challenge teachers in college courses to become aware of certain ethnic factors. When studying cultures, universals are rare, and knowledge is often situated in a real place or context. One must experience the culture and become part of it. Knowledge is not the same for each culture.

The fourth element: high standards and high expectations

High standards and high expectations are important components of culturally responsive pedagogy. The teacher

- creates learning experiences that make the content meaningful
- uses multiple representations and explanations and links them to students' prior understandings
- understands and appreciates cognitive processes involved in academic learning, including diverse learning styles
- is sensitive to diverse cultural groups globally, and understands how ethnicity, class, gender and other socio-cultural factors influence students' learning and classroom climate
- understands students' families, cultures and communities and connects to students' experiences
- implements a variety of instructional and assessment strategies appropriate to diverse learners
- diagnoses and builds upon the personal, cultural and historical experiences of learners
- communicates in ways that demonstrate sensitivity to cultural and gender differences
- plans learning opportunities that meet the developmental and individual
- uses a variety of assessment techniques, including observation, portfolios, self- and peer-assessment
- reflects on his/her life experiences in order to develop culturally responsive curricula and instructional practices
- understands the influence of family participation on students' learning
- identifies and uses community resources in the classroom and understands teaching as situated in schools and communities.

However, it takes a community to raise a child successfully: and the community, as well as the family, share a responsible, responsive role if a multicultural approach is to be effective.

Pre-service teachers' university preparation

Fuller (1999) proposes the following elements for effective multicultural teacher training programs:

- school-based field experiences with multi-ethnic populations in college and in lower schools
- community-based experiences, e.g. tutoring American-Indian students, working with recent immigrant families, tutoring low-income, culturally diverse students, working with residents at a homeless shelter
- opportunities to see films that provide exposure to particular groups
- use of texts that provide accurate perceptions
- experience at a reservation or inner city school with time to reflect and discuss
- visits to an international center where students share their cultures.

Finally, universities and colleges need to model a multicultural community, provide knowledge, skills and attitudes not only for good pedagogy, but also to provide background on cultures, poverty, family structure and ethnographic and sociological principles. Students must be encouraged to experience the multicultural environment on the campus and in the classroom. In these ways the global awareness of diversity and difference will be enhanced.

Key questions

1   Is there a plurality of thought about the most effective ways universal teacher education programs can be planned?
2   What recruitment techniques can be used to encourage teachers of various ethnic groups to become teachers?
3   Is there a global agreement on the definition of multiculturalism?

References

American Association of Colleges for Teacher Education (AACTE) (1995) *SCDE Enrollments by Race and Ethnicity: AACTE Survey of Teacher Education Enrollments by Race/ethnicity and Gender, Fall 1989, 1991, 1995.* Washington, DC: AACTE, 12 May 2003 http://www.aacte.org/Multicultural/enrollment_ethnicity_yr89-91-95.htm.

Baldwin, A. Y. (1999) An annotated bibliography of multicultural resources with curriculum and Instruction applications, unpublished manuscript.

Baldwin, A. Y. (2001) Informal survey using Pohan, C. A. and Aguilar, T. E. (1999) The *Personal and Professional Beliefs about Diversity Scales.* San Diego, CA: College of Education. Unpublished data.

Bandura, A. and Walters, R. N. (1963) *Social Learning and Personality Development.* New York: Holt, Rinehart and Winston.

Banks, J. (1989) Multicultural education: characteristics and goals, in J. Banks and C. Banks (eds) *Multicultural Education: Issues and Perspectives*. Needham Heights, MA: Allyn and Bacon.

Borland, J. and Wright, L. (1994) Identifying young, potentially gifted, economically disadvantaged students. *Gifted Child Quarterly*, 33(4): 164–171.

Cruickshank, D. (1990) *Research that Informs Teachers and Teacher Educators*. Bloomington, IN: Phi Delta Kappa.

Fuller, M. L. (1992) Teacher education programs and increasing minority school populations, in C. Grant (ed.) *Research and Multicultural Education: From the Margins to the Mainstream*. London: Falmer Press.

Fuller, M. L. (1994) The monocultural graduate in a multicultural environment: a challenge to teacher education. *Journal of Teacher Education*, 43(4): 269–278.

Fuller, M. L. (1999) Becoming a researcher: it's the trip not the destination and studying the monocultural pre-service teachers, in C. A. Grant (ed.) *Multicultural Research*. Philadelphia, PA: Falmer Press.

Fuller, M. L. and Ahler, J. C. (1991) Pre-service multicultural education: progressing through developmental stages. *Multicultural Teaching*, 9(2): 33–40.

Hillard, A. G. (1992) Behavioral style, culture, and teaching and learning. *Journal of Negro Education*, 61(3): 370–377.

Irvine, J. J. (1990) Beyond role models: an examination of cultural influences on the pedagogical perspective of black teachers. *Peabody Journal of Education*, 66(4): 51–63.

Irvine, J. J. and Armento, B. J. (2001) *Culturally Responsive Teaching*. Boston, MA: McGraw-Hill Higher Education.

Kahaney, P. and Liu, J. (2001) *Contested Terrain: Diversity, Writing and Knowledge*. Ann Arbor, MI: University of Michigan Press.

King, J. E. (1991) Unfinished business: black students alienation and black teacher's emancipatory pedagogy, in M. Foster, *Qualitative Investigations into Schools and Schooling*. New York: AMS Press.

Liu, W. T. and Yu, E. H. (1995) Asian American Studies, in J. Banks and C. Banks (eds) *Handbook of Research on Multicultural Education*. New York: Simon and Schuster.

Manning, M. L. and Baruth, L. G. (eds) (2000) *Multicultural Education of Children and Adolescents*. Boston, MA: Allyn and Bacon.

Pohan, C. and Agulilar, T. (1999) *The Personal and Professionals Beliefs about Diversity Scales*. San Diego, CA: San Diego State University.

Yarrow, P. (2000) *Don't Laugh at Me*. New York: Operation Respect, Inc.

10.3 Personal perspective: gifted global nomad – home is where you hang your hat

Achim Runnebaum

'Where are you from?' This question is difficult to answer without going into a long dissertation about my personal history. I am originally from Germany, but moved to the United States when I was 12 years old, which means that I am neither fully German, nor completely American. To this day this question still makes me think twice since I've lived in three different countries with very different cultures – Germany, the United States and currently Japan.

In the new setting, I initially felt a lot of isolation and loneliness, since I didn't know many people. This made me self-sufficient and I became much more tolerant of other people. Some initial challenges were studying in English; even though I found the actual work easy, I was put down a grade from Germany because I had to translate everything, even though I could do the work quite well. After-school options are extensive in the United States, less so in Germany. In Germany, schedules are very precise, punctuality is essential and plans are adhered to; in the United States plans remain flexible and guests may or may not arrive when invited. The sense of privacy is stricter in Germany; closed doors are respected, unlike in the United States where an open door policy is common. When we first came to the United States, I felt very uncomfortable whenever somebody told me that 'the fridge is over there – help yourself' because going through somebody's refrigerator is considered extremely rude in Germany. Despite this, US relationships appear temporary compared to my long-term German friends; I felt my friendships were taken for granted. Since Germans are direct and love facts, they don't like boasting and exaggeration; Americans enjoy self-praise. It amazes me how wasteful and disrespectful of nature Americans can be; in Germany lights are turned off, resources are used and reused, books are valued and trash is carefully recycled. However, I have learned to keep an open mind and not give in to stereotypes. I knew that to be able to fit in, I would have to change my previous beliefs and adapt to the different way of thinking. Living in a different culture will undoubtedly open up your eyes to different philosophies on life.

On the negative side, no matter how well you learn to speak, read and write another language, or how long you live in a different culture, or how many good friends you make, you always feel a little different. Most people go through different phases of 'uniqueness':

- At first you try to fit in and be exactly like everyone else.
- In time, you realize that you will never be completely 'local' and you might go through some rough times and dissatisfaction.
- Eventually, you accept the fact that you're different in thought, in appearance, and lifestyle.
- Finally, you acknowledge that being different is not necessarily such a bad thing.
- That's when you truly find inner strength as you accept yourself for who you are. You no longer feel the need to impress anybody and you start living for yourself. You start to really enjoy life in your surroundings.

Of course I also experienced hardships. I speak English fluently, and I don't look any different than the average American male, but I have to watch what I say or do because I might accidentally promote a stereotype. I'm also bound by different legal issues than 'natives' are. If I want to travel internationally, I have to fill out much more paperwork than a regular citizen. I think I'm almost an expert on American immigration law. If I want to rent an apartment, or buy a car, or do anything which involves legal documents asking for my nationality, I have to provide extra paperwork, which can get quite frustrating (especially in Japan since it's such a homogenous country, and foreigners are still treated very differently).

What does it actually take to be 'a global nomad' and live and work in different countries?

- have a basic familiarity with the local laws and immigration procedures
- need to be truly independent and self-sufficient
- need to have a strong and persistent character
- have an extremely flexible and open mind
- stay true to yourself
- have a true and genuine interest in the culture/country you will live in
- be able to adapt to a completely different culture and different customs.

Before moving to Japan, I read many books about Japanese customs, festivals and manners because I wanted to prepare myself. In the western world, we generally tend to associate direct eye contact with expressing an interest in the narrator, but in the eastern countries, this is not the case. So when I started teaching in Japan, I was very frustrated at first because I thought that most of my students didn't pay attention to me since they tended to look away if stared at directly. I had to adjust my teaching methods to make my students more comfortable.

Exposure to diverse people can further our understanding of differences, which will ultimately make us more effective teachers. So whether we are from a different culture, or dream about living in a different country, or our job takes us to a different place, or we have lots of multicultural students in our classes, we need to keep an open mind and not judge someone just because they look or act differently. Chances are, they have the same dreams, hopes, fears and goals as we do. The word 'home' has taken on a different meaning for me over the years; I now believe that home is where you hang your hat. As long as you're comfortable living in a certain place, you can feel at home anywhere in the world.

10.4 Conflict resolution 9: infusing global education and LGBT realities

Trae Stewart

Regardless of empirical findings by respected scientists in the field of human sexuality, gays and lesbians as a group are still not extended the civil rights that heterosexuals enjoy, unless they masquerade their sexual identities. This holds true in the majority of the world, excluding a handful of countries that have taken progressive leaps forward in social policy to protect, include and, in some cases, celebrate their LGBT citizenry (e.g. The Netherlands, Denmark, Canada). The number of countries that outlaw and penalize homosexual behavior far outweighs their progressive neighbors: death (e.g. Iran, Pakistan, Yemen, Nigeria), life in prison (e.g. Saudi Arabia, India, Singapore, Nepal), 10–15 years' incarceration (e.g. Bahrain, Brunei, Fiji, Kenya) and 1–10 years' imprisonment (e.g. Cuba, Botswana, Zimbabwe, Uzbekistan, Tunisia). Bearing in mind this repugnance, consider the following news stories about the experiences of LGBT peoples worldwide.

- *Australia:* Five youths kicked and punched a gay youth, and stripped him of most of his clothes; one was brandishing a 70cm machete like he was opening a coconut. (Ansley 2002)
- *United States:* Laughing, three men attacked a 17-year-old female in Denver, Colorado, by carving derogatory words into her flesh with a razor. (Crecente 2002)
- *Nigeria:* Fourteen teens were arrested for allegedly beating a schoolmate to death because they suspected that he was gay. (Aribike and Kudu 2002)
- *Africa:* '[Homosexuality] is against African tradition and biblical teachings.' (Kenyan President Arap Moi in McGreal 1999)
- *Brazil:* More than 100 gays, lesbians and transsexuals were killed in 2001 as a result of hate crimes, the largest number recorded of any nation. (Report: Brazil a leader in gay hate crimes 2002)
- *Mexico:* A privately operated swimming pool in Aguascalientes displayed the entry sign: 'No Dogs, No Homosexuals.' (Patterson 2000)
- *China:* 'I thought I was mentally sick. . . . I took a lot of herbs, and even followed some traditional prescriptions by eating baked scorpions, lizards, and toads.' (Huang 2001)
- *India:* 'If you are a woman and gay, you are really at the bottom of the totem pole.' (Lloyd 1999)
- *Israel/West Bank:* A 17-year-old refugee spent months in a [Palestinian] prison, was cut with glass, and had toilet cleaner poured into his wounds. (Halevi 2002)
- *Croatia:* Fifteen supporters of homosexual rights were attacked at Croatia's first Gay Pride parade, even amid tight security. (Croatian homosexuals step out from shadow to demand equal civil rights 2002)
- *United Kingdom:* 'From the moment I came out to a friend when I was 14, I was subjected to beating, taunts, and punches. I was a straight-A student before. . . . I began to drink to escape my troubles. I considered suicide many times.' (Ross 2001)

Key questions

1   How do teachers reduce homophobic prejudice in their gifted students?
2   What strategies could be used by teachers to prevent such violent attacks from occurring in their schools?

References

Ansley, G. (2002) Vicious attacks on gays in Australia like a 'sport'. *New Zealand Herald*, 14 August.

Aribike, S. and Birnin, K. (2002) Pupils arrested for killing suspected gay school-mate. *African Eye News Service* (Nelspruit), 15 April.

Crecente, B. D. (2002) 17-year-old female reports mutilation as anti-gay crime. *Rocky Mountain News*, 28 March.

Croatian homosexuals step out from shadow to demand equal civil rights (2002) *Agence France-Presse*, 18 July.

Halevi, Y. K. (2002) Refugee status. *The New Republic*, 19 August.

Huang, W. (2001) China's gay community in half fight. *Boston Globe*, 29 April.

Lloyd, M. (1999) Out of India's antigay closet. *Boston Globe*, 24 October.

McGreal, C. (1999) Debt? War? Gays are the real evil, say African leaders. *Guardian* (UK), 2 October.

Patterson, W. (2000) A life of fear for gays. *San Francisco Chronicle*, 12 October.

Report: Brazil a leader in gay hate crimes (2002) *United Press International*, 23 April.

Ross, G. (2001) Beating the bullies. *Pink Paper* (UK), 28 September.

11 International profiles

11.1 International and comparative issues in educating gifted students

Barbara Clark

Programs and services for gifted children around the world differ not only in terms of cross-cultural conceptions of giftedness and resultant identification procedures, but also in terms of program objectives, structure and organization, and community support. The use of surveys to report these practices not only demonstrates diverse and limited methods of identification, but also points out the need for access to appropriate education that takes into account divergent views of giftedness.

Under the auspices of the World Council for Gifted Children, two international surveys were conducted to examine cross-cultural conceptions, practices and programs. These are admittedly a selective reporting from particular individuals from a small sample of countries at a specific time, but provide a window into exploring issues in gifted education internationally.

Worldwide survey 2000: cross-cultural identification of gifted students

A survey regarding practices used in identifying gifted students in countries around the world was conducted in 2000 (Clark 2000, 2003). The results included thirty-two responses representing seventeen countries: Australia, Brazil, Canada, Denmark, Germany, Indonesia, Israel, Jamaica, Macedonia, Nigeria, Saudi Arabia, South Africa, Thailand, Turkey, United Kingdom, United States and (former) Yugoslavia. Most of those responding were psychologists, lecturers and government administrators affiliated with a university or center for gifted studies in their countries. The findings below are reported as they were stated in 2002.

Which methods are used in your country to identify gifted children?

Identification practices most commonly used for screening by the countries reporting were high levels of achievement ascertained from class grades or achievement testing and/or teacher recommendation. Tests used include the Stanford-Binet Intelligence Scales, Wechsler Intelligence Scale (in forms specific to various countries), Raven's Advanced Progressive Matrices, Cognitive Abilities Test, Leiter, Peabody Picture Vocabulary Test, Thurston Primary Abilities Test, Test of Non-Verbal Intelligence and the Otis-Lennon School Abilities Test. Many respondents used national tests designed and normed in their own countries. The cut-off scores reported most frequently ranged from 130 to 140 on the Stanford-Binet; from 120 to 140+ on the Wechsler and the 95th percentile on achievement tests. The subjects used for achievement scores were math and science, with reading and language arts used less frequently. Reflecting new trends in education, some countries reported the use of portfolios, interviews, non-verbal instruments, peer and self-nomination, and multiple criteria in the identification process.

What definition is most commonly used for children identified as gifted and talented in your country?

Seven countries reported using intellectual, academic, creative, leadership and/or fine and performing arts abilities to define gifted students (Australia, Brazil, Jamaica, Thailand, Nigeria, Saudi Arabia and the United States). A focus on intellectual ability was currently being used to define giftedness in Germany, Indonesia and the United Kingdom. Canada, Israel and the United States reported the use of academic and intellectual ability to define giftedness. England and Ireland reported using the term 'gifted and talented', while Wales, Scotland and Northern Ireland prefer 'more able' or 'highly able' as their identifier for this population.

What placement would be most common for a child identified as gifted and talented in your country?

Clusters in general education classrooms (found in Australia, Canada, Jamaica, Turkey, the United Kingdom and the United States), resource rooms (found in Australia, Brazil, Denmark, Canada, Turkey and the United States) and special classes (found in Australia, Indonesia, Israel, Thailand, Turkey and the United States) were reported as the commonly used forms of placement. Special schools can be found in Australia, Indonesia, Nigeria, South Africa, Thailand, Turkey and the United States. The most frequent form of placement was stated as the adjunct program that includes clubs, seminars, summer programs and before or after school programs found in Australia, Brazil, Canada, Denmark, Germany, Indonesia, Jamaica, Macedonia, Saudi Arabia, South Africa, Thailand, Turkey, the United States and Yugoslavia.

Table 11.1.1 Comparative 'gifted' identification methods

Country	Teacher referral	Parent referral	Individual standardized intelligence tests	Group standardized intelligence tests	Standardized achievement tests	High academic achievement	Checklist	Creativity tests
Australia	S ID	S ID	ID	S ID	S	ID	S	S ID
Brazil	S	S	ID	S	S	S	ID	ID
Canada	IS	S	ID	ID		S ID	S ID	S
Denmark	S	S	ID			S		
Germany	S	S	ID		S	S	S	S
Indonesia	S		ID		S	S	ID	S ID
Israel			ID	ID	S		ID	ID
Jamaica	ID	S	ID	S	S	S	S	
Macedonia	S		ID				ID	ID
Nigeria	ID					ID		
Saudi Arabia	S	ID	ID	ID		S	ID	ID
South Africa	S	S	ID			S	ID	
Thailand	S		ID		S	ID	ID	ID
Turkey	ID		ID	ID	S	ID		S
United Kingdom	ID	ID	S (rarely)	ID	S ID	ID	ID	ID
United States	S	S	ID	ID	S ID	S	S ID	ID
Yugoslavia	ID		S			ID	ID	ID

Notes: S = used for screening; ID = used for identification assessment.

Of special note are the following comments made regarding programs in various countries:

- Denmark has an egalitarian education system and private or after school programs are the favored arrangements for gifted students.
- Canada offers many alternatives including week-long mini-course enrichment, Math Olympiads, science fairs and university mentors to provide for gifted students.
- Australia is involved in early entrance programs, mentoring, discovery programs, distance education, Future Problem-Solving and Tournament of the Minds.
- Yugoslavia offers small additional scholarships/stipends for about 10,000 children age 15 to 20 years of age from the country-level through the National Foundation for Gifted Students and from local levels. About 3000 children (12 to 17 years old) attend summer or winter camps for gifted students in science, math, sports, and music.

Worldwide survey 2003: cross-cultural programs and services

An additional survey in 2003 aimed at understanding the specific programs and services provided to gifted students worldwide. Members from fourteen countries responded: Australia, Brazil, Canada, Germany, Hong Kong, Indonesia, Jamaica, Korea, New Zealand, Philippines, South Africa, Spain, Taiwan and the United States.

Some interesting issues were noted specific to a single country at the time of the survey:

- New Zealand reported legislation for the mandating of gifted programs only at the local level as their educational system is organized so that individual schools are largely autonomous and any directive for service must originate at that level.
- From Spain, a member commented that the Spanish National Educational System has excellent legislation, but there are very serious problems applying the legislation in practice.
- In Korea a law to provide for gifted students was implemented in 2002. In addition, private efforts accommodate the education of gifted students in Korea.
- Private schools in the Philippines offer gifted programming in science, math, art and music.
- South Africa's new education system has discontinued much of the infra-structure that was previously serving gifted children. 'Outcomes Based Education', now in place, is presumed to cater to all children.

What services for gifted students are available in your country?

All fourteen countries reported the provision of educational services, although some were regional or otherwise limited. Only seven countries provided counseling services – Australia, Germany, Indonesia, Jamaica, Spain, Taiwan and the United States. Programs for early learning were provided in seven countries – Australia, Canada, Jamaica, Korea, Philippines, Spain and the United States.

How are services for gifted students funded in your country?

The funding for gifted programs at a national level was found in only six countries – Brazil, Germany, Indonesia, Spain, Taiwan and the United States (on a limited basis). Five countries provided state or provincial level appropriations – Australia, Canada, Germany, Taiwan and the United States. Local level appropriations funded gifted programs in nine countries – Australia, Brazil, Hong Kong, Indonesia, New Zealand, Philippines, Spain, Taiwan and the United States. In Australia fees were being paid to schools for gifted programs and conference profits from local organizations provide for other program costs. Private funding was an important source of support in nine countries – Brazil, Canada, Germany, Indonesia, Jamaica, Korea, Philippines, South Africa and Spain. In Jamaica parents currently pay fees for gifted programming.

Is service mandated in your country?

National level legislation mandates service to gifted students in six countries reporting – Brazil, Indonesia, Korea, Philippines, Spain and Taiwan. State level legislation can be found in Canada, Germany and the United States (not mandated in all states or provinces).

Where are the gifted students served in your country?

Public schools currently provide service for gifted students in eleven countries – Australia, Brazil, Canada, Hong Kong, Indonesia, Jamaica, New Zealand, Philippines, Spain, Taiwan and the United States. Gifted students are being served in private schools in eleven countries – Australia, Canada, Germany, Hong Kong, Indonesia, Jamaica, New Zealand, Philippines, South Africa, Spain and the United States. In Indonesia this was reported as the primary site for gifted programs. Gifted centers provide service for gifted students in ten countries – Australia (in selective centers and programs provided by the gifted associations), Brazil, Canada, Hong Kong, Indonesia, Korea, New Zealand, Philippines, Spain and the United States.

What program modifications are provided for gifted students in your country?

Eleven countries reported the use of both content acceleration and enrichment as ways to modify curriculum – Australia, Canada, Germany, Indonesia, Jamaica, Korea, New Zealand, Philippines, Spain, Taiwan and the United States. Brazil also reported the use of enrichment. Grade skipping and/or early entrance were being used by ten countries – Australia, Brazil, Canada, Germany, Jamaica, Korea, New Zealand, Spain, Taiwan and the United States. Six countries reported the use of compacting, ability grouping, and differentiation in their programs – Australia, Canada, Indonesia, New Zealand, Taiwan and the United States. In addition, Germany and Spain reported the use of compacting, and Hong Kong and the Philippines the use of ability grouping and differentiation. Only four countries use cross-grading – Australia, Canada, New Zealand and the United States.

Is teacher training in gifted education available in your country?

Only seven countries reported having specific credentials available for teachers of the gifted – Australia, Canada, New Zealand, Philippines, Spain, Taiwan and the United States. Degree programs at universities are currently available to some extent in nine countries – Australia, Brazil, Canada, Indonesia, Korea, Philippines, South Africa, Taiwan and the United States. In-service in public schools was reported as available in nine countries – Australia, Brazil, Canada, Germany, Indonesia, New Zealand, Spain, Taiwan and the United States. Teachers receive their knowledge of gifted education at teacher centers in six countries – Australia, Canada, New Zealand, Spain, Taiwan and the United States.

How are parents involved in gifted programs in your country?

Parents are involved in the identification process in eleven countries – Australia, Brazil, Canada, Hong Kong, Indonesia, Jamaica, New Zealand, Philippines, Spain, Taiwan and the United States. It was stated that they were involved in the implementation of programs in only five countries – Canada, Indonesia, New Zealand, South Africa and Spain.

Does your country have groups that advocate in the interest of gifted students?

Parent organizations devoted to advocacy for gifted students are to be found in ten of the countries reporting – Australia, Canada, Germany, Hong Kong, New Zealand, South Africa, Spain, Taiwan, United Kingdom and the United States. Teacher organizations advocating for gifted issues were reported in Australia, Philippines and the United States. Twelve countries have national organizations in the area of gifted advocacy – Australia, Brazil, Germany, Indonesia, Jamaica,

Korea, New Zealand, Philippines, South Africa, Spain, Taiwan and the United States. Australia, Canada, Indonesia and the United States have gifted associations at the state or province level.

While these surveys of countries represent a small sample, it is clear that there is a wide range of programming being offered to gifted children worldwide. It is equally clear that there is much work ahead in every country if we are to give this unique population of children consistently appropriate educational experiences. As advocates, we need to provide them with opportunities and challenges that will allow their growth and assure that their abilities will not be lost to themselves or to the world.

Key questions

1 How are gifted students identified in your county, state or country? What types of diversity are of particular concern and what modifications should be made to accommodate the needs of these gifted students?
2 Does your county, state or country demonstrate any of the issues or problems addressed in these surveys? What actions can be taken?
3 What further research needs to be conducted on a global scale to address issues that impact diverse gifted students?

Reference

Clark, B. (ed.) (2000, 2003) Worldwide Survey 2000: Cross-cultural identification of gifted students. Reported in *World Gifted*. The Newsletter of the World Council for Gifted and Talented Children (WCGTC). Website online at http://www.worldgifted.org

---

11.2 China: psychological research on gifted and talented 'supernormal' children

Qiong Zhang and Jiannong Shi

While modern China has encouraged development in the areas of agriculture and industry, scientific research has also been undertaken with regard to the education of gifted children. In 1978, Liu Fan (1983) proposed the term of 'supernormal children' considering that:

• 'gifted', in Chinese *tian cai*, means the gods' bestowal upon humankind, and Chinese psychologists do not think that high ability is totally inborn
• 'super-normal' means some children are relatively superior to most normal children; hence, 'supernormal' is a term with statistical meaning.

(Shi and Xu 1998: 298–305)

Meanwhile, the Cooperative Research Group of Supernormal Children of China (CRGSCC) was set up under the leadership of Professor Zha and colleagues, as well as a special class for intellectually gifted adolescents in the University of Science and Technology of China (Shi and Xu 1999). Since then, a new research project has been undertaken which aims to identify and distinguish extraordinary children who are gifted intellectually, and to explore factors which accelerate the development of intelligence in order to improve the education of all children. There are now more than thirty experimental schools including kindergartens, primary and middle schools with hundreds of gifted children identified and taught in special classes.

Areas of research

A number of themes are being studied.

Thinking skills

A set of analogical reasoning tests, including geometrical or figural analogy, numerical analogy, and verbal or semantic analogy, has been developed.

Cognition

The abilities of memory monitoring and memory organization of gifted children have been tested and the relationship between memory performance and meta-memory of gifted and normal children has been analysed. Elementary cognitive tasks have been developed which include choice reaction time, logo matching, mental rotation and abstract matching between intellectually super-normal children and intellectually normal children. In addition, there have been studies on the relationship between intelligence test performance and visual inspection time, and a group of academics have extended these studies into brain functioning.

Creativity

A creativity test has been developed and included in the Cognitive Ability Test for Identifying Supernormal Children (Zha 1986). Cross-cultural research on technical creativity of gifted and normal children between China and Germany has also been conducted under the support of the Volkswagen Foundation: the relationships between creativity, intelligence and personality traits are currently under investigation. A theoretical model about creativity, the system model of creativity, has been proposed (Shi 1995; Shi and Xu 1997, 1999).

Psychological measurement

Zhou (1996) revised the Creativity Attitude Survey to assess the validity of children's creative expression. While intellectual aspects of development are important, non-intellectual factors form an increasing focus where the effects of school organization, curriculum provision and teacher approach are viewed in relation to self-confidence, self-concept and motivation. The questionnaire for adolescents, Chinese Adolescents Non-intellectual Personality Inventory was compiled and used to investigate ambition, independence, perseverance, curiosity and self-awareness (Yuan and Hong 1990; Hong 1998). Li (2004) has explored the multiple forms of self-concept and self-confidence and the avoidance of failure in intellectually super-normal children and intellectually normal children.

Hong Kong

In Hong Kong, the Gifted Education Council was formed in 1988, but the governmental policies for provision for gifted education were not issued until 1990 (Shi and Zha 2000). Since then, several enrichment programs for the gifted have been created and university researchers have been involved in psychological and educational projects. In addition, the School for Gifted and Talented Children was established in 1996.

In Hong Kong, initially a battery of tests in addition to self/peer nominations was used in identifying and selecting gifted students, but recently, Gardner's multiple intelligence theory has been considered, and a three-tier operation model has been adopted: school-based whole-class activity, school-based pull-out activity and off-site support.

Research into giftedness in Hong Kong falls into several categories: parent-involved enrichment programs, in-service training programs and research into self-concept, learning attitudes, creativity and leadership.

Current issues

In the intervening years since the gifted movement developed in China in the early 1980s, there has been an increased awareness of the needs of gifted children and a demand for schools to respond with more appropriate provision. There are, however, several pressing issues that need to be addressed if sustained progress is to be made:

- Great efforts should be made to establish a sound theoretical basis of gifted research and education.
- The governmental budgets are limited, as are professional researchers and research instruments in the field.
- The teachers of gifted children need to be supported and encouraged through professional development programs.
- The study of visual and performing arts, athletics in talented children also demands considerate attention.

References

Hong, D. (1998) Issues of the application and revision of CA-NPI, in Z. Zha and J. Shi (eds) *The Mystery of the Development of Supernormal Children*. Beijing: Chong Qing Publishing House.

Li, Y. (2004) The differences of nonintellectual factors between gifted and normal children. *Chinese Mental Health Journal*, 18(8): 561–563.

Liu, F. (1983) On supernormal children, in *CRGSCC; Monograph of Study on Supernormal Children*. Xining: Qinhai Publishing House.

Shi, J. (1995) A system model of creativity. *Journal of Developments in Psychology*, 3(3): 1–5.

Shi, J. and Xu, F. (1997) Interest, motivation and creative thinking of supernormal and normal children. *Acta Psychologica Sinica*, 29(3): 271–277.

Shi, J. and Xu, F. (1998) Progress and problems of studies on supernormal children in China in the last 20 years. *Acta Psychologica Sinica*, 30(3): 298–305.

Shi, J. and Xu, F. (1999) *Recognizing the Gifted Children*. Beijing: Esperanto Publishing House of China.

Shi, J. and Zha, Z. (2000) Psychological research on and education of gifted and talented children in China, in K. Heller, F. Monks, R. J. Sternberg and R. Subotnik (eds) *International Handbook of Giftedness and Talent*, 2nd edn. Oxford: Pergamon.

Yuan, J. and Hong, D. (1990) A report from the investigation on intellectual gifted adolescents with CA-NPI, in CRGSCC (eds) *The Selected Works on Supernormal Children of the Last Ten Years in China*. Beijing: Unity Publishing House.

Zha, Z. (1986) *Manual of Cognitive Ability Test of Identifying the Super-normal Children*. Beijing: Institute of Psychology, Chinese Academy of Sciences.

Zhou, L. (1996) The revision of creative attitude survey (CAS). *Psychological Development and Education*, 12(1): 22–25.

11.3 Egypt: the challenges of gifted and talented education in the Arab Republic of Egypt

Ahmed Hassan Hemdan Mohamed

There are a few gifted programs in Egypt: the first two gifted schools were Ain Shams Gifted School, founded in 1960, and later Helwan School of Gifted Girls. Some sports and military schools also educate gifted students. Other initiatives include some gifted classrooms in different areas of the country, grants and incentives given to gifted students, local and national contests, some gifted centres in science, as well as some legislation that states the special needs of gifted students. However, most public schools do not have programmes for gifted education.

One of the problems in gifted education is the gap between theory and practice. Although the Ministry of Education recommends methods for identification of gifted and talented students, most of these methods are limited to narrow achievement tests, and some tests of creativity. Also, although there are qualified professors in the field of giftedness in Egyptian universities such as Cairo, Ain Shams, Alexandeia and Assiut, more research is needed to identify the particular problems facing Egyptian schools. Moreover, the class density and the rigid curriculum for most subjects, represent a huge obstacle for effective identification and education procedures. School psychologists are not sufficiently prepared to use standardized tests such as IQ, creativity and personality attributes. For example, identifying a gifted student in the high school is through a written test consisting of three short tests of 'general intelligence': a pictorial test, the identifying of interests and attitudes, and creative production. Gifted students are identified in the light of their scores – a most unscientific procedure.

In Egyptian public schools, students obtaining high scores in the final year of middle school attend special classes in the high school. In these classrooms, students get better teachers and more opportunities to excel. However, there are no other methods of identification, and no special strategies are employed in teaching them. Acceleration is not recommended by the ministry so students cannot skip grades. Also, there are no Gifted and Talented Education directories or departments in the school districts. Each school district has a department of 'Special Education' that takes care of special needs students; however, most of the supervisors are not well prepared in the field of gifted education. Moreover, there are no classroom teachers who are well qualified in the field of identifying and educating gifted students.

Yet another problem facing gifted education in Egypt is that the curricula are not addressing the problem-solving abilities of students. Each classroom teacher must cover specified content, and does not have the flexibility to create opportunities that help students reveal their potential. Class size can reach seventy; in some impoverished areas, diverse teaching methods cannot be used, and teachers conduct lectures. Due to time constraints, the teacher does not have the opportunity to use formative assessment to ascertain current achievement levels and to monitor progress across the school year. Most of the tests or examinations tend to measure rote memory rather than the application of knowledge. Moreover, students in impoverished areas do not have access to technology resources such as computers and Internet. Although there have been some improvements, limited funds constitute the major obstacle towards providing students with basic computer needs.

The colleges of education generally do not prepare teachers in the field of gifted education. In the few that do, little attention is given to recent changes in the concept of giftedness and theories in the field.

The system of education in Egypt is centralized. So, textbooks are identical all over the nation, and curriculum developers do not differentiate the content that is relevant for a rural area as distinct from an urban one.

According to the National Education Plan for All (2002–2003), the challenges that face Egypt in developing provisions for gifted students are lack of funds, expenditure imbalances, the difficulty of reaching remote and slum areas, lack of professional training for teachers, increasing dropout rates for impoverished areas, the gender-gap problem in rural areas, and the gap between rural and urban resources resulting in high illiteracy rates in rural areas. Wealthy families resort to private tutoring, increasing the gap between rich and poor families.

Reference

The National Plan for Education for All in the Arab Republic of Egypt (2003). Retrieved 25 August 2004 from http://www.unesco.org

---

11.4 England: issues in education for gifted and talented pupils

Michele Paule

It was not until 1997 that the education of England's most able pupils was made the subject of national scrutiny and strategic development, when a House of Commons Select Committee was set up to investigate the area. From this starting point, development has been rapid and far-reaching, and the needs of these pupils are now a factor in government initiatives across all stages of education. The various strands and developments are united under a National Gifted and Talented (G&T) Strategy focusing on three key areas: intensive area-based programmes in disadvantaged areas through 'Excellence in Cities', resources that support teaching and learning nationally and are dispersed via local training, government websites and national publications, and regional support (Department for Education and Skills (DfES) 2004a).

What perhaps makes England's approach under the strategy distinctive is its underpinning commitment to provision for the most able within mainstream schooling. While the establishment of a National Academy for Gifted and Talented Youth (NAGTY) after the Johns Hopkins model may seem to be at odds with this, it also represents an acknowledgment that individual schools may lack the resources to meet all the needs of their most able pupils, and thus their provision might include funding opportunities for pupils to participate in NAGTY summer schools.

After five years of high-profile national focus since 1999, areas of success and priorities for development emerged.

Identification of able pupils

'Excellence in Cities' guidelines require schools to draw up a register of their most able 10 percent, and this register must be broadly representative of the school cohort in terms of socio-economic status, gender, ethnicity etc. The National Academy, on the other hand, provides for a defined national cohort and has clear criteria for inclusion. The difference between these two approaches illustrates a core anxiety for many schools and teachers regarding exactly who and what is meant by 'gifted and talented'. There is a need for local as well as national discussion around norm and criterion referenced approaches, and how these marry with the nature and purpose of provision.

While schools show increasingly sophisticated use of attainment data in identifying able pupil cohorts (Haight 2004), there is a growing interest in the development of more qualitative approaches. Such development could help in the identification of underrepresented groups, not least through the involvement of the underrepresented themselves in the processes (DfES 2004b).

Achievement and underachievement

When England's National Curriculum was designed in the mid-1980s there was little awareness of the varying nature and degrees of high ability. This has resulted in a ceiling on expectation for the most able: too often they have nowhere to go in formal attainment terms. While some schools are experimenting with curriculum compacting and fast tracking for groups and individuals, such ameliorative measures are piecemeal, and the current exam board practice of adding 'stars' to A grades in an attempt to differentiate between high achieving students is a sticking plaster approach. We need to open up our notions of what the most able can do, reconsider our expectations at each age or key stage, and conceive of a more flexible curriculum that does not keep the gifted in lock-step with their peers.

The underachievement of particular groups remains an urgent priority both for research and resources. Taking participation in higher education as a measure, one study shows that while the proportion of school leavers entering university has risen, the most economically and socially deprived groups continue to be significantly underrepresented (Galindo-Rueda et al. 2004). Worryingly, there is already evidence that the introduction of university tuition fees is deterring students from the poorest backgrounds (Machin 2003). While national initiatives are in place to try to raise the aspirations of secondary school students, interesting work involving much earlier interventions is taking place in some areas, such as the study of the Peers Early Education Partnership (PEEP) project, a pre-school intervention, initiated in 1995, that works with adults who live and work with 0–5 year olds in an area of low economic status in Oxford (Sylva et al. 2005).

Within the broader definition of underrepresented students, certain groups merit further attention. The lower attainment of boys relative to girls has been a national focus since the mid-1990s, although this low attainment is relative – middle class boys, for example, still achieve more highly than working class girls. Research by the Universities and Colleges Admissions Service (UCAS 2003) shows that 7 percent more female than male applicants were accepted on to undergraduate courses in 2004, with the gap widening year on year. And while there are now significantly more girls than boys entering university, the academic and professional aspirations of able girls continue to be too often influenced by expectations associated with gender rather than ability (Taylor 2005).

Underperformance among and differences in performance between ethnic minority groups continue to trouble practitioners and policy makers. The establishment of Gifted and Talented registers has brought the issue to the foreground in many schools, and while teachers recognize that such underachievement may be grounded in social and cultural exclusion, they are keen to engage with research and guidance which will help them develop their understanding and practices.

Teacher development

Given the speed and volume of change involved in Gifted and Talented initiatives, and the competition with other agendas, teacher response has been generally positive, if anxious.

A study of 'Excellence in Cities' teachers reveals that while pre-training conceptions of provision are largely concerned with school operations such as grouping and extracurricular classes, there is genuine interest in developing understanding of learning needs and pedagogical approaches (Paule 2004). At present there seems to be little consensus among teachers as to what appropriate provision might look like, and while several internationally derived models are being imaginatively adopted, there is a need for more home-grown models, particularly at the secondary level.

Reservations expressed by teachers tend to reflect ethical concerns, and to exist in the absence of a clear philosophical rationale for the G&T strategy. This highlights the importance of giving teachers opportunities to air their views and anxieties, and to reach consensus in establishing vision and aims, as a vital first stage of professional development.

References

Department for Education and Skills (DfES) (2004a) *National Gifted and Talented Strategy*. Retrieved 6 March 2005 at http://www.standards.dfes.gov.uk/giftedandtalented/strategyandstrands/

Department for Education and Skills (DfES) (2004b) Identification approaches at the George Mitchell School in Waltham Forest and Halewood School in Knowlsey. *Nord Anglia Research Project for DfES: An Evaluation of the Gifted and Talented Strand of Excellence in Cities During its Pilot Year (1999–2000)*. Retrieved 6 March 2005 at http://www.standards.dfes.gov.uk/giftedandtalented/publications/

Galindo-Rueda, F., Marcenaro-Gutierrez, O. and Vignoles, A. (2004) *The Widening Socio-economic Gap in UK Higher Education*. London University's Institute of Education and London School of Economics. Retrieved 6 March 2005 at http://www.lse.ac.uk/collections/pressAndInformationOffice/PDF/HigherEducationPaperJuneAmended.pdf

Haight, A. (2004) *A Review of Identifying the Gifted in Mainstream Secondary Schools: the Experience of England's Excellence in Cities Programme*. Retrieved 6 March 2005 at http://www.brookes.ac.uk/schools/education/rescon/cpdgifted/wie-research.html!

Machin, S. (2003) 'Unto them that hath . . .' *Centrepiece*, Winter. Centre for Economic Performance, London School of Economics. Retrieved 20 February 2005 at http://cep.lse.ac.uk/centrepiece/v08i1/machin.pdf

Paule, M. (2004) Teacher views on teaching and learning models for the gifted and talented in Excellence in Cities and schools in England. Paper given at ECHA Conference, Pamplona, Spain, September. Retrieved 20 February 2005 at: http://www.brookes.ac.uk/schools/education/rescon/cpdgifted/docs/research/teacherviewson-t&l-models-mpaule.pdf!

Sylva, K., Evangelou, M., Brooks, G. and Taylor, R. (2005) *A Study of The Peers Early Education Partnership (PEEP) Project* (Oxon and Bucks. Learning and Skills Council). Conducted by Oxford University Department of Educational Studies. Oxford University. Retrieved 6 March 2005 at: http://www.edstud.ox.ac.uk/Research/fell2.html

Taylor, M. (2005) University gender gap widens as women increase their lead, interview with National Union of Students' Women's Officer, Jo Salmon, *Education Guardian*, 27 January.

UCAS (2003) *Higher Education Statistics*. Universities and Colleges Admissions Service (UCAS). Gender and Innovation G+I. Retrieved 6 March 2005 at http://www2.set4women.gov.uk/set4women/statistics/tables/

11.5 Germany: identification and encouragement of talents (*Begabungen*)

Albert Ziegler

The report Forum Bildung (2001) highlighted three issues in the field of gifted education: potential or achievement, promotion of talented persons in the regular German educational system and the goal of talent promotion.

Potential or achievement?

As far back as 1916, Götze said 'Talent can only be measured on achievements'. Even today promotional measures are mainly made available to those who achieve highly in school examinations or competitions (Manstetten 1992). Stern, also in 1916, counterbalanced this by arguing for diagnostic identification of potential, calling for counseling centers which could supply support and guidance. One can see Götze as an early supporter of the 'expertise' approach, while Stern, in contrast, advocated the 'developmental' approach, stressing factors such as persistence, self-discipline, ambition and social awareness (Gruber and Ziegler 1996). This conflict between performance criteria, as against potential, is reflected in the range of programs presented in Germany: there are now special schools for students demonstrating superior performance, as well as special schools for students demonstrating superior talent potential.

Promotion of talented persons in the regular German educational system

A second issue revolves around whether the promotion of talented persons is feasible within the regular educational system. Differential answers are to be found in Germany arising from the particulars of its educational system. Traditionally, it seemed that the German educational system was one of the most effective in the world with an elaborate system of tracking and the existence of Gymnasia, attended by the 20 percent top achievers. German Nobel prize recipients were prolific in the early days of the Third Reich. The failure of the German educational system to produce top achievers following the Second World War was attributed to the emigration of Germany's intellectual elite and the massive difficulties of rebuilding a devastated nation. While many industrialized nations made early endeavors to promote gifted and talented persons, countries such as the Federal Republic of Germany and Austria emphasized the identifying, counseling and support of children with learning deficits. It was only in the 1980s that it became clear that students at the other end of the talent spectrum were also in need of encouragement. Although good promotional instruments for gifted students of grades 5 through 13 seemed to have been established in the form of the Gymnasia with consequent access to university placement, this was not the case for preschool and elementary education in Germany, where ability grouping is not practiced.

As this shortfall was recognized, a sharp debate revolved around three proposals for rectifying this deficit:

- The radical approach that maintains that the current educational system cannot support gifted persons and additional institutions must be established. For example, in each of the sixteen German administrative states there is at least one state run counseling center specifically catering for the gifted and talented.
- The specialization approach that maintains that no new institutions are necessary, but existing institutions should specialize. A proportion of nursery schools, elementary schools and secondary schools would specialize in the fostering of gifted and talented pupils, some of which already focus on sport or music.
- The modification approach which sees the existing educational institutions as completely adequate and able to differentiate learning for the gifted. For example, almost all German federal states have established various forms of acceleration in their schools. Pupils in primary school can skip grades, participate in early enrollment programs or in '2 in 1' classes, where the material usually covered in two grades will be taught in one school year.

Which of these three approaches is to be given preference is largely left to the individual German states. The general consensus, however, is that the traditional educational systems are not in the position to adequately encourage and support gifted pupils.

The goal of talent promotion

The third issue in the current situation in Germany is concerned with the goal of talent promotion. The formation of personality factors which encourage social responsibility and social awareness are emphasized in comprehensive education which establish proficiency in a broad range of subjects, thus allowing pupils to discover the field which best corresponds to their talents. However, it has become increasingly obvious that this notion is rather naive, and that a broad education is not a guarantee for the development of a personality with positive social values. Furthermore, the talented are in need of expert support in the field of activities which correspond to their talents, and the breadth of the education they receive stands in direct conflict with necessary, early specialization in their field. A controversial discussion of various solutions emerges here: these range from the partial exemption from school instruction to enable early university specialization, to obligatory internships at social institutions for gifted students regarding the development of personality traits bound to socially responsible citizens.

References

Forum Bildung (2001) *Finden und Fördern von Begabungen* [Identification and encouragement of talents]. Bonn: Arbeitsstab Forum Bildung.

Götze, C. (1916) Schulbegabung und lebensbegabung [School giftedness and life giftedness], in P. Petersen (ed.) *Der Aufstieg der Begabten. Vorfragen.* Berlin, Germany: Teubner.

Gruber, H. and Ziegler, A. (eds) (1996) *Expertiseforschung: Theoretische und methodische Grundlagen* [Expertise research: theoretical and methodological fundamentals]. Opladen: Westdeutscher Verlag.

Manstetten, R. (ed.) (1992) *Begabung im Spannungsfeld von Bildung und Beruf* [Talent and the conflict between education and career]. Bad Heilbrunn: Klinkhardt.

Stern, W. (1916) Psychologische begabung und begabungsdiagnose [Psychological giftedness and its diagnosis], in P. Petersen (ed.) *Der Aufstieg der Begabten.* Leipzig, Germany: Teubner.

11.6 Hungary: education for diverse talented students

Maria Herskovits

National provisions

The 1993 Act of Education includes principles that directly apply to *gifted* education:

- All children have the right to receive recognition and development of his/ her abilities, interests, talents (para. 10.3).
- The pedagogical programs of the schools should contain activities that develop the potentials of the gifted (para. 48.1).

In practice this means that most elementary schools introduce a foreign language and/or ICT earlier, and children are selected according to their abilities or attainment. Some highly selective secondary schools prepare the most able children for national or international competitions. In addition, different schools provide extra opportunities for languages, advanced maths, sciences and arts.

The Arany Program for socially disadvantaged children

The Arany program 'Disadvantaged Talented Students' is named after Arany János, a talented nineteenth-century writer from a rural village. The program started in 2000 to help minimalize social disadvantages in Hungarian society, and to help rural, talented students aged 14–18 to get into colleges. Previously, only a small number of graduating students came from rural settlements, whereas from September 2004, nearly 3000 students will have entered colleges. The best secondary boarding schools have joined the program and now there are 23 such schools. The programs have been developed by professionals in gifted education, but the management of the courses is carried out by the participating institutions.

> We believe that the whole country is responsible for finding and developing talents, so we use a wide range of strategies to select students for the program. Primary teachers are the key personnel and they use observation schedules and psychological tests. The 5 year program aims to prepare students for higher education. In the first year we help students to bridge any gaps in their education, since many parents (and teachers) in rural areas do not value and support formal education. The students have special programs in communication and learning strategies; and we emphasise the development of emotional intelligence. All courses are carefully structured and teachers receive special in-service training in order to work effectively with very able students. We are trying to create a traditional system of Arany classes.
>
> (The Arany Program 2000)

The Tudor Foundation program for disadvantaged minority students

The most disadvantaged minority in Hungary are the Gypsies, and the issues are complex with huge unemployment and social problems. Although there are local schools trying to help the Gypsy children, the national non-profit-making Tudor Foundation aims to help all talented underprivileged children from ages 8 to 10 through primary school. The Foundation, relying on voluntary subscriptions, was announced through the press in 2001. The signatories were well-known scientists, artists and priests, and the Tudor Workshop educators support the children in their lives outside school and help them to make it secondary school. They provide the appropriate social environment: the infrastructure, expert education, attention and care, which is not provided for them at home nor in the general educational system.

There are several other foundations that sponsor college and secondary school students. In most cases, however, the poorest and most disadvantaged do not even reach secondary school despite their potential talent. The Tudor Foundation decided to help the 8–10 age group because

- disadvantages set in well before secondary school
- it is easier for the teachers to identify the most gifted children above age 8.

The Tudor Workshops provide intellectual inspiration after school: children take part in skills development classes, are given help with their schoolwork and homework, and have opportunities for developing their talent. The children work in small groups of eight under the guidance of tutors: they have their own study desks, books and toys. On weekends or in school holidays, they go on excursions and visit museums, the cinema or the theatre. They are provided with all that is vital for their intellectual development and would be accessible to them, had they been born in a better environment.

Programs for gifted handicapped or for gifted children with learning disabilities

For children in this category, there is the greatest lack of proper support. There are special boarding schools for deaf and blind children, but the associations have limited funds, and most schools do not have elevators for children in wheelchairs. There is one private school in Budapest for gifted children with learning disabilities, and/or social adaptation problems, called Gyermekház (Children's House) for students 6–18 years. It was established in the early 1990s and is subsidized by the City. Private schools have been established for children aged 10 to 15 years, but because of their high fees they are available only for privileged families.

11.7 New Zealand: gifted and talented Maori learners

Roger Moltzen and Hikairo Angus Macfarlane

The issues facing gifted Maori young people are common to many of the world's indigenous peoples and the continued under-representation of Maori students in educational programmes is a New Zealand concern (Bevan-Brown 2000, 2002; Moltzen 1999; Reid 1992).

Considerable effort has been directed at equipping New Zealand teachers to better cater for the increasing student diversity in their classrooms (Hill and Hawk 2000; Ministry of Education 2003). Consequently, many teachers are now more knowledgeable about Maori culture and practices, and how this might be reflected in their teaching. However, the views and values of the dominant culture remain disproportionately influential in many schools. Approaches to giftedness are essentially Eurocentric, with many areas of Maori ability unrecognized and neglected. Also, it is important to recognize that Maori is not a homogenous group and that while the issues may be common to many Maori, they will not apply to all.

A central issue here is the difference between the traditional view of giftedness and how Maori perceive the concept. The conceptualization of giftedness in many western European societies has tended to emphasize academic success, and is seen as the preserve of a small minority; in Maoridom the concept is much broader. Both abilities and 'qualities' are valued by Maori, including spiritual, cognitive, affective, artistic, psychomotor, social, intuitive, creative and leadership domains. Contrasting with the western European tradition, the Maori approach to giftedness is more holistic and intertwined with other Maori concepts. It is the Maori culture that allows for the emergence and development of special gifts. The gifts may be individual, or can be 'owned' by the group, and there is an expectation that a person's talents will be used to benefit others (Bevan-Brown 2004).

The implications for educators of Maori giftedness are extensive: teachers must provide Maori children opportunities and encouragement to develop their talents in a Maori-relevant context (Bevan-Brown 2004). Children who are strong in their cultural identity, in an environment where their culture is valued, are much more likely to feel confident about expressing their special abilities.

This does not mean that Maori young people do not possess abilities in the more traditional areas of talent: New Zealand is replete with Maori who have achieved as scientists, mathematicians and writers. Nor does this mean incorporating approaches to giftedness that are out-of-step with contemporary models. The Maori concept is similar to Gagné's (1999) differentiated Giftedness-Talent Model and Gardner's (1993) multiple intelligences approach. The differences lie in the cultural-specificity of Maori talents, traditions and values, and in the interpretation of qualities and abilities.

An ongoing issue in the non-identification of many able Maori students is low teacher expectations, with some teachers not expecting to find giftedness among their Maori students. The most important message for teachers in identifying gifted Maori is the provision of a culturally safe and valuing environment. Teachers need to work in partnership with Maori to identify the potential of gifted Maori learners and use culturally appropriate methods of identification (Bevan-Brown 2004). The *whanau* (extended family) and *kaumatua* (elders) need to play a dominant role. Also, it is important that Maori are consulted in the design of programmes for gifted Maori students, and need to be involved in supporting this group of students. While an individualistic approach to developing talent may work for many non-Maori students, it may be counterproductive for gifted Maori students. Programmes that isolate gifted Maori children from their peers may result in these children dropping out. Providing for gifted Maori students in an inclusive setting is more appropriate than placing them in a separate environment.

Jenkins (2002) argues that central to providing appropriately for gifted Maori students are matters of power and control. She contends that increasing the visibility of Maori giftedness is not about adding a Maori dimension to existing constructs and practices, it is about changing the very essence of the system itself. From this position, the realization of Maori achievement requires fundamental shifts in order to break down the power imbalances and subordination inherent within many New Zealand schools. In her view, anything short of addressing these basic issues represents only a 'tinkering' with a flawed structure, and will fall short of seeing the talents of Maori students truly valued, appropriately identified and provided for.

While in New Zealand we have begun the journey of better understanding of a Maori concept of giftedness, we still have a long way to go before our approaches can be considered bicultural and equitable. Part of the challenge is to unpack the legacy of colonization and co-construct new approaches to education within an authentic bicultural discourse – a discourse valid for, and validating of, the cultural realities of both Maori and non-Maori.

References

Bevan-Brown, J. (2000) Running the gauntlet: a gifted Maori learner's journey through secondary school. *Proceedings of the Now is the Future, the Gifted Student in Today's Secondary School Conference* [October]. Auckland: George Parkyn Centre.

Bevan-Brown, J. (2002) Culturally appropriate, effective provision for Maori learners with special needs: He waka tino whakarawea, unpublished doctoral thesis, Massey University, Palmerston North, New Zealand.

Bevan-Brown, J. (2004) Gifted and talented Maori learners, in D. McAlpine and R. Moltzen (eds) *Gifted and Talented: New Zealand Perspectives*, 2nd edn. Palmerston North: Kanuka Grove Press.

Gagné, F. (1999) My convictions about the nature of abilities, gifts and talents. *Journal for the Education of the Gifted*, 22(2): 109–136.

Gardner, H. (1993) *Multiple Intelligence: The Theory in Practice*. New York: Basic Books.

Hill, J. and Hawk, K. (2000) *Making a Difference in the Classroom: Effective Teaching Practice in Low Decile, Multicultural Schools*. Wellington: Ministry of Education Research Division.

Jenkins, H. (2002) Culturally responsive pedagogy: embracing Maori giftedness, unpublished master's project, Waikato University, Hamilton, New Zealand.

Ministry of Education (2003) *Te Kotahitanga: The Experiences of Year 9 and 10 Maori Students in the Mainstream Classroom*. Wellington: Ministry of Education.

Moltzen, R. (1999) Young, gifted and living in New Zealand. *Proceedings of Inside–Out: Understanding the Needs of the Gifted Conference*. Christchurch College of Education, April. Christchurch: Christchurch Association for Gifted Children and North Canterbury Support for Gifted and Talented Children.

Reid, N. (1992) Correcting cultural myopia, in E. Le Sueur (ed.) *Proceedings of Guiding the Gifted Conference* (July). Auckland: Conference Publishing Limited.

11.8 Saudi Arabia: key issues regarding the education of gifted students

Omar M. Muammar

Great minds make a great nation! The need for education of gifted students in Saudi Arabia at this time is crucial. In 1999, His Majesty Abdullah Bin Abdulaziz (who was the Crown Prince, but has now become the King of Saudi Arabia) announced the establishment of King Abdulaziz and his Companion Foundation for the Gifted (KACFG) as a non-profit-making organization. The organization aims to identify gifted individuals throughout the country and to provide them with high quality educational services so they can contribute to their society and the world. KACFG is chaired by His Majesty, King Abdullah, and led by the Minister of Education. Top level executive leaders and business people in the country make the policies for KACFG.

Thus, in Saudi Arabia, the education of gifted students receives strong support from the government, private sector, educational institutions, and other profit and non-profit organizations. Since 1999, the KACFG has served significant numbers of students from public schools and communities across the country, through summer programs for enrichment; the establishment of prizes in science and technology; support of gifted centers across the country; scholarships and conferences; professional development of teachers; translated publications for teachers and students; and the encouragement of inventors and creative people by assisting them in developing original ideas, patenting and marketing them around the world.

However, the education of the gifted in Saudi Arabia faces critical challenges. The main challenge derives from the complexity of the concept of giftedness, and how the education of gifted students can be best linked to national development. Obviously, the new conceptualization of giftedness as a multifaceted concept of multiple abilities adds to the overall problem. Therefore, establishing priorities in the education of the gifted regarding who will be served at this time, together with the stages of development, is an immediate challenge. Types of giftedness and services need to be prioritized on the basis of defensible criteria and rationale; hence a vision needs to be developed by the policy makers in Saudi Arabia to provide a road map of development for the education of the gifted.

Another key issue is the broader mission of the KACFG, which needs to include not only students in K–12 grades, but also gifted individuals regardless of age and occupation. The plan for the complex task of administering and developing a national program needs to be comprehensive across all forms of giftedness within all grade levels and inclusive with regard to gender. Furthermore, the development of gifted education in Saudi Arabia should be carried out in partnership with educational, industrial and governmental institutes across the nation.

Another issue regarding the role of the KACFG and other related organizations is whether they should play an essential role in developing, implementing and administering the gifted programs across the country, or whether this role should be delegated to key professionals and institutions so that the developmental process and effort is shared. In 2001, KACFG started a series of gifted summer programs for eleventh grade students: it took more than one semester to select 500 students from a talent pool of 65,000 male students. Surely this process could be delegated to relevant organizations.

Another key issue of concern is that the education system in Saudi Arabia adopts a segregation policy with regard to gender. Providing gifted services for both genders requires careful consideration of the cultural and social values within the society. Not all types of gifted programs are socially acceptable, nor are all types of giftedness of cultural interest. For example, most of the residential programs and special schools do not accept girls. Also, kinesthetic and musical giftedness that involve performing arts such as dance and singing are excluded in our programs.

Saudi Arabia is the largest country in the Gulf region: it occupies land one-quarter the size of the United States of America. A few cities could be considered metropolitan, but the country mainly consists of small sparsely populated towns and villages. It is very difficult for KACFG to reach out to serve potentially gifted individuals in remote parts of the country.

In conclusion, adapting educational alternatives for the gifted that have been developed in different parts of the world would only partially solve the problem. There are complex issues regarding the educational system, and social and cultural roles. Saudi Arabian experience in the field of gifted education is young, but there is huge potential for success in the light of the determination of the KACFG to arrive at, and fund, a strategic plan that accommodates the nation's vision and needs.

11.9 Serbia: diversity and giftedness

Jasmina Šefer

In 1986, national regulations (backed by financial support) provided guidelines for identification and encouragement, in-service training and research in gifted education. Schools were required to organize extra-curricular activities, provide opportunities for acceleration, additional subjects and special awards. Some special grammar and vocational schools were also initiated. However, many gifted and talented students were not included in this initiative, and financial support for extra work in schools was not provided (Milovanović 1992). The identification procedure was usually based on exams in the domain, achievement tests and competitions. Few seminars were organized for teacher in-service training, and the strong academic tradition promoted reproduction of knowledge rather than creative thinking and problem-solving.

A few special secondary schools were established: for music talent (in 1973), for advanced mathematicians (1988), for modern and classic languages (1988) and also for arts and crafts, and sport. Schools for ballet, visual arts and design already existed. Special classes in science and technology, math and languages in secondary grammar and vocational schools were developed and still exist. Classes in these schools have more complex curricula and higher standards: content may be added and adapted according to the student interests and needs. Optional subjects and extra-curricular activities are also available (Milovanović 1992). Various centers and associations have been promoting giftedness. However, currently during the democratic and political changes in the country, there is reform of *general* education; gifted and talented are being left for later.

Particular issues in Serbia

There has always been a lack of organized work with gifted and talented students who are handicapped, poor or who come from educationally and economically disadvantaged groups (Romanies, for example). Serbia embraces a number of nationalities, and all are included in the regular educational system, including their mother languages and elements of cultural history. There are also curricula available in their mother languages or in bilingual schools. Therefore, students have the possibility of recognition as gifted and talented regardless of gender or nationality. Only if cultural background negatively affects economic status, and consequently achievement, do the students not have equal chances to succeed. Poverty, however, is an obstacle for all students. Low economic income during the period of economic sanctions in the 1990s, negatively affected all spheres of social and cultural life, especially education and certain subgroups of population, including gifted and talented.

Although the possibility of being identified as intellectually and academically gifted in is equal for all, the reality is limited due to the criteria used. Psychological tests and school achievement are biased criteria (Šefer 1981, 2000; Maker 1992, 2003; Malušić 2000), particularly for gifted from disadvantaged groups. Some local experts recommended qualitative and process oriented methodology for identification in regular schools. Talent in music, art and movement are identified usually in special schools based on personal interests, and by parents and experts. Exams are eliminatory and required at the beginning and during education in the art and sport domains. However, teachers are not yet trained to identify gifted and talented (Koren 1990), particularly not by using multiple abilities criteria.

Research on the local population

The studies in gifted education have been mainly theoretical, experimental, statistically and test-oriented or have provided a review of work (Kvaščev 1976; Djordjević 1979; Krnjajić 2002; Maksić and Djurišić-Bojanović 2004); studies of qualitative approaches, action research into educational process and creativity have been rare. Although *creativity*, *personality* and *development* are key words in educational documents, the reproductive learning approach is dominant.

However, there have been trials of new methodology, curricula approaches, and teaching methods for all in regular schools, for example active learning (Ivić et al. 2001) and critical thinking (Plut et al. 2001). A longitudinal study of curriculum design and creative development in the elementary school has been completed and interpreted (Šefer 1995, 1996, 2005). Šefer has shown that Gardner's multiple intelligence model combined with five types of problem-solving situations (Maker 1992) and the idea of synthetic, analytic and practical production (Sternberg et al. 1997) in developing play/research interdisciplinary/ thematic curriculum at the elementary level will contribute positively to the development of cognitive skills, knowledge, creative behavior, social and emotional skills, motivation, expression and leadership.

References

Djordjević, B. (1979) *Individualiyacija vaspitanja darovitih* [Individualized education of the gifted]. Beograd: Prosveta.

Ivić, I., Pešikan, A. and Antić, S. (2001) *Aktivno učenje – priručnik za primenu metode aktivnog učenja-nastave* [Active learning – a textbook for curriculum implementation of the active learning method]. Beograd: Institut za psihologiju.

Koren, I. (1990) *Nastavnik i nadareni učenici* [A teacher and gifted students]. Beograd: 'Arhimedes', Matematička tribina.

Krnjajić, Z. (2002) *Intelektualna nadarenost mladih* [Intellectual giftedness of the young]. Beograd: Institut za psihologiju.

Kvaščev, R. (1976) Razvijanje stvaralačkih sposobnosti kod učenika [Development of creative potential among students]. *Psihološka istraživanja* [Psychological research]. Beograd: Institut za psihologiju.

Maker, C. J. (1992) Intelligence and creativity in multiple intelligences: identification and development. *Education Able Learners*, 17: 12–19.

Maker, C. J. (2003) Kreativnoist, rešavanje problema, višestruka inteligencija i različitost [Creativity, problem solving, multiple intelligences and diversity], in *Uvažavanje različitosti i obrazovanje* [Recognition of diversity and education]. Beograd: Institut za pedagoška istraživanja.

Maksić, S. and Djurišić-Bojanović (2004) Kreativnost, znanje i školski uspeh [Creativity, knowledge and school achievement], *Zbornik Instituta za pedagoška istraživanja*, 36. Beograd: Institut za pedagoška istraživanja.

Malušić, S. (2000) *Daroviti učenici i rad s njima* [Talented pupils and work with them]. Beograd: EMKA.

Milovanović, L. J. (1992) Activities with talented children in Serbia, The Ninth World Conference *Talented for Future*. The Hague, The Netherlands, July/August 1991.

Plut, D., Gošović, R., Grahovac, V., Janković, S., Krnjajić, Z., Lazarević, D., Moskovljević, J., Pavlović, D., Pešić, J. and Stepanović, I. (2001) *Kultura kritičkog mišljenja – bazični priručnik* [The culture of critical thinking – basic handbook]. Internal written material. Beograd: Institut za psihologiju i grupa MOST.

Šefer, J. (1981) Psihološko dijagnostikovanje mentalne zaostalosti učenika iz socijalno ugroženih sredina [Psychological diagnosis of mentally handicapped children from the socially deprived groups]. *Psihologija*, 3: 130–134.

Šefer, J. (1995) The effects of play oriented curriculum on creativity in elementary school, *Gifted Education International*, 11: 3–14.

Šefer, J. (1996) A curriculum which stimulates creative behaviour, in G. Zindović-Vukadinović, B. Trebješanin and S. Krnjajić (eds) *Towards a Modern Learner Centred Curriculum*. Beograd: Institute for Educational Research and UNESCO-UNICEF.

Šefer, J. (2000) *Kreativnost dece – problemi vrednovanja* [Children's creativity – problems of evaluation]. Beograd: Institut za pedagoška istraživanja.

Šefer, J. (2005) *Kreativne aktivnosti u tematskoj nastavi* [Creative activities in thematic oriented curriculum]. Beograd: Institut za pedagošska istraživanja.

Sternberg, R. J., O'Hara, A. L. and Lubart, I. T. (1997) Creativity as investment. *California Management Review*, 40(1): 8–21.

11.10 Turkey: education for gifted students

Ugur Sak

Currently there are no *special* programs for gifted students at primary (K–8) levels in public schools. Private schools provide the only chance for gifted students to receive differentiated education appropriate for their needs. These schools offer better education for highly able students, particularly in science and mathematics: students win many international science and maths competitions. Unfortunately, students from low or middle income families seldom attend these prestigious, expensive schools unless they win scholarships. However, the Ministry of Education has undertaken a reform to benefit gifted students at middle school level. Starting in 2005, the new system, called the 'corridor system', inspired by Gardner's theory of multiple intelligences, is expected to provide interest based education for middle school students. There will be at least three major corridors: hard sciences, social sciences and vocational areas. Students can choose any of these corridors or switch between corridors from sixth to eighth grade, depending on their intellectual strengths and academic interest.

Secondary level of education (public and private) has a few schools specializing in math and science, and the Anatolia high schools for foreign languages. Their curricula have both depth and breadth, providing opportunities for individual explorations. Their academic success also is high, in that 90–100 percent of graduates of these schools get into the best university programs. However, these schools are very selective, accepting less than the top 1 percent of students who take the middle school aptitude-achievement test (ÖSYM 2004). This is partly because the demand exceeds the capacity of the schools. For example, from nearly 700,000 applicants, only 4608 students were placed in science schools funded by the Ministry of Education: many able students scoring in the top 1 percent were unable to get a place.

Another major problem is the underrepresentation of girls and students from diverse backgrounds in these prestigious public high schools for science and languages. The east, southeast and north regions of Turkey are economically disadvantaged, with Turkish as the second language for many students from the southeast region. The rate of schooling also is low in these regions. In the 2003 public school examinations taken by eighth graders, there was no northern city in the first 20 highest achieving cities, and no eastern city in the first 30 cities among the 81 major cities of Turkey. Even more problematic is the fact that the lowest achieving 13 cities were from the east or southeast region. The low achievement of students from these regions is inevitably reflected in their underrepresentation in schools for high ability students. Furthermore, the distribution of high quality schools for gifted students varies unequally from region to region. For example, there are few schools of this kind in the east region compared to the west region. From the total number of students who took public examinations in science in 2003, only 49 percent were girls: of these, only 32 percent were placed in science schools, the remaining 68 percent were boys.

Another major problem arises from the trend of middle or low income families to prefer 'job-orientated high schools', since vocational-technical education provides better job opportunities. Many high ability students do not even attempt to go to universities because of poverty. For the students who would like to pursue a higher degree after high school, another problem arises because the curriculum in vocational schools emphasizes technical skills rather than academic subjects. In addition, the current legislation reduces students' national tests scores for university acceptance if they choose a university major that is not related to their high school major: this legislation disqualified over 500 such students who came top in the vocational schools. Moreover, 1500 top students from vocational schools could not get into *any* university program in 2003 (Kahraman 2004).

The mismatch between identification, curriculum and instruction is also a source of problems in Turkey. Teachers teach in lecture style for memory of facts, while the new diagnostic tests to identify high ability students focus on conceptual knowledge and analytical reasoning. Even some high achieving students, taught in the traditional way, have dramatically failed the diagnostic tests of ability. Almost 43 percent of high school graduates who were top in their schools could not get into a university program in 2004 because they did not score high enough in the diagnostic tests.

In summary, although Turkey has provided some opportunities for gifted students at the secondary level, such as science and Anatolia schools, these are the only chances for economically disadvantaged gifted students to receive special education. Gifted students have almost no opportunity at the elementary level. Underrepresentation of gifted girls, and the numbers of economically and regionally disadvantaged gifted students in schools for high abilities, also remain serious problems.

References

Kahraman, S. (2004) Birinciler baraji asamadi [High school champions could not pass the cut-off]. *Milliyet Gazetesi*, 8 May. Retrieved 12 August 2004 from http://www.milliyet.com/2004/05/08/guncel/gun03.html

Ögrenci Secme ve Yerlestirme Merkezi (ÖSYM) (2004) *2004 yili sayisal biligiler* [Data for 2004]. Retrieved 20 August 2004 from http://www.osym.gov.tr/BelgeGoster.aspx

Conclusion

A glimpse of life poised and open in expectancy

Belle Wallace

The eyes of a newly born child focus gradually on an awareness of a world of colours, shapes and shadows. The dawning and recognition of faces that smile and welcome, and the scent and warmth of supporting arms in the close intimacy of nurturing and caring – the first knowing of the self. The self – parted from the time of preconscious thought yet still linked to it for a brief all-knowing time. A gift to adults – these newly opened eyes – a glimpse into eternity – a glimpse of life poised and open in expectancy.

What experiences then clarify and colour in the outline of the child's new world of knowing?

What feelings quickly network through the brain's potential brilliance?

What confirming sense of being in the world confirms the premonition of joy and self as one dimension?

What will the old, worn, gnarled and cynical world of experience offer to the newly born child?

We are living at a time of such rapid change that many people are overwhelmed by the changing values, lifestyles and currently fashionable, or unfashionable, 'norms' of our society. So-called 'developed' countries are confronted with new technologies that have taken over what were essentially 'human' skills of living and communicating. Machines have made life fast and easy, so there is a surfeit of human energy which is not always used constructively for the benefit of the self and the community. Money, or easy credit, can buy immediate material dreams for many; leaving a vast empty space devoid of those big dreams that set the pathway for life fulfilment. Consequently, many young people are beginning to search to find a deeper meaning to life that is different from the 'moneyed rat race' that is symptomatic of their superficially rich world. Yet alongside this powerful material world, low socio-economic communities stand in stark contrast, often just surviving and unable to buy the luxuries of easy living. In so-called 'developing' countries, the contrast is even greater, with many families barely surviving – set bleakly against the powerful privilege of wealth and consequent opportunity.

Other contrasts are equally stark: the dominant language, usually the language of the colonists, takes precedence over a range of indigenous languages. The dominant culture, again often that of the colonizing empire, determines what is worthy of 'status' in the community, determining also which social, ethnic and religious practices are acceptable.

This text, however, conveys both hope and determination to work towards a democratic and global world: the book has brought together a wide selection of people committed to the education of the young – the next generation of world citizens. The contributors bring experience and life commitment, and share their knowledge willingly with the reader – inspiring and supporting the development of an education that seeks to empower and provide opportunities for all children to develop their full potential; both for their self-fulfilment and also for the benefit of their immediate and wider, global community. The collective wisdom of the contributors is, indeed, full of hope and guidance for all concerned with education.

A recurring theme throughout this book is the need to build the self-esteem of all learners as a necessary requisite for effort and persistence. All learners need to feel that their background, language, gender and culture are of worth and value in their learning. Learners' experiences need to form the central base of further learning: they move from acceptance and understanding of what they are, and what they already know, to wider and deeper understanding of themselves and others. If the self is negated by word or deed, then the learner is disabled rather than enabled, denied rather than empowered. This holds true for all learners, but for those with exceptional potential it is essential that they are truly empowered to persevere with the big life challenges, the macro issues, the global concerns. If our most able people accept the challenge, their life pathway is long and arduous, but they also need to learn that the same pathway is full of joyous discoveries.

While we can think and communicate in many ways, for example, through body language, dance, architecture, music and so on, language is still our dominant mode for most transactions of meaning. Language, thought and emotions are inseparable, and throughout the book, writers comment on the denial of the use of pupils' home languages for learning – especially early learning when young children are struggling to express themselves and establish their identities. Language lies at the very foundation of our emerging selves, as we endeavour to make sense of the world: moreover, our first language remains in the core of us even when we become bilingual or multilingual. Constructing meaning in a second language is a most demanding cognitive and emotional experience – especially when we feel that our language is perceived as inferior. In our increasingly global, multilingual world, so many pupils are faced with this challenge; yet children in multilingual classrooms can and do construct meaning when they perceive that their language is not only accepted but also celebrated. Our global world needs our most able linguists to negotiate meaning and understanding.

Another theme centres on the universally stubborn adherence to a content curriculum, and the urgent global need to change this to a process based curriculum. In our rapidly changing world, knowledge is exploding at a rate often too fast for textbooks to be written and published. How can we predict what challenges will face 5 year olds when they are mature adults? Throughout this book, writers urge that teaching learners the skills of how to learn and how to assess their learning should be the universal aim of education. The greatest gift educators can give to all children is the gift of a repertoire of problem-solving skills and strategies which are brought to bear on relevant challenges.

In a number of countries, 'intelligence' is still viewed in the old paradigm of testing and quantifying a person's mental capacity which emerges without need of intervention and nurturing. All the contributors in this volume who discuss the concept of 'intelligence' maintain that mental capacity is not a 'fixed commodity': we can only identify and crudely estimate a range of skills needed for learning as promoted by the existing school tests of achievement. Our wonderful human brain is dynamic and capable of lifelong growth, but the brain needs active learning that engages learners in exploring issues that are relevant and understandable. The brain also needs a range of activities across the full spectrum of human abilities: language, mathematics, sciences, somatic-movement, sonal-musical, visual-spatial, mechanical-technical, emotional, social and spiritual. Moreover, different cultures promote different styles of learning across this interrelated range of human abilities, ranging from cooperative, mainly oral, group sharing of ideas, to individualistic, competitive modes. In addition, different cultures place different values on the development of the range of human abilities.

Why is it that in the light of greater understanding of how all children learn, the old paradigm of the nineteenth century 'fill up the empty child with an immutable and set body of knowledge' still exists? Why is it that so many educators feel that they need to be authoritarian dispensers and testers of inert, old, established knowledge? Why are so many educators perpetuating outdated, 'colonial' and often irrelevant curricula? Why do intolerance, injustice and inequity pervade when there is a global concern for democracy and peace?

Let's reflect on some possible reasons.

One of the most basic human drives is to seek safety and to maintain that state of feeling safe and secure. Change and risk-taking require courage and creativity. The belief that one can step on to a new path and follow a new direction, solving as yet unknown problems encountered along the way, needs the firm belief and commitment that the self is capable. All people need this assurance, but our most able young people, as future leaders and innovators, need to be supported and assured that they can seek, find and implement new solutions and approaches. However, young teachers are being trained by teachers who were trained by the previous generation of teachers: this pattern of training spans three generations. Since behaviour is largely the result of the modelling of social interactions, we need to consider whether our young teachers are being trained with appropriate skills for teaching the young who will need to be expert communicators, negotiators and problem-solvers on a global scale. How can teachers learn to manage classrooms and facilitate learning if the experiences of their own learning are top-down, knowledge based and set in a static content driven curriculum?

Huge bureaucracies perpetuate themselves only because people follow the rules, and again it takes courage to question the 'way things are always done'. Certainly communities need an acceptable order and consensus of fair discipline, but bureaucracies promote conformity, and the leaders often feel threatened when confronted with major change. It is safer to tinker with and patch the system than to reconceptualize and transform it: transformation takes leadership, vision, huge energy and lifetime commitment. But although schools need to model transformation both to parents and to pupils, the current form of education is perceived by many as the gateway to power and wealth; therefore, transformation needs to be acceptable to both parents and pupils. They need to understand and participate in the process as partners and collaborators. Moreover, 'successful' pupils and their parents generally come from the dominant culture, and have usually succeeded within the system as it is currently; change is often perceived as a challenge to their current ideologies and power.

Throughout this book, writers have celebrated the rich and exciting canvas of human differences. Is this the dream of only a few committed people? Is it impossible to help all people to experience the joy of living in a global world of diverse beliefs, customs and languages? Contributors have shared their vision, and poignantly argued their case for education which is accepting of the diversity and the uniqueness of individuals. Although they have argued the case for an empowering education for all – they have also made a case for empowering those who can see further, and travel faster than others – the potentially very able in all fields of human abilities. We believe, however, that the case made for developing the emotional, social and spiritual strengths of learners is supreme. We seem to have lost the essential qualities of being human and humane as we function globally at the beginning of this twenty-first century, and need to develop the strength of our most able – if they are to begin to meet the challenges we have bequeathed to them.

Appendix

Strategies for conflict resolution: possible solutions

Suzanne Rawlins and Gillian Eriksson

The conflicts presented throughout this book stem from real situations faced by teachers. For many of these incidents, teachers and administrators negotiated these conflicts and the solutions provided here were ones that were actually implemented.

We recommend that a problem-solving strategy be used to address these conflicts. The TASC problem-solving wheel (Figure A.1) indicates the stages of thinking that are appropriate (Wallace 2000).

Actual solution: 2.4 Bilingual

Lesson learned: bilingual communication is only as good as its clarity. Volunteer parents of the community involved now preview all presentations and

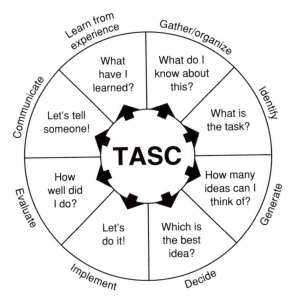

Figure A.1 TASC: Thinking Actively in a Social Context the TASC problem-solving wheel. Source: Wallace 2000.

communications that are addressing more than one language. Questions that arise during the preview are noted and added to the communication and/or presentations. Certainly the time spent in previewing is worth the investment in assuring that the intended message is clearly communicated.

Actual solution: 3.4 Cultural prejudice

The new principal began with cultural awareness and prejudice reduction training for the office staff. Then, she instituted a different version of the conferences. During the third week of school, each grade level was given one day to meet with parents. The gymnasium was converted to a large meeting room: tables, chairs and desks were arranged all around the periphery; the center contained seats for a waiting area, games for smaller siblings, refreshments and soft music. No matter how many family members appeared, the gymnasium would hold them all. The new configuration also allowed families of the community to meet as they waited their turn for the student conference. Soon, the new procedure became a community gathering that everyone enjoyed, including the office staff.

Actual solution: 4.4 Classism

The chairperson asked the father if he would agree to be on the agenda for the next meeting. He agreed. At the next meeting, he shared these words:

> I know that our boys and girls all learn together every day. I know they share their hopes and their dreams. I know I want the most for my daughter. I know they will lead our country tomorrow. I work in the fields each day from sun-up to sun-down. I must drive in my old truck over 75 miles to be here. I must ask permission to leave my duties, but I come because it is important. I feel bad that my coming later than others makes them feel bad. My daughter, she is the winner. I am sorry for my lateness. My boss says I can come, but I must work on Sunday afternoon to make up the time.

All the parents erupted into a standing ovation as the demure father took his seat. A motion to the floor came from the primary complainer:

> Let us begin our meetings with our social time rather than our program. Each of us can take turns bringing some refreshments. Then, the program can begin later . . . because it is important. And let's make sure that there are plenty of goodies for later-arrivers to enjoy during the program . . . because it is important.

Actual solution: 5.5 Racism

This teacher used and modified the techniques used in the well-known simulation on prejudice and discrimination created by Jane Elliott in 1968, an elementary fourth–fifth grade teacher from Riceville, Iowa, an all-white community. Jane Elliott's lesson was conducted the day after Martin Luther King had been killed, and students did not understand the impact of this racism. Elliott divided the class into blue eyes and brown eyes (with others as bystanders); the latter were given privileges while the former were denied these. After three days, the roles were reversed; Elliott demonstrated that prejudice is quickly internalized into poor self-concept and racism can be taught. She identified the hidden assumptions of white privilege. She has since received worldwide acclaim for the videos (*Eye of the Storm, A Class Divided* and *The Essential Blue-Eyed*) and workshops conducted to train those not exposed to prejudice about its impact. (Note that this would not be appropriate with a mixed race group as ethnicity is defined by eye color: most minorities have brown eyes, and this could foster actual prejudice. Randomized grouping or use of neutral symbols for preferential groups is one alternative method.)

Resources

Frontline (2003) PBS video – *A Class Divided* – footage available at: http://www.pbs.org/ wgbh/pages/frontline/shows/divided/etc/view.html

H2G2 (2003) *Jane Elliott and the Brown Eyes, Blue Eyes Exercise.* Available at: http:// www.bbc.co.uk/dna/h2g2/A1132480

Kral, B. (2005) *The Eyes of Jane Elliott.* Available at: http://www.horizonmag.com/4/ jane-elliott.asp

Actual solution: 6.4 Religious intolerance

The teacher realized that this student was experiencing a series of challenges. Not only was this student trying to "fit in" and acculturate in a new culture, but also she was trying to make friends and feel accepted. In addition, this student was very proud of her English ability and was trying to enrich her knowledge of American culture. Her high level of intelligence was being attacked as well in that she was accused of being ignorant. This comment not only was insulting but also immediately excluded her from the other students.

The teacher informed the student that everyone has diverse beliefs and that the other students had no right to make personal accusations, that she was proud of the achievements the student showed, and that she would meet with her parents. In the meeting, the teacher discussed the incident and suggested that the student complete an enrichment unit on diverse comparative religions. She suggested that the parents participate in this, so that it would be a family project. She also decided that this would be a good time to include a curriculum unit on diverse cultures and religious heritage. In order to maintain objectivity, she chose cultures that were not directly related to the actual classroom, but covered the main religions around the world. Parents were invited to participate and agree to their student's participation. The unit did much to dispel religious ignorance and prevent future prejudice.

Actual solution: 7.6 Sexism

Celeste found four other girls who wanted to attend the math and science classes. The five girls requested a hearing with the local school board. Celeste's mother testified that she was able to teach Celeste anything that she wanted to know about running a home, but that she knew nothing about chemistry. Celeste wanted the policy changed. Celeste's mother supported her desires. The five man board denied the schedule change, until one gentleman on the board spotted his granddaughter at the back of the room, waiting to testify at the hearing. With a soft voice, he said, "If these girls want to change the world, I think we better give them a chance to do so." With that, Celeste and four other girls began Chemistry I Honors and Honors Geometry the following week. (Celeste now teaches science at a middle school. Two of the girls teach mathematics at their local high schools. The "fifth girl" is now a lobbyist for her state legislator. Her specialty is educational issues.)

Actual solution: 8.4 Twice exceptional

No magic solutions have happened for Raymond. His father was allowed to take custody of him while his mom is in rehabilitation. The father tried boot-camp and an alternative educational setting (reforming) for him. Grades were improved with the structure of those settings. However, due to family issues, Raymond moved away. Not all stories end like a fairy tale. Everyone hopes that Raymond will one day realize his potential.

Actual solution: 9.4 Ageism

Kumalo was referred to the school psychologist, who assessed his abilities, and developed a profile of his strengths, weaknesses and interests. A team was formed that included his teachers, the principal and parents to plan an individual curriculum for him. They obtained books and resources from central libraries. He began a newspaper for the school, did surveys using the students in the school, and was paired up with mentors in the community. He studied what a community needed. He made up a play about the characters in his village that was performed at school. His heroes were firefighters and he prepared a project for his age peers on safety, and organized a field trip to the closest fire station. There he got to know the firefighters and started volunteering, learning about issues of safety and building codes. He was hoping to receive a scholarship to attend a school in the town where his father worked that would allow him to accelerate and work on his interests.

References

Wallace, B. (2000) *Teaching the Very Able Child: Developing a Policy and Adopting Strategies for Provision.* London: David Fulton.

Index